STUDIES IN THE ECONOMIC DEVELOPMENT
OF INDIA

Edited by Professor P. N. Rosenstein-Rodan

6

Planning for Growth

STUDIES IN THE ECONOMIC DEVELOPMENT OF INDIA

PLANNING FOR GROWTH

Multisectoral, Intertemporal Models Applied to India

Richard S. Eckaus and Kirit S. Parikh

The M.I.T. Press
Massachusetts Institute of Technology
Cambridge, Massachusetts, and London, England

Preface

Scholarly books on economic development as well as the programs prepared by planning commissions frequently begin with admonitions that the development process is an intricate interaction of many economic, political, and cultural factors. Scholars then proceed, by simplifying assumptions, to develop both general theories of the growth process and explanations of its particular aspects. Practical planners also simplify the development process, for they are no more successful than are academic scholars in understanding the process or in integrating their partial and incomplete insights. The published economic plans for many countries often treat many aspects of development and contain a great amount of detail. Nevertheless such plans are, for the most part, collections of separate programs the real interactions of which are not fully worked out and taken into account in the making of policy. The inadequacies of the planning methods practiced are only partly due to the limitations of the development theories available, and most development plans could be improved by a more consistent and intensive application of these theories. Moreover, the development of high-speed computers has made it possible to apply these theories more effectively. An awareness of the gap between the practice of economic planning and the tools available was part of the inspiration of the project leading to this book.

The central issues of over-all development policy and growth theory are the mobilization and optimum use of resources. These issues are analyzed here by means of linear programming models in which intersectoral and intertemporal relationships are made explicit. These models may be considered as extensions and applications of the multisectoral theories of capital accumulation and growth and the one- or two-sector models now current in growth theory. The models are elaborated in several versions. Each solution of the models, in maximizing the value of the objective function and meeting all the production and behavioral constraints imposed, determines all the necessary resource allocations including intersectoral flows and capital formation. The sensitivity of the results to errors in estimation and alternative policies are investigated by means of successive solutions with different values of parameters and exogenous quantities.

The models remain highly abstract versions of a real economy, in part because we have not exploited all the potential of modern growth theory and in part because that theory is still far from being realistic. Many of the complexities of economic growth such as external economies, changes in foreign trade specialization, and induced innovation are still not effectively embodied in growth theory. Furthermore, the information and computation required to implement much of the theory place it beyond the possibility of immediate use. But there are aspects and versions of growth theory the information requirements of which are hardly greater than those of the planning methods now being used. The computational requirements are great but still within the feasible range of high-speed, digital computers.[1]

While we have tried to construct a bridge between some areas of economic theory and economic policy, we have not attempted to be either as comprehensive or as specific as required by the real tasks of planning. We believe, however, that even a modest version of the type of analysis presented can add important insights into economic policy. Moreover, in concrete applications, the models can be both extended and made more specific depending on the information available, the detail desired, and the computational capacity available.

Chapters 1 and 6, the Introduction and Summary and Conclusions, are more or less self-contained and make no particular demands in terms of analytical economic techniques. They are intended to make available to the general reader the approach and the results of the analyses in the book. Deeper understanding, unfortunately, will require trekking through rather than around the swamps of the intermediate chapters.

The project on which this book is based provides, we believe, an example of the principle of critical minimum effort that operates in economic research organization as in physics and in economic development. That critical minimum in this case was the support of several organizations and a large number of people for various periods. The project had its origins in the winter of 1961-62 in the individual and cooperative research of N. Andreatta, R. S. Eckaus, and P. Sevaldson, then members of the India Project of the Center for International Studies, Massachusetts Institute of Technology, and S. Chakravarty, who had previously been a Research Associate of the Center and was a consultant to the group. In this initial stage the adequacy of existing and potential sources of empirical information was established, and alternative theoretical model structures were described. Dr. Ashish Chakravarti, then of the Indian Statistical Institute in New Delhi, gave invaluable advice on empirical problems in this early phase. Work on the project continued in 1962-63 both in New Delhi and in Cambridge, Massachusetts. In India James Mirrlees, of Cambridge University, and Sevaldson continued efforts to improve the empirical information, and Sevaldson prepared a paper describing a linear programming model. In Cambridge, Kirit Parikh assumed complete responsibility for computations and participated with Eckaus and Louis Lefeber, now of Brandeis University, who joined the project, in data preparation and model formulation. In 1963-64 Chakravarty, who was then visiting the M.I.T. Department of Economics, resumed his association with the project. By the end of the 1963-64 academic year, when Chakravarty and Lefeber left Cambridge, most of the computations of the short-term Target and Transit Models for the Indian Third Plan period had been completed. Subsequently Eckaus and Parikh applied the models to the Fourth Plan period and developed

---

[1] The five decimal places in some of the numerical results should not be interpreted as an indication of the authors' faith in the quality of the data on which the calculations are based. The detail is required not because of its economic significance but to achieve accuracy in the approximative computational procedures necessarily involved in finding solutions to the models.

and calculated the long-term Guidepath Models and the Guidepost Models. In its early stages in particular, therefore, the project was a group effort to which a number of persons made important contributions, and those of Chakravarty and Lefeber deserve special emphasis.

Jaleel Ahmad, Michel Bonneau, Mrinal Datta-Chaudhuri, George DeMenil, T. Krishnan, Hari Raina, Jayant Shah, and Thomas Weisskopf provided research assistance that often went far beyond routine performance of their duties and gave critical help in some difficult spots. We are grateful to Miss Grace Locke and Mrs. Mary Jane Shubow for their efficiency and forbearance in dealing with a difficult manuscript.

The advice and encouragement of Shri Tarlok Singh, formerly Additional Secretary and Member of the Planning Commission, Government of India, was important in encouraging the undertaking of the project in its earliest and formative stages. Professors Max Millikan and P. N. Rosenstein-Rodan of the Center for International Studies gave continuing support. The analysis has also benefited from the criticism of a large number of persons, but we would particularly like to acknowledge the useful comments and cooperation of Professor Alan S. Manne of Stanford University both on theoretical and empirical problems. Because so many people have been involved at various stages we feel we must stress that only the authors are responsible for the presentation of this volume.

Support for the research on which this book is based was provided first by the India Project of the Center for International Studies, financed by a grant from the Ford Foundation, and later by the U.S. Agency for International Development. The M.I.T. Computation Center was generous and cooperative in providing computation facilities. None of these organizations bear any responsibility for the analyses and opinions presented here.

Richard S. Eckaus
Kirit S. Parikh

April 1966

Contents

6. Summary and Conclusions   197

Tables

Figures

1. Introduction

A beggar to the graveyard hied
And there "Friend corpse, arise," he cried;
"One moment lift my heavy weight
Of poverty; for I of late
Grow weary, and desire instead
Your comfort: you are good and dead."
The corpse was silent. He was sure
'Twas better to be dead than poor.

The Panchatantra

1.1 Planning Models as Analytical Tools

The intersectoral and intertemporal allocation of resources are among the major determinants of the costs and benefits of economic growth and therefore are central issues in development policy. In this book we present a set of linear programming models for planning and analyzing these allocations. The models are applied to development planning in India to illustrate their scope and utility. The project on which this book reports has been primarily a pilot study of the potentiality of linear programming techniques in over-all development planning. However, we believe that the analyses also provide some new insights into Indian economic policy and the operation of the Indian economy.

Development planning always has many different economic and social goals. In general, these goals conflict with each other to varying degrees. A greater achievement with respect to one goal often means a lesser achievement with respect to another, so that compromises are necessary. For example, if a higher growth rate of the gross national product is desired, it may be necessary to accept a lower rate of improvement in the average standard of living. Similarly, a reduction in inequality of the distribution of income may result in a lower growth rate for total income. Making compromises among conflicting objectives requires political value judgments, which in turn, implies the existence of at least an ordinally defined social welfare function embodying these objectives. Yet in practice, comprehensive and precisely stated goals for development are rarely created by social-decision processes. Thus, if economists confine themselves to their conventionally defined role in policy-making of analyzing the consequences of well-defined objectives, they have only narrowly and inexactly defined terms of reference. In such circumstances, the economist can contribute to economic policy-making not only in the conventional manner, but also by describing alternative economic policies corresponding to different feasible combinations of objectives. For example, economic analysis may show that a 7 per cent growth rate of national income can be achieved if the rate of increase in the standard of living is limited to 2 per cent, but that only a 5 per cent growth rate can be achieved if the standard of living is to rise by 3 per cent. Unless such alternatives and their implications are made explicit, informed choices cannot be made. The models presented here are designed to generate policy alternatives and explore the implications of any given set of objectives. Consequently, the models can also be used to test the feasibility, consistency, and political acceptability of plans made by other, less formal methods.

1

The complexity of development processes and the limitations of data necessitate the formulation of models, or conceptual simplifications, of real relationships for both theoretical analysis and formulation of policy. Models are intended to bring the most relevant issues into focus without doing irreparable damage to our understanding of them through the means by which other problems are put into the background. The more implications of a model which can be deduced, the more useful the model will be. Modern, high-speed computers can carry out detailed investigations of relatively large and complex quantitative models, which otherwise could either not be analyzed at all or only in a qualitative manner. An improvement in the speed with which the process of logical deductions can be performed is, therefore, a potential increase in our powers of analysis and adds insight and flexibility to policy-making.

The linear programming technique used here has become familiar in theoretical models of capital accumulation and intersectoral resource allocation.[1] In this technique a specific objective or criterion function is maximized subject to constraints that describe the relevant technological, economic, and social behavior relationships.[2] There is a substantial and rapidly growing literature on the application of linear programming to development problems.[3] In these applications the models, though multisectoral, have been almost exclusively in static terms. The models presented in this book include a number of separate sectors and also take intertemporal relations explicitly into account. They are analytical innovations only in that they are structured to the requirements of development planning and are therefore relatively detailed in some aspects.

The explicit recognition of both intertemporal and intersectoral relationships in a planning model has a number of advantages. It is, first of all, a better approximation to the real context in which policy is made than are static and aggregative models. Such a formulation also permits and even forces the premises about such relationships, which usually remain implicit, to be brought into the open and to be examined. The model solutions include period-by-period calculations of the uses of capital and of the requirements of other inputs in each sector, the level of investment in each sector, the deliveries by each sector of goods for consumption and investment, and other final demands. These results, in temporal and sectoral detail, make possible a more effective analysis of many important issues of development policy, such as the savings and investment

---

[1] Since other bibliographies of linear programming are available and its intellectual origins are well known (see G. B. Dantzig, *Linear Programming and Extensions,* the RAND Corporation, Santa Monica, Calif., Aug. 1963) we need only record our most immediate inspiration, R. Dorfman, P. A. Samuelson, and R. Solow, *Linear Programming and Economic Analysis,* McGraw-Hill, New York, 1958. The models used are generalizations of the one presented in R. S. Eckaus and L. Lefeber, "Capital Formation: A Theoretical and Empirical Analysis," *Review of Economics and Statistics, 44,* 1962, pp. 113-122, but have been modified in many particulars by S. Chakravarty, L. Lefeber, and the authors and have benefited from the suggestions of others

[2] A linear programming solution of any planning model is optimal *only* with respect to the objectives embedded in the specified criterion function and constraints. The question whether the objectives themselves are appropriate for maximizing some all-inclusive concept of social welfare is beyond the scope of such models.

[3] See, for example: H. B. Chenery and K. S. Kretchmer, "Resource Allocation for Economic Development," *Econometrica, 24,* 1956, pp. 365-399, and other articles by Chenery; J. Sandee, *A Long-Term Planning Model for India,* Calcutta, 1960; and M. Bruno, *Interdependence, Resources Use, and Structural Change in Israel,* Jerusalem, 1962.

implications of particular goals, the effectiveness of foreign aid, and the content of "balanced" growth.

Finally, it should be noted that the models in themselves imply neither a particular ideological outlook nor a commitment to a particular program of implementation. Their use is consistent with either considerable centralization or decentralization of decision-making and with any combination of direct and indirect means of influencing production. Having an economic policy is inevitable, and it would appear to be desirable to try to improve all types of analytical tools that might help in forming policy. The results presented here need no more justification than this.

In the remainder of this chapter we first describe briefly the techniques used in Indian economic planning. This provides a background against which to judge the methods to be presented subsequently and the computations to be carried out with Indian data. We do not attempt to provide an evaluation of the strategies of the Indian Plans at this point, except to note where these have been influenced by the techniques used. A brief description of the various models is then given, followed by some comment on their structure. Some remarks on the adequacy of the data available for applying the models conclude the chapter.

1.2 Overview of Planning Techniques in India

The accomplishments of the Indian economy since independence, in the face of an extraordinary number of all but overwhelming difficulties, are remarkable in themselves and especially so in comparison with conditions prior to August 1947 when India became independent. The First Five Year Plan of economic development was started in 1951-52. It was followed by the Second Five Year Plan in 1956-57 and the Third Five Year Plan in 1961-62. The degree to which the Plans have achieved their goals has been quite uneven with general shortfalls averaging 20 to 25 per cent of the targets. Yet the Plans represent a sustained effort toward economic development through consent rather than coercion, which is a tribute to the determination of the Indian political leadership and the Indian people. The achievements of this effort have been amply recorded as have been the failures.[4] In Chapter 4 one of the models is used to evaluate the Plans. At this point, therefore, we shall concentrate on describing the techniques of planning that have actually been used.

The Indian Plans, the methodology of which is widely regarded as being among the most sophisticated of the less developed areas, have provided the general framework for the evolution of the Indian economy. While the Plans may better be regarded as statements of intent rather than rigid blueprints, they are the backbone of government economic policy. The Plans provide the output and investment targets for the various branches of the economy on the basis of which investment and import licenses are granted to the private sector and new projects are started in the public sector. The national and the state plans are prepared at the same time, and efforts are made to coordinate them. The Plans have also served as the basis for negotiation of foreign assistance.

---

[4]For a balanced account, see J. P. Lewis, *Quiet Crisis in India,* The Brookings Institution, Washington, D.C., 1962.

The strength of the Indian Plans is in their abundant detail of specific government sectors projects. In addition, targets are set for sectors that are predominantly in private hands, though for these sectors less detail is provided. However, careful plans are made for a wide variety of government activities designed to assist, stimulate, or regulate private enterprise. For example, there are extensive programs of government activity to promote agriculture and to establish centers of private industry.

In the formulation of the Indian Plans a comprehensive set of social and economic goals have been articulated. These include immediate alleviation of poverty to some degree and achievement of a rate of growth that will provide for a substantially improved standard of living in the future. An increase in employment opportunities is regarded not only as a means of achieving these goals, but also as an end in itself, as is a less disparate distribution of income and greater equality of social and economic opportunities. Improved educational, medical, and other welfare facilities are also proposed in the Plans. These and other goals are to be achieved in the context of a free and socialist economy, in which there will also be a substantial role for private enterprise. Though the process of making these general goals specific has not been clear and straightforward, in this deficiency Indian planning is not unique.

There has been intensive debate in India over the Plans. The newspapers and journals of opinion reflect this debate as it occurs within the government before the Plans are made public, and the debate continues in the national arena afterward. The debate, which itself constitutes consideration of alternatives, focuses on the size of the Plan and on the relative emphasis to be placed on the various sectors. Unfortunately, the debate has not been well informed with respect to the relationships among these issues and with respect to the intertemporal distribution of benefits. The view seems to have been widely accepted that the bigger the Plans are the better they are, and the controversy has focused on the feasibility of achieving the required levels of taxation and foreign aid.

The output goals of the Plans are specified for the final Plan year. The projected supplies and demands of the major commodities for the final Plan year are brought into equality in an attempt to insure over-all consistency. Demands are projected for private and government consumption, exports, and domestic industrial requirements. The sectoral targets are set by experts of the relevant ministries, the Planning Commission, and the Finance Ministry. These experts meet in interagency committees, which overlap and pyramid in order to take sectoral interrelationships and over-all limitations and objectives into account. These committees bring a great deal of practical experience to bear on the problems of expanding capacity and output in each sector and of integrating the sectoral plans. The economic guidelines provided to the committees appear to be based on macroeconomic balances of saving, investment, and foreign exchange resources and on commodity balances of supplies and requirements. However, there are many alternative sectoral compositions of output and investment which are compatible with the totals, and the precise criteria and techniques which are used by the committees in determining the Plan proportions are not apparent.

1.2.1 First Five Year Plan

The First Plan was, for the most part, a rather hastily organized program of government projects. It did contain, however, a projection of over-all economic growth to be generated by capital accumulation financed largely by domestic saving. With a projected marginal savings rate higher than the average savings rate, the reliance on foreign aid was expected to diminish in spite of growing rates of investment. Although this simple model had a few implications for over-all policy, it was more of a projection than a plan that could be implemented. Sectoral investment allocations in the public sector were determined more by the availability of projects than by explicit long-term policy considerations, although the over-all analysis did show an explicit concern for the future. Considering both the knowledge of economic planning at this time and the circumstances in India, it is not surprising that more detailed analyses were not made. The First Plan was generally considered to be a success. Roughly speaking, the projected output levels were achieved in many sectors. Major projects were started, and while they did not progress as rapidly as programmed, the Plan as a whole was believed to have gone well.

1.2.2 Second Five Year Plan

The objectives of the Second Five Year Plan were clearly stated in the Plan document. They were (1) a growth of 25 per cent in national income over five years, which was considered attainable from historical comparisons with other countries, and (2) the creation of 11 million new jobs, so that no rise in unemployment would take place. This statement of objectives appears to have been made on an a priori basis without an exploration of alternative goals in a quantitative manner. As a result, it is conceivable that they were not optimal; i.e., it may have been possible to exceed either or both of the targets. The targets, indeed, may even have been inconsistent or infeasible in that one or both of the goals may have been unrealizable.

The macroeconomic framework of the Second Plan, like that of the First, was a model of growth generated by capital accumulation based on domestic saving and foreign capital. In this model, aggregate investment multiplied by an aggregate marginal output-capital ratio produced increases in aggregate output. From these increases, an ever greater proportion was to be saved and invested in order to achieve further growth. The sources of domestic saving in the household, business, and government sectors were analyzed separately in the more detailed calculations.

The only formal techniques of relating aggregate and sectoral investment allocation that are apparent in the preparations for the Plan are the well-known two- and four-sector models of Mahalanobis.[5] In order to demonstrate the relationships between the allocation of investment among the sectors and the over-all growth rate,

---

[5]P. C. Mahalanobis, "The Approach of Operational Research to Planning in India" and "Draft Plan Frame for the Second Five Year Plan," *Sankhya, 16,* 1955, pp. 3-89.

Mahalanobis used a two-sector model reminiscent of the Fe'ldman model,[6] which distinguished only consumption and investment goods, the latter usable to create capacity in either sector. A constant marginal utility of consumption was assumed so that future and present consumption would provide the same benefits. The structure of production was also assumed to be linear. Foreign trade was ignored, as were the requirements for consumption maintenance for labor. In this model, the long-run rate of growth depended on the relative allocation of investment to the capital goods producing sector. This conclusion and its acceptability for policy would not necessarily be maintained if the assumptions were modified. Yet the model served the purpose of emphasizing the significance of the choice of planning horizon. The four-sector model of Mahalanobis was intended to indicate the investment allocations that would achieve prescribed growth rates and employment levels. Here also a closed economy was assumed and investment gestation lags were ignored. Demand conditions for investment and consumption were taken into account by adopting the investment allocations suggested by the two-sector model. Both of the Mahalanobis models were too limited in scope to indicate the most desirable allocation of resources among interdependent sectors. No attempt was made to find optimal allocations, dynamic interrelations were not taken into account, and the targets were defined in highly aggregative terms. The models were not employed to examine the significance of alternative long-term programs and in fact could have been used for that purpose only with substantial modification.[7]

The achievements of the Second Plan were less than the targets. Over 5 years a 20 per cent increase in national income was attained, and 8 million new jobs were created. The effective capital-output ratios and gestation lags were higher than assumed, and a foreign exchange crisis developed during the Plan.

1.2.3 Third Five Year Plan

The Third Plan added the objective of self-sufficiency to the growth and employment objectives of the Second Plan. It aimed at achieving (1) an increase in national income of over 5 per cent per year, (2) self-sufficiency in food grains by the end of the Plan, (3) self-sustaining growth in 10 years, and (4) the creation of 14 million new jobs.

The technique of commodity balances seems to have been used in an attempt to achieve consistency among sectoral output goals for the terminal year of the Plan. For this year, demands for private consumption were estimated on the basis of consumption-expenditure elasticities and the expected growth rate of income. Exports and government consumption were projected independently. Investment requirements for the last Plan year, which must include those for the post-Plan period, were estimated separately. Indirect requirements were then computed by an iterative procedure by means of "consumption norms," which, like the

---

[6]See E. Domar, "A Soviet Model of Growth," *Essays in the Theory of Economic Growth*, Oxford University Press, New York, 1957, pp. 223-262.

[7]These models have been the subject of a number of critical analyses, which will not be repeated here. See S. Tsuru, "Some Theoretical Doubts on India's Plan Frame," *Economic Weekly, 5*, (Annual Number), 1957; S. Chakravarty, *The Logic of Investment Planning*, North Holland Press, Amsterdam, 1959, pp. 43-48; R. Komiya, "A Note on Professor Mahalanobis' Model of Indian Economic Planning," *The Review of Economics and Statistics, 41*, 1959, pp. 29-35.

input-output ratios of interindustry matrices, relate current input requirements to sectoral output levels.

There is no indication in the Plan of the methods used to establish the over-all income targets. The investment requirements for the Plan period itself were calculated from the sectoral targets by means of capital-output coefficients. Different capital-output coefficients were used for new units and for expansion of existing units. This made it possible to account for economies of scale, which are significant in some industries; for example, in electricity and transportation, once the transmission lines or roads are built, further expansion of capacity requires a proportionally much smaller investment.

The achievements of the Third Plan were far short of the targets. Again, there was a foreign exchange crisis, and the capital-output ratios and investment lags were higher than assumed. The Chinese invasion, military engagements with Pakistan, and unfavorable agricultural conditions placed special burdens on the Indian economy and its foreign exchange position. In general, it has been assumed in assessments of the Plan that the targets were originally based on realistic estimates of prospects and parameters. The reasons given for lack of success include not only unforeseeable exigencies of weather and increased defense spending, but also inadequacies in implementation, which may mean either too little, too much, or the wrong kind of government intervention, depending on the source of criticism. We will explore the issues of feasibility and consistency of the Third Plan targets with the help of our models in Chapter 4.

1.2.4 Proposed Fourth Five Year Plan

The Fourth Five Year Plan, scheduled to begin in 1966-67, is now planned to begin in 1968-69. All references to the Fourth Five Year Plan in this book pertain to the one proposed in *Notes on Perspective of Development, India: 1960-61 to 1975-76.*[8]

The objectives stated for the Fourth Plan period were (1) attainment of a 7 per cent growth rate of national income in order to provide a minimum per capita consumption of Rs. 20 per month even in rural areas, (2) achievement of a self-sustaining growth at a rate of 7 per cent per year beginning in 1975-76, and (3) creation of 50 million new jobs by the end of the Plan. Sectoral targets and allocations were again made on the basis of commodity-balance analysis. However, the analysis was more detailed than in the previous plans. These targets also will be analyzed for their allocational implications in Chapter 4.

The macroeconomic models used in preparing the Indian Plans were able, at best, to determine only the aggregate savings and investment implications of a growth path. Yet, there are many alternative sectoral compositions of output and investment compatible with the totals. The commodity balance methods are potentially capable of achieving consistency only after sectoral final demand targets have been determined. In themselves, they cannot provide a rationale for choosing the targets. Intertemporal planning which takes investment gestation lags into account has been almost completely lacking in the Indian Plans. Yet such

---

[8]Perspective Planning Division, Planning Commission, New Delhi, April 1964. The Fourth Five Year Plan Draft outline, published in August 1966 when this manuscript was already in final draft, is not examined here.

accounting is necessary to avoid domestic resource and foreign exchange bottlenecks that result from, as well as lead to, longer gestation lags and higher capital-output ratios.

1.2.5 Indian Policy Methods

The patterns of the Indian economy are still evolving, but from the first three Five Year Plan periods a "mixed economy" is emerging. Some sectors such as rail transport and electric power have been entirely reserved for public enterprise; in other sectors, such as steel, coal, and heavy machinery, public and private enterprise coexist. The Indian government has attempted to guide the private sector by means of a variety of direct and indirect controls. Direct regulation of investment and imports is pervasive. Output controls exist in some sectors and are supplemented by extensive price controls. There are also specific controls on the use of certain commodities in production. An extensive range of government activities from community development to government research laboratories provide assistance and leadership to the economy. In addition to its veto and control powers, the government, through purchases and sales by its public enterprises, creates incentives for private enterprise to pursue the goals of the Plans.[9] Private enterprise has not been forced where it does not want to go, however, and it has substantial freedom in its control of day-to-day activity. The vigorous private entrepreneurship evident in India is eloquent testimony to the opportunities that exist for the private sector.

The demands of private consumers are not controlled directly, and both the public and private sectors respond to these private market generated stimuli. Consumer demands create a set of incentives not necessarily consistent with those required to achieve the targets established in the Plans. However, both fiscal and monetary policy have been used extensively in attempts to bring privately generated demands into consistency with Plan objectives. This is seen in the rising marginal savings rates, achieved to a large extent through continuing increases in the scope and level of indirect taxes. These fiscal measures must be given credit for keeping the changes in price levels to relatively modest proportions until recent years.

1.3 Brief Description of the Models

Having described for purposes of contrast the practice of Indian planning, we turn now to a brief survey of the planning models that will be presented in the following chapters. The models are addressed to the problems of determining the optimal levels of savings and investment over time, and the related problems of intersectoral and intertemporal distribution of investment and output and use of foreign exchange resources. They are linear programming models that are adapted in various ways in specific applications. There is a basic structure common to all of them. Production processes in all sectors require fixed capital and intermediate inputs in fixed proportions and have constant returns to scale. Many sectors need imports as inputs in fixed proportions to output. Imports are also permitted in varying amounts to supplement domestic production in certain sectors. Private consumption is a composite commodity and is consumed in proportions that are

---

[9]There has been substantial progress toward decontrol of the economy in recent months.

fixed in each period. Furthermore, aggregate consumption must increase monotonically with time. Investments for creating new capacity have to be made up to three years before the capacity can be put into use. In any period, stocks of inventories depend on the output of the next period. Fixed capital and foreign exchange are the only scarce factors. Labor supply is assumed to be unlimited and, thus, not a constraint on output. The economy is defined by the following elements:

1. *The objective or criterion function,* which is maximized, is the sum of aggregate consumption in each of the plan periods, discounted by a social discount rate. The solution of each model achieves the highest value of this function that is consistent with all the constraints. This particular objective is chosen because it reflects directly, through comparison with population levels, one of the major objectives of development: improvement in the average standard of living. Other types of criteria, such as maximizing the growth of the industrial sector or expanding agricultural production as fast as possible, prejudge the means by which social welfare is advanced. It should be noted, however, that in a programming model, goals of economic policy can be stipulated not only by what is chosen to be maximized, but also by the content of the constraints.

2. *A consumption growth constraint* requires that aggregate consumption grow by at least a stipulated minimum rate. This rate, when compared to the population growth rate, indicates a required minimum rate of growth in the average standard of living.

3. *A savings constraint,* imposed in some of the models, relates the maximum permissible level of net savings to the net national product. It is yet another way of introducing social goals and a behavioral constraint into the models, for it describes, though indirectly, the limits on the willingness of society to sacrifice present for future consumption.

4. *Consumption proportions* are specified exogenously for each period in some models but are varied endogenously from period to period by means of consumption-expenditure elasticities in other models.

5. *Production accounting relationships* stipulate that the total requirements for each commodity in each period not exceed its availability in that period. The total demand consists of the requirements for the good as an intermediate input, which are determined by use of an input-output matrix, and of a number of final demands. These include the demands for inventories, new fixed investment, replacement investment, public and private consumption, and exports. The availability is the sum of domestic production and imports.

6. *Capacity restraints* insure by means of capital-output ratios that the output of each sector in each period does not exceed that producible with the fixed capacity available in the sector at the beginning of that period.

7. *Capital accounting relationships* determine capacity at the beginning of each period as the capacity previously available, less depreciation, plus the newly completed additions to capacity, plus that part of the depreciated capacity which is restored.

8. *New capital creation* takes place in each sector with a separate gestation lag for the contribution from each of the capital goods producing sectors.

The different gestation lags for each sector are specified externally to the model.

9. *Inventory requirements* are determined by inventory-output matrices.

10. *Exports and public consumption* are estimated outside the model and supplied to it as data.

11. *Imports* are divided into two categories. "Noncompetitive" imports for each sector are determined by stipulated import-output ratios, but the stipulations may change over time. "Competitive" imports are allocated by the model with limits set, in some versions, on the extent to which this type of import can be absorbed in any one sector.

12. *Balance of payments constraints* require that total imports in each period not exceed the foreign exchange availability as determined by exports and the stipulated net foreign capital inflow in that period. A goal of national self-sufficiency can also be imposed in this constraint through the time pattern stipulated for the decline and eventual elimination of the net foreign capital inflow.

13. *Initial conditions* are estimates of production capacities, stocks of inventories, and the unfinished capital-in-process actually available at the beginning of the plan period.

14. *Terminal conditions* must be provided in some manner, in order to relate the events of the plan period to the postplan period, so the model will not behave as if time stopped at the end of the plan. These terminal conditions are the final capital stocks on hand and in process of completion. They are either completely specified from some source outside the model, or they are partially derived in the solution of the model. The manner in which terminal conditions are determined is one of the major features differentiating the various models.

This basic structure is combined in various ways and over different planning periods to develop four different models illustrating different aspects of model building and analyzing different problems.

In the first, which we call the *Target Model,* the terminal conditions are stipulated in the form of required minimum terminal capital stocks in each sector. In the solutions calculated, the target stocks are taken from the Third Five Year Plan and from the proposed Fourth Five Year Plan. The model solution determines the maximum amount of consumption that can be produced within the plan period consistent with these targets and the other constraints. It also indicates the total amount of investment and domestic savings required by the targets, as well as an exhaustive calculation of the sectoral input requirements and outputs in each year.

The model is useful in testing the feasibility of a prescribed target set of output capacities. The targets are considered feasible if a transition from the initial capacity levels to the target capacities can be made within the prescribed time period of the Plan. The targets may have been determined, as in the case of the Indian Plans, by using a method such as commodity balances. They may or may not be statically consistent in the sense that, if achieved, they can be maintained. Static consistency however, is not enough to insure that targets are attainable within the prescribed Plan period. Comparison of the investment requirements as

Fig. 1.1. Target Model Illustration.

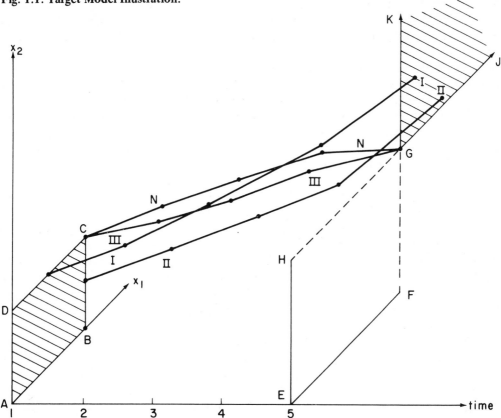

calculated in the model solutions with the planned allocations provides a test of the over-all feasibility as well as the consistency of the Plans.

Figure 1.1 illustrates the operation of the Target Model in the simple case of a five-year plan in which there are only two goods, x_1 and x_2. The maximum amounts of x_1 and x_2 that can be produced in the first period are indicated by the length of the line segments AB and AD, respectively. These are determined by the capacities available at the beginning of the first period. Even though not all the capacities available in the first period need be used, the shaded area ABCD contains all the possible combinations of initial outputs of x_1 and x_2.[10] The terminal-year capacity targets can also be described by the maximum potential outputs that they make possible in the first postterminal year. The goal specified for x_1 is EF and for x_2 is EH. Final capacities that exceed EF and EH would also be acceptable outcomes, so the shaded quadrant KGJ, whose origin is at G, indicates all acceptable terminal points. Any technically feasible time path of outputs must begin from a point in ABCD and reach a point in KGJ. Lines I, II, III, · · ·, N represent all such feasible paths. Paths I and II exceed the targets. If none of the paths can reach a point in KGJ, that region represents a technically infeasible set of targets. Any one of the time paths I, II, III, · · ·, N may be

[10]Not all of the points in ABCD are necessarily feasible.

optimal, depending on the criteria applied, which may be enforced by constraints restricting the set of acceptable paths. For example, x_1 may represent consumer goods and x_2 capital goods. Path I sacrifices some potentially available consumer goods production in the first period but finally reaches a higher terminal level of capital goods capacity than does path II with the opposite set of sacrifices and achievements. Whether path I or II is preferred depends on time preference and the relevant social welfare function or set of social judgments.

The second model, which we call the *Transit Model,* is one in which the terminal conditions are set endogenously from a specification of required postterminal growth rates of consumption, exports, and imports. It is used to find the optimal path of transition to these growth rates from the initial capacity levels. Solutions are carried out corresponding to the Fourth Plan period. The model is used to demonstrate the technique of endogenous determination of targets and to explore the implications of alternative targets. In the Transit Model for example, it may be required that in the postplan period consumption grow by 7 per cent per year, exports by 6 per cent, and imports by 5 per cent. The Transit Model is constrained to attain a terminal composition of stocks that satisfies such requirements. However, in our solutions it is not necessary to reach a particular final level of capacities on such a path. The terminal capacities actually attained are determined in the process of solution. This freedom to select the final set of capacities makes the Transit Model an open-ended system as compared to the Target Model, in which both the initial and the terminal conditions are completely specified. This distinction, though not intrinsic to the models, is important in our applications. It is possible to specify such low terminal requirements for the Target Model that it is virtually an open-ended system. Similarly the Transit Model can be constrained to reach terminal conditions equivalent to particular output targets.

Figure 1.2 illustrates the Transit Model. The starting point of any feasible path is again confined to the shaded quadrant ABCD, representing all possible initial combinations of outputs of x_1 and x_2. The terminal conditions may now be anywhere in quadrant KEJ. Here too lines I, II, III, $\cdots$, N represent all possible feasible paths, with terminal conditions now determined by specifying the postterminal growth rates that must be achievable at the end of the planning period. These postterminal growth rates are indicated by the arrows at the ends of the paths in the terminal quadrant KEJ.[11]   A feasible path may have high growth in the plan period and relatively low growth in the postplan period, or vice versa. Designation of an optimal path again depends on the criteria applied. In this model also it is possible to apply some criteria by constraints restricting the set of acceptable paths. For example, minimum terminal output capacities may be specified at levels of EF and EH for x_1 and x_2 so that all paths leading to a point in EFGH would be ruled out.

In path I, production of x_1 in each plan year is weighted so heavily in the criterion function that x_2 is sacrificed in all years, and the productive capacity of

---

[11] The arrows representing the postterminal growth rates will have different slopes even when they represent the same growth rates. Constant growth rates imply exponentially growing paths, and the various terminal points are at different positions on such paths.

Fig. 1.2. Transit Model Illustration.

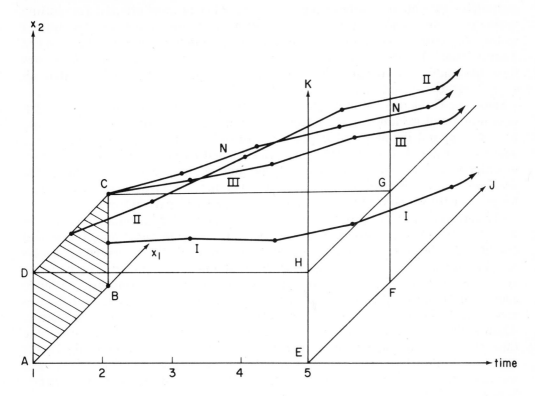

x_1 in later years actually declines. In path II, production of x_2 is weighted so heavily that the production of x_1 is reduced to below the initial capacity levels. Path III has constant relative weights for x_1 and x_2 but with a requirement that the output of both increase monotonically. Paths III and N start by fully utilizing the initial capacities and end by achieving the same goals, but they provide different amounts of x_1 and x_2 at different times within and at the end of the plan period.

The implications for society of many objectives can be evaluated adequately only in the context of a long perspective. For example, the sacrifices that the current generation makes for the next generation depend both upon the burden of those sacrifices and on the magnitude of future rewards. These issues arise most concretely in terms of the content specified for targets of short plans. Ideally the analysis of such issues should be done in the context of an infinite planning horizon since there is no natural way of truncating the future time span considered. Since this is not currently practical, one of the issues to be resolved is whether a planning horizon of, say, twenty to thirty years is adequate for a long-run study. The *Guidepath Models* are formulated in order to investigate issues that require a long planning horizon. To accomplish this, the time span of the Guidepath Models is stretched to eighteen and thirty years in alternative solutions. In order to do this and stay within the bounds of computational capacity, each successive time period is aggregated to three-years' duration. In addition, in order to take into account some of the long-term shifts that occur in an economy in the process of development, the Guidepath Models embody techniques for endogenously changing consumption proportions and for shifting resources from traditional to modern methods in the important agricultural sector. The terminal conditions in the Guidepath Models are determined, as in the Transit Model, by specifying minimum postterminal growth rates for the various final demands. The *Guidepath-I* and *Guidepath-II* versions differ in that an explicit savings constraint is enforced in the latter model.

Since the Guidepath Models are used primarily for the purpose of providing orientation and guidance in the selection of objectives and long-term strategy, the loss of temporal detail is not important. For operational purposes however, the year-by-year details for the early years of a desired long-term path are important in order to provide guidance for nearby periods. A short-term model, called the *Guidepost Model* is used to obtain such detail for the early years of a desired long-term path which is obtained as a solution of a Guidepath Model.

The illustration of Guidepath Model solutions in Fig.1.3 is generally similar to that for the Transit Model with respect to the determination of terminal conditions. However, the initial capacities now refer to the projected capacities for the second year as an average for the first three-year period. The planning period is now much longer, and the solutions indicate outputs, resource allocations, etc., for each three-year period. The provisions for structural changes which the Guidepath Model contains cannot be shown in the schematic picture. Again paths I, II, III, $\cdots$, N illustrate the range of alternative, technically feasible time paths that can be generated. Some, such as path II, would be eliminated if minimum terminal output capacities of both EF and EH were required for x_1 and x_2, respectively. Choice among the other paths again depends on the criteria imposed.

Fig. 1.3. Guidepath and Guidepost Model Illustrations.

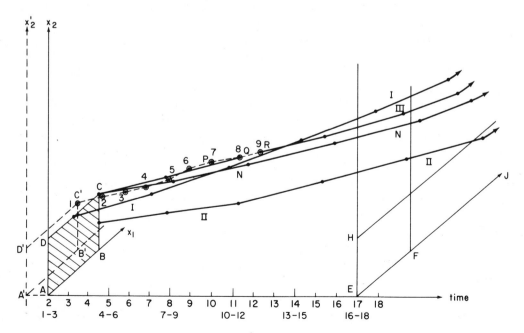

The operation of the Guidepost Model is illustrated in Fig. 1.3 by the broken lines. This shows a year-by-year path consistent with a set of targets taken from a Guidepath Model solution. The capacities represented by point Q refer to the third period of Guidepath-II. These capacities are taken as the capacities for the eighth year, and the capacities P and R for the seventh and ninth years are interpolated. The capacities corresponding to P are stipulated as the required terminal capacities. Moreover, terminal capital-in-process is to be sufficient so that capacities Q and R may be realized in the postplan period. The initial feasible region is now confined to A′B′C′D′. The year-by-year plan is shown by the broken line C′PQR.

Each model is solved for a variety of alternative specifications of behavioral, technical, and policy parameters in order to determine the sensitivity of the results to changes in such parameters and to illustrate the range of issues that the models can analyze. Each solution of a model generates for each sector and each period all the uses of capacity, foreign exchange, and output that are consistent with the maximum value of the objective functions and the constraints. Detailed, period-by-period national income accounts are compiled to show the over-all workings of the economy.

In addition each solution provides a set of shadow prices, corresponding to the various constraints, which indicate the value, in terms of the maximand, of a marginal adjustment in a constraint with all other constraints remaining unchanged. For example, when the production accounting constraint on the agricultural sector is modified by one unit, say, by external provision of one unit of agricultural output, the allocations will be reorganized and the maximum consumption provided will increase. This increase in consumption is the shadow price on the production accounting constraint on Agriculture. Since, in the objective function of these models consumption is a composite commodity, the increment in consumption must also be in the form of the composite commodity. The shadow prices are therefore also determined in terms of this composite commodity.

The shadow prices are analogous to real prices. They represent the true worth to society of a change in availabilities or in structure. They differ from real prices not only because of "imperfections" in the world that are not in the models, such as monopolies, but also because the shadow prices reflect rigorously the models' particular and inevitably somewhat unrealistic structure.

1.4 Preliminary Evaluation of the Models

Finding solutions to the models just described is practicable only with a high-speed computer with large memory, and even so requires relatively large amounts of computer time.[12] Many of the simplifications embodied in the models' descriptions of the economy are required because of limitations of computer capacity. Others are due to unavailability of data. Every simplification has a cost in terms of the realism and usefulness of the models, and one of the most important aspects of model building and use is appreciation of the

---

[12] The development of the models and the computations presented in this book required, over a period of 3 years, 150 hours of computer time on an IBM 7094. With a core memory of 32,768 words, it was the largest commercially available computer at the time.

consequences of simplification. We shall constantly be concerned with this problem, but some of its aspects can be usefully reviewed at this point on the basis of the brief summary of the models which has already been presented.

Although consumption is the only criterion in the objective function of the models, some additional social goals, such as steady growth in average consumption levels and in national self-sufficiency, are introduced as linear constraints, and still others could be. For example, government consumption, which is specified externally, provides for expenditure on education, medical, and other welfare goals and can also be specified to account for changes in military defense expenditures. Similarly, the savings constraint reflects the limits of the willingness of the present generation to sacrifice for the future. If sectoral employment coefficients are available, a minimum employment constraint can easily be introduced. Income distribution goals can also be introduced as a constraint by means of data relating the distribution of income generated in each sector to the output of the sector.

The form of the objective function has a major influence on the intertemporal distribution of consumption and investment. A linear objective function, as in the models just described, will unless modified by other relationships, result in a solution in which consumption tends to be concentrated either at the beginning or at the end of the plan. However, this "flip-flop" or "bang-bang" tendency is modified by means of the constraints specifying a minimum consumption growth rate and those relating savings and net national product. Such constraints have an effect on the solution similar to nonlinearities in the objective function. With suitable specification of these constraints, any desired time path of consumption which is feasible can be obtained. We believe that the present formulation has the advantage that the significance of the constraints is more readily apparent and meaningful and, in the absence of any empirical data on the social utility of consumption, involves no more arbitrariness than would be required by the specification of a social utility function.

The sectoral composition of consumption is stipulated in the models in externally fixed proportions or is determined endogenously by fixed elasticity relations with total consumption. No opportunity is provided for variations in the composition of consumption depending on price elasticities, mainly due to lack of empirical data. The only means of adjusting sectoral demands for consumption is through changes in total consumption. As a result, bottleneck situations in a particular sector can have the effect of constraining over-all consumption. While this may be troublesome in short-run models, over longer periods such situations are avoided in the model solutions. On the other hand, the high degree of aggregation in these models makes substitution only marginally important, and in a practical application on a more disaggregated basis some amount of flexibility can be permitted with additional computational costs.

In these models the availability of natural resources can be assumed to be reflected in the productivity of capital in the primary goods sectors. Labor is assumed to be free except that education expenditures are subsumed in government consumption. The gestation period specified for capital provides another device for taking into account the problems of developing new organizations, of training labor, and of developing managerial skills. It would be a fairly simple matter to expand the models to require various types of labor inputs for production and to specify the methods of their supply in models of this type. These additional production relationships have not been introduced in the present analyses, mainly because data on the types of labor skills required in the different sectors are limited, and there is even less information on how these skills are acquired in the Indian economy. Furthermore, scarcity of labor with limited skills is not critical in India, and the effects of neglecting such labor as an input to production would be marginal. The types of labor skills which are most likely to be bottlenecks in expanding production, i.e., those of foremen, technicians, engineers, and managers, are the most difficult to quantify and take into account in any type of planning framework.

The production functions in the models are homogeneous of the first degree, i.e., they show constant returns to scale and have fixed input coefficients. In addition, all production relationships are accounted for directly in inputs and outputs, so there are no external economies or diseconomies. Thus, there is no provision for increasing or decreasing returns to scale, substitution of relatively scarce factors, or increasing productivity by learning-by-doing. Decreasing returns to scale can easily be incorporated into a linear model, and we have done this for Agriculture in the Guidepath and Guidepost Models. As far as they can be predicted in advance, marginal rather than average capital-output ratios can be used to treat increasing returns.[13] Similarly, in order to account for the effects of learning-by-doing and "teething troubles," a higher capital-output ratio can be used for capacity in the first few years after its creation than in subsequent years. At the high level of aggregation of eleven sectors with which all our calculations have been made, substitution among the outputs of different sectors may be unimportant. The explicit accounting of interindustry interdependences in the models is a satisfactory treatment of the so-called pecuniary externalities.

Though inventory coefficients are fixed, inventory accounting is an explicit part of the models' framework rather than being omitted or estimated in a completely arbitrary manner as has often been done in planning exercises. In some solutions, inventory coefficients are progressively reduced to illustrate the effects of a policy of economizing on this type of investment.

The estimation of depreciation externally to the model follows from the assumption that the wearing out of capital is a function of time rather than of use, and that capital lifetimes are long in relation to planning periods. The alternative assumption that depreciation is a linear function of the use of capital could easily be introduced wherever the data would justify it.

The structure of the foreign trade sector in the models is less sophisticated, because it is linear with fixed coefficients, than much of current trade theory. Yet the models do have the virtue of relating foreign trade to the rest of the economy quantitatively and in considerable detail.

To plan a program of import substitution by means of the models requires a level of sectoral aggregation which is far more detailed than the eleven-sector aggregation. However, by externally specifying noncompetitive import coeffi-

---

[13] There are promising developments in integer and mixed-integer techniques which can be adapted to handle increasing returns satisfactorily. However, in the current state of knowledge, solution of such problems takes relatively large amounts of computer time.

cients that diminish with time, planned programs of import substitution can be introduced in the models. Exports were specified externally using projections based on studies for particular commodities. The wealth of detail produced by the solutions throws a great deal of light on the significance of each assumption and provides guidelines for the iterative testing of alternative assumptions.

In view of the importance in economic development of changing production techniques, externalities, import substitution, variations in inventory-holding relations and in capital maintenance, a special comment is required on the simple treatment of these issues in the models. As already pointed out, that treatment is usually determined not so much by theoretical preference as by limited data and computational necessity. The stringencies of these necessities would be less serious in a full-scale application of the techniques than in this pilot project. Moreover, present research efforts are making progress in opening the way to a more satisfactory theoretical formulation of these aspects of the models. Therefore, we do not believe that an evaluation of the potentiality of the models should be based on the present restricted treatment of these issues. However, it is necessary to keep these limitations in mind when assessing the empirical results to be presented here for their insights into past and future Indian economic policy; we shall try to respect this requirement.

An issue frequently raised in connection with the use of programming models for development is whether the information available in the less developed countries is sufficient in quantity and quality to justify the use of the techniques. The answer is surely different for different countries, and few generalizations on this issue are possible. However, the view of economic conditions in less developed areas as unmapped and unexplorable *terra incognita* is unwarranted. There are some enclaves, the "modern sectors" usually, which may be relatively well known even when compared to the more advanced countries, simply because of their small size and newness. Sectors that have been major sources of exports have often been studied intensively in less developed areas because of their importance as foreign exchange earners. Consequently, considerable input-output and other data may exist even if the productive units are small and "unorganized."

In India and some other countries, the extensive systems of controls and public enterprise generate a substantial amount of useful information. Investment and import license applications frequently require supporting documents listing the production information that will be used by government agencies in making their decisions. In addition, there may be price control procedures such as those of the Indian Tariff Commission, which produce valuable data. For some commodities there are direct controls on use which generate a mass of detail in the various applications. In India a substantial bureaucracy has developed to administer these controls and regulations. Though the degree and ease of contact of this bureaucracy with private industry varies, a system of regular reports has helped to create a cadre of well-informed persons. In addition, there have been industrial censuses in India, the most recent of which is for 1960, and a number of sample surveys. There are grave problems of compatibility of the census and the survey material, but they are valuable data sources. Large areas remain that are nearly blank in terms of statistical information, especially the mass of agricultural, handicraft, and service sectors, which are only partially and loosely tied to markets. In many underdeveloped countries, as in India, these sectors are often among the largest in terms of output, so the information inadequacies are serious.

In the models presented here, all sectors were treated as if data of equal quality were available. This was done mainly because stochastic programming is not sufficiently developed for the purposes of these models and partly because the significance of errors in specification could be explored by testing the sensitivity of the solutions to changes in parameters. It should be noted that less consistent and theoretically satisfactory planning procedures make no smaller claims for data if they are to be used for the same purposes as the models presented here. On the other hand, it is possible to use the models flexibly and integrate less formal procedures for some sectors with the more rigorous procedures for other sectors.

Given the drawbacks described, what then can be said for the use of programming models for making development policy? We believe that no other known method does as well in providing a consistent analysis of intertemporal and intersectoral relationships and economic goals. Whatever the means of implementation, decisions will have to be made on amounts of government saving, on whether to start another steel plant next year, or build more power facilities, or allocate foreign exchange to importing mining equipment, etc. These decisions should be coordinated with all the sectoral development plans and the national goals. We believe the models indicate how this can be done in a manner superior to that of existing techniques and work on similar models now under way in a number of institutions will lead to still further improvements.

Moreover, there are likely to be some important by-products associated with the techniques presented here. First, they make the issues involved in planning more explicit than do informal and partial techniques. For example, the problems involved in setting plan targets may be glossed over in using comparative-statics analyses, e.g., commodity balances, because they do not force an explicit and thorough consideration of the issues. Second, the models inspire the development of data that might otherwise be ignored. Finally, the models emphasize the importance of exploring alternatives and designing planning methods for high-speed computation, rather than, as has generally been the case, concentrating on the preparation of only a single plan. With these techniques using high-speed computation it becomes possible to trace the outlines of a number of alternative plans and to substantially increase knowledge as to the choices available. In economic policy, as in other areas, informed choices can be made only when the alternatives are known. Furthermore, planning is a continuous process, even though it has usually been explicitly organized in discrete and intensive phases every four to seven years. There are often unexpected shortfalls in production and delays in completion of new facilities. There are occasionally unexpected increases in output and windfalls in foreign exchange earnings. Political circumstances change and, in turn, force changes in government budgets and economic policy. The formality of the quinquennial debates should not be allowed to obscure the reality of continuous adjustment and readjustment of means and ends, which should, and do, go on, and which require quick and flexible techniques of analysis.

The programming models of this book should be considered as tools which can be used continuously in a variety of forms designed for particular problems. The use of high-speed computers is both a necessity and a virtue, because it can produce with greater speed a range of alternative policies the implications of which are developed in much greater detail than otherwise possible. Finally, however, models will always be simplifications of reality, and not all the relevant considerations can be embodied in computable models.

In practical application, the limits of computational cost, which have been a constraint to the enlargement of the scope of this project, would be much less important. Even so, there is no question of the next five-year plan for India or any other country rolling off the computer intact. Though the use of the computer can provide much more detailed information about alternative policies than has been available, the computer, itself, never makes the final choice.

1.5 Outline of the Chapters

The subsequent order of presentation will be as follows: In Chapter 2 the structure of the models will be described in detail, as well as some of the reasons for choosing the particular relationships used. In Chapter 3 the data used in implementing the models, their sources, and the adjustments performed on them will be discussed. The use of the programming models for short-term planning will be demonstrated in Chapter 4 with tests of plans for the Indian Third and Fourth Five Year Plan periods. In Chapter 5 the Guidepath and Guidepost models will be presented and alternative long-term growth paths generated. Chapter 6 will be a brief summary and evaluation of the methods and results.

2. Target and Transit Models

Since verbal science has no final end,
Since life is short, and obstacles impend,
Let central facts be picked and firmly fixed,
As swans extract the milk with water mixed.

The Panchatantra

Since the methods of linear programming are well known, the description of the models' analytic framework can be relatively brief with attention concentrated on issues related to the particular applications. First, the structure common to both the Target and the Transit Model is presented and discussed. This consists of the behavioral and structural constraints and is called the Basic Model. Then the terminal conditions distinguishing each of the specific models are described. A general appraisal is made of the analytical formulation of the models and of the character of their solutions. Finally, we discuss the shadow prices, which constitute the solution of the cost-minimizing problem which is the dual to the optimizing problem.

2.1 Basic Model

The Basic Model defines an economy with the following characteristics:

1. Production in all sectors requires fixed capital and intermediate inputs in specified fixed proportions to output and is characterized by constant returns to scale.
2. Most sectors require imports in exogenously fixed proportions to output.
3. Additional imports are permitted in certain sectors to supplement domestic production in amounts determined endogenously within specified ceilings.
4. A balance of payments constraint must be met in each period, which limits total imports to the total amount of exports and net foreign capital inflow in that period.
5. Private consumption is a composite commodity the sectoral proportions of which are fixed exogenously. Furthermore, consumption is required to increase monotonically in successive periods at least at specified minimum rates.
6. In order to create new capacity, investment must be made in the periods immediately preceding the period when the new capacity becomes available, as determined by a fixed gestation process, which varies among sectors but can be as long as three periods.
7. In each period, investment in inventories in each sector is linearly related to the change in output to be realized in the next period.
8. Fixed capital stocks and foreign exchange are the only scarce factors. Labor and new materials are assumed to be adequate and exogenous to the models.

2.1.1 Objective Function

Ideally, the objective function should be a social welfare function. Since this is unknown, we choose for explicit maximization aggregate private consumption, which is surely one of the most important determinants of welfare.

The specific objective function maximized is the present discounted value of aggregate private consumption W over the planning period $t = 1, \cdots, T$;

$$(1.0) \quad W = \sum_{t=1}^{T} \frac{C(t)}{(1 + w)^{t-1}}$$

where $C(t)$ is aggregate consumption in period t and w is the social discount rate applied to future private consumption.[1]

The multiplicity of economic goals that characterizes the real world of policy-making can be described by a model whose objective function embodies only one criterion, other goals being enforced via the model's constraints. A goal imposed via a constraint is equivalent to one that has an infinite weight in the objective function until it is satisfied, after which the weight is zero. When the goals are naturally formulated as inequalities, it is most convenient to have them appear as constraints. This, for example, is the case when it is desired that consumption growth be monotonic with a certain minimum rate. Alternatively, it is possible to incorporate the content of a variety of goals in the objective function with suitable weights. The approach chosen is, to some extent, dictated by the character of the goals. In either formulation, the possibilities of trade-off can be explored by means of repeated solutions with different weights in the objective function and different limits in the constraints.

The model solutions have implications, moreover, for goals that are not specified either in the objective function or as constraints. The employment implications of a solution, for example, can be examined by dividing output results by labor productivity coefficients. Other implications of the solutions, such as those for income distribution and national self-sufficiency, can also be developed by additional analysis.

2.1.2 Consumption Growth Constraints

Constraints are applied in most solutions that require the monotonic growth of aggregate consumption between successive periods; i.e.,

$$(2.0) \quad C(t + 1) \geqslant C(t)[1 + \rho(t)], \quad \text{for } t = 0, \cdots, T - 1$$

$$(2.1) \quad C(0) = \overline{C(0)},$$

where $\rho(t)$ is the prescribed minimum growth rate for aggregate private consumption in period t and $\overline{C(0)}$ is the aggregate private consumption in the preplan period. Constraints 2.0 permit parametric investigation of the influences

---

[1]We could have put the objective function on a per capita basis by dividing aggregate consumption in each period by a projection of the population in that period. In such a formulation, the change in the population deflator has the same effect as a discount rate. As a result, the rate of growth in population would itself create a tendency in the solutions to concentrate aggregate consumption in the early plan years, when the population deflator would be smaller than in the later plan years. Per capita results can be obtained in the present formulation by dividing the consumption values in the solutions by projected population figures.

on over-all growth and output of policy decisions with respect to minimum intraplan growth rates of consumption. There is no reason why, in the absence of such constraints, the model solutions would generate monotonic growth, rather than some other pattern. Though the preplan consumption level is a historic fact that can be estimated empirically, Eq. 2.1 permits us to specify it at any arbitrary level $\overline{C(0)}$ as a way of setting $C(1)$. When $C(0)$ is set at a nonzero value, the levels, as well as the rate of growth of consumption, are constrained to minimum values in the solutions. However, in many of the calculations to be presented, when there are grounds for believing that otherwise no feasible solution would exist, $C(0)$ is set at zero. This makes the Constraint 2.1 redundant and helps to insure the achievement of a solution by permitting the solution to determine the level of consumption in the first period.

The objective function implies constant marginal utility of aggregate consumption. With this type of objective function, solutions to the model, unless otherwise constrained, would exhibit the flip-flop characteristic of solutions to linear models. In this case, the characteristic would lead to a concentration of output of consumption goods either at the beginning or at the end of the planning period. The consumption growth constraints counter the tendency to concentrate consumption at the beginning, since increasing consumption in the early plan periods would only force still higher consumption in the later ones. On the other hand, if the solution tended to concentrate consumption in the later plan periods anyway, that behavior would not be restrained by the constraints on the growth of consumption. However, terminal conditions can be set so that they also moderate the tendency to crowd consumption into the final plan years. Therefore, although a nonlinear utility function, reflecting diminishing marginal utility of aggregate consumption, would be preferable on theoretical grounds to the simple objective function chosen, with suitable constraints some of the effects of having such a utility function can be achieved.[2] A nonlinear utility function could be introduced by linear approximations, but it would impose somewhat greater computational burdens. Even if these could be borne in a more ambitious scheme, the fundamental difficulty would still remain of making reasonable estimates of the utility function. Solutions, moreover, are certain to be sensitive to the rate at which marginal utility declines. Of course, the approach could be adopted on this issue, as in other similar cases, of experimenting with various utility functions and then offering the results as a menu of alternatives.

An arbitrary utility function would not necessarily be more satisfactory for the purposes of calculation than a linear objective function. The coefficients of an arbitrary function would most likely be derived from an assumed desirable, intertemporal distribution of consumption, in which case it is as well to use the linear objective function and to specify the distribution of consumption directly, as in the constraints. Nonetheless, it must be admitted that the monotonicity

---

[2]Optimizing a linear objective function leads to a point on the bounding feasible surface. Whereas in the general case of a nonlinear objective function, the true optimum may be an interior point in the feasible space. However, the true utility function of aggregate consumption is likely to be monotonic in all dimensions. Furthermore, the true maximum is outside the feasible region. These two conditions are sufficient to insure that the true optimum is on the feasibility surface. A piecewise linear approximation of the true utility function would lead the solution to one of the corners of the facet of the feasibility surface on which the true optimum lies.

constraints are "black boxes," i.e., mechanisms providing desirable results, but whose mode of operation, in this case the relationship of the constraints to a theoretically more satisfactory utility function, is not apparent. Practical planners, however, are not concerned with the latter question, and models are judged by their meaningfulness.

2.1.3 Production Accounting Relationships

Such relationships require that the total demand for each commodity in each period not exceed the availability of the commodity in that period. Each of the terms in Eq. 3.0 represents a column vector of n elements where n is the number of sectors.

(3.0) $J(t) + H(t) + N(t) + Q(t) + F(t) + G(t) + E(t) \leqslant M(t) + X(t),$

for $t = 1, \cdots, T.$

The first seven terms represent uses of the output of each sector: $J(t)$ intermediate inputs, $H(t)$ deliveries for inventory accumulation, $N(t)$ deliveries of investment goods for new fixed capital, $Q(t)$ deliveries of investment goods for restoring depreciated fixed capital, $F(t)$ private consumption, $G(t)$ government consumption, and $E(t)$ exports. The last two terms, $M(t)$ imports and $X(t)$ domestic production, are the sources of availability of the products.

2.1.4 Intermediate Products

The intermediate requirements for output in each period are determined, Leontief-like, by an $n \times n$ matrix of input-output coefficients $a(t)$ where $a_{ij}(t)$ is the amount of good i required as an intermediate input in period t to produce one unit of good j.

(3.1) $J(t) = a(t) X(t),$ for $t = 1, \cdots, T.$

Input-output coefficients reflect technology, relative factor prices, the degree of plant integration, and the internal composition of the sectors. A certain amount of stability has been found for these coefficients in a number of countries, mainly for the organized, industrial sectors.[3] For other sectors, however, the input ratios have a substantial variance, and it is reasonable to expect some changes in these coefficients in the process of development. The time subscript t of the $a(t)$ matrix indicates that it is possible to change the intermediate requirements ratios over time. This possibility is exploited in this study, as in other approaches to planning, only to a limited degree because of lack of information.

2.1.5 Inventory Accumulation

Inventory accumulation is determined in a set of accelerator-type relationships using an $n \times n$ matrix of inventory coefficients $s(t)$. An element $s_{ij}(t)$ is the amount of good i required as inventory in period $t - 1$ to produce one unit of good j in period t.

---

[3]H. B. Chenery and T. Watanabe, "International Comparisons of the Structure of Production," *Econometrica, 24*, No. 4, 1956, pp. 487-521.

(3.2) $H(t) = s(t) \{X(t + 1) - X(t)\}$,   for $t = 2, \cdots, T$.

(3.3) $H(1) = s(1) \{X(2) - (I + \alpha_0) \overline{X(0)}\}$,

where I is the identity matrix.

   Thus, deliveries in period t for inventory are a function of the forward difference of output $[X(t + 1) - X(t)]$. This is preferable to making current deliveries for inventory purposes depend on the backward difference in output, i.e., $[X(t) - X(t - 1)]$, but a case might be made for the combination of the two formulations. Production for inventory in the first period $H(1)$ is based on the difference between output levels in the second period and output levels in the first period as anticipated in the preplan period. With α_0 the diagonal matrix of anticipated sectoral growth rates and $\overline{X(0)}$ the preplan year output levels, $s(1) (I + \alpha_0) \overline{X(0)}$ gives total stocks of inventories at the beginning of the plan. Inventory coefficients are only partially determined by technical requirements. To a considerable degree they are behavioral coefficients and respond to both price and nonprice influences; the latter include the reliability of communications and transport. Such factors may be expected to change over time, and this possibility is embodied in the formulation by giving a time subscript to the inventory coefficients.

2.1.6 Private Consumption

   The vector $F(t)$ of deliveries to private consumption is related to aggregate consumption $C(t)$ by a coefficient vector $c(t)$, which defines the proportions of sectoral consumption in the aggregate.

(3.4) $F(t) = c(t)C(t)$,   for $t = 1, \cdots, T$.

$c_i(t)$ is the amount of good i in one unit of aggregate consumption $C(t)$ and so $\Sigma_{i=1} c_i(t) = 1$. The specification of $c(t)$ thus fixes the composition of aggregate private consumption in period t. Since substantial variability in consumption composition is unlikely in the short run, $c(t)$ is kept constant for all the periods of the plan in the solutions of the Target and the Transit Models. At low levels of income, and under the still powerful influence of tradition, there is likely to be little substitution, particularly among such grossly defined sectors as those used in the solutions. The Indian market basket of consumption goods, like that of other countries at such low income levels, is relatively simple and dominated by staples. While the income and expenditure elasticities of consumption for metal or plastic items may be quite high, they are consumed in such small quantities that their total consumption is not likely to become substantial within five years. It would be particularly mistaken to believe that such products would be substituted for staples if the latter goods should become relatively scarce. In any case, the formulation of the models with fixed consumption proportions is not meant to be a permanent commitment. The proportions can be changed exogenously from solution to solution to study the effects of alternative compositions. In fact, in the Guidepath and Guidepost Models described in Chapter 5, the sectoral proportions of consumption are determined by consumption-expenditure elasticities. The latter modification could easily be introduced in the Target and Transit Models as well, but was not, mainly because it would have little effect on the general character of the solutions. The consumption proportions could also be allowed to vary within specified limits, and the optimizing mechanism would then choose the set of limits permitting the greater total of consumption goods to be produced; or only the minimum amounts of each type of consumption could be specified, and the solution would decide in which types of consumption goods production the limits would be exceeded and relative specialization would occur. The latter formulation is likely to create in actual solutions a concentration of consumption on services once minimum requirements are met in other sectors, since the service sector is far and away the easiest to expand. So a combination of the latter two approaches might be more desirable than either separately.

None of these formulations makes the consumption composition responsive to relative prices and, thus, to relative scarcities. However, the empirical information on cross-elasticities required to formulate a utility function including the possibility of substitution among sectors is not available. The additional computational costs of solving models embodying substitutability were not considered justified for an arbitrarily specified utility function. Furthermore, as we have already pointed out, at the high level of sectoral aggregation at which we work, and at India's low level of income, cross-elasticities between sectors are relatively unimportant, though within the sectors they are important. In a mixed economy, decisions within most sectors are delegated to the market mechanism, so that the neglect of intrasectoral cross-elasticities in making intersectoral allocations is of less significance in a macroeconomic policy model.

2.1.7 Government Consumption

The amounts required from each sector for government consumption in each period are specified externally. If $G(t)$ is the vector of government consumption in period t, then

(3.5) $G(t) = \overline{G(t)}$,   for $t = 1, \cdots, T$.

This projection includes a wide variety of welfare expenditures, administrative costs, defence expenditures, and other items.

Government consumption is not independent of the level and growth rate of output, either on the demand or supply side. The area of education provides a good example of the interdependence of private output and government consumption. Private demand for education certainly rises with income, and the government responds by trying to meet it, even though much of the demand can hardly be considered an increment to productive capacity. On the other hand, government engineering colleges, for example, provide additional, scarce inputs without which the system would not run nearly so well. Similar observations can be made about government health services. We do not attempt to introduce these considerations into the model by relating government consumption to other variables.

2.1.8 Exports

$E(t)$, the vector of exports in period t, is determined outside the model structure, and

(3.6) $E(t) = \overline{E(t)}$,   for $t = 1, \cdots, T$.

This is not a fully satisfactory procedure, since, except in extreme cases, exports depend on domestic prices, which in turn depend on the amount and composition of productive resources and, finally, on comparative advantage. Though the separate projection of exports is not a grave deficiency for short-period plans, it is a more serious shortcoming in models with a long planning horizon, since the model solution itself should reflect changing comparative advantage. Yet to determine comparative advantage, an analysis of the world economy would be required.

If a demand schedule for exports is estimated outside the model, then the choice between export promotion or import substitution can be made within the model solution. For this purpose, however, a higher degree of disaggregation is desirable than is contained in our models.

2.1.9 Capacity Restraints

These insure, by means of the diagonal matrix b of aggregate capital-output ratios, that output in each sector in each period does not exceed the amount producible with the fixed capital in that sector available at the beginning of that period. If $K(t)$ is the vector of fixed capital available at the beginning period t,

$$(4.0) \quad b(t)X(t) \leqslant K(t), \qquad \text{for } t = 1, \cdots, T.$$

A different b matrix might be associated with each specific "vintage" of capital, but that is not done here.[4]

2.1.10 Investment Requirements

The total capital in each sector, represented by an element of the vector $K(t)$, is a composite commodity with a fixed composition. This composition is defined by a proportion matrix p, in which element p_{ij} represents the good i held as fixed capital by sector j per unit of composite fixed capital K_j.

Sectoral capacities may be increased in any period t by the delivery of additions to capacity $Z(t)$. These increments of capacity, in turn, are formed by deliveries of investment goods from the sectors that produce them. The deliveries are in fixed proportions and with fixed time leads of one, two, and three periods prior to the completion of the addition to capacity. The amount of $Z(t)$ that must be furnished by each sector in each period is determined by the three investment lag proportions matrices p', p'', p'''. The coefficients p'_{ij}, p''_{ij}, p'''_{ij} in these matrices indicate the proportions of the total increment to capacity in sector j in period t that must be supplied by sector i in periods $t - 1$, $t - 2$, and $t - 3$.[5] Thus, the total amount of deliveries of investment goods in each period is

$$(5.0) \quad N(t) = p'Z(t + 1) + p''Z(t + 2) + p'''Z(t + 3), \qquad \text{for } t = 1, \cdots T.$$

The constancy of the terms in the matrices p', p'', and p''' imply assumptions of fixed proportions of the various components of capital, e.g., of equipment and

---

[4]By stipulating a different capital coefficient for capital of different ages, learning-by-doing can be introduced into the model. This can be done without adding further restraints, if the capital accounting Relationships 5.4 are formulated as strict equalities and substituted into 4.0.

[5]The matrices p', p'', and p''' have a simple relationship to p, p_{ij} being equal to $p'_{ij} + p''_{ij} + p'''_{ij}$.

construction, in finished capital of each sector and of fixed-time sequences in which these components must be provided to create the capital. Such fixity is again not an accurate description of reality. The fixed-proportions assumption is an aspect of the assumption of given technology. If the choice of technology is to be made by the model solution, a set of alternative p's must be stipulated. With respect to the fixed-sequences assumption, since the output of each sector is homogeneous, it would be possible as an alternative procedure to make capital-in-process nonspecific and to indicate only the total contribution of each capital goods sector to output. This would allow investment goods to be produced in advance of the actual increment in capacity whenever the model decided it was most convenient. The latter formulation would provide for flexibility in the sequence of capital formation, making it possible for the model to stretch out the lags beyond the specified minimum lags if it would be preferable to do so. This, in turn, would undoubtedly somewhat improve the over-all performance of the model solutions. It would require, however, a more careful accounting of the production of capital goods by each sector, their movement into use or into an inventory of "unfinished capacity," and their withdrawal from that inventory. That would, in turn, increase the number of restraints. Since the model is likely to use the additional freedom only in the initial periods, the additional computational burden was not considered worthwhile. Moreover, if the model were given this additional freedom in scheduling investment, it would use it, if at all, by totally interrupting investment in some year. Since the costs of such a complete interruption are not easily accounted for in a linear framework and, in reality, the output of each sector is not completely homogeneous, we chose not to provide the model with the freedom to reschedule the investment sequence.

2.1.11 Depreciated Capital

Real depreciation in this model depends on passage of time rather than on rate of use. The depreciation pattern chosen is the "one hoss shay" type, again because of the desire for simplicity and the limitation of factual ignorance. In this pattern capital can produce services at a constant rate over a lifetime independent of the rate of use of the capital. At the end of this lifetime, all the productive capability of the capital disappears. Since the lifetimes of plant and equipment are chosen to be, respectively, thirty-three and twenty years, the disappearance of productive capacity through depreciation is predetermined in full for twenty years and in part for thirteen more years.

The capital originating in sector i that wears out in sector j is $D_{ij}(t)$. The total depreciated capital in each sector in each period is then $D_j = \Sigma_i D_{ij}(t)$, and for all sectors

(5.1) $D(t) = \overline{D(t)}$, for $t = 1, \cdots, T + 3$.

2.1.12 Depreciated Capacity

Different lifetimes for different components of capital imply that plant and equipment depreciate in an "unbalanced" manner. This, in turn, provides the opportunity for restoring capacity by an unbalanced production of capital of the plant or equipment type. Since the components of capital stock in each sector wear out at different rates, the capacity immobilized by the depreciation of the components must be computed. The depreciation composition matrix r is defined with element $r_{ij} = D_{ij}/D_j$. Then if $D_j(t)$ is multiplied by r_{ij}/p_{ij}, the amount of capacity that would be lost due to depreciation on each component $D_{ij}(t)$ in sector j can be computed. The actual amount of capacity lost through depreciation in sector j is the largest loss due to the wearing out of any component and is determined by the maximum of $(r_{1j}/p_{1j}, r_{2j}/p_{2j}, \cdots, r_{nj}/p_{nj})D_j$. Therefore, the diagonal matrix d can be formed whose element $d_{jj} \equiv$ Max $(r_{1j}/p_{1j}, r_{2j}/p_{2j}, \cdots, r_{nj}/p_{nj})$. The capacity lost through depreciation in each sector is, therefore,

(5.2) $V(t) = [d] D(t)$, for $t = 1, \cdots, T + 3$.

2.1.13 Restoration Requirements

It is up to the optimizing mechanism to determine R(t), the amount of the capacity lost through depreciation that will be restored. The model solution may, in fact, provide for restoration of only part of the depreciated capacity. This is likely to happen only when the patterns of depreciating capacity are substantially different from the proportions in which capacity is desired in the future.

The deliveries Q(t) from each sector for capacity restoration R(t) are assumed, like new capital formation, to require up to three periods. So the deliveries for this purpose in any one period look three periods ahead.

Where r', r'', and r''' are restoration lag proportions matrices similar to p', p'', and p''',

(5.3) $Q(t) = r'[d]^{-1} R(t + 1) + r''[d]^{-1} R(t + 2) + r'''[d]^{-1} R(t + 3)$,

for $t = 1, \cdots, T$.

The coefficients r'_{ij}, r''_{ij}, and r'''_{ij} indicate the proportions of the total *capital* replacement $R_j(t)/d_{jj}$ to restore *capacity* $R_j(t)$ that must be supplied by sector i in periods $t - 1, t - 2$, and $t - 3$.

2.1.14 Capital Accounting Relationships

Having described the manner in which capital is created, wears out, and is replaced, we can now write the accounting relationships for capacity in each sector as

(5.4) $K(t + 1) \leqslant K(t) + Z(t + 1) + R(t + 1) - V(t + 1)$, for $t + 1, \cdots, T + 2$.

This merely states that K(t + 1), the capital available at the beginning of period t + 1, cannot be greater than the capital available in the preceding period plus the new, completed additions to capacity, plus that part of depreciated capacity that is restored, less the capacity depreciating in period t. Since both the restored capacity R(t + 1) and new capacity Z(t + 1) can be zero, decumulation of capital to the extent of V(t + 1) is possible.

We have assumed in this formulation that if capacity is to be restored when any component of capital depreciates, the restoration must take place in the same period in which the depreciation occurs. This means that undepreciated components of capital are lost if restoration is not carried out in that period.[6]

2.1.15 Restoration ceilings

Since a unit of capacity can be created more cheaply by restoring a worn-out component than by supplying the entire set of components of the composite capital, the model has to be restrained from restoring more capacity than is depreciated in any period.

$$(6.0) \quad R(t) \leqslant V(t), \quad \text{for } t = 1, \cdots, T + 3.$$

2.1.16 Balance of Payments Constraints

The total amount of imports $\sum_{i=1}^{n} M_i(t)$ in each period is limited by the availability of foreign exchange. This in turn depends on the total amount of exports $\sum_{i=1}^{n} E_i(t)$, foreign aid from government sources, private foreign investment, and whatever changes in reserves will be tolerated. The latter three components, lumped together, are designated net foreign capital inflow and are specified exogenously as $\overline{A(t)}$. The balance of payments is

$$(7.0) \quad uM(t) \leqslant \overline{A(t)} + uE(t), \quad \text{for } t = 1, \cdots T.$$

where u is a unit row vector $[1, 1, 1, \cdots, 1]$. By changing A(t) over time, a schedule of progress toward a condition of self-sufficiency can be enforced in this constraint.

2.1.17 Composition of Imports

The next step is to provide for the allocation of the total import potential among the various sectors. First, some sectors, such as construction and electric power generation, are not allowed to import at all, so the import terms in those sectors are set at zero. Second, in each period some imports are noncompetitive in the sense that these are goods for intermediate as well as final use for which no domestic capacity exists, and for which no substitution by domestic output is possible, whatever the relative prices of imports and domestic outputs. Few imports are strictly noncompetitive in the long run for a country such as India, which contains a wide variety of resources and climates. In the short run, however, capacities and institutions create distinct limits to many types of domestic production. Competitive imports are goods for which domestic capacity can be created. They are, therefore, allocated among consuming sectors, depending on the relative costs of the imports and domestic production.

The vector of noncompetitive imports $M'(t)$ is related to output levels by fixed coefficients. The vector of competitive imports $M''(t)$ merely supplements the output of the corresponding domestic sectors. Total imports in each sector are the sum of the two types:

$$(8.0) \quad M(t) = M'(t) + M''(t), \quad \text{for } t = 1, \cdots T.$$

---

[6]It would be possible to avoid this limiting assumption by changing the Constraints 6.0 on restoration ceilings, described next, to

$$\sum_{t=1}^{t} R(t) \leqslant \sum_{t=1}^{t} V(t), \quad t = 1, \cdots, T + 3.$$

This would provide the freedom to restore depreciated capital in any period subsequent to its depreciation.

2.1.18 Noncompetitive Imports

Noncompetitive imports are determined by multiplying the diagonal matrix $m'(t)$ of fixed import coefficients by the vector of domestic outputs:

$$(8.1) \quad M'(t) = m'(t)X(t), \qquad \text{for } t = 1, \cdots, T.$$

Noncompetitive imports are essential and must be made if there is to be any domestic production. They thus complement domestic production. The requirements for such imports must be satisfied before other, supplementary imports are allowed. Because of these conditions, the foreign exchange available to purchase noncompetitive imports can, in some circumstances, set a limit to domestic output. However, noncompetitive import coefficients can be changed period by period to take into account planned programs of import substitution.

2.1.19 Competitive Import Ceilings

Equation 8.1 has the effect of determining the minimum amount of imports necessary for producing domestic output $X(t)$. Once the minimums are satisfied, the remaining foreign exchange should be used where it is most valuable; the creation of domestic capacity depends on this use. Competitive imports make use of whatever foreign exchange is left after noncompetitive imports are satisfied.

While noncompetitive imports are complements to domestic production, competitive imports $M''(t)$ are substitutes. In the absence of diminishing returns however, the model solution would tend to concentrate the use of competitive imports in only a few sectors. To the extent that diminishing returns exist, this would unduly restrict domestic capacity formation in these sectors. To avoid this possibility the maximum use of foreign exchange for competitive imports is stipulated for each sector in

$$(8.2) \quad M''(t) \leqslant m''(t) \left[A(t) + uE(t) - uM'(t) \right], \qquad \text{for } t = 1, \cdots, T.$$

where the vector of coefficients $m''(t)$ is exogenously prescribed so that $\Sigma_i m_i''(t) > 1$. This formulation provides some scope for choice among sectors in the allocation of foreign exchange to competitive imports, but recognizes limitations on such choice. In some of the solutions, the constraint in Eq. 8.2 will be nullified by setting all the m_i'' equal to unity so that the model has complete freedom to allocate foreign exchange for competitive imports.

The treatment of competitive and noncompetitive imports recognizes the technical, political, and administrative obstacles to changes in the pattern of use of foreign exchange resources from period to period. Yet the distinctions as made are probably more rigid than as they exist in reality. Bottlenecks, due to indivisibilities in production and the lack of specific material resources and of technical skills, do exist and must be introduced in the model. Though they may be absolute in the short run, they are often subject to substantial modification within several years. This possibility now exists in the model to only a limited degree. It would be more valid to formulate the model so that the creation of domestic capacity for all imported goods would be determined by the optimizing mechanism with constraints that perhaps reflect increasing costs but are less completely rigid than in the present framework. While this is less important for short-run than for long-run models, it would represent a desirable extension of the analysis.

2.1.20 Initial Capital Stock and Capital-in-Process

Events within the plan period are related both to what has gone before and what comes after, as can be seen explicitly in a number of the relationships of the Basic Model. In the capacity restraints in Eq. 4.0, for example, the capital stocks available at the outset of the plan period must be known. Eq. 5.4 also indicates the need for somehow determining the levels of capital-in-process at the beginning and end of the plan. To the Basic Model core, we must now add the description of how the model is started.

The capital stock available at the beginning of the first year of the plan is greater than that which produced the output of the preplan period, since additional investment will mature and become available by the end of the preplan period, i.e., by the beginning of the first plan period. This capital capacity is the initial capacity for the plan. In addition, the investment undertaken in the preplan period to mature in the first and second periods must also be specified. Alternatively, the maximum gross increments in capacity deliverable in the first and second periods can be stipulated since they are rigidly linked to preplan investment. This does not commit the solution to the completion of the projects started before the plan period; that is a matter to be determined by the optimization procedure.

These initial conditions ought to be based on empirical information available before the plan begins. Practically, however, no information has been available to us as to the amounts of uncompleted capital-in-process at the beginning of each plan period. Even though the Third Five Year Plan refers to projects started during the Second to be completed during the Third, the information in the Plan is not sufficient to estimate either the sectoral composition or the degree of completion of such projects at the beginning of the Third Plan. Similarly, adequate information about initial conditions is not publicly available for the Fourth Plan period.

It would have been possible to estimate the capital stocks available during the first three periods of the Third Plan from the output levels achieved in these three years. Yet our objective is to simulate the planning process as it is confronted before the beginning of the plan. Consequently, initial conditions are estimated by assuming that in the preplan period for each sector a growth rate, α_{0i}, has been projected for the creation of capital. The initial conditions thus become

$$(9.0) \quad K(1) = b(1)(I + \alpha_0)\overline{X(0)},$$

$$(9.1) \quad Z(2) + R(2) \leqslant b(2)\,\alpha_0\,(I + \alpha_0)\,\overline{X(0)} + V(2),$$

$$(9.2) \quad Z(3) + R(3) \leqslant b(3)\,\alpha_0\,(I + \alpha_0)^2\,\overline{X(0)} + V(3),$$

where α_0 is a diagonal matrix of sectoral growth rates α_{0i}.

2.1.21 Terminal Requirements

An optimum short-run plan is a detailed working-out of a longer plan that embodies distant as well as current goals of society. Making longer plans, however, requires information hidden by the future. Therefore the choice of the plan period depends, among other factors, on the uncertainties associated with the future. Analytical and computational problems also force the truncation of the planning period. In Chapter 5, techniques of making and coordinating long and short plans will be presented. In this chapter we confine ourselves to the conventional five-year plan period.

Our objective function is a weighted sum of aggregate consumption provided during the plan years. But current economic policy decisions should reflect the reality of an unbroken chain of economic relationships leading from the past into the future. In our models the stocks of fixed capital, of inventories, and of capital-in-process are the only links in that chain. Specification of these stocks at the end of the plan period determines the future alternatives available to the economy. It is therefore the function of the terminal requirements, formulated as constraints, to reflect the goals of the postplan future into the plan period. Alternatively, terminal conditions could have been embodied in the objective function.

In general then, the terminal requirements state the desired minimum levels of the final capital stocks:

(10.0) $K(T + 1) \geqslant \overline{K(T + 1)}$,

(10.1) $K(T + 2) \geqslant \overline{K(T + 2)}$,

(10.2) $K(T + 3) \geqslant \overline{K(T + 3)}$,

and

(10.3) $s(T)X(T + 1) \geqslant X_s(T + 1)$,

where $\overline{X_s(T + 1)}$ is the vector of stocks of inventories at the beginning of the first postplan period $T + 1$, i.e., at the end of the plan. $\overline{K(T + 1)}$, $\overline{K(T + 2)}$, $\overline{K(T + 3)}$, and $\overline{X_s(T + 1)}$ are prescribed in two alternative ways in the Target and Transit Models.

2.2 Target Model

In this model, the *levels* of the terminal stocks are determined independently and specified as constraints which the model solution must satisfy. Neither the methods of determining the particular levels, nor the reasons for desiring them, is the concern of the Target Model. It merely investigates the allocational implications of the targets for the plan period. The required minimum capital-in-process at the end of period T is determined by $K(T + 2)$ and $K(T + 3)$ because of the assumed lag of up to three periods between investment and maturity of capital. Alternatively, the levels of terminal stocks may be defined in terms of $\overline{X(T)}$, the levels of output for the terminal year that are set as targets, for example, as in Indian planning.

There are no postterminal conditions explicit in the specifications of $X(T)$, although the logic of planning requires that they be considered. It is, therefore, necessary to project postterminal conditions in order to operate the model. The assumption adopted here is simply that each sector grows postterminally at the annual sectoral growth rate, $\alpha_{\tau i}$, which is implied between $\overline{X(T)}$ and $\overline{X(0)}$. We obtain $K(T + 1)$, $K(T + 2)$, and $K(T + 3)$ from $X(T + 1)$, $X(T + 2)$, and $X(T + 3)$ by using the diagonal matrix b of capital-output ratios:

(11.0) $K(T + 1) \geqslant b(T)(I + \alpha_\tau)\overline{X(T)}$,

(11.1) $K(T + 2) \geqslant b(T)(I + \alpha_\tau)^2 \overline{X(T)}$,

(11.2) $K(T + 3) \geqslant b(T)(I + \alpha_\tau)^3 \overline{X(T)}$,

and

(11.3) $s(T)X(T + 1) \geqslant s(T)(I + \alpha_\tau)\overline{X(T)}$.

With these terminal conditions added to the Basic Model core, we have a model that can be used to investigate the implications of a set of specified plan targets. The solution calculates all the direct and indirect requirements implied by the targets, allocates resources to their production, and simultaneously distributes the use of resources over time in such a way as to maximize the discounted consumption in the objective function. If the solution indicates the targets are not feasible, no allocation of resources can be found to meet them. If the targets are feasible, no other allocation of resources will reach the targets and produce a larger value of discounted consumption.

2.3 Transit Model

This, like the Target Model, is a short-term model covering the conventional planning period of five years. In this case, however, the targets are determined as part of the solution. The technique used for this purpose is a variation of that presented by Chakravarty and Eckaus and by Stone and Brown.[7]

The terminal conditions provided guarantee the achievement, in the postterminal period, of *growth rates* of deliveries for private consumption, replacement, government consumption, exports, and imports exogenously specified from the levels and composition of these deliveries in the last year of the plan. The fixed-capital capacities and inventory investment consistent with these stipulations are deduced. The level of aggregate consumption C(T) and the composition of imports M(T) in the last period are endogenously determined by the model solution. Consequently, the levels of terminal stocks are themselves determined as part of the solution. If the minimum level of consumption is also specified by means of the consumption growth constraint and a prescribed $\overline{C(0)}$, then a minimum postterminal consumption level and growth rate is stipulated for the postterminal period as well. While it is desirable to allow the composition of imports to be determined by the optimizing mechanism during the plan period this mechanism does not work in the postplan period. Thus it becomes necessary to provide some basis for extrapolating the composition of imports, and in this case that composition is taken to be the import levels of the final plan period.

Again, three postterminal periods must be accounted for because of the three-period gestation lag in investment. The presentation that follows will initially assume a constant postterminal composition of consumption by using the same growth rate in each sector. Thus with postterminal growth rates ϕ, δ, γ, ϵ, and μ for consumption, replacement, government, exports, and imports, respectively, we have for $t \geqslant T$

(12.0) $F(t) = F(T)(1 + \phi)^{t-T}$,

(12.1) $G(t) = \overline{G(T)}(1 + \gamma)^{t-T}$,

[7]S. Chakravarty and R. S. Eckaus, "An Approach to a Multisectoral Planning Model," in *Capital Formation and Economic Development*, P. N. Rosenstein-Rodan (ed.), M.I.T. Press, Cambridge, Mass., 1964; R. Stone and A. Brown, *A Computable Model of Economic Growth*, M.I.T. Press, Cambridge, Mass., 1962.

(12.2) $E(t) = \overline{E(T)}(1 + \epsilon)^{t-T}$,

(12.3) $D(t) = \overline{D(T)}(1 + \delta)^{t-T}$,

(12.4) $M(t) = M(T)(1 + \mu)^{t-T}$

With these assumptions, the distribution equation in the postterminal periods becomes

$$
\begin{aligned}
(12.5) \quad X(t) = \ & a(T)X(t) + (s(T) + b(T)p')[X(t + 1) - X(t)] \\
& + b(T)p'' [X(t + 2) - X(t + 1)] \\
& + b(T)p''' [X(t + 3) - X(t + 2)] \\
& + F(T)(1 + \phi)^{t-T} + \overline{G(T)}(1 + \gamma)^{t-T} \\
& + \overline{E(T)}(1 + \epsilon)^{t-T} + \overline{D(T)}(1 + \delta)^{t-T} \\
& - M(T)(1 + \mu)^{t-T} \qquad \text{for } t > T.
\end{aligned}
$$

The postterminal output levels can then be found as a particular solution of the distribution Eq. 12.5:

$$
\begin{aligned}
(13.0) \quad X(t) = \ & [I - a(T) - (b(T)p'(T) + s(T))\phi - b(T)p''(T)(1 + \phi)\phi \\
& - b(T)p'''(T)(1 + \phi)^2\phi]^{-1}F(T)(1 + \phi)^{t-T} \\
& + [I - a(T) - (b(T)p'(T) + s(T))\gamma - b(T)p''(T)(1 + \gamma)\gamma \\
& - b(T)p'''(T)(1 + \gamma)^2\gamma]^{-1}\overline{G(T)}(1 + \gamma)^{t-T} \\
& + [I - a(T) - (b(T)p'(T) + s(T))\epsilon - b(T)p''(T)(1 + \epsilon)\epsilon \\
& - b(T)p'''(T)(1 + \epsilon)^2\epsilon]^{-1}\overline{E(T)}(1 + \epsilon)^{t-T} \\
& + [I - a(T) - (b(T)p'(T) + s(T))\delta - B(T)p''(T)(1 + \delta)\delta \\
& - b(T)p'''(T)(1 + \delta)^2\delta]^{-1}\overline{D(T)}(1 + \delta)^{t-T} \\
& - [I - a(T) - (b(T)p'(T) + s(T))\mu - b(T)p''(T)(1 + \mu)\mu \\
& - b(T)p'''(T)(1 + \mu)^2\mu]^{-1}M(T)(1 + \mu)^{t-T} \\
& \qquad\qquad\qquad\qquad \text{for } t = T + 1, T + 2, T + 3.
\end{aligned}
$$

From which, using b(T) and s(T) and defining

$$
\begin{aligned}
q_\eta \equiv \ & [I - a(T) - (b(T)p'(T) + s(T))\eta - b(T)p''(T)(1 + \eta)\eta \\
& - b(T)p'''(T)(1 + \eta)^2\eta], \quad \text{for } \eta = \phi, \gamma, \epsilon, \delta, \mu,
\end{aligned}
$$

the terminal requirements for the Transit Model are obtained.
  Terminal capital stocks are

$$
\begin{aligned}
(14.0) \quad K(T) \geqslant \ & b(T)q_\phi^{-1}F(T)(1 + \phi)^{t-T} + b(T)q_\gamma^{-1}\overline{G(T)}(1 + \gamma)^{t-T} \\
& + b(T)q_\epsilon^{-1}\overline{E(T)}(1 + \epsilon)^{t-T} + b(T)q_\delta^{-1}\overline{D(T)}(1 + \delta)^{t-T} \\
& - b(T)q_\mu^{-1}M(T)(1 + \mu)^{t-T}, \quad \text{for } t = T + 1, T + 2, T + 3.
\end{aligned}
$$

Terminal inventories are

$$
\begin{aligned}
(15.0) \quad s(T)X(T + 1) = \ & s(T)q_\phi^{-1}F(T)(1 + \phi) + s(T)q_\gamma^{-1}\overline{G(T)}(1 + \gamma) \\
& + s(T)q_\epsilon^{-1}\overline{E(T)}(1 + \epsilon) + s(T)q_\delta^{-1}\overline{D(T)}(1 + \delta) \\
& - s(T)q_\mu^{-1}M(T)(1 + \mu).
\end{aligned}
$$

The assumption that in any one use all sectors grow at the same rate can easily be dropped. In the general case, the growth rate ϕ, δ, γ, ϵ, and μ may each be vectors of growth rates. As a result the solution becomes only somewhat more tedious than before and, in fact, Eq. 12.0 could be reinterpreted for this case.

Each of vectors F(t), D(t), G(t), E(t), and M(t) can be represented as a sum of n vectors, each with its own scalar growth rate; e.g.,

$$F(t) = \begin{Bmatrix} F_1(T) \\ 0 \\ 0 \\ \vdots \\ 0 \end{Bmatrix} (1 + \phi_1)^{t-T} + \begin{Bmatrix} 0 \\ F_2(T) \\ 0 \\ \vdots \\ 0 \end{Bmatrix} (1 + \phi_2)^{t-T} + \cdots +$$

$$\begin{Bmatrix} 0 \\ \vdots \\ 0 \\ F_i(T) \\ 0 \\ \vdots \\ 0 \end{Bmatrix} (1 + \phi_i)^{t-T} + \cdots + \begin{Bmatrix} 0 \\ 0 \\ \vdots \\ 0 \\ F_n(T) \end{Bmatrix} (1 + \phi_n)^{t-T}.$$

Then one would just evaluate Eq. 13.0 n times taking each of the n terms of the foregoing representation in turn. Dropping the equiproportional growth rate assumption permits the exercise of discretion as to possible variation in the postterminal growth rates for the sectors' outputs.

During the plan period the level, though not the composition, of imports is effectively determined by the specification of the level of exports and net foreign capital inflow in each period and the balance of payments constraint. By the stipulation of a postterminal growth rate for exports different from the postterminal growth rate for imports, the trade gap can be made to decrease or increase in the postterminal period. The postterminal requirements for foreign aid, changes in gold reserves, or debt repayment can all be built into the solution of the model in this way. The statement of the Transit Model is completed with the addition of its terminal conditions to the Basic Model core.

It cannot be assumed that a feasible solution to the Transit Model always exists. As already pointed out, if the minimum initial level of consumption is not prescribed, the model has freedom to determine the level from which consumption growth will start while satisfying the growth constraints and achieving the terminal conditions. This will ordinarily be enough to guarantee a feasible solution. For example, zero aggregate consumption in each period would satisfy the monotonicity constraints, and thus, only enough capacity would be necessary in the plan and postplan periods to satisfy the exogenous demands.

Table 2.1 brings together all the symbols used in the Target and Transit Models. Table 2.2 sets out all the relationships of the Basic Model and the terminal conditions for the Target and Transit Models.

The computer time required to solve a linear programming problem is primarily dependent on the number of constraints in the problem. The number of columns, i.e., the number of unknowns, has a comparatively negligible effect on the time required for a solution. Therefore in order to reduce the number of constraints, all constraints formulated as strict equalities are substituted into the various inequalities. The final form of the constraints as programmed for the computer as the Target Model are given in Table A.1 in Appendix A at the end of this chapter.

Table 2.1. Symbols Used in the Target and Transit Models

Variables and Parameters[*]		Dimensions for n sectors, k activities T periods
$A(t)$	net foreign capital inflow in period t	T
$a(t)$	matrix of interindustry current flow coefficients appropriate to period t	n × k
$b(t)$	diagonal matrix of capital-output ratios	k × k
$c(t)$	column vector, each term of which indicates the proportion of the sector's output in total consumption	n
$C(t)$	aggregate consumption in each period	T
$D(t)$	vector of the amount of fixed capital (components) in each sector that is completely depreciated in period t	k
d	diagonal matrix transforming depreciation into capacity immobilized, each of whose terms d_{jj} is the maximum of $\left(\dfrac{r_{1j}}{p_{1j}}, \dfrac{r_{2j}}{p_{2j}}, \ldots, \dfrac{r_{nj}}{p_{nj}}\right)$; (r's and p's are explained further on in the list)	k × k
$E(t)$	column vector of exports by each sector	n
$F(t)$	column vector of deliveries by each sector for private consumption purposes	n
$G(t)$	column vector of deliveries by each sector for government consumption	n
$H(t)$	column vector of deliveries by each sector for inventory accumulation	n
I	identity matrix	n × n or k × k
$J(t)$	column vector of deliveries of intermediate inputs by each sector	n
$K(t)$	column vector of fixed-capital capacity in each sector	k
$M(t)$	column vector of total imports	n
$M'(t)$	column vector of noncompetitive imports	k
m'	diagonal matrix of import coefficients relating non-competitive imports to sectoral output	k × k
$M''(t)$	column vector of competitive imports	n
m''	column vector of coefficients indicating in each sector maximum use of the foreign exchange available after competitive import requirements have been satisfied	n
n	number of sectors	
$N(t)$	column vector of deliveries by each sector of investment goods for new capital formation	n
$\left.\begin{array}{l} p' \\ p'' \\ p''' \end{array}\right\}$	investment lag proportions matrices for capital; elements p'_{ij}, p''_{ij}, and p'''_{ij} indicate the proportions of fixed capital in sector j supplied by sector i for new capacity 1, 2, or 3 periods ahead, respectively	n × k
p	capital composition matrix where each element is $\sum_k p^k_{ij}$, and $\sum_i p_{ij} = 1.0$	n × k

Table 2.1. (cont.)

Variables and Parameters		Dimensions for n sectors, k activities T periods
$Q(t)$	column vector of deliveries by each sector to restore depreciated capacity	n
q_η	$[I - a(T) - (b(T)p'(T) + S(T))\eta - b(T)p''(T)(1 + \eta)$ $-b(T)p'''(T)(1 + \eta)^2\eta]$ for $\eta = \phi, \delta, \gamma, \epsilon$, or ν	n $\times$ n
$R(t)$	vector of depreciated capital capacities that are restored	k
r' r'' r'''	matrices of coefficients, each of which indicates the proportion of depreciated capacity in each sector j supplied by sector i for restored capacity in period $t - 1$, $t - 2$, or $t - 3$, respectively, to become effective in period t	n $\times$ k
r	depreciation compostion matrix, each element of which is D_{ij}/D_j, where D_{ij} is the ith type of capital depreciated in in sector j	n $\times$ k
s	matrix of inventory coefficients, each element s_{ij} of which indicates the deliveries for inventory purposes by sector i to sector j per unit of additional output in sector j	n $\times$ k
T	length of the plan in periods	
t	time, in periods	
u	unit row vector $[1, 1, 1, \cdots, 1]$	1 $\times$ n
$V(t)$	column vector of capacities lost in each sector due to the depreciation of some component of its capital stock	k
W	value of the objective function, which is equal to the present discounted value of aggregate consumption over the plan period	1
w	social discount rate applied to aggregate private consumption	1
$X(t)$	column vector of gross domestic outputs	k
$Z(t)$	column vector of new additions to fixed-capital capacity in each sector	k
ϕ	postterminal growth rate for consumption	1
δ	postterminal growth rate for depreciation	1
γ	postterminal growth rate for government	1
ϵ	postterminal growth rate for exports	1
μ	postterminal growth rate for imports	
$\rho(t)$	minimum rate of growth of aggregate consumption $C(t)$ over $C(t - 1)$	1
α_0	diagonal matrix of growth rates used in calculating inventory investment in first period and maximum new investment in second and third periods	T
α_τ	diagonal matrix of growth rates used in calculating terminal capital requirements	k $\times$ k

*Variables in capital letters; parameters in small letters.

Table 2.2. Target and Transit Models

1. Objective Function
   Maximize:

   $$(1.0) \quad W = \sum_{t=1}^{T} \frac{C(t)}{(1 + w)^{t-1}}$$

   Subject to:

2. Consumption Growth Constraints
   $(2.0) \quad C(t + 1) \geqslant C(t)[1 + \rho(t)]$,   for $t = 0, \cdots, T - 1$,
   Initial consumption:
   $(2.1) \quad C(0) = \overline{C(0)}$,

3. Production Accounting Relationships
   $(3.0) \quad J(t) + H(t) + N(t) + Q(t) + F(t) + G(t) + E(t) \leqslant M(t) + X(t)$,   for $t = 1, \cdots, T$.
   Intermediate products:
   $(3.1) \quad J(t) = a(t)X(t)$,   for $t = 1, \cdots, T$,
   Inventory requirements:
   $(3.2) \quad H(t) = \dot{s}(t) \{X(t + 1) - X(t)\}$,   for $t = 2, \cdots, T$,
   $(3.3) \quad H(1) = s(1) \{X(2) - (I + \alpha_0)\overline{X(0)}\}$,   for $t = 1$,
   Private consumption:
   $(3.4) \quad F(t) = c(t)C(t)$,   for $t = 1, \cdots, T$,
   Government consumption:
   $(3.5) \quad G(t) = \overline{G(t)}$,   for $t = 1, \cdots, T$,
   Exports:
   $(3.6) \quad E(t) = \overline{E(t)}$,   for $t = 1, \cdots, T$,

4. Capacity Restraints
   $(4.0) \quad b(t)X(t) \leqslant K(t)$,   for $t = 1, \cdots, T$,

5. Capital Accounting Relationships

   Investment requirements:
   $(5.0) \quad N(t) = p'Z(t + 1) + p''Z(t + 2) + p'''Z(t + 3)$,   for $t = 1, \cdots, T$,

   Depreciated capital:
   $(5.1) \quad D(t) = \overline{D(t)}$,   for $t = 2, \cdots, T + 3$,

   Depreciated capacity:
   $(5.2) \quad V(t) = [d] D(t)$,   for $t = 2, \cdots, T + 3$,

   Restoration requirements:
   $(5.3) \quad Q(t) = r'[d]^{-1}R(t + 1) + r''d^{-1}R(t + 2) + r'''d^{-1}R(t + 3)$,   for $t = 1, \cdots, T$,

   Capital accounting:
   $(5.4) \quad K(t + 1) \leqslant K(t) + Z(t + 1) + R(t + 1) - V(t + 1)$.   for $t = 1, \cdots, T + 2$,

6. Restoration Ceilings
   $(6.0) \quad R(t) \leqslant V(t)$,   for $t = 2, \cdots, T + 3$,

7. Balance of Payments Constraints
   $(7.0) \quad uM(t) \leqslant \overline{A(t)} + uE(t)$,   for $t = 1, \cdots, T$,

8. Imports
   Import composition:
   $(8.0) \quad M(t) = M'(t) + M''(t)$ for $t = 1, \cdots, T$,
   Noncompetitive imports:
   $(8.1) \quad M'(t) = m'(t)X(t)$,   for $t = 1, \cdots, T$,
   Competitive import ceilings:
   $(8.2) \quad M''(t) \leqslant m''(t) [\overline{A(t)} + uE(t) - uM'(t)]$,   for $t = 1, \cdots, T$,

9. Initial Capital-in-Process Restraints
   $(9.0) \quad K(1) = b(1)(I + \alpha_0)\overline{X(0)}$,
   $(9.1) \quad Z(2) + R(2) \leqslant b(2)\alpha_0 [I + \alpha_0] \overline{X(0)} + V(2)$,
   $(9.2) \quad Z(3) + R(3) \leqslant b(3)\alpha_0 [I + \alpha_0]^2 \overline{X(0)} + V(3)$,

Table 2.2. (cont.)

10. Terminal Requirements in General
    (10.0) $K(T + 1) \geqslant \overline{K(T + 1)}$,
    (10.1) $K(T + 2) \geqslant \overline{K(T + 2)}$,
    (10.2) $K(T + 3) \geqslant \overline{K(T + 3)}$,
    (10.3) $s(T)X(T + 1) \geqslant \overline{X_s(T + 1)}$.

11. Target Model Specification of Terminal Requirements
    Terminal capital stocks:
    (11.0) $K(T + 1) \geqslant b(T)(I + \alpha_r)\overline{X(T)}$,
    (11.1) $K(T + 2) \geqslant b(T)(I + \alpha_r)^2 \overline{X(T)}$,
    (11.2) $K(T + 3) \geqslant b(T)(I + \alpha_r)^3 \overline{X(T)}$,
    Terminal inventories:
    (11.3) $s(T)X(T + 1) \geqslant s(T)(I + \alpha_r)\overline{X(T)}$.

12. Transit Model Specification of Terminal Requirements
    Postterminal growth rates of demands and imports:
    (12.0) $F(t) = F(T)(1 + \phi)^{t-T}$,
    (12.1) $G(t) = \overline{G(T)}(1 + \gamma)^{t-T}$,
    (12.2) $E(t) = \overline{E(T)}(1 + \epsilon)^{t-T}$, $\left.\right\}$ for $t > T$.
    (12.3) $D(t) = \overline{D(T)}(1 + \delta)^{t-T}$,
    (12.4) $M(t) = M(T)(1 + \mu)^{t-T}$,

    This implies
    (12.5) $X(t) = a(T)X(t) + (s(T) + b(T)p')[X(t + 1) - X(t)]$
    $+ b(T)p''[X(t + 2) - X(t + 1)]$
    $+ b(T)p'''[X(t + 3) - X(t + 2)]$

    $+ F(t)(1 + \phi)^{t-T} + \overline{G(T)}(1 + \gamma)^{t-T} + \overline{E(T)}(1 + \epsilon)^{t-T}$
    $+ D(T)(1 + \delta)^{t-T} - M(T)(1 + \mu)^{t-T}$,   for $t > T$.

13. Solution of (12.5)
    (13.0) $X(t) = [I - a(T) - (b(T)p'(T) + s(T))\phi - b(T)p''(T)(1 + \phi)\phi - b(T)p'''(T)(1 + \phi)^2\phi]^{-1}F(t)(1 + \phi)^{t-T}$
    $+ [I - a(T) - (b(T)p'(T) + s(T))\gamma - b(T)p''(T)(1 + \gamma)\gamma - b(T)p'''(T)(1 + \gamma)^2\gamma]^{-1}\overline{G(T)}(1 + \gamma)^{t-T}$
    $+ [I - a(T) - (b(T)p'(T) + s(T))\epsilon - b(T)p''(T)(1 + \epsilon)\epsilon - b(T)p'''(T)(1 + \epsilon)^2\epsilon]^{-1}\overline{E(T)}(1 + \epsilon)^{t-T}$
    $+ [I - a(T) - (b(T)p'(T) + s(T))\delta - b(T)p''(T)(1 + \delta)\delta - b(T)p'''(T)(1 + \delta)^2\delta]^{-1}\overline{D(T)}(1 + \delta)^{t-T}$
    $- [I - a(T) - (b(T)p'(T) + s(T))\mu - b(T)p''(T)(1 + \mu)\mu - b(T)p'''(T)(1 + \mu)^2\mu]^{-1}M(T)(1 + \mu)^{t-T}$,
    for $t = T + 1, T + 2, T + 3$.

    Define:
    $q_\eta \equiv [I - a(T) \quad (b(T)p'(T) + s(T)\eta - b(T)p''(T)(1 + \eta)\eta - b(T)p'''(T)(1 + \eta)^2\eta]$, for $\eta = \phi, \gamma, \epsilon, \delta, \mu$.

14. Terminal Capital Stocks
    (14.0) $K(t) \geqslant b(T)q_\phi^{-1}F(T)(1 + \phi)^{t-T}$
    $+ b(T)q_\gamma^{-1}\overline{G(T)}(1 + \gamma)^{t-T}$
    $+ b(T)q_\epsilon^{-1}\overline{E(T)}(1 + \epsilon)^{t-T}$
    $+ b(T)q_\delta^{-1}\overline{D(T)}(1 + \delta)^{t-T}$
    $- b(T)q_\mu^{-1}M(T)(1 + \mu)^{t-T}$ for $t = T + 1, T + 2, T + 3$.

15. Terminal inventories
    (15.0) $s(T)X(T + 1) = s(T)q_\phi^{-1}F(T)(1 + \phi)$
    $+ s(T)q_\gamma^{-1}\overline{G(T)}(1 + \gamma)$
    $+ s(T)q_\epsilon^{-1}\overline{E(T)}(1 + \epsilon)$
    $+ s(T)q_\delta^{-1}\overline{D(T)}(1 + \delta)$
    $- s(T)q_\mu^{-1}M(T)(1 + \mu)$

Table 2.3 shows the corresponding tableau. Table A.2, also in Appendix A, presents the final form of the constraints of the Transit Model as programmed for computation after the equalities were substituted into inequalities; Table 2.4 is the corresponding tableau.

2.4 Solutions and Shadow Prices

For any set of values of the parameters, a solution of the model, if it exists, will be a point in consumption space defined by the intersection of the binding constraints. Variation of the relative weights on consumption in each period in the objective function will move the solution to a different point on the production feasibility surface. Variation of the postterminal conditions will change the solution by shifting the feasibility surface. Likewise, changes in the production parameters will change the production feasibility surface itself and consequently the value of the maximand for any given objective function. For each value of the maximand there is a specific allocation of resources and outputs in each period. A solution of the model determines the unknown variables remaining after all the possible substitutions have been made. These are the gross domestic outputs $X(t)$, the level of aggregate consumption $C(t)$, competitive imports $M''(t)$, capital stocks $K(t)$, new capital $Z(t)$, and restored capacity $R(t)$. With the solution values of these variables, it is possible to generate for each period a detailed list of gross-output levels, imports and final demands, interindustry transactions, investment allocations, and capital stock uses that will achieve the maximand. This sectoral and temporal detail, along with the associated set of national income accounts, facilitates over-all appraisal of the implications of each solution.

In addition to allocations of "physical quantities," a solution includes a set of shadow prices, each of which is related to one of the constraints. These shadow prices are the variables of the minimizing valuation problem, which is the dual of the maximizing problem. In the minimizing problem, prices are found for the scarce resources, in this case the sectoral capacities and foreign exchange, which exhaust the value of the total product and minimize the cost of production within the behavioral as well as technological constraints.

From the solution of the model and its dual, the following shadow prices are determined: $V_{X(t)}$, vector of shadow prices associated with the production accounting relationships and interpretable as shadow prices of output $X(t)$; $V_{K(t)}$, vector of shadow rentals of capital $K(t)$ obtained as values associated with the capacity constraints; $V_{Z(t)}$, vector of shadow prices of new capital stock $Z(t)$ obtained as values associated with the capital accounting relationships; $V_{CR(t)}$, shadow prices associated with the consumption growth constraints; $V_{FX(t)}$, shadow prices associated with the foreign exchange balance requirements; $V_{M''C(t)}$, vector of shadow prices associated with the ceilings imposed on the competitive imports; $V_{R(t)}$, vector of shadow prices of restorable capacity obtained as values associated with the restoration ceilings; $V_{IK(t)}$, vector of shadow prices of initial capital-in-process obtained as values associated with initial capital-in-process constraints.

Since the optimal solutions of the primal and the dual describe the same state of the economy, the quantity allocations and the valuations must be considered

Table 2.3. Tableau for the Target Model

Variables / Constraints		X(1)	C(1)	M″(1)	X(2)	C(2)	M″(2)	K(2)	Z(2)	R(2)	X(3)	C(3)	M″(3)	K(3)	Z(3)	R(3)	X(4)	C(4)	M″(4)
(1) Objective			1.0			$(1+w)^{-1}$						$(1+w)^{-2}$						$(1+w)^{-3}$	
(2) Consumption Growth Constraints	1		-1																
	2		$(1+\rho)$			-1													
	3					$(1+\rho)$						-1							
	4											$(1+\rho)$							
	5																	-1	$(1+\rho)$	
(3) Distribution Relations	1	$\lfloor a\cdot l\cdot m'\rfloor$	$\lfloor c\rfloor$	$-\lfloor l\rfloor$	$\lfloor s\rfloor$			$\lfloor p'\rfloor$	$\lfloor r'\rfloor\lfloor d\rfloor^{-1}$						$\lfloor p''\rfloor$	$\lfloor r'\rfloor\lfloor d\rfloor^{-1}$			
	2				$\lfloor a\cdot l\cdot m'\cdot s\rfloor$	$\lfloor c\rfloor$	$-\lfloor l\rfloor$				$\lfloor s\rfloor$				$\lfloor p'\rfloor$	$\lfloor r'\rfloor\lfloor d\rfloor^{-1}$			
	3										$\lfloor a\cdot l\cdot m'\cdot s\rfloor$	$\lfloor c\rfloor$	$-\lfloor l\rfloor$						
	4																$\lfloor s\rfloor$		
	5																$\lfloor a\cdot l\cdot m'\cdot s\rfloor$	$\lfloor c\rfloor$	$-\lfloor l\rfloor$
(4) Capacity Restraints	1	$\lfloor b\rfloor$																	
	2				$\lfloor b\rfloor$			$-\lfloor l\rfloor$											
	3										$\lfloor b\rfloor$			$-\lfloor l\rfloor$					
	4																$\lfloor b\rfloor$		
	5																		
(5) Capital Accounting Relations	1							$\lfloor l\rfloor$	$-\lfloor l\rfloor$	$-\lfloor l\rfloor$									
	2							$-\lfloor l\rfloor$						$\lfloor l\rfloor$	$-\lfloor l\rfloor$	$-\lfloor l\rfloor$			
	3													$-\lfloor l\rfloor$					
	4																		
	5																		
	6																		
	7																		
(6) Restoration Ceilings	2									$\lfloor l\rfloor$									
	3															$\lfloor l\rfloor$			
	4																		
	5																		
	6																		
	7																		
	8																		
(7) Foreign Trade Balance	1	um'		u															
	2				um'		u												
	3										um'		u						
	4																um'		u
	5																		
(8) Competitive Import Ceilings	1	um'		$\lfloor m''\rfloor^{-1}$															
	2				um'		$\lfloor m''\rfloor^{-1}$												
	3										um'		$\lfloor m''\rfloor^{-1}$						
	4																um'		$\lfloor m''\rfloor^{-1}$
	5																		
(9) Initial Capital in Process	2							$\lfloor l\rfloor$	$\lfloor l\rfloor$										
	3													$\lfloor l\rfloor$	$\lfloor l\rfloor$				

K(4)	Z(4)	R(4)	X(5)	C(5)	M''(5)	K(5)	Z(5)	R(5)	Z(6)	R(6)	Z(7)	R(7)	Z(8)	R(8)	≷	R.H.S.
				$(1+w)^{-4}$											≤	$-(1+\rho(o))\overline{C(o)}$
															≤	0
															≤	0
				-1											≤	0
															≤	0
	$[p'']$	$[r''][d]^{-1}$					$[p'']$	$[r''][d]^{-1}$							≤	$-\overline{E(1)}-\overline{G(1)}+s(1)[1+\alpha_0]\overline{X(o)}$
	$[p'']$	$[r''][d]^{-1}$					$[p'']$	$[r''][d]^{-1}$	$[p''']$	$[r'''][d]^{-1}$					≤	$-\overline{E(2)}-\overline{G(2)}$
	$[p']$	$[r'][d]^{-1}$	$[s]$				$[p']$	$[r'][d]^{-1}$	$[p'']$	$[r''][d]^{-1}$	$[p'']$	$[r''][d]^{-1}$			≤	$-\overline{E(3)}-\overline{G(3)}$
			$[a{-}l{-}m'{-}s]$	$|c|$	$-[1]$				$[p']$	$[r'][d]^{-1}$	$[p']$	$[r'][d]^{-1}$	$[p''']$	$[r'''][d]^{-1}$	≤	$-\overline{E(4)}-\overline{G(4)}$
															≤	$-\overline{E(5)}-\overline{G(5)}-s(6)[1+\alpha_T]\overline{X(5)}$
															≤	$[b][1+\alpha_0]\overline{X(0)}$
															≤	0
															≤	0
$-[1]$			$[b]$			$-[1]$									≤	0
															≤	0
$[1]$	$-[1]$	$-[1]$				$[1]$	$-[1]$	$-[1]$							≤	$-[d]\overline{D(2)}+[b][1+\alpha_0]\overline{X(0)}$
$-[1]$						$-[1]$									≤	$-[d]\overline{D(3)}$
						$-[1]$									≤	$-[d]\overline{D(4)}$
						$-[1]$									≤	$-[d]\overline{D(5)}$
									$-[1]$	$-[1]$					≤	$-[d]D(6)-[b][1+\alpha_T]\overline{X(5)}$
									$-[1]$	$-[1]$	$-[1]$	$-[1]$			≤	$-[d]D(6)-[d]\overline{D(7)}-[b][1+\alpha_T]^2\overline{X(5)}$
									$-[1]$	$-[1]$	$-[1]$	$-[1]$	$-[1]$	$-[1]$	≤	$-[d]D(6)-[d]\overline{D(7)}-[d]\overline{D(8)}-[b][1+\alpha_T]^3\overline{X(5)}$
		$[1]$													≤	$[d]\overline{D(2)}$
															≤	$[d]\overline{D(3)}$
															≤	$[d]\overline{D(4)}$
								$[1]$							≤	$[d]\overline{D(5)}$
										$[1]$					≤	$[d]\overline{D(6)}$
												$[1]$			≤	$[d]\overline{D(7)}$
														$[1]$	≤	$[d]\overline{D(8)}$
															≤	$\overline{A(1)}+u\overline{E(1)}$
															≤	$\overline{A(2)}+u\overline{E(2)}$
															≤	$\overline{A(3)}+u\overline{E(3)}$
			um'	u											≤	$\overline{A(4)}+u\overline{E(4)}$
															≤	$\overline{A(5)}+u\overline{E(5)}$
															≤	$\overline{A(1)}+u\overline{E(1)}$
															≤	$\overline{A(2)}+u\overline{E(2)}$
															≤	$\overline{A(3)}+u\overline{E(3)}$
			um'		$|m'''|{-}1$										≤	$\overline{A(4)}+u\overline{E(4)}$
															≤	$\overline{A(5)}+u\overline{E(5)}$
															≤	$[d]\overline{D(2)}+[b][\alpha_0][1+\alpha_0]\overline{X(0)}$
															≤	$[d]\overline{D(3)}+[b][\alpha_0][1+\alpha_0]^2\overline{X(0)}$

Table 2.4. Tableau for the Transit Model

Constraints	X(1)	C(1)	M''(1)	X(2)	C(2)	M''(2)	K(2)	Z(2)	R(2)	X(3)	C(3)	M''(3)	K(3)	Z(3)	R(3)	X(4)	C(4)	M''(4)
(1) Objective		1.0			$(1+w)^{-1}$						$(1+w)^{-2}$						$(1+w)^{-3}$	
(2) Consumption Growth Constraints 1		-1																
2		$(1+\rho)$			-1													
3					$(1+\rho)$						-1							
4											$(1+\rho)$						-1	
5																	$(1+\rho)$	
(3) Distribution Relations 1	$[a\text{-}l\text{-}m']$	$|c|$	$-[l]$	$[s]$				$[p']$	$[r'][d]^{-1}$					$[p'']$	$[r''][d]^{-1}$			
2				$[a\text{-}l\text{-}m'\text{-}s]$	$|c|$	$-[l]$				$[s]$				$[p']$	$[r'][d]^{-1}$			
3										$[a\text{-}l\text{-}m'\text{-}s]$	$|c|$	$-[l]$				$[s]$		
4																$[a\text{-}l\text{-}m'\text{-}s]$	$|c|$	$-[l]$
5																		
(4) Capacity Restraints 1	$[b]$																	
2				$[b]$			$-[l]$											
3										$[b]$			$-[l]$					
4																$[b]$		
5																		
(5) Capital Accounting Relations 1							$[l]$	$-[l]$	$-[l]$									
2							$-[l]$						$[l]$	$-[l]$	$-[l]$			
3													$-[l]$					
4																		
5																		
6																		
7																		
(6) Restoration Ceilings 2									$[l]$									
3															$[l]$			
4																		
5																		
6																		
7																		
8																		
(7) Foreign Trade Balance 1	$u\,m'$		u															
2				$u\,m'$		u												
3										$u\,m'$		u						
4																$u\,m'$		u
5																		
(8) Competitive Import Ceilings 1	$u\,m'$		$[m'']^{-1}$															
2				$u\,m'$		$[m'']^{-1}$												
3										$u\,m'$		$[m'']^{-1}$						
4																$u\,m'$		$[m'']^{-1}$
5																		
(9) Initial Capital in Process 2								$[l]$	$[l]$									
3														$[l]$	$[l]$			

$|s_{\phi 1}| = sq_\phi^{-1}(1+\phi)c(T)$; $|s_{\phi 2}| = sq_\phi^{-1}(1+\phi)^2 c(T)$; $|s_{\phi 3}| = sq_\phi^{-1}(1+\phi)^3 c(T)$

$|b_{\phi 1}| = bq_\phi^{-1}(1+\phi)c(T)$; $|b_{\phi 2}| = bq_\phi^{-1}(1+\phi)^2 c(T)$; $|b_{\phi 3}| = bq_\phi^{-1}(1+\phi)^3 c(T)$

$|s_*|, |s_s|, |s_r|, |s_\mu|$ etc. and $|b_*|, |b_s|, |b_r|, |b_\mu|$ etc. are analogously defined.

q_ϕ, etc. are defined in (13.0) in Table 2.2.

K(4)	Z(4)	R(4)	X(5)	C(5)	M"(5)	K(5)	Z(5)	R(5)	Z(6)	R(6)	Z(7)	R(7)	Z(8)	R(8)	⋛	R.H.S.
				$(1+w)^{-4}$											≤	$-(1+\rho(o))\bar{C}(o)$
															≤	0
															≥	0
				-1											≥	0
															≤	0
	$[p''']$	$[r''][d]^{-1}$													≤	$-\bar{E}(1)-\bar{G}(1)+s(1)[1+\infty_0]\,\bar{X}(o)$
	$[p'']$	$[r'][d]^{-1}$				$[p''']$	$[r''][d]^{-1}$		$[p''']$	$[r''][d]^{-1}$	$[p'']$	$[r''][d]^{-1}$			≤	$-\bar{E}(2)-\bar{G}(2)$
	$[p']$	$[r'][d]^{-1}$	$[s]$			$[p'']$	$[r'][d]^{-1}$		$[p'']$	$[r''][d]^{-\frac{1}{2}}$	$[p']$	$[r''][d]^{-1}$			≤	$-\bar{E}(3)-\bar{G}(3)$
						$[p']$	$[r'][d]^{-1}$		$[p']$	$[r'][d]^{-1}$			$[p''']$	$[r''][d]^{-1}$	≤	$-\bar{E}(4)-\bar{G}(4)$
			$[a-l-m'\cdot s-s_\mu m']$	$[c+s_{cl}]$	$[l+s_\mu]$										≤	$-\bar{E}(5)-\bar{G}(5)-s_\epsilon-s_x-s_\delta$
															≤	$[b][1+\infty_0]\,\bar{X}(o)$
															≤	0
															≤	0
		$[b]$													≤	0
$-[1]$					$-[1]$										≤	0
															≤	$-[d]\,\bar{D}(2)+[b][1+\infty_0]\,\bar{X}(o)$
															≤	$-[d]\,\bar{D}(3)$
	$-[1]$	$-[1]$													≤	$-[d]\,\bar{D}(4)$
$[1]$						$[1]$	$-[1]$	$-[1]$							≤	$-[d]\,\bar{D}(5)$
$-[1]$			$-[b_\mu m']$	$[b_\phi]$	$[b_\mu]$	$-[1]$			$-[1]$	$-[1]$					≤	$-[d]\,\bar{D}(6)-b_\epsilon-b_x-b_\delta$
			$-[b_{\mu2}m']$	$[b_{\phi2}]$	$[b_{\mu2}]$	$-[1]$			$-[1]$	$-[1]$	$-[1]$	$-[1]$			≤	$-[d]\,\bar{D}(6)-[d]\,\bar{D}(7)-b_\epsilon2-b_x2-b_\delta2$
	$[1]$		$-[b_{\mu3}m']$	$[b_{\phi3}]$	$[b_{\mu3}]$				$-[1]$	$-[1]$	$-[1]$	$-[1]$	$-[1]$	$-[1]$	≤	$-[d]\,\bar{D}(6)-[d]\,\bar{D}(7)-[d]\,\bar{D}(8)-b_\epsilon3-b_x3-b_\delta3$
															≤	$[d]\,\bar{D}(2)$
															≤	$[d]\,\bar{D}(3)$
															≤	$[d]\,\bar{D}(4)$
							$[1]$								≤	$[d]\,\bar{D}(5)$
										$[1]$					≤	$[d]\,\bar{D}(6)$
												$[1]$			≤	$[d]\,\bar{D}(7)$
														$[1]$	≤	$[d]\,\bar{D}(8)$
															≤	$\bar{A}(1)+u\,\bar{E}(1)$
															≤	$\bar{A}(2)+u\,\bar{E}(2)$
			$u\,m'$	u											≤	$\bar{A}(3)+u\,\bar{E}(3)$
															≤	$\bar{A}(4)+u\,\bar{E}(4)$
															≤	$\bar{A}(5)+u\,\bar{E}(5)$
															≤	$\bar{A}(1)+u\,\bar{E}(1)$
															≤	$\bar{A}(2)+u\,\bar{E}(2)$
			$u\,m'$	$[m"]^{-1}$											≤	$\bar{A}(3)+u\,\bar{E}(3)$
															≤	$\bar{A}(4)+u\,\bar{E}(4)$
															≤	$\bar{A}(5)+u\,\bar{E}(5)$
															≤	$[d]\,\bar{D}(2)+[b][\infty_0][1+\infty_0]\,\bar{X}(o)$
															≤	$[d]\,\bar{D}(3)+[b][\infty_0][1+\infty_0]^2\,\bar{X}(o)$

equally valid. However, because of the unfortunate nomenclature of "shadow prices" for the variables of the dual problem, there is a tendency to identify the shadow prices either with real-world prices or with prices in some other ideal competitive system.

As was noted in Chapter 1, the shadow price associated with a constraint is the value of change in the objective function when there is a marginal change in the right-hand side of the particular constraint and all other constraints are left unchanged.

A constraint reflecting the same real restriction can be written with different right-hand sides by means of transpositions and substitutions. In the alternative formulations, a marginal variation actually is a change of different quantities or of a different magnitude. The shadow price associated with each formulation of the same restriction will also be different. The shadow prices are in terms of the maximand, in this case the composite consumption commodity.

Whenever a restraint represents an inequality which stipulates that requirements must be less than or equal to availabilities, the shadow price associated with the constraint can be interpreted as the shadow price of the quantity, because in this case a marginal modification in the right-hand side of the constraint amounts to a marginal change in the availability of the quantity. Most of the constraints are descriptions of real technical or physical relationships that must be met if any economic system is to function viably. These descriptions are not completely accurate because of limitations of data or computational capacity, or because of analytical restrictions, such as the assumption of linearity. The deficiencies create undesirable results in the solutions. For example, due to the linear form of the objective function, there will be flip-flop tendency in the solutions. In order to avoid such undesirable features other constraints are invented. These invented constraints are "artifacts," effective in compensating for limitations in other parts of the models' structure only if the quantity results obtained in the solutions are the results that would have been obtained if the limitations were not present. The artifact constraints can be given an economic interpretation, although their primary purpose is not the addition of the economic content they may be interpreted to embody. The shadow prices associated with these artifact constraints can also be given an economic interpretation; such interpretation must be made, however, with the source and precise meaning of the constraint constantly in mind.

In fact there may be several alternative sets of artifact constraints that lead the system to the same results. Each set of such constraints would have a different set of shadow prices with a different meaning. Since the shadow prices on the artifact constraints are an integral part of the entire system of shadow prices, their existence will affect the shadow prices associated with the "real" structural or behavioral constraints as well. This effect is not objectionable but is necessary and desirable. However, the interaction does create difficulties in interpretation. An example of this interaction is in the relationship of the shadow prices of the competitive import constraints and the foreign exchange balance constraints. The constraints on the use of foreign exchange for competitive imports compensate for inability to describe diminishing returns to the use of foreign exchange in the various sectors. These constraints and their shadow prices have a direct influence on the shadow price associated with the foreign exchange balance constraint, which is not an artifact but a direct description of a real resource constraint.

The meaning of a shadow price can be best appreciated by referring to the corresponding constraint in the dual problem. The constraints of the dual can be read from Table 2.3 for the Target Model and from Table 2.4 for the Transit Model by reading down the columns.

The prices associated with the production accounting relationships are the shadow prices of the outputs. From Table 2.3, reading down the column of X(2), for example, we can write the dual relationship as follows:

$$s^T(2)[V_{X_1} - V_{X(2)}] + [a - m]^T V_{X(2)} + bV_{K(2)} + m'V_{FX(2)} + m'V_M''C(2)$$
$$- V_{X(2)} \geqslant 0;{}^8$$

i.e.,

$$\left\{ \begin{array}{c} \text{Value of} \\ \text{changes in} \\ \text{inventories} \\ \text{in period 1} \end{array} \right\} + \left\{ \begin{array}{c} \text{Value of} \\ \text{indirect} \\ \text{inputs} \\ \text{for X(2)} \end{array} \right\} + \left\{ \begin{array}{c} \text{Rental of} \\ \text{capital} \\ \text{to produce} \\ \text{X(2)} \end{array} \right\} + \left\{ \begin{array}{c} \text{Value} \\ \text{of} \\ \text{imported} \\ \text{inputs} \end{array} \right\}$$

$$+ \left\{ \begin{array}{c} \text{Shadow price} \\ \text{associated with} \\ \text{competitive} \\ \text{import ceilings} \end{array} \right\} + \left\{ \begin{array}{c} \text{Shadow} \\ \text{price} \\ \text{of} \\ \text{X(2)} \end{array} \right\} \geqslant 0.$$

It should be noted that the constraints corresponding to X(1), the vector of output in period 1, are different from the constraints for X(2) in that they do not have any inventory term. For the Transit Model, Table 2.4 shows that the constraints corresponding to X(5), the outputs of terminal years, include values of postterminal capital stocks. This is so because in the Transit Model the postterminal stocks are dependent on the levels of consumption C(5) and noncompetitive imports M'(5) and hence on X(5)

The prices associated with the capacity constraints are the shadow rentals of capital in the period of the constraint. For example, column K(2) in Table 2.3 or 2.4 gives us

$$-V_{K(2)} + V_{Z(1)} - V_{Z(2)} \geqslant 0;$$

i.e.,

$$- \left\{ \begin{array}{c} \text{Shadow} \\ \text{rental} \\ \text{of} \\ \text{capital} \\ \text{in period 2} \end{array} \right\} + \left\{ \begin{array}{c} \text{Value} \\ \text{of} \\ \text{capital} \\ \text{in} \\ \text{period 1} \end{array} \right\} - \left\{ \begin{array}{c} \text{Value} \\ \text{of} \\ \text{capital} \\ \text{in} \\ \text{period 2} \end{array} \right\} \geqslant 0.$$

Since capital services are in perfectly inelastic supply in any one period, the shadow prices on these services are either positive, if all the capacity is in use, or zero, if it is to any degree in excess supply.

---

^{8}Here the superscript T indicates the transpose of the matrix.

Since foreign exchange can always be used indirectly to increase the maximand, it should always have a positive shadow price. As we have pointed out, the shadow prices on the balance of payments constraints reflect not only the shadow prices of imports, but also the shadow prices on the constraints on the use of foreign exchange for competitive imports. When they bind, these constraints may prevent the use of foreign exchange in the sectors in which it would contribute most to the maximand. The shadow prices on the competitive import constraints indicate the value, in terms of the maximand, of an additional unit of foreign exchange in the particular sector.

The relationship between the shadow prices associated with the foreign exchange balance constraints and the shadow prices of the competitive import ceilings and of output can be obtained from Table 2.3 by reading down the column $M''(t)$. For example, for $M''(2)$ we have:

$$-V_{X(2)} + V_{FX(2)} + [m'']^{-1}V_{M''C(2)} \geq 0;$$

i.e.,

$$-\left\{\begin{array}{l}\text{Shadow}\\\text{price}\\\text{of}\\\text{output}\\X(2)\end{array}\right\} + \left\{\begin{array}{l}\text{Shadow price}\\\text{associated}\\\text{with}\\\text{foreign exchange}\\\text{balance}\end{array}\right\} + \left\{\begin{array}{l}\text{Shadow price}\\\text{associated with}\\\text{competitive import}\\\text{ceilings in}\\\text{period 2}\end{array}\right\} \geq 0.$$

This indicates that the shadow prices on the balance of payments constraints should not be identified with what is usually meant by the shadow price of foreign exchange. All of the supply and demand forces that in reality affect the foreign exchange rate are by no means taken into account in the model. The shadow price also reflects the availability of the stipulated foreign aid and of private capital flows from all sources. Thus, there is no easy translation from this shadow price on foreign resources to the shadow price of the rupee against the dollar.

The shadow price of consumption is, of course, the weight of $C(t)$ in the objective function, namely $(1 + w)^{t-1}$. It is affected by the consumption growth constraints and therefore is not simply the value of the components that make up the composite consumption. From the column of $C(2)$ in Table 2.3 we have:

$$-V_{CR(2)} + (1 + \rho)V_{CR(3)} + [c]^T V_{X(2)} \geq (1 + w)^{-1};$$

i.e.,

$$-\left\{\begin{array}{l}\text{Value of}\\\text{consumption in}\\\text{meeting consumption}\\\text{growth constraint}\\\text{in period 2}\end{array}\right\} + \left\{\begin{array}{l}\text{Value of additional}\\\text{consumption that will}\\\text{have to be provided in}\\\text{period 3 to meet the}\\\text{consumption growth}\\\text{constraint in period 2}\end{array}\right\} + \left\{\begin{array}{l}\text{Value}\\\text{of}\\\text{inputs to}\\\text{consumption}\\\text{in period 2}\end{array}\right\} \geq \left\{\begin{array}{l}\text{Discount}\\\text{rate}\\\text{applied to}\\\text{consumption}\\C(2)\end{array}\right\}$$

It may be seen from this that if consumption in the objective function is discounted, the shadow prices on output also embody the discount rate.

The shadow price of new investment in a sector does not reflect the usefulness of the capacity over the entire future, but instead reflects the cost of the new investment in terms of discounted consumption over the plan period. It should be noted, however, that all the shadow prices, including those of the inputs required to produce the new capital, are affected by the postterminal conditions imposed. The dual constraint corresponding to column $Z(4)$, for example, from Table 2.3 is as follows:

$$[p']^T V_{X(3)} + [p'']^T V_{X(2)} + [p''']^T V_{X(1)} - V_{Z(3)} \geqslant 0,$$

i.e.,

$$\{\text{Cost of inputs}\} \quad - \quad \left\{ \begin{array}{c} \text{Value} \\ \text{of} \\ \text{new} \\ \text{capital} \end{array} \right\} \geqslant 0.$$

The shadow prices are no worse and no better a part of the solution than are the real variables. They are an intrinsic aspect of the solution, and if one accepts the solution of the allocation problem, one must accept the associated shadow prices. But, as we have pointed out, in some cases these are prices having no exact counterpart in reality. Since there has been discussion as to the potential usefulness of shadow prices in microeconomic decision-making, we turn briefly to two questions related to the analysis here. First, can the shadow prices be used in project evaluation? Second, would the enforcement of these shadow prices by a central authority lead an otherwise uncontrolled economy to the optimum allocation?

2.4.1 Use of Shadow Prices in Project Evaluation

The shadow prices can be used for project evaluation provided the following three conditions are met:

1. All the relevant shadow prices are used in the evaluation.
2. The size of the project being considered does not violate the linearity and divisibility assumptions of the model. This may happen if the project is so small that different technical coefficients do not materially alter the technical coefficients of the sector to which it belongs. On the other hand, a project having the same technical coefficients can be as big as the sector itself and still not violate the linearity assumptions.
3. The model includes all the constraints and goals, and only those, of the society. If objectives are left out that are nonetheless considered important in practice, then the solution of the model is not the true optimum solution with respect to the larger set of goals but is just a point on the feasibility surface. The prices then correspond to this efficient point and not to the true optimum point.

2.4.2 Shadow Prices and Decentralization

The enforcement of the shadow prices by a central authority would not lead, in general, to the optimum allocation for the following reasons:

1. The real world is neither linear nor divisible in all sectors.
2. Neither does everyone have the same discounted objective function as that of the planners, nor can the interaction of different individual

objective functions necessarily be expected to lead to the results desired by planners. Different objectives or different discount rates would affect the choice of investments, and the projects corresponding to the model solution may not be selected by a decentralized price system.

3. The dynamic nature of the economy requires that a complete year-by-year price specification be made in advance and that this specification be credible. Even then the existence of an equilibrium is not assured, and oscillations may result.[9] For example, if over-investment occurs in a sector, it is realized only at the end of the gestation period when again everyone would want to disinvest.

4. Finally, the artifact constraints may not reflect the goals of individual profit maximizing competitors, and the corresponding constraint prices may not be enforceable. For example, consumption growth constraints can be imposed by an expenditure tax on consumption in those years when the solution indicates that the constraints are binding. On the other hand, competitive import ceilings, which may reflect the policy of import substitution or national self-sufficiency, may be difficult to impose by prices alone without actually specifying the levels of imports.

In describing the models we have tried to present their economic rationale as well as their formal structure, to make clear their weaknesses as well as their strengths. The test of any planning method, however, is not only its analytical sophistication, but also its relative effectiveness in dealing with important issues. A planning framework with an elaborate treatment of relatively minor problems may not be as useful as a cruder approach to the central issues. Some appreciation of the usefulness of the models is possible based on the discussion so far. This appreciation can be improved by examining the results of applying the models, and it is that to which we shall turn.

---

[9] See K. Arrow and G. Debreu, "Existence of an Equilibrium for a Competitive Economy," *Econometrica*, 22, pp. 265-290.

APPENDIX A

Table A.1. Target Model Constraints after Substitutions

1. Objective function
   Maximize:

   (1.0) $\quad W = \sum\limits_{t=1}^{T} \dfrac{C(t)}{(1+w)^{t-1}}$

   Subject to:

2. Consumption Growth Constraints
   (2.01) $\quad -C(1) \leqslant -(1 + \rho(0))\overline{C(0)}$,
   (2.02) $\quad -C(t+1) + (1 + \rho(t))C(t) \leqslant 0, \qquad t = 1, \cdots, T-1$,

3. Distribution Relationships
   (3.01) $\quad [a(1) - I - m'(1)]X(1) + s(1)X(2) + p'Z(2) + p''Z(3) + p'''Z(4)$
   $\quad\quad + r'd^{-1}R(2) + r''d^{-1}R(3) + r'''d^{-1}R(4) + c(1)C(1) - M''(1)$
   $\quad\quad \leqslant s(1)[I + \alpha_0]\overline{X(0)} - \overline{E(1)} - \overline{G(1)}$,
   (3.02) $\quad [a(t) - I - m'(t) - s(t)]X(t) + s(t)X(t+1) + p'Z(t+1) + p''Z(t+2) + p'''Z(t+3)$
   $\quad\quad + r'd^{-1}R(t+1) + r''d^{-1}R(t+2) + r'''d^{-1}R(t+3) + c(t)C(t) - M''(t)$
   $\quad\quad \leqslant -\overline{E(t)} - \overline{G(t)}, \qquad \text{for } t = 2, \cdots, T-1$,
   (3.03) $\quad [a(T) - I - m'(T) - s(T)]X(T) + p'Z(T+1) + p''Z(T+2) + p'''Z(T+3)$
   $\quad\quad + r'd^{-1}R(T+1) + r''d^{-1}R(T+2) + r'''d^{-1}R(T+3) + c(T)C(T) - M''(T)$
   $\quad\quad \leqslant -\overline{E(T)} - \overline{G(T)} - s(T)(I + \alpha_r)\overline{X(T)}$,

4. Capacity Restraints
   (4.01) $\quad b(1)X(1) \leqslant b(1)(I + \alpha_0)\overline{X(0)}$,
   (4.02) $\quad b(t)X(t) - K(t) \leqslant 0$,

5. Capital Accounting Relationships
   (5.01) $\quad K(2) - Z(2) - R(2) \leqslant b(1)(I + \alpha_0)\overline{X(0)} - d\overline{D(2)}$,
   (5.02) $\quad K(t+1) - Z(t+1) - R(t+1) - K(t) \leqslant -d\overline{D(t+1)}, \qquad \text{for } t = 2, \cdots, T-1$,
   (5.03) $\quad -Z(T+1) - R(T+1) - K(T) \leqslant -d\overline{D(T+1)} - b(T)(I + \alpha_r)\overline{X(T)}$,
   (5.04) $\quad -Z(T+2) - R(T+2) - Z(T+1) - R(T+1) - K(T) \leqslant -d\overline{D(T+1)} - d\overline{D(T+2)}$
   $\quad\quad\quad\quad - b(T)(I + \alpha_r)^2\overline{X(T)}$,
   (5.05) $\quad -Z(T+3) - R(T+3) - Z(T+2) - R(T+2) - Z(T+1) - R(T+1) - K(T)$
   $\quad\quad \leqslant -d\overline{D(T+1)} - d\overline{D(T+2)} - d\overline{D(T+3)} - b(T)(I + \alpha_r)\overline{X(T)}$,

6. Restoration Ceilings
   (6.01) $\quad R(t) \leqslant dD(t), \qquad \text{for } t = 2, \cdots, T+3$,

7. Balance of Payments Constraints
   (7.01) $\quad um'(t)X(t) + uM''(t) \leqslant \overline{A(t)} + u\overline{E(t)}, \qquad \text{for } t = 1, \cdots, T$,

8. Competitive Import Ceilings
   (8.01) $\quad [m''(t)]^{-1}M''(t) + um'(t)X(t) \leqslant \overline{A(t)} + u\overline{E(t)}, \qquad \text{for } t = 1, \cdots, T$,

9. Initial Capital-in-Process Restraints
   (9.01) $\quad Z(2) + R(2) \leqslant b(2)\alpha_0(I + \alpha_0)\overline{X(0)} + d\overline{D(2)}$,
   (9.02) $\quad Z(3) + R(3) \leqslant b(3)\alpha_0(I + \alpha_0)^2\overline{X(0)} + d\overline{D(3)}$.

Table A.2. Transit Model Constraints after Substitutions

1. Objective Function
   Maximize:

   (1.0) $\quad W = \sum\limits_{t=1}^{T} \dfrac{G(t)}{(1 + w)^{t-1}}$

   Subject to:

2. Consumption Growth Constraints
   (2.01) $\quad -C(1) \leqslant -(1 + \rho(0))\overline{C(0)}$
   (2.02) $\quad -C(t + 1) + (1 + \rho(t))C(t) \leqslant 0, \quad t = 1, \cdots, T \quad 1.$

3. Distribution Relationships
   (3.01) $\quad [a(1) - I - m'(1)]X(1) + s(1)X(2) + p'Z(2) + p''Z(3) + p'''Z(4)$
   $\quad + r'd^{-1}R(2) + r''d^{-1}R(3) + r'''d^{-1}R(4) + c(1)C(1) - M''(1)$
   $\quad \leqslant s(1)[I + \alpha_0]\overline{X(0)} - \overline{E(1)} - \overline{G(1)},$
   (3.02) $\quad [a(t) - I - m'(t) - s(t)]X(t) + s(t)X(t + 1) + p'Z(t + 1) + p''Z(t + 2) + p'''Z(t + 3)$
   $\quad + r'd^{-1}R(t + 1) + r''d^{-1}R(t + 2) + r'''d^{-1}R(t + 3) + c(t)C(t) \quad M''(t)$
   $\quad \leqslant -\overline{E(t)} - \overline{G(t)}, \quad \text{for } t = 2, \cdots, T - 1,$
   (3.03) $\quad [a(T) - I - m'(T) - s(T)] X(T) + p'Z(T + 1) + p''Z(T + 2) + p'''Z(T + 3) + r'd^{-1}R(T + 1)$
   $\quad + r''d^{-1}R(T + 2) + r'''d^{-1}R(T + 3) + [c(T) + s(T)q_\phi^{-1}(1 + \phi)c(T)]C(T)$
   $\quad -[I + s(T)q_\mu^{-1}(1 + \mu)]M''(T) - s(T)q_\mu^{-1}(1 + \mu)m'(T)X(T)$
   $\quad \leqslant -\overline{E(T)} \quad \overline{G(T)} - s(T)q_\gamma^{-1}\overline{G(T)}(1 + \gamma) - s(T)q_\epsilon^{-1}\overline{E(T)}(1 + \epsilon)$
   $\quad - s(T)q_\delta^{-1}D(T)(1 + \delta),$

4. Capacity Restraints
   (4.01) $\quad b(1)X(1) \leqslant b(1)(I + \alpha_0)\overline{X(0)},$
   (4.02) $\quad b(t)X(t) - K(t) \leqslant 0,$

5. Capital Accounting Relationships
   (5.01) $\quad K(2) - Z(2) - R(2) \leqslant b(1)(I + \alpha_0)\overline{X(0)} - d\overline{D(2)},$
   (5.02) $\quad K(t + 1) - Z(t + 1) - R(t + 1) - K(t) \leqslant -d\overline{D(t + 1)}, \quad \text{for } t = 2, \cdots, T - 1,$
   (5.03) $\quad -Z(T + 1) - R(T + 1) - K(T) + b(T)q_\phi^{-1}(1 + \phi)c(T)C(T) - b(T)q_\mu^{-1}(1 + \mu)m'(T)X(T)$
   $\quad + b(T)q_\mu^{-1}(1 + \mu)M''(T) \leqslant -d\overline{D(T + 1)} \quad b(T)q_\gamma^{-1}(1 + \gamma)\overline{G(T)} \quad b(T)q_\epsilon^{-1}(1 + \epsilon)\overline{E(T)}$
   $\quad - b(T)q_\delta^{-1}(1 + \delta)\overline{D(T)},$
   (5.04) $\quad Z(T + 2) - R(T + 2) - Z(T + 1) - R(T + 1) - K(T) + b(T)q_\phi^{-1}(1 + \phi)^2c(T)C(T)$
   $\quad -b(T)q_\mu^{-1}(1 + \mu)^2m'(T)X(T) + b(T)q_\mu^{-1}(1 + \mu)^2 M''(T) \leqslant -d\overline{D(T + 1)} - d\overline{D(T + 2)}$
   $\quad -b(T)q_\gamma^{-1}(1 + \gamma)^2\overline{G(T)} - b(T)q_\epsilon^{-1}(1 + \epsilon)^2\overline{E(T)} - b(T)q_\delta^{-1}(1 + \delta)^2\overline{D(T)},$
   (5.05) $\quad -Z(T + 3) - R(T + 3) - Z(T + 2) - R(T + 2) \quad Z(T + 1) - R(T + 1) - K(T)$
   $\quad + b(T)q_\phi^{-1}(1 + \phi)^3c(T)C(T) - b(T)q_\mu^{-1}(1 + \mu)^3m'(T)X(T) + b(T)q_\mu^{-1}(1 + \mu)^3 M''(T)$
   $\quad \leqslant -d\overline{D(T + 1)} - d\overline{D(T + 2)} - d\overline{D(T + 3)} - b(T)q_\gamma^{-1}(1 + \gamma)^3\overline{G(T)} - b(T)q_\epsilon^{-1}(1 + \epsilon)^3\overline{E(T)}$
   $\quad - b(T)q_\delta^{-1}(1 + \delta)^3 \overline{D(T)},$

6. Restoration Ceilings
   (6.01) $\quad R(t) \leqslant d\overline{D(t)}, \quad \text{for } t = 2, \cdots, T + 3,$

7. Balance of Payments Constraints
   (7.01) $\quad um'(t)X(t) + uM''(t) \leqslant A\overline{(t)} + u\overline{E(t)}, \quad \text{for } t = 1, \cdots, T,$

8. Competitive Import Ceilings
   (8.01) $\quad [m'(t)]^{-1}M''(t) + um'(t)X(t) \leqslant A\overline{(t)} + u\overline{E(t)}, \quad \text{for } t = 1, \cdots, T,$

9. Initial Capital-in-Process Restraints
   (9.01) $\quad Z(2) + R(2) \leqslant b\alpha(I + \alpha_0)\overline{X(0)} + d\overline{D(2)},$
   (9.02) $\quad Z(3) + R(3) \leqslant b\alpha(I + \alpha_0)^2\overline{X(0)} + d\overline{D(3)}.$

3. Data for the Third and Fourth Five Year Plan Periods

The firefly seems a fire, the sky looks flat;
Yet sky and fly are neither this nor that.
The true seem often false, the false often true;
Appearances deceive, so think it through.

The Panchatantra

3.1 Data Requirements

Once the theoretical structure of the models has been specified, it is relatively easy to describe the kind of information necessary to fill in that structure. It has been our experience, however, that our appreciation of the difficulties in the empirical problems has increased as we have confronted them. The process of providing the relevant data has been laborious, and we shall present only the end results.

Our source materials have been confined to generally available public documents. We have modified and extrapolated the data in these documents when it appeared to us that there was a reasonable basis for doing so. On occasion, we have proceeded with inadequate information, if we believed that it would be possible to prepare improved data and that a case for developing such data would be demonstrated by the potential usefulness of the results. For example, at the outset of this project, only one ten-year-old input-output table existed for India. After extensive investigation of basic sources, we concluded that there was sufficient data available for the preparation of a new and substantially improved interindustry flow matrix. At the stage of final computation, we were able to make use of two, more recent input-output tables, which had by then been made public. Since these input-output tables and most other available data were estimated in 1959-60 prices, this price level was maintained throughout in all estimations and projections. Where international comparisons of the rupee with other currencies are made, the exchange rate used is that prevailing prior to the devaluation of June 6, 1966.

In order to apply the models described in the previous chapter, data are required to define the technology of production and also to stipulate the various externally specified demands. On the production side, the following information is needed for each period:

1. $a(t)$, interindustry flow coefficient matrix.
2. $s(t)$, stock-flow matrix.
3. b, diagonal matrix of aggregate capital coefficients.
4. p, capital proportions matrix.
5. p', p'', and p''', proportions matrices for investment lags.
6. m', diagonal matrix of noncompetitive import coefficients.
7. m'', competitive import coefficients for exchange allocation ceilings.

To specify the demands for output, the following have to be estimated for each period:

1. $c(t)$, vector of consumption coefficients.
2. $\rho(t)$, minimum growth rate of consumption in period t.
3. $D(t)$, vector of the fixed capital that depreciates in period (t).
4. r, composition matrix for the depreciated capital.
5. $\overline{E(t)}$, vector of exports.
6. $\overline{G(t)}$, vector of government consumption.
7. $\overline{A(t)}$, net foreign capital inflow.
8. δ, ϵ, γ, postterminal growth rates for D, E, and G.

Initial and terminal conditions are prescribed by the following:

1. $\overline{X(0)}$, vector of domestic output levels in the preplan period. This is used to estimate $\overline{K(1)}$.
2. α_0, diagonal matrix of implicit yearly growth rates projected for the early periods of the plan in the preplan years. α_0, along with $\overline{X(0)}$ is used to determine the initial capital stocks and the initial capital-in-process.
3. $\overline{X(T)}, \alpha_\tau$, vector of domestic output levels for the target year T, $\overline{X(T)}$, and matrix of projected postterminal growth rates, α_τ, are used to determine the terminal capital stocks and the terminal capital-in-process for the Target Model.
4. ϕ, μ, postterminal growth rates for consumption and imports, respectively. $\phi, \mu, \delta, \epsilon$ and γ are used to determine the postterminal capital stocks for the Transit Model.

3.2 Description of the Sectors

The sectoral classification for use in computation had to be decided on the basis of the input-output tables available. At the start of the project in 1963, the most recent input-output table available was for 1955-56 and was on a fifty-sector basis. It was compiled at the Indian Statistical Institute by A. Chakravarti. Computation on a fifty-sector basis using this input-output table exceeded the amount of computational capacity at our disposal. Some rough calculations indicated that computations on the basis of a thirty-two-sector table would still exceed the acceptable computation time. Further aggregation was necessary. Unfortunately, there was no possibility of carrying out the aggregation in a way that would be certain to satisfy the theoretical criteria for avoiding bias.[1] This was due partly to lack of the empirical information that the criteria require and partly to inadequate knowledge of the procedures used in the previous aggregation. In this instance the thirty-two sectors already represent a high degree of aggregation, and, lacking a full description of the tables, we were ignorant of the detailed sectoral composition. Experimentation with various classification systems led us to choose an eleven-sector level of detail. Table 3.1 indicates the manner in which the sectors were aggregated.

---

[1] For a survey of aggregation problems in production data, see A. A. Walters, "Production and Cost Functions: An Econometric Survey," *Econometrica, 31,* Nos. 1-2, 1963, pp. 5-11.

Table 3.1. Sectoral Classification Compared with I.S.I. Classification

Aggregated Sectors	I.S.I. Sectors	Descriptive Notes
1. Agriculture and Plantations AG. PL.	11 Plantations	Natural rubber, tea, coffee
	13 Animal Husbandry and Fishery	Including hides and skins, wool
	15 Food Grains	Including cereal substitutes and pulses
	18 Other Agriculture	Including cotton, jute, sugarcane, oil seeds, tobacco, fruits and vegetables, spices
	21 Forestry Products	Including timber, firewood, resins
2. Mining and Metals M.M.	6 Iron and Steel	Including ferroalloys and special steel
	7 Iron Ore	
	9 Other Metals	Nonferrous metals and alloys, including precious metals
	10 Other Minerals	
	20 Coal and Coke	
3. Equipment EQIPMT	3 Electrical Equipment and Machinery	Including domestic electrical appliances
	4 Transport Equipment and Accessories	Including tractors and bulldozers
	5 Nonelectrical Equipment and Machinery	Including instruments such as surgical tools and water meters, and consumer goods such as furniture and fixtures, cutlery, utensils, clocks, razor blades
4. Chemicals CHEMIC	19 Chemical Fertilizers	
	23 Petroleum Products	
	24 Crude Oil	
	25 Rubber Products	Including tires and tubes, belting, rubber footwear
	26 Synthetic Rubber	
	27 Chemicals	Including matches, paper, newsprint, artificial silk yarn, soaps and cosmetics, drugs and pharmaceuticals, dyestuffs and inks, paints and varnishes, plastics; excluding synthetic rubber and chemical fertilizers
5. Cement and Nonmetals (Glass, Wooden Products, etc.) CMGLWD	8 Cement	
	20 Glass, Wooden, and Nonmetallic Mineral Products	Including glass and glassware, structural clay products and refractories, china, asbestos, hume pipes, plywood, cane products, strawboard
6. Food, Clothing, and Leather FOODCL	12 Leather and Leather Products	Leather tanning, leather footwear, and leather components
	14 Food Industries	Including tobacco and products, alcoholic and nonalcoholic beverages, salted, preserved, and prepared foods
	16 Cotton and Other Textiles	Including hosiery and knitted fabrics, cordage, twine, rope, carpets
	17 Jute Textiles and Coir Products	
7. Electricity ELECTR	29a Thermal Electricity	Generation, transmission, and distribution of thermal electricity
	29b Hydroelectricity	Generation, transmission, and distribution of hydroelectricty
8. Transport TRANS	22 Motor Transport	Transport of goods and passengers
	28 Railways	Transport of goods and passengers
9. Construction CONSTR	1 Construction	Urban and industrial
	2 Construction	Rural
10. Housing HOUS.	Housing	
11. Others and Margin OTHMAR	Others, Margin	Including other industries, transport, commerce, services

3.3 Production Data

As indicated in the description of the models, the Leontief input-output assumption of "fixed coefficients" of production has been adopted. The production data are a set of ratios for each sector that indicate input requirements per unit of output. The ratios can be changed from period to period and from one solution to the next. However, the Target and Transit Models are not provided with technological alternatives. The general structure and logic of input-output tables have been discussed in detail elsewhere,[2] and so we shall not review that material. Since we utilize only secondary sources and published information we shall not repeat the detailed descriptions of the data in the original documents. The following discussion will be limited to brief accounts of the data used and to explanations of the adjustments made.

3.3.1 Interindustry Flow Coefficient Matrices a(t)

In early 1964, two new Indian input-output tables became available for 1959-60. One was prepared at the Indian Statistical Institute under the direction of A. S. Manne and A. Rudhra. The second table was prepared by the Inter-Industry Study Group of the Planning Commission under the direction of K. S. Khrisnaswamy of the Economic Growth Section. These two tables were intended for somewhat different purposes and differ with respect to a number of features. Without the details of their construction, it was not possible to reconcile the differences in the tables. In most cases however, the variations do not appear to represent different estimates of the same quantities but rather somewhat different concepts of these quantities. Inasmuch as more information and other supporting data were available for the I.S.I. table, it has been used in all our computations. The I.S.G. table has been used only to supply information, not contained in the I.S.I. table, on the distribution of inputs in the Transport sector and the use of imports.

The 1960-61 I.S.I. table used is that presented in *Notes on Perspective of Development, India: 1960-61 to 1975-76*[3] and is shown in Table 3.2. It is a thirty-sector table with inputs valued at producers' prices. The final uses of output are for the Household, Government, and Export sectors, Others, a miscellaneous sector, Inventory Stocks, and Gross Fixed Capital Formation. Total domestic production is obtained after subtracting Imports. In addition to the inputs of the intermediate producing sectors, Wages and Salaries, Gross Profit and Margins are distinguished. The latter includes wholesale and retail trade margins and indirect taxes and subsidies.

In the I.S.I. table only five sectors produce fixed capital: Urban and Rural Construction, and Electrical, Transport, and Nonelectrical Equipment. Industrial sectors such as Cement, Iron and Steel, and Other Metals, rather than supplying outputs directly for fixed-capital formation, deliver to the Construction sectors, which in this table are processing rather than service industries. They receive inputs, process them, and deliver fixed capital.

---

[2]W. Leontief and others, *Studies in the Structure of the American Economy,* Oxford University Press, New York, 1953; H. B. Chenery and P. G. Clark, *Interindustry Economics,* John Wiley, New York, 1959.

[3]Perspective Planning Division (P.P.D.), Planning Commission, Government of India, April 1964, pp. 183-187.

Inasmuch as the purpose in the experiments with empirical information is the analysis and demonstration of generally applicable techniques, a number of modifications have been made in the I.S.I. table:

1. In several sectors of the I.S.I. table, there is a negative input entered in the Others sector as an aggregate correction to overestimation of inputs to other sectors. Such a negative input is eliminated by allocating it along the row among the deliveries of the sector using the proportions of the positive deliveries as a guide, so that

$$a_{ij}^{new} = \tilde{a}_{ij} - a_i \frac{a_{ij}}{\sum\limits_{j=1}^{30} a_{ij}}$$

   where $\tilde{a}_i$ is the negative input from the ith sector.

2. The undistributed inputs of Railways and Motor Transport were allocated using the proportions from the I.S.G. table.

3. A major change made in the I.S.I. table was the creation of a (Residential) Housing sector that provides rental services. This sector constitutes approximately 7 per cent of the consumer budget; it is also the sector with the largest capital-output ratio. Initial experiments with the 1955-56 I.S.I. table strongly suggested that over-all results would be sensitive to the size and growth rate of this sector. It was therefore decided to isolate Housing from the Others sector. In order to construct a residential property row, it was assumed that this sector would deliver only to Private Consumption, and the amount of the delivery would be the Rs. 520 crores estimated as the output of the sector in the official national income accounts for 1959-60. This amount was subtracted from the delivery of the Others sector to Private Consumption. The Housing column was formed by allocating the row total among the input sectors, using the relevant coefficients of the 1955-56 I.S.I. input-output table.

4. The Margins sector was made into a source of intermediate inputs rather than being treated, as were Wages and Salaries, as payments to a primary factor. This was done to conform to the usual practice for wholesale and retail trade. In the absence of any other basis for establishing an empirical relationship, it would, in any case, have been necessary to relate outputs of the trade sectors to other sectors by fixed coefficients.

Table 3.3 presents the modified 1960-61 I.S.I. table, now on a thirty-two-sector basis. Tables 3.4 and 3.5 present the matrix of interindustry coefficients aggregated to eleven sectors, using as weights the gross domestic outputs in 1960-61 and projected gross domestic outputs in 1965-66, respectively. The former is used for the Third Plan period, and the latter for the Fourth Plan period.

3.3.2 Stock-Flow Coefficients

The patterns of inventory-holding in the less developed areas have not been studied intensively, and relatively little empirical information is available. Such information is notoriously difficult to collect and the statistical reporting systems

Table 3.2. I.S.I. Input-Output Table for 1960-61 (Rs. crores, 1959-60 prices)

Sector	1	2	3	4	5	6	7	8	9	10	11	12	13
1. Construction, urban and industrial													
2. Construction, rural													
3. Electrical Equipment			2.3	0.6	1.6	1.6							
4. Transport Equipment				7.0									
5. Nonelectrical Equipment	23.0	3.0	6.0	1.0	6.0	2.7	0.2			1.1			
6. Iron and Steel	214.0	26.0	4.0	22.0	71.0	43.0							
7. Iron Ore						3.5							
8. Cement	44.0	5.4						5.7					
9. Other Metals			10.0	3.0	44.0	12.0			8.3				
10. Other Minerals			0.3			6.7			5.4				
11. Plantations													
12. Leather and Leather Products			0.3	0.4						0.2			
13. Animal Husbandry												46.0	55.0
14. Food Industries												42.0	
15. Food Grains												2.0	97.0
16. Cotton, Other Textiles			0.3			0.6		7.8			1.0	0.2	
17. Jute Textiles			0.5										
18. Other Agriculture											6.3		
19. Chemical Fertilizers													
20. Glass, Wooden, and Nonmetallic Mineral Products	280.0	35.0	2.1	0.6	1.0					0.3	3.3		
21. Forestry Products	61.3	7.6	0.5	11.0			0.1						
22. Motor Transport									0.1			9.0	
23. Petroleum Products			0.8	2.0	1.0	2.4		0.3	0.3	0.4	0.4	0.6	
24. Crude Oil				8.0	0.1								
25. Rubber Products			0.3										
26. Rubber													
27. Chemicals			2.8	4.4	5.2	6.0		3.1	0.4	0.8	1.6	12.0	19.0
28. Railways			1.5	3.0	4.0	6.0	0.1	5.8	0.6		0.2	1.3	
29. Electricity			0.1	0.4	2.5	6.4	0.3	3.7	0.4		0.6	0.2	
30. Coal									0.1	1.7	11.4	5.5	
31. Others			40.0	27.0	27.5	27.6							
32. Total, rows 1-31	622.3	77.0	71.8	90.4	163.9	118.6	0.7	26.4	15.7	4.1	24.8	118.8	171.0
33. Value Added	327.9	308.7	45.4	90.6	129.7	110.8	7.0	19.5	12.8	40.8	168.0	47.3	932.0
34. Margin	250.8	30.3	8.8	20.0	49.9	39.6	0.1	6.7	3.5	0.5	3.2	22.0	27.0
35. Value of Output	1201.0	416.0	126.0	201.0	343.5	269.0	7.8	52.0	32.0	45.4	196.0	189.0	1130.0

Source: Planning Unit, Indian Statistical Institute, New Delhi.

Table 3.2. (cont.)

Sector	14	15	16	17	18	19	20	21	22	23	24	25
1. Construction, urban and industrial												
2. Construction, rural												
3. Electrical Equipment												
4. Transport Equipment												
5. Nonelectrical Equipment	6.6			0.5			1.2			7.7		0.3
6. Iron and Steel												
7. Iron Ore												
8. Cement							3.2					
9. Other Metals												
10. Other Minerals							6.0					
11. Plantations												15.5
12. Leather and Leather Products	16.4		4.0									
13. Animal Husbandry	48.4		10.0									
14. Food Industries	23.0	421.0	5.6									
15. Food Grains												
16. Cotton, Other Textiles	6.6	2.9	18.0	0.4		0.9	0.4					7.0
17. Jute Textiles		2.7	3.9	3.0								
18. Other Agriculture	772.0		300.0	61.0	84.0							
19. Chemical Fertilizers		15.0			9.0							
20. Glass, Wooden, and Nonmetallic Mineral Products	0.9		6.4			0.1	8.4					
21. Forestry Products												
22. Motor Transport	4.5	11.9	7.2	0.3			59.0		130.0			
23. Petroleum Products					6.3		10.0			0.1		0.1
24. Crude Oil									21.0	43.6		0.7
25. Rubber Products												1.4
26. Rubber												4.4
27. Chemicals	7.3	3.8	34.0	2.9	2.1	4.2	26.0		36.0	1.2		
28. Railways	5.8	5.6	22.0	3.5		0.3	7.0	9.0			0.3	
29. Electricity	2.9	0.4	6.0	0.5	2.2	1.2	6.4			2.4		0.8
30. Coal		8.9	72.0	6.0		3.1						0.1
31. Others	90.1						39.0			25.6		5.0
32. Total, rows 1-31	984.4	472.2	489.5	78.1	103.6	9.8	166.6	9.0	187.0	80.6	0.3	35.3
33. Value Added	271.2	3489.0	277.0	48.6	1992.0	9.2	198.0	171.0	216.0	55.0	2.9	24.7
34. Margin	67.4	12.8	33.5	3.3	1.4	1.7	33.4		3.0	2.8		7.5
35. Value of Output	1323.0	3974.0	800.0	130.0	2097.0	20.7	398.0	180.0	406.0	139.0	3.2	67.5

+98.1 taxes

Table 3.2. (cont.)

Sector	26	27	28	29	30	$\sum_{j=i}^{30} X_{ij}$ 31	32	House-hold 33	Govern-ment 34	Stock 35	Exports 36	Imports 37	Gross Fixed Capital Formation 38	Output 39
1. Construction, urban and industrial							153.0		104.0				944.0	1201.0
2. Construction, rural													416.0	416.0
3. Electrical Equipment						6.1		33.4	16.9	1.8	0.8	57.0	124.0	126.0
4. Transport Equipment		1.7				7.0		39.2	45.9	4.6	0.5	69.2	173.0	201.0
5. Nonelectrical Equipment					3.8	64.8		112.8	31.0	15.7	2.9	228.7	345.0	343.5
6. Iron and Steel						380.0	-4.2			4.0	10.1	120.9		269.0
7. Iron Ore						3.5	1.5			-0.2	2.4			7.8
8. Cement						52.6				1.7	0.3			52.6
9. Other Metals		3.1				80.4	-1.0				0.2	0.1		32.0
10. Other Minerals		8.2				32.3	-1.2				24.5	49.3		45.4
11. Plantations						15.5		73.7		5.8	109.5	10.0		196.0
12. Leather and Leather Products						50.5	18.3	96.0		0.8	23.7	8.5		189.0
13. Animal Husbandry		2.8				71.2		1057.4	93.6	102.3	20.6	0.3		1130.0
14. Food Industries		10.9				121.9		978.6		57.8	36.1	19.2		1323.0
15. Food Grains						541.0		3520.1		9.2		9.5		3974.0
16. Cotton, Other Textiles		0.3				26.4		702.6	11.3	1.6	54.5	144.9		800.0
17. Jute Textiles		1.7				29.5	4.6				94.4	4.0		130.0
18. Other Agriculture		0.3				1220.0	172.0	761.4		19.1	49.3	0.1		2097.0
19. Chemical Fertilizers						30.3	-0.2			1.3		124.8		20.7
20. Glass, Wooden, and Nonmetallic Mineral Products												10.7		
21. Forestry Products		6.8				344.9	11.7	63.2		-1.9	2.4	10.6		398.0
22. Motor Transport		12.5				161.0	73.0	113.0			12.4	5.1		180.0
23. Petroleum Products					0.1	220.0		81.4	27.3		4.1	82.8		406.0
24. Crude Oil		2.8				207.1						40.4		237.1
25. Rubber Products						43.6				0.2		3.3		3.2
26. Rubber			23.0	2.9		30.1		39.9		0.9	0.6	2.3		67.5
27. Chemicals		63.0				200.3		179.2		5.8	9.9	111.2		284.0
28. Railways						278.0	87.0	89.0						454.0
29. Electricity		6.2	3.4	13.5	3.2	83.0	6.3	11.1	4.7	-2.1†	1.8	0.1		103.0
30. Coal		3.1	31.7	12.7	7.3	89.9	9.0	6.1		2.3	7.3	11.1		109.0
31. Others		14.0	17.7	29.1	4.7	488.8	185.3‡							
32. Total, rows 1-31		137.4	75.8	65.5	19.1	4383.3*	529.8	7958.1	520.0	231.1	468.1	1090.5	2002.0	13734.2§
33. Value Added		121.8	378.0	8.4	89.2	9650.2	3224.0	860.0						
34. Margin		24.8	0.2		0.7	664.2		4646.8ǁ			164.8	276.0		
35. Value of Output		284.0	454.0	103.0	109.0	14697.7	529.8	12604.9	1380.0	231.1	632.9	1090.5	2278.0	14795.8

+98.1 taxes on petroleum products

* Row total is less than column total by 498.0 if entries in rows 22 and 28 are considered.
† Adjusted for exaggerated industrial consumption.
‡ Inclusive of Margin.
§ Gross value added.
ǁ Inclusive of Others.

Table 3.3. Modified I.S.I. Input-Output Table for 1960-61 (Rs. crores, 1959-60 prices) (Rs. crores, 1959-60)

	1 CONSTU	2 CONSTR	3 ELEQIP	4 TRANEQ	5 NEEQIP	6 IRONST	7 IRONOR	8 CEMENT	9 O METL	10 O MIN.	11 PLATN	12 LEATHR	13 ANIMLS	14 FCCEIA	15 FCCDGR	16 COTEXT	17 JUTEXT	18 O AGRI
1 CONSTU																		
2 CONSTR																		
3 ELEQIP			2.3CC	.600	1.6CC	1.6CC												
4 TRANEQ		3.000		7.CCC	1.CCC													
5 NEEQIP	23.0CC		6.CCC	1.CCC	69.793	2.7CC	.2CC			1.1CC				.6CC			.500	
6 IRONST	210.361	25.558	3.932	21.626	42.269	3.5CC												
7 IRONOR																		
8 CEMENT	42.171	5.175	9.876	2.963	43.453	4.792		5.372	8.197									
9 O METL			.283			6.314	.031		5.089									
10 O MIN.																		
11 PLANTN																		
12 LEATHR			.3CC							.2CC		46.000				4.CCC		
13 ANIHUS												42.000		16.4CC		10.CCC		
14 FOODIN												2.000	55.CCC	48.4CC		5.600		
15 FOODGR													97.CCC	23.CCC	+21.CCC			
16 COTEXT			.3CC	.4CC				7.800	.032		1.000	.2CC				18.CCC	.4CC	
17 JUTEXT			.500													3.9CC	3.000	84.000
18 O AGRI														772.CCC	2.7C3	61.CCC		
19 FERTIL														-14.9C1	-.C			8.941
20 GLASWD	275.055	34.382	2.063	.589	.982	.6CC	-.059		.1CC	-.295	6.258			-.884		6.287		
21 FOREST	61.300	7.600	.5CC	11.CCC	19.5CC			7.620	3.410		3.242	9.000						
22 MOTRAN	17.150		6.570	13.720	19.5CC	39.6CC	.525			3.150	3.410			29.250	12.650	34.300	5.500	22.450
23 PETPRO	13.500		.800	2.000	1.CCC	2.4CC		.3CC	.3CC		.4CC	.6CC		4.5CC	11.900	7.200	.3CC	6.3CC
24 CR.OIL																		
25 RUBPRD			.3CC	8.0CC	.1CC													
26 RUBBER																		
27 CHEMIC			2.800	4.4CC	5.2CC	6.CCC		1.170	.4CC	7.520	1.600	12.000	19.CCC	7.300	3.800	34.CCC	2.900	2.1CC
28 RAILS	25.400		3.530	2.590	3.C5C	3.290	.24C	3.1CC	2.590	.800	3.530	1.300		24.700	3.530	22.700	3.650	7.760
29 ELECTR			1.500	3.CCC	4.CCC	6.CCC	.14C	5.800	.600	.045	.2CC	.2CC		5.8CC	5.600	22.CCC	3.500	2.2CC
30 COAL			.1CC	.4CC	2.5CC	11.4CC	.CC8		.4CC		.600			2.9CC	.4CC	6.4CC		
31 HOUS.																		
32 OTHERS	151.408	22.030	28.137	22.313	39.879	13.C21	-0.	1.172			5.737	21.270	20.221	77.478	4.134	36.324	.112	
34 OUTPUT	1201.0	416.0	126.0	201.0	343.5	269.0	7.8	52.6	32.0	45.4	196.0	189.0	1130.0	1323.0	3974.0	800.0	130.0	2097.0

Table 3.3 (cont.)

	19 FERTIL	20 GLASWD	21 FOREST	22 MOTRAN	23 PETPRO	24 CR.OIL	25 RUBPRO	26 RUBBER	27 CHEMIC	28 RAILS	29 ELECTR	30 COAL	31 HOUS.	32 OTHERS	33 SUM	34 OUTPUT
1 CONSTU	0.	0.	0.	0.	0.	0.	0.	0.	0.	0.	0.	0.	0.	153.000	153.000	1201.000
2 CONSTR	0.	0.	0.	0.	0.	0.	0.	0.	0.	0.	0.	0.	0.	0.	0.	416.000
3 ELEQIP	0.	0.	0.	0.	0.	0.	0.	0.	0.	0.	0.	0.	0.	0.	6.100	126.000
4 TRANEQ	0.	1.200	0.	0.	0.	0.	0.	0.	0.	0.	0.	0.	0.	0.	7.000	201.000
5 NEEGIP	-0.	-0.	-0.	-0.	0.	0.	.300	0.	1.700	0.	0.	0.	2.261	0.	64.800	343.500
6 IRONST	-0.	0.	-0.	0.	7.700	0.	0.	0.	0.	0.	0.	3.800	0.	0.	382.300	269.000
7 IRONOR	-0.	0.	-0.	-0.	-0.	-0.	-0.	-0.	-0.	-0.	-0.	-0.	0.	0.	3.500	7.800
8 CEMENT	-0.	3.067	-0.	-0.	0.	0.	0.	0.	0.	0.	0.	0.	2.425	0.	60.130	52.600
9 O METL	-0.	-0.	-0.	-0.	-0.	-0.	-0.	-0.	3.061	-0.	-0.	-0.	-0.	0.	80.400	32.000
10 O MIN.	-0.	5.655	-0.	0.	-0.	-0.	-0.	-0.	7.728	-0.	-0.	-0.	.660	0.	33.000	45.400
11 PLANTN	0.	0.	0.	0.	0.	0.	15.500	0.	0.	0.	0.	0.	0.	0.	15.500	196.000
12 LEATHR	0.	0.	0.	0.	0.	0.	0.	0.	2.800	0.	0.	0.	0.	0.	50.531	189.000
13 ANIHUS	0.	0.	0.	0.	0.	0.	0.	0.	10.900	0.	0.	0.	0.	18.300	89.500	1130.000
14 FOODIN	0.	0.	0.	0.	0.	0.	0.	0.	0.	0.	0.	0.	0.	0.	121.900	1323.000
15 FOODGR	0.	0.	0.	0.	0.	0.	7.000	0.	0.	0.	0.	0.	0.	0.	541.000	3974.000
16 COTEXT	0.	0.	0.	0.	0.	0.	0.	0.	.300	0.	0.	0.	0.	4.600	26.400	800.000
17 JUTEXT	.900	.400	0.	0.	0.	0.	0.	0.	1.700	0.	0.	0.	0.	0.	34.132	130.000
18 O AGRI	0.	0.	0.	-0.	0.	0.	-0.	-0.	.300	-0.	-0.	-0.	0.	172.000	392.000	2097.000
19 FERTIL	-0.	-0.	0.	-0.	0.	0.	0.	0.	0.	0.	0.	0.	0.	0.	30.300	20.700
20 GLASWD	-0.	8.252	-0.	0.	-0.	-0.	-0.	-0.	-0.	0.	0.	0.	0.	0.	351.070	398.000
21 FOREST	0.	59.000	0.	0.	0.	0.	0.	0.	6.680	0.	0.	0.	6.100	0.	172.700	180.000
22 MOTRAN	2.360	16.350	0.	104.100	10.550	0.	3.940	.005	12.500	4.470	12.150	4.470	2.890	11.700	364.385	325.000
23 PETPRO	.100	10.000	0.	16.800	43.600	0.	.100	.000	26.400	23.000	2.900	.100	0.	62.000	207.100	237.100
24 CR.OIL	0.	0.	0.	0.	0.	0.	0.	0.	2.800	0.	0.	0.	0.	12.400	43.600	3.200
25 RUBPRD	0.	0.	0.	0.	0.	0.	.700	0.	0.	0.	0.	0.	0.	0.	30.100	67.500
26 RUBBER	0.	0.	0.	0.	0.	0.	1.400	0.	0.	0.	0.	0.	0.	4.200	1.400	.010
27 CHEMIC	4.200	0.	0.	0.	0.	0.	4.700	.000	63.000	0.	0.	0.	0.	0.	200.305	284.000
28 RAILS	1.410	6.590	0.	18.800	1.200	0.	0.	0.	5.880	9.400	0.	2.350	.940	59.600	229.620	454.000
29 ELECTR	.300	7.000	0.	0.	4.700	0.	.800	.000	6.200	3.400	0.	3.200	0.	6.300	89.340	103.000
30 COAL	1.200	6.400	0.	0.	2.400	0.	.100	.000	3.100	31.700	13.500	7.300	0.	4.000	98.953	109.000
31 HOUS.	0.	0.	0.	0.	0.	0.	0.	0.	0.	0.	0.	0.	0.	0.	0.	569.280
32 OTHERS	.810	38.901	7.079	9.753	10.343	.236	3.036	0.	5.128	3.170	7.039	7.300	25.384	0.	743.900	5854.600
34 OUTPUT	20.7	398.0	180.0	325.0	237.1	3.2	67.5	.01	284.0	454.0	103.0	109.0	569.28	5854.6		

Table 3.4. Input-Output Coefficient Matrix, a, for Third Plan Period

	1 AG.PL.	2 M.M.	3 EQIPMT	4 CHEMIC	5 CMGLWD	6 FOODCL	7 ELECTR	8 TRANS	9 CONSTR	10 HOUS.	11 OTHMAR
AG.PL.	.080	.000	.017	.051	.131	.505	0.	0.	.043	0.	.035
M.M.	.000	.208	.231	.025	.052	.004	.131	.041	.146	.005	.001
EQIPMT	0.	.020	.037	.016	.003	.003	0.	0.	.016	0.	0.
CHEMIC	.010	.020	.037	.199	.081	.028	.028	.185	.008	0.	.003
CMGLWC	.000	.011	.005	.011	.025	.003	0.	0.	.221	.015	0.
FOODCL	.008	.002	.002	.034	.018	.057	0.	0.	0.	0.	.001
ELECTR	.001	.023	.013	.016	.022	.013	0.	.004	0.	0.	.001
TRANS	.007	.145	.073	.098	.070	.049	.118	.042	.026	.007	.021
CONSTR	0.	0.	0.	0.	C.	0.	0.	0.	0.	0.	0.
HOUS.	0.	0.	0.	0.	C.	0.	0.	0.	0.	0.	0.
OTHMAR	.005	.028	.135	.032	.089	.055	.068	.017	.107	.045	0.
SUM	.111	.458	.550	.480	.491	.710	.346	.288	.567	.071	.061

Table 3.5. Input-Output Coefficient Matrix, a, for Fourth Plan Period

	1 AG.PL.	2 M.M.	3 EQIPMT	4 CHEMIC	5 CMGLWD	6 FOODCL	7 ELECTR	8 TRANS	9 CONSTR	10 HOUS.	11 OTHMAR
AG.PL.	.079	.000	.010	.048	.134	.502	0.	0.	.035	0.	.035
M.M.	.000	.235	.263	.027	.048	.004	.131	.037	.118	.005	.001
EQIPMT	0.	.018	.033	.014	.003	.003	0.	0.	.013	0.	0.
CHEMIC	.010	.023	.030	.198	.082	.029	.028	.202	.006	0.	.003
CMGLWD	.000	.013	.005	.011	.026	.003	0.	0.	.180	.015	0.
FOODCL	.008	.002	.002	.034	.015	.056	0.	0.	0.	0.	.001
ELECTR	.001	.023	.012	.016	.022	.014	0.	.004	C.	0.	.001
TRANS	.007	.150	.071	.099	.068	.050	.118	.043	.018	.007	.021
CONSTR	0.	0.	0.	0.	0.	0.	0.	0.	0.	0.	0.
HOUS.	0.	0.	0.	0.	0.	0.	C.	0.	0.	0.	C.
OTHMAR	.005	.033	.132	.032	.090	.055	.068	.018	.090	.045	0.
SUM	.110	.498	.558	.479	.488	.715	.346	.304	.459	.071	.061

Table 3.6. Aggregate Inventory-Output Coefficients $s_j(t)$

| | 32 Sectors | | | 11 Sectors[‡] | | | | |
| | | | | | Reference Set | | Lower Set | |
Sector	C.S.O.[*]	P.P.D[†]	Refer-ence Set	Sector	Third Plan	Fourth Plan	Third Plan	Fourth Plan
1. Construction, urban and industrial			.068	1. AG.PL.	.393	.393	.131	.131
2. Construction, rural			.068	2. M.M.	.240	.236	.240	.236
3. Electrical Equipment	.361	.336	.34	3. EQIPMT	.384	.384	.384	.384
4. Transport Equipment	.399	.233	.40	4. CHEMIC	.528	.527	.259	.259
5. Nonelectrical Equipment	.425	.389	.39	5. CMGLWD	.237	.236	.237	.236
6. Iron and Steel	.352	.230	.23	6. FOODCL	.361	.359	.181	.181
7. Iron Ore		.200	.20	7. ELECTR	.129	.129	.129	.129
8. Cement	.292	.070	.29	8. TRANS	.020	.018	.020	.018
9. Other Metals	.261	.240	.24	9. CONSTR	.068	.068	.068	.068
10. Other Minerals			.24	10. HOUS.				
11. Plantations			.368	11. OTHMAR	.008	.008	.008	.008
12. Leather and Leather Products	.302		.30					
13. Animal Husbandry and Fishery			.020					
14. Food Industries	.326		.33					
15. Food Grains			.430§					
16. Cotton and Other Textiles	.283	.123	.28					
17. Jute Textiles	.251		.25					
18. Other Agriculture			.430					
19. Chemical Fertilizers	.514	.500	.50					
20. Glass, Wooden, and Non-metallic Mineral Products	.279	.231	.23					
21. Forestry Products			.020					
22. Motor Transport			.016					
23. Petroleum Products	.141		.14					
24. Crude Oil			.60					
25. Rubber Products	.230	.230	.23					
26. Synthetic Rubber			.30					
27. Chemicals	.305	.275	.28					
28. Railways			.022					
29. Electricity, total	.147		.129					
30. Coal		.187	.190					
31. Housing								
32. Others and Margin			.008					

[*]Central Statistical Organization, *Annual Survey of Industry 1960*.

[†]P.P.D. *Notes*, Table M. Individual sectors are not necessarily complete.

[‡]A. K. Sen, in "Working Capital in The Indian Economy: A conceptual Framework and Some Estimates," estimated the following coefficients:

| 1. Agriculture | .14 | 3. Small Industries | .40 to .60 |
| 2. Manufacture | 1.05 | 4. Trading | 1.10 |

§An unpublished estimate by J. Mirrlees of the inventory-output ratio in Agriculture was 0.860.

of these areas have not been able to cover this aspect of investment in a thorough manner. Data that do exist suggest that inventory accumulation may be a relatively significant part of total investment in the less developed areas. The limitations of transport and communications and other uncertainties associated with deliveries would contribute to such a pattern.

The inventory coefficient s_j, the ratio of total inventories held by sector j to annual output of the sector j, is calculated from two sources: the P.P.D. *Notes*, Table M, and the Central Statistical Organization's *Annual Survey of Industry, 1960*, except in Transport Equipment, Cement, Cotton and Other Textiles. The P.P.D. *Notes* are not comprehensive, so "typical" coefficients have to be used. Neither source covers all sectors, and in the remaining sectors the coefficients are simply guessed. These guesses are based on two estimates, one made by A. K. Sen[4] and the other, unpublished, by A. Chakravarti, but they are usually much

[4]A. K. Sen, "Working Capital in the Indian Economy: A Conceptual Framework and Some Estimates," in *Pricing and Fiscal Policies,* P. N. Rosenstein-Rodan (ed.), M.I.T. Press, Cambridge, Mass., 1964, pp. 125-146.

lower than either of these two sources suggest. Table 3.6 shows the aggregate inventory-output coefficients. From these aggregate coefficients an inventory-output coefficient matrix is constructed. The aggregate inventory-output ratio in each sector is distributed along a column in the proportions of the storable elements of the input column in the corresponding matrix, a. Before doing this, the coefficients of the Others and Margin sector are eliminated, on the grounds that the contribution of this sector is so miscellaneous that it would be difficult to know what would in fact be storable.

Tables 3.7 and 3.8 present the inventory-output coefficient matrices for the Third and Fourth Plan periods, respectively.

In carrying out calculations for alternative values of the parameters, several of the larger inventory coefficients are reduced in order to provide tests of sensitivity of the results to changes. This reduces the investment requirements for growth. In the alternative set, the aggregate inventory coefficients are changed for Agriculture, Food, Clothing, and Leather, and Chemicals. This alternative set of inventory coefficients is also shown in Table 3.6. A corresponding matrix, s, of inventory-output coefficients is created for the matrices in Tables 3.7 and 3.8, in the manner just described.

Table 3.7. Inventory-Output Coefficient Matrix s for Third Plan Period

	1 AG.PL.	2 M.M.	3 EQIPMT	4 CHEMIC	5 CMGLWD	6 FOODCL	7 ELECTR	8 TRANS	9 CONSTR	10 HOUS.	11 OTHMAR
AG.PL.	.318	.C00	.023	.C31	.101	.298	0.	0.	.C07	0.	.C07
M.M.	.001	.162	.258	.C19	.039	.002	.106	.012	.023	0.	.C00
EQIPMT	0.	.044	.046	.C54	.002	.002	0.	0.	.C03	0.	0.
CHEMIC	.041	.014	.046	.394	.062	.018	.023	.009	.C01	C.	.001
CMGLWD	.002	.014	.007	.C07	.019	.002	0.	0.	.C35	0.	0.
FOODCL	.031	.005	.003	.C23	.013	.040	0.	0.	0.	0.	.000
ELECTR	0.	0.	0. .	0.	0.	0.	0.	0.	0.	0.	0.
TRANS	0.	0.	0.	C.	0.	0.	0.	0.	0.	0.	0.
CONSTR	0.	0.	0.	0.	0.	0.	0.	0.	0.	0.	0.
HOUS.	0.	0.	0.	0.	0.	0.	0.	0.	0.	0.	0.
OTHMAR	0.	0.	0.	0.	0.	0.	0.	0.	0.	0.	0.
SUM	.393	.240	.384	.528	.237	.361	.129	.020	.068	0.	.008

Table 3.8. Inventory-Output Coefficient Matrix s for Fourth Plan Period

	1 AG.PL.	2 M.M.	3 EQIPMT	4 CHEMIC	5 CMGLWD	6 FOODCL	7 ELECTR	8 TRANS	9 CONSTR	10 HOUS.	11 OTHMAR
AG.PL.	.318	.000	.011	.076	.102	.302	0.	0.	.007	0.	.007
M.M.	.001	.190	.295	.042	.037	.003	.106	.003	.123	0.	.000
EQIPMT	0.	.015	.037	.023	.002	.002	0.	0.	.003	0.	0.
CHEMIC	.041	.019	.033	.315	.063	.017	.023	.016	.031	0.	.001
CMGLWD	.002	.010	.006	.018	.020	.002	0.	0.	.035	0.	0.
FOODCL	.031	.002	.002	.054	.012	.034	0.	0.	0.	0.	.000
ELECTR	0.	0.	0.	0.	0.	0.	0.	0.	0.	0.	0.
TRANS	0.	0.	0.	0.	0.	0.	0.	0.	0.	0.	0.
CONSTR	0.	0.	0.	0.	0.	0.	0.	0.	C.	0.	0.
HOUS.	0.	0.	0.	0.	0.	0.	0.	0.	0.	0.	0.
OTHMAR	0.	0.	0.	0.	0.	0.	0.	0.	0.	0.	0.
SUM	.393	.236	.384	.527	.236	.359	.129	.018	.068	0.	.008

3.3.3 Fixed-Capital Formation and Output

Much of what was said in qualification of the current flow matrices is applicable to the capital formation relationships as well; thus the remarks on aggregation problems and technological change will not be repeated.

As pointed out previously, there is no detailed accounting of capital stock by vintages in the model. The capital-output ratio for all past accumulations of fixed capital is assumed to be the same as that for new investment. The capital-output ratios estimated are intended to be marginal, rather than average, coefficients. Marginal coefficients are the most common type of data available, and interest centers on the new investments required during a plan period. These marginal coefficients are used to estimate the initial capital stocks from known output levels, rather than vice versa. As a result, the capital stock levels are scaled up or down from their "true" levels, depending on the unknown relationship between the average and the marginal coefficients. This, in turn, may throw off the capital accounting relationships somewhat, since depreciation is based on historical estimates of capital formation.

There is a substantial amount of information on capital-output ratios for the Indian economy that has not yet been fully utilized. For modern industry in particular, the data potentially available are quite comprehensive, and even for the traditional and agricultural sectors a good deal of partial and sample survey data exists. In the latter sectors, however, the relation of capital accumulation to capacity changes may be less reliable than in industry and certainly warrants much more investigation. The estimation procedure followed has been to establish aggregate capital-output ratios for each sector, then to determine the relative contribution of each of the capital-supplying sectors, and finally to distribute this over the entire gestation period. This was first done independently using a wide variety of sources of information. The estimation procedures were not sophisticated, and there have never been enough observations of the same quality to warrant the use of econometric methods based on the assumption of stochastic processes. In general, an attempt was made to rely almost entirely on Indian data to estimate the aggregate capital-output ratios.

In 1964 a matrix of capital coefficients was estimated in the Indian Statistical Institute by V. Prakash. These estimates also give the breakdown of capital coefficients in four types of capital, Urban Construction, Rural Construction, Transport Equipment, and Other Equipment. The estimates, based on numerous studies "released or undertaken by the various official and nonofficial agencies," are the most recently available authoritative estimates. The Prakash matrix is used as the basis of most of our computations. Since the coefficients are in producers prices, they are modified to include trade margins assumed to be 13 per cent of the equipment portion of capital in the sector. These aggregate capital-output coefficients and their composition are shown in Table 3.9. The eleven-sector coefficients are aggregated; the weights used are the capital stocks as implied by these coefficients and by the output levels in 1960-61 and 1965-66, in Tables 3.10 and 3.11, which also show the proportions matrices, p, implicit in these coefficients for the Third and Fourth Plan periods, respectively.

The set of capital coefficients just described will be referred to as the "reference" set. They appear to us to be reasonable but moderate, in the sense that they reflect a somewhat optimistic view of the requirements for increasing

Table 3.9. Aggregate Capital-Output Coefficients Matrix b

		Fixed-Capital Coefficients				
		Construction		Equipment		Others
						and
Sector	Total	Urban and Industrial	Rural	Electrical and Nonelectrical	Transport	Margin
1. Construction, urban and industrial	0.153	0.04	–	.10	–	.013
2. Construction, rural	–	–	–	–	–	–
3. Electrical Equipment	0.695	0.30	–	0.35	–	.045
4. Transport Equipment	0.752	0.30	–	0.40	–	.052
5. Nonelectrical Equipment	1.072	0.45	–	0.55	–	.072
6. Iron and Steel	2.252	0.93	–	1.17	–	.152
7. Iron Ore	1.993	0.75	–	1.10	–	.143
8. Cement	1.788	0.85	–	0.83	–	.108
9. Other Metals	2.825	1.30	–	1.35	–	.175
10. Other Minerals	2.673	1.17	–	1.33	–	.173
11. Plantations	1.586	0.40	0.15	0.90	–	.136
12. Leather and Leather Products	0.369	0.20	–	0.15	–	.019
13. Animal Husbandry and Fishery	1.591	0.80	0.50	0.20	–	.091
14. Food Industries	0.412	0.13	–	0.25	–	.032
15. Food grains	1.591	0.80	0.50	0.20	–	.091
16. Cotton and Other Textiles	0.964	0.25	–	0.72	–	.094
17. Jute Textiles	1.051	0.35	–	0.62	–	.081
18. Other Agriculture	1.591	0.80	0.50	0.20	–	.091
19. Chemical Fertilizers	1.565	1.00	–	0.50	–	.065
20. Glass, Wooden and Nonmetallic Mineral Products	0.689	0.35	–	0.30	–	.039
21. Forestry Products	1.591	0.80	0.50	0.20	–	.091
22. Motor Transport	1.356	*	–	–	1.20	.156
23. Petroleum Products†	0.475	0.26	–	0.19	–	.025
24. Crude Oil	7.137	3.95	–	2.82	–	.367
25. Rubber Products	0.539	0.20	–	0.30	–	.039
26. Synthetic Rubber	1.621	0.83	–	0.70	–	.091
27. Chemicals	0.892	0.35	–	0.48	–	.062
28. Railways	2.599	*	–	–	2.30	.299
29a. Thermal Electricity	6.133	2.80	–	2.95	–	.383
29b. Hydroelectricity	6.947	4.80	–	1.90	–	.247
30. Coal	2.117	1.10	–	0.90	–	.117
31. Housing	10.00	10.00	–	–	–	–
32. Others and Margin	0.157	.10	–	–	.502	.066

*Not required because of its exogenous nature.   †Including lubricating oils and naphtha.

Table 3.10. Aggregate Capital-Output Ratios b and Capital Proportions Matrix p for Third Plan Period

Sector / Capital Type	1 AG.PL.	2 M.M.	3 EQIPMT	4 CHEMIC	5 CMGLWD	6 FOODCL	7 ELECTR	8 TRANS	9 CONSTR	10 HOUS.	11 OTHMAR
1. AG.PL.	-	-	-	-	-	-	-	-	-	-	-
2. M.M.	-	-	-	-	-	-	-	-	-	-	-
3. EQIPMT	.138	.496	.516	.490	.471	.628	.404	.885	.654	0.	.319
4. CHEMIC	-	-	-	-	-	-	-	-	-	-	-
5. CMGLWD	-	-	-	-	-	-	-	-	-	-	-
6. FOODCL	-	-	-	-	-	-	-	-	-	-	-
7. ELECTR	-	-	-	-	-	-	-	-	-	-	-
8. TRANS	-	-	-	-	-	-	-	-	-	-	-
9. CONSTR	.844	.441	.418	.446	.468	.290	.543	0.	.261	1.0	.639
10. HOUS.	-	-	-	-	-	-	-	-	-	-	-
11. OTHMAR	.018	.064	.066	.064	.061	.082	.053	.115	.085	0.	.042
Sum	1.000	1.000	1.000	1.000	1.000	1.000	1.000	1.000	1.000	1.000	1.000
Capital-Output Ratio Reference Set	1.511	2.416	.905	.875	.894	.551	6.259	2.222	.153	10.000	.156
Lower Set	1.000	2.416	.905	.875	.894	.551	6.259	2.222	.153	7.5000	.156

Table 3.11. Aggregate Capital-Output Ratios b and Capital Proportions Matrix p for Fourth Plan Period

Sector Capital Type	1 AG.PL.	2 M.M.	3 EQIPMT	4 CHEMIC	5 CMGLWD	6 FOODCL	7 ELECTR	8 TRANS	9 CONSTR	10 HOUS.	11 OTHMAR
1. AG.PL.	-	-	-	-	-	-	-	-	-	-	-
2. M.M.	-	-	-	-	-	-	-	-	-	-	-
3. EQIPMT	.138	.503	.515	.471	.444	.629	.404	.885	.654	0.	.319
4. CHEMIC	-	-	-	-	-	-	-	-	-	-	-
5. CMGLWD	-	-	-	-	-	-	-	-	-	-	-
6. FOODCL	-	-	-	-	-	-	-	-	-	-	-
7. ELECTR	-	-	-	-	-	-	-	-	-	-	-
8. TRANS	-	-	-	-	-	-	-	-	-	-	-
9. CONSTR	.844	.432	.418	.468	.498	.289	.543	0.	.261	1.000	.639
10. HOUS.	-	-	-	-	-	-	-	-	-	-	-
11. OTHMAR	.018	.065	.067	.061	.058	.082	.053	.115	.085	0.	.042
Sum	1.000	1.000	1.000	1.000	1.000	1.000	1.000	1.000	1.000	1.000	1.000
Capital-Output Ratio Reference Set	1.510	2.477	.955	1.056	.862	.557	6.259	2.173	.153	10.0	.156
Lower Set	1.000	2.477	.955	1.056	.862	.557	6.259	2.173	.153	7.5	.158

output. In sensitivity tests the coefficient in Agriculture is reduced from 1.5 to 1.0 and the coefficient in Housing from 10.0 to 7.5. These alternative capital coefficients are also shown in Table 3.10 as the "lower" set.

The capital-output ratio in Transport for the Third and Fourth Plan periods is relatively low, since the Prakash assumption that no substantial additional construction would be necessary in these sectors during these periods was adopted. The capital coefficient in Housing, which is the highest, depends on the relative weights of Urban and Rural Construction in total output, which were not known to us. No information on changes in capital-formation relationships, which reflect changing technology and industrial composition, was available to us. The capital coefficients were therefore treated as constants but changed parametrically in some alternative solutions.

3.3.4 Lag Proportions Matrices

The next step in data preparation is the disaggregation of the capital formation by periods. The fact that there are gestation periods of varying lengths is a major source of the difficulty in coordinating the growth of different sectors in development programs. In addition, since delays in making capital effective have a particularly high cost in the less developed regions, the ability to analyze such delays is important.

Published empirical information about the gestation periods of capital projects is relatively scarce for developed as well as for less developed regions. There is a substantial body of informal comment which holds that gestation periods in the less developed countries are quite different from those prevailing in the developed areas. Although the existence of several studies of the time patterns of capital creation indicates the feasibility of such investigations, secondary sources are completely inadequate for this purpose, and no independent estimation is attempted.

We have adopted a simple pattern to represent the gestation process, which can easily be modified as more information becomes available. It is assumed that the Construction component of investment required to achieve an increment of capacity in period t has to be made in three equal installments over the three preceding periods, $t-1$, $t-2$, and $t-3$. For the Equipment component of investment, it is assumed that half of the total requirements has to be provided in each of the two periods preceding the period in which capacity is to become effective. With these assumptions, the matrices showing proportions of total requirements of each sector in periods $t-1$, $t-2$, and $t-3$ for capacity that will mature in period t are estimated for India for the 1960's and are shown in Tables 3.12 and 3.13 for the Third and Fourth Plans, respectively.

Again for sensitivity tests, the gestation lag structure is changed in a manner that facilitates the adjustments of the system. The alternative lag proportions matrices are based on our judgment of the potential for reducing the time lag in capital creation in some sectors. The investment lag in Construction and in Others and Margin is reduced to one year. In Mining and Metals and in Electricity, the

Table 3.12. Lag Proportions Matrices p′, p″, p‴ for Third Plan Period

p'

	1 AG.PL.	2 M.M.	3 EQIPMT	4 CHEMIC	5 CMGLWD	6 FCODCL	7 ELECTR	8 TRANS	9 CONSTR	10 HOUS.	11 OTHMAR
AG.PL.	0.	0.	0.	0.	0.	0.	0.	0.	0.	0.	0.
M.M.	0.	0.	0.	0.	0.	0.	0.	0.	0.	0.	0.
EQIPMT	.069	.248	.258	.245	.222	.314	.202	.442	.327	0.	.160
CHEMIC	0.	0.	0.	0.	0.	0.	0.	0.	0.	0.	0.
CMGLWD	0.	0.	0.	0.	0.	0.	0.	0.	0.	0.	0.
FOODCL	0.	0.	0.	0.	0.	0.	0.	0.	0.	0.	0.
ELECTR	0.	0.	0.	0.	0.	0.	0.	0.	0.	0.	0.
TRANS	0.	0.	0.	0.	0.	0.	0.	0.	0.	0.	0.
CONSTR	.282	.147	.139	.149	.166	.097	.181	0.	.087	.333	.213
HOUS.	0.	0.	0.	0.	0.	0.	0.	0.	0.	0.	0.
OTHMAR	.009	.032	.034	.032	.029	.041	.026	.057	.042	0.	.021
SUM	.359	.427	.431	.425	.417	.452	.409	.500	.456	.333	.393

p''

	AG.PL.	M.M.	EQIPMT	CHEMIC	CMGLWD	FCODCL	ELECTR	TRANS	CONSTR	HOUS.	OTHMAR
AG.PL.	0.	0.	0.	0.	0.	0.	0.	0.	0.	0.	0.
M.M.	0.	0.	0.	0.	0.	0.	0.	0.	0.	0.	0.
EQIPMT	.069	.248	.258	.245	.222	.314	.202	.442	.327	0.	.160
CHEMIC	0.	0.	0.	0.	0.	0.	0.	0.	0.	0.	0.
CMGLWD	0.	0.	0.	0.	0.	0.	0.	0.	0.	0.	0.
FOODCL	0.	0.	0.	0.	0.	0.	0.	0.	0.	0.	0.
ELECTR	0.	0.	0.	0.	0.	0.	0.	0.	0.	0.	0.
TRANS	0.	0.	0.	0.	0.	0.	0.	0.	0.	0.	0.
CONSTR	.282	.147	.139	.149	.166	.097	.181	0.	.087	.333	.213
HOUS.	0.	0.	0.	0.	0.	0.	0.	0.	0.	0.	0.
OTHMAR	.009	.032	.034	.032	.029	.041	.026	.057	.042	0.	.021
SUM	.359	.427	.431	.425	.417	.452	.409	.500	.456	.333	.393

p'''

	AG.PL.	M.M.	EQIPMT	CHEMIC	CMGLWD	FCODCL	ELECTR	TRANS	CONSTR	HOUS.	OTHMAR
AG.PL.	0.	0.	0.	0.	0.	0.	0.	0.	0.	0.	0.
M.M.	0.	0.	0.	0.	0.	0.	0.	0.	0.	0.	0.
EQIPMT	0.	0.	0.	0.	0.	0.	0.	0.	0.	0.	0.
CHEMIC	0.	0.	0.	0.	0.	0.	0.	0.	0.	0.	0.
CMGLWD	0.	0.	0.	0.	0.	0.	0.	0.	0.	0.	0.
FOODCL	0.	0.	0.	0.	0.	0.	0.	0.	0.	0.	0.
ELECTR	0.	0.	0.	0.	0.	0.	0.	0.	0.	0.	0.
TRANS	0.	0.	0.	0.	0.	0.	0.	0.	0.	0.	0.
CONSTR	.282	.147	.139	.149	.166	.097	.181	0.	.087	.333	.213
HOUS.	0.	0.	0.	0.	0.	0.	0.	0.	0.	0.	0.
OTHMAR	0.	0.	0.	0.	0.	0.	0.	0.	0.	0.	0.
SUM	.282	.147	.139	.149	.166	.097	.181	0.	.087	.333	.213

Table 3.13. Lag Proportions Matrices p′, p″, p‴ for Fourth Plan Period

p′

	1 AG.PL.	2 M.M.	3 EQIPMT	4 CHEMIC	5 CMGLWD	6 FOODCL	7 ELECTR	8 TRANS	9 CONSTR	10 HOUS.	11 OTHMAR
AG.PL.	0.	0.	0.	0.	0.	0.	0.	0.	0.	0.	0.
M.M.	0.	0.	0.	0.	0.	0.	0.	0.	0.	0.	0.
EQIPMT	.069	.251	.257	.235	.222	.315	.202	.442	.327	0.	.160
CHEMIC	0.	0.	0.	0.	0.	0.	0.	0.	0.	0.	0.
CMGLWD	0.	0.	0.	0.	0.	0.	0.	0.	0.	0.	0.
FOODCL	0.	0.	0.	0.	0.	0.	0.	0.	0.	0.	0.
ELECTR	0.	0.	0.	0.	0.	0.	0.	0.	0.	0.	0.
TRANS	0.	0.	0.	0.	0.	0.	0.	0.	0.	0.	0.
CONSTR	.281	.144	.139	.156	.166	.096	.181	0.	.087	.333	.213
HOUS.	0.	0.	0.	0.	0.	0.	0.	0.	0.	0.	0.
OTHMAR	.009	.033	.033	.031	.029	.041	.026	.057	.042	0.	.021
SUM	.359	.428	.430	.422	.417	.452	.409	.500	.456	.333	.393

p″

	AG.PL.	M.M.	EQIPMT	CHEMIC	CMGLWD	FOODCL	ELECTR	TRANS	CONSTR	HOUS.	OTHMAR
AG.PL.	0.	0.	0.	0.	0.	0.	0.	0.	0.	0.	0.
M.M.	0.	0.	0.	0.	0.	0.	0.	0.	0.	0.	0.
EQIPMT	.069	.251	.257	.235	.222	.315	.202	.442	.327	0.	.160
CHEMIC	0.	0.	0.	0.	0.	0.	0.	0.	0.	0.	0.
CMGLWD	0.	0.	0.	0.	0.	0.	0.	0.	0.	0.	0.
FOODCL	0.	0.	0.	0.	0.	0.	0.	0.	0.	0.	0.
ELECTR	0.	0.	0.	0.	0.	0.	0.	0.	0.	0.	0.
TRANS	0.	0.	0.	0.	0.	0.	0.	0.	0.	0.	0.
CONSTR	.281	.144	.139	.156	.166	.096	.181	0.	.087	.333	.213
HOUS.	0.	0.	0.	0.	0.	0.	0.	0.	0.	0.	0.
OTHMAR	.009	.033	.033	.031	.029	.041	.026	.057	.042	0.	.021
SUM	.359	.428	.430	.422	.417	.452	.409	.500	.456	.333	.393

p‴

	AG.PL.	M.M.	EQIPMT	CHEMIC	CMGLWD	FOODCL	ELECTR	TRANS	CONSTR	HOUS.	OTHMAR
AG.PL.	0.	0.	0.	0.	0.	0.	0.	0.	0.	0.	0.
M.M.	0.	0.	0.	0.	0.	0.	0.	0.	0.	0.	0.
EQIPMT	0.	0.	0.	0.	0.	0.	0.	0.	0.	0.	0.
CHEMIC	0.	0.	0.	0.	0.	0.	0.	0.	0.	0.	0.
CMGLWD	0.	0.	0.	0.	0.	0.	0.	0.	0.	0.	0.
FOODCL	0.	0.	0.	0.	0.	0.	0.	0.	0.	0.	0.
ELECTR	0.	0.	0.	0.	0.	0.	0.	0.	0.	0.	0.
TRANS	0.	0.	0.	0.	0.	0.	0.	0.	0.	0.	0.
CONSTR	.281	.144	.139	.156	.166	.096	.181	0.	.087	.333	.213
HOUS.	0.	0.	0.	0.	0.	0.	0.	0.	0.	0.	0.
OTHMAR	0.	0.	0.	0.	0.	0.	0.	0.	0.	0.	0.
SUM	.281	.144	.139	.156	.166	.096	.181	0.	.087	.333	.213

three-year gestation lags are kept. In all remaining sectors, the lag is reduced to two years. These matrices are shown in Table 3.14 as the "Alternative Lag Proportions Matrices."

3.3.5 Imports

The only readily available information on noncompetitive imports, as defined in Chapter 2, has been that presented in the Inter-Industry Group's transactions matrix. In a single column, it estimates that quantity of imports which, though classifiable in one of the grossly defined producing sectors, could be considered as noncompetitive. A separate row for all noncompetitive imports allocated them to each producing sector. Since this treatment blurred the desired distinction considerably, it was decided to adjust the matrix by absorbing the noncompetitive import row into the body of the transactions matrix as if they were competitive imports. The noncompetitive imports are treated as fixed fractions of the total output of the sectors in which they were assigned. The ratios of noncompetitive imports to output were calculated from the Inter-Industry Group's input-output matrix and used as noncompetitive import coefficients. Table 3.15 lists these coefficients by sector.

As noted previously, ceilings are set in the models on the use in each sector of the foreign exchange left over after the satisfaction of noncompetitive import needs. These ceilings are in the form of ratios of uncommitted foreign exchange. The ratios are based on the import information in the I.S.I. and Inter-Industry Group input-output tables, with some adjustments based on guesses as to the sectors in which government policy would be more or less restrictive in permitting import substitution for domestic production. These ratios are also shown in Table 3.15.

Table 3.14. Alternative Lag Proportions Matrices p', p'', p'''–Shortened Lags

p'

	1 AG.PL.	2 M.M.	3 EQIPMT	4 CHEMIC	5 CMGLWD	6 FOODCL	7 ELECTR	8 TRANS	9 CONSTR	10 HOUS.	11 OTHMAR
AG.PL.	0.	0.	0.	0.	0.	0.	0.	0.	0.	0.	0.
M.M.	0.	0.	0.	0.	0.	0.	0.	0.	0.	0.	0.
EQIPMT	.069	.251	.257	.235	.222	.315	.202	.442	.654	0.	.320
CHEMIC	0.	0.	0.	0.	0.	0.	0.	0.	0.	0.	0.
CMGLWC	0.	0.	0.	0.	0.	0.	0.	0.	0.	0.	0.
FCODCL	0.	0.	0.	0.	0.	0.	0.	0.	0.	0.	0.
ELECTR	0.	0.	0.	0.	0.	0.	0.	0.	0.	0.	0.
TRANS	0.	0.	0.	0.	0.	0.	0.	0.	0.	0.	0.
CONSTR	.422	.144	.209	.234	.249	.144	.181	0.	.262	.500	.639
HOUS.	0.	0.	0.	0.	0.	0.	0.	0.	0.	0.	0.
OTHMAR	.009	.033	.033	.031	.029	.041	.026	.057	.084	0.	.041
SUM	.500	.428	.500	.500	.500	.500	.409	.500	1.000	.500	1.000

p''

	AG.PL.	M.M.	EQIPMT	CHEMIC	CMGLWD	FOODCL	ELECTR	TRANS	CONSTR	HOUS.	OTHMAR
AG.PL.	0.	0.	0.	0.	0.	0.	0.	0.	0.	0.	0.
M.M.	0.	0.	0.	0.	0.	0.	0.	0.	0.	0.	0.
EQIPMT	.069	.251	.257	.235	.222	.315	.202	.442	0.	0.	0.
CHEMIC	0.	0.	0.	0.	0.	0.	0.	0.	0.	0.	0.
CMGLWC	0.	0.	0.	0.	0.	0.	0.	0.	0.	0.	0.
FOODCL	0.	0.	0.	0.	0.	0.	0.	0.	0.	0.	0.
ELECTR	0.	0.	0.	0.	0.	0.	0.	0.	0.	0.	0.
TRANS	0.	0.	0.	0.	0.	0.	0.	0.	0.	0.	0.
CONSTR	.422	.144	.209	.234	.249	.144	.181	0.	0.	.500	0.
HOUS.	0.	0.	0.	0.	0.	0.	0.	0.	0.	0.	0.
OTHMAR	.009	.033	.033	.C31	.029	.041	.026	.057	0.	0.	0.
SUM	.600	.428	.500	.500	.500	.500	.409	.500	0.	.500	0.

p'''

	AG.PL.	M.M.	EQIPMT	CHEMIC	CMGLWQ	FOODCL	ELECTR	TRANS	CONSTR	HOUS.	OTHMAR
AG.PL.	0.	0.	0.	0.	0.	0.	0.	0.	0.	0.	0.
M.M.	0.	0.	0.	0.	0.	0.	0.	0.	0.	0.	0.
EQIPMT	0.	0.	0.	0.	0.	0.	0.	0.	0.	0.	0.
CHEMIC	0.	0.	0.	0.	0.	0.	0.	0.	0.	0.	0.
CMGLWC	0.	0.	0.	0.	0.	0.	0.	0.	0.	0.	0.
FOODCL	0.	0.	0.	0.	0.	0.	0.	0.	0.	0.	0.
ELECTR	0.	0.	0.	0.	0.	0.	0.	0.	0.	0.	0.
TRANS	0.	0.	0.	0.	0.	0.	0.	0.	0.	0.	0.
CONSTR	0.	.144	0.	0.	0.	0.	.181	0.	0.	0.	0.
HOUS.	0.	0.	0.	0.	0.	0.	0.	0.	0.	0.	0.
OTHMAR	0.	0.	0.	0.	0.	0.	0.	0.	0.	0.	0.
SUM	0.	.144	0.	0.	0.	0.	.181	0.	0.	0.	0.

Table 3.15. Noncompetitive Import Coefficients m' and Ratios of Competitive Imports to Uncommitted Foreign Exchange m''

	SECTOR	m'	m''
1	AG.PL.	.301000	.016000
2	M.M.	.199000	.145000
3	EQIPMT	.348000	.235000
4	CHEMIC	.162000	.261000
5	CMGLWD	.020000	.004000
6	FOODCL	.027000	.000080
7	ELECTR	0.	0.
8	TRANS	0.	0.
9	CONSTR	0.	0.
10	HUUS.	0.	0.
11	OTHMAR	.020000	0.

Table 3.16. Decreasing Noncompetitive Import Coefficients m' for Fourth Plan Period

SECTOR	1966-67	1967-68	1968-69	1969-70	1970-71
1 AG.PL.	.0160	.0160	.0160	.0160	.0160
2 M.M.	.1150	.1450	.1300	.1000	.0850
3 EQIPMT	.2250	.2350	.2300	.2200	.2100
4 CHEMIC	.2000	.2610	.2300	.1700	.1300
5 CMGLWD	.0040	.0040	.0040	.0040	.0040
6 FOODCL	.0001	.0001	.0001	.0001	.0001
7 ELECTR	0.	0.	0.	0.	0.
8 TRANS	0.	0.	0.	0.	0.
9 CONSTR	0.	0.	0.	0.	0.
10 HOUS.	0.	0.	0.	0.	0.
11 OTHMAR	0.	0.	0.	0.	0.

The P.P.D. *Notes* place a strong emphasis on the import substitution aspects of their Fourth Plan targets. Sectoral projections of imports for 1965-66 and 1970-71 are also given. However, this information is not sufficient to generate the noncompetitive import coefficients that are presumed for 1970-71. In some solutions, in order to investigate the effects of import substitution, the noncompetitive import coefficients are reduced from year to year. The coefficients assumed for this purpose are shown in Table 3.16.

3.4 Demand Data

3.4.1 Depreciation

The operating lifetime of many types of capital is 20 to 25 years or more, which is substantially longer than the planning horizon of the short-term models. Given such life spans and the "one hoss shay" pattern of capital decay, depreciation is exogenous to these models, being determined by the investment that took place in the years previous to the start of the plan period. The problem of calculating depreciation is thus transformed into one of estimating investment during the early postwar years, for which relatively little statistical information exists.

An estimate of depreciating capital is made as follows:

1. We assume lifetimes of 25 and 33 years for equipment and construction, respectively.
2. We assume further that prior to 1951 a steady state prevailed in which all extensive magnitudes grew at the same rate of 1.5 per cent per year, the rate of growth of population. Then depreciating capital D(t) in period t is given by

$$D(t) = D(0)e^{0.015t}$$

3. The Central Statistical Organization of the Government of India has estimated that in 1948-49 total replacement was Rs. 611 crores in current prices. This has to be converted to 1959-60 prices. For this we have the C.S.O. estimates in current prices of gross investments in 1948-49 in the forms of construction and equipment at Rs. 755 crores and Rs. 403 crores, respectively. To find what proportion of total replacement is made up of construction and equipment replacement, we

use the ratio of gross investment in the form of construction in 1915-16 to gross investment in the form of equipment in 1928-29, both of which come up for replacement in 1948-49.

$$\frac{\text{Construction component of replacement in } 1948\text{-}49}{\text{Equipment component of replacement in } 1948\text{-}49} = \frac{755e^{-.015(33)}}{403e^{-.015(20)}} = \frac{1.5}{1.0}$$

Price indices for 1948-49 (1959-60 = 100) for construction and equipment are 86.8 and 72.1, respectively. Then the 1948-49 replacement in 1959-60 prices is

$$R(0) = (611) \frac{(1.5)(.866) + (.721)}{(2.5)} = \text{Rs. 755 crores.}$$

Assuming that all depreciated capital was replaced in 1948-49, we have

$$D(0) = R(0) = \text{Rs.755 crores.}$$

It follows that

$$D(t) = 755e^{0.015t}, \qquad \text{with } t = 0 \text{ in } 1948\text{-}49$$

The over-all levels of depreciation estimated with this formula have checked reasonably well with aggregate depreciation estimated by the Central Statistical Organization for various years[5] and with other order of magnitude calculations, in which we assumed steady states with different life spans and savings rates.

Replacement requirements by sectors have been estimated by V. Prakash for the decade of 1961-71.[6] However, replacements in a number of sectors, including Railways, Roads, and Housing, are not given by Prakash and have been separately estimated by us. This sectoral distribution of depreciated capital is assumed unchanged from year to year for the Third and the Fourth Plan periods. The depreciated capital is shown in Table 3.17. The corresponding matrix of proportions r is given in Table 3.18. Table 3.19 shows the matrices r', r'', and r''', which are obtained from lag requirements similar to those of p', p'', and p'''.

3.4.2 Exports

For the Third Plan period, exports are projected assuming constant sectoral composition from the 1960-61 levels using a single annual growth rate. These projections are given in Table 3.20.

Estimates of exports are given in the P.P.D. *Notes.* Assuming a constant growth rate and the same composition of exports as that in the year 1970-71, the yearly vectors of exports are obtained for 1965-71. These are given in Table 3.21.

3.4.3 Government Consumption

The government sector in our models is assumed to consist entirely of "public consumption," so that resources delivered for this purpose neither contribute to productive capacity nor act as intermediate inputs to producing sectors.

---

[5] Estimates of Gross Capital Formation in India from 1948-49 to 1960-61, New Delhi, 1961.

[6] A. S. Manne, "A Consistency Model of India's Fourth Plan," Report No. 1, *Studies in the Structure of the Indian Economy,* M.I.T. Center for International Studies, July 28, 1964.

Table 3.17. Depreciated Capital D for Third and Fourth Plan Periods
(Rs. crores, 1959-60 prices)

	SECTOR	1961-62	1962-63	1963-64	1964-65	1965-66
1	AG.PL.	143.6563	145.8519	148.0475	150.2431	152.4388
2	M.M.	65.8512	66.8577	67.8642	68.87C6	69.8771
3	EQIPMT	14.6194	14.8428	15.0662	15.2897	15.5131
4	CHEMIC	47.9160	48.6483	49.3806	50.113C	50.8453
5	CMGLWD	13.0896	13.2897	13.4898	13.6898	13.8899
6	FOODCL	30.2738	30.7365	31.1992	31.6619	32.1246
7	ELECTR	40.5330	41.1525	41.7720	42.3915	43.0110
8	TRANS	84.5926	85.8855	87.1784	88.4713	89.7642
9	CONSTR	1.2641	1.2834	1.3027	1.3220	1.3414
10	HOUS.	186.8274	189.6828	192.5382	195.3937	198.2491
11	OTHMAR	134.1757	136.2264	138.2771	140.3278	142.3786
12	SUM	916.0000	930.0000	944.0000	958.0000	972.0000

	SECTOR	1966-67	1967-68	1968-69	1969-70	1970-71	1971-72	1972-73
1	AG.PL.	154.7912	157.1437	159.4961	161.8486	164.3578	166.8671	169.3764
2	M.M.	70.9554	72.0338	73.1121	74.1905	75.3407	76.4910	77.6412
3	EQIPMT	15.7525	15.9919	16.2313	16.4707	16.7261	16.9814	17.2368
4	CHEMIC	51.6300	52.4146	53.1993	53.9839	54.8209	55.6578	56.4948
5	CMGLWD	14.1042	14.3186	14.5329	14.7473	14.9759	15.2046	15.4332
6	FOODCL	32.6203	33.1161	33.6118	34.1076	34.6364	35.1652	35.6940
7	ELECTR	43.6747	44.3385	45.0022	45.6660	46.3740	47.0820	47.7900
8	TRANS	91.1494	92.5347	93.9199	95.3052	96.7828	98.2604	99.7380
9	CONSTR	1.3621	1.3828	1.4035	1.4242	1.4462	1.4683	1.4904
10	HOUS.	201.3085	204.3679	207.4273	210.4867	213.7501	217.0134	220.2768
11	OTHMAR	144.5758	146.7730	148.9702	151.1674	153.5110	155.8547	158.1984
12	SUM	987.0000	1002.0000	1017.0000	1032.0000	1048.0000	1064.0000	1080.0000

Table 3.18. Depreciation Composition Matrix r for Third and Fourth Plan Periods

	1 AG.PL.	2 M.M.	3 EQIPMT	4 CHEMIC	5 CMGLWD	6 FOODCL
AG.PL.	0.	0.	0.	0.	0.	0.
M.M.	0.	0.	0.	0.	0.	0.
EQIPMT	.265	.538	.568	.519	.549	.679
CHEMIC	0.	0.	0.	0.	0.	0.
CMGLWD	0.	0.	0.	0.	0.	0.
FOODCL	0.	0.	0.	0.	0.	0.
ELECTR	0.	0.	0.	0.	0.	0.
TRANS	0.	0.	0.	0.	0.	0.
CONSTR	.700	.391	.357	.413	.379	.231
HOUS.	0.	0.	0.	0.	0.	0.
OTHMAR	.035	.071	.075	.068	.072	.090
SUM	1.000	1.000	1.000	1.000	1.000	1.000

	7 ELECTR	8 TRANS	9 CONSTR	10 HOUS.	11 OTHMAR
	0.	0.	0.	0.	0.
	0.	0.	0.	0.	0.
	.311	.885	.812	0.	.308
	0.	0.	0.	0.	0.
	0.	0.	0.	0.	0.
	0.	0.	0.	0.	0.
	0.	0.	0.	0.	0.
	0.	0.	0.	0.	0.
	.648	0.	.080	1.000	.652
	0.	0.	0.	0.	0.
	.041	.115	.109	0.	.041
	1.000	1.000	1.000	1.000	1.000

Table 3.19. Lag Proportions Matrices for Restoration r′, r″, r‴

r′	1 AG.PL.	2 M.M.	3 EQIPMT	4 CHEMIC	5 CMGLWD	6 FOODCL	7 ELECTR	8 TRANS	9 CONSTR	10 HOUS.	11 OTHMAR
AG.PL.	0.	0.	0.	0.	0.	0.	0.	0.	0.	0.	0.
M.M.	0.	0.	0.	0.	0.	0.	0.	0.	0.	0.	0.
EQIPMT	.133	.269	.284	.259	.275	.339	.156	.442	.406	0.	.154
CHEMIC	0.	0.	0.	0.	0.	0.	0.	0.	0.	0.	0.
CMGLWD	0.	0.	0.	0.	0.	0.	0.	0.	0.	0.	0.
FOODCL	0.	0.	0.	0.	0.	0.	0.	0.	0.	0.	0.
ELECTR	0.	0.	0.	0.	0.	0.	0.	0.	0.	0.	0.
TRANS	0.	0.	0.	0.	0.	0.	0.	0.	0.	0.	0.
CONSTR	.233	.130	.119	.138	.126	.077	.216	0.	.027	.333	.217
HOUS.	0.	0.	0.	0.	0.	0.	0.	0.	0.	0.	0.
OTHMAR	.017	.035	.038	.034	.036	.045	.021	.057	.054	0.	.023
SUM	.383	.435	.441	.431	.437	.461	.392	.500	.487	.333	.391

r″	1 AG.PL.	2 M.M.	3 EQIPMT	4 CHEMIC	5 CMGLWD	6 FOODCL	7 ELECTR	8 TRANS	9 CONSTR	10 HOUS.	11 OTHMAR
AG.PL.	0.	0.	0.	0.	0.	0.	0.	0.	0.	0.	0.
M.M.	0.	0.	0.	0.	0.	0.	0.	0.	0.	0.	0.
EQIPMT	.133	.269	.284	.259	.275	.339	.156	.442	.406	0.	.154
CHEMIC	0.	0.	0.	0.	0.	0.	0.	0.	0.	0.	0.
CMGLWD	0.	0.	0.	0.	0.	0.	0.	0.	0.	0.	0.
FOODCL	0.	0.	0.	0.	0.	0.	0.	0.	0.	0.	0.
ELECTR	0.	0.	0.	0.	0.	0.	0.	0.	0.	0.	0.
TRANS	0.	0.	0.	0.	0.	0.	0.	0.	0.	0.	0.
CONSTR	.233	.130	.119	.138	.126	.077	.216	0.	.027	.333	.217
HOUS.	0.	0.	0.	0.	0.	0.	0.	0.	0.	0.	0.
OTHMAR	.017	.035	.038	.034	.036	.045	.021	.057	.054	0.	.023
SUM	.383	.435	.441	.431	.437	.461	.392	.500	.487	.333	.391

r‴	1 AG.PL.	2 M.M.	3 EQIPMT	4 CHEMIC	5 CMGLWD	6 FOODCL	7 ELECTR	8 TRANS	9 CONSTR	10 HOUS.	11 OTHMAR
AG.PL.	0.	0.	0.	0.	0.	0.	0.	0.	0.	0.	0.
M.M.	0.	0.	0.	0.	0.	0.	0.	0.	0.	0.	0.
EQIPMT	0.	0.	0.	0.	0.	0.	0.	0.	0.	0.	0.
CHEMIC	0.	0.	0.	0.	0.	0.	0.	0.	0.	0.	0.
CMGLWD	0.	0.	0.	0.	0.	0.	0.	0.	0.	0.	0.
FOODCL	0.	0.	0.	0.	0.	0.	0.	0.	0.	0.	0.
ELECTR	0.	0.	0.	0.	0.	0.	0.	0.	0.	0.	0.
TRANS	0.	0.	0.	0.	0.	0.	0.	0.	0.	0.	0.
CONSTR	.233	.130	.119	.138	.126	.077	.216	0.	.027	.333	.217
HOUS.	0.	0.	0.	0.	0.	0.	0.	0.	0.	0.	0.
OTHMAR	0.	0.	0.	0.	0.	0.	0.	0.	0.	0.	0.
SUM	.233	.130	.119	.138	.126	.077	.216	0.	.027	.333	.217

Table 3.20. Export Projections E for Third Plan Period (Rs. crores, 1959-60 prices)

SECTOR	1961-62	1962-63	1963-64	1964-65	1965-66
1 AG.PL.	198.188	206.370	214.552	223.037	231.826
2 M.M.	40.090	41.745	43.400	45.117	46.894
3 EQIPMT	4.336	4.515	4.694	4.880	5.072
4 CHEMIC	15.088	15.711	16.334	16.980	17.649
5 CMGLWD	2.793	2.908	3.023	3.143	3.267
6 FOODCL	215.656	224.560	233.463	242.696	252.259
7 ELECTR	0.	0.	0.	0.	0.
8 TRANS	0.	0.	0.	C.	0.
9 CONSTR	0.	0.	0.	0.	0.
10 HOUS.	0.	0.	0.	0.	0.
11 OTHMAR	177.836	185.178	192.519	200.133	208.019
12 SUM	654.000	681.000	708.000	736.000	765.000

Table 3.21. Export Projections E for Fourth Plan Period (Rs. crores, 1959-60 prices)

SECTOR	1966-67	1967-68	1968-69	1969-70	1970-71
1 AG.PL.	195.922	210.328	228.026	249.430	276.389
2 M.M.	159.650	171.389	185.812	203.252	225.221
3 EQIPMT	62.356	66.941	72.574	79.386	87.966
4 CHEMIC	48.457	52.020	56.397	61.691	68.359
5 CMGLWD	6.759	7.256	7.867	8.605	9.535
6 FOODCL	355.953	382.126	414.281	453.167	502.148
7 ELECTR	0.	0.	0.	0.	0.
8 TRANS	0.	0.	0.	0.	0.
9 CONSTR	0.	0.	0.	0.	0.
10 HOUS.	0.	0.	0.	0.	0.
11 OTHMAR	122.903	131.940	143.043	156.469	173.381
12 SUM	952.000	1022.000	1108.000	1212.000	1343.000

The value added directly by government operations is external to the models and projected as a constant fraction of government consumption.

For the Third Plan period, government expenditures are extrapolated using an assumed growth rate of 4 per cent from the sectoral levels of government demand presented in the I.S.I. table. This sectoral composition is also applied to the projections of aggregate government expenditure made in the P.P.D. *Notes* in order to obtain estimates for the Fourth Plan period. These estimates are shown in Tables 3.22 and 3.23.

3.4.4 Total Consumption

The models require specification of the proportions in which the total consumer budget is allocated among the outputs of the producing sectors. The specifications of the initial and subsequent consumption proportions are based on the I.S.I. table for 1960-61. These proportions are shown in Table 3.24.

3.4.5 Net Foreign Capital Inflow

For most of the solutions, net annual foreign capital inflows are set at Rs. 500 crores, approximately the amounts projected in the Third Plan. The consequences of changes in availability are analyzed in alternative solutions. As we have already noted, the allotment of foreign aid on an annual basis, as has been the practice, will lead to different results from those if a total amount to be available over the entire Plan is specified.

Table 3.22. Government Consumption G for Third Plan Period (Rs. crores, 1959-60 prices)

SECTOR	1961-62	1962-63	1963-64	1964-65	1965-66
1 AG.PL.	0.	0.	0.	C.	0.
2 M.M.	0.	0.	0.	C.	0.
3 EQIPMT	97.596	101.2C4	104.993	108.601	112.209
4 CHEMIC	28.402	29.452	30.555	31.605	32.655
5 CMGLWD	0.	0.	0.	C.	0.
6 FCCDCL	109.120	113.154	117.389	121.423	125.457
7 ELECTR	4.923	5.105	5.296	5.478	5.660
8 TRANS	0.	0.	0.	0.	0.
9 CCNSTR	108.2^0	112.200	116.400	12C.4C0	124.400
10 HOUS.	0.	0.	0.	0.	0.
11 OTHMAR	192.758	199.884	207.367	214.493	221.619
12 SUM	541.000	561.0C0	582.0CC	602.C00	622.000

Table 3.23. Government consumption G for Fourth Plan Period (Rs. crores, 1959-60 prices)

SECTOR	1966-67	1967-68	1968-69	1969-70	1970-71
1 AG.PL.	0.	0.	0.	0.	0.
2 M.M.	0.	0.	0.	0.	0.
3 EQIPMT	199.883	212.331	226.222	241.195	257.611
4 CHEMIC	58.170	61.792	65.835	70.192	74.970
5 CMGLWD	0.	0.	0.	0.	0.
6 FOODCL	223.484	237.401	252.932	269.673	288.028
7 ELECTR	10.083	10.711	11.411	12.167	12.995
8 TRANS	0.	0.	0.	0.	0.
9 CONSTR	221.600	235.400	250.800	267.400	285.600
10 HOUS.	0.	0.	0.	0.	0.
11 OTHMAR	394.780	419.365	446.800	476.373	508.796
12 SUM	1108.000	1177.000	1254.000	1337.000	1428.000

Table 3.24. Consumption Proportions c

1	AG.PL.	.38790
2	M.M.	.00047
3	EQIPMT	.02416
4	CHEMIC	.03005
5	CMGLWD	.03589
6	FOODCL	.14318
7	ELECTR	.00103
8	TRANS	.01752
9	CONSTR	0.
1	HOUS.	.04617
11	OTHMAR	.34363

3.4.6 Initial and Terminal Capital Stocks

The initial capital stocks are the results of events in the pre-Plan period. Similarly, the amounts of uncompleted capital, construction of which was started prior to the Plan period with a view to completion during the Plan, are exogenous. These endowments of completed and uncompleted capital are the means by which events in the Plan period are related to events in the preceding Plan period. In any actual planning procedure, these initial conditions will be estimates based on whatever empirical information is available prior to the beginning of the new Plan period. In applying the models, we attempt to simulate the planning process by placing ourselves in the position of the planners and therefore rely only on data for the pre-Plan period in setting initial conditions. However, since we do not have detailed empirical information with which to estimate the initial capacities and capital goods in process at the outset of the Third and Fourth Plans, a somewhat arbitrary procedure is adopted to overcome this obstacle. The initial conditions are projected using the output levels in the pre-Plan year X(0) and the sectoral growth rates as shown in Eqs. 9.0, 9.11, and 9.12 in Chapter 2, Table 2.2. As explained there, these equations embody the assumption that the sectoral growth rates projected for the *succeeding* Plan period determined the investments made in the three pre-Plan years. With respect to capital-in-process, it is thus assumed that enough is created in the pre-Plan years to maintain the sectoral growth rates projected for the succeeding Plan period.

On the other hand, it is assumed that output levels in the year just prior to the Plan, from which initial capital stocks were projected, are based on full use of existing capacity. The adjustment for less than full use of capacity in order to determine initial effective capital endowment could be a significant one, since even small errors here may correspond to a substantial portion of the annual amounts of investment, and there has been repeated citation of the existence of unused capacity in the Indian economy. However, this adjustment could not be made because of the inadequacy of data on idle capacity. The well-known problems of defining capacity occur in an aggravated form in sectors such as Traditional Agriculture. Changes in effective capacity may also occur due to improvements in operating efficiency as personnel become more skilled. Where new projects are a substantial fraction of the total capital as in the Indian steel industry, this can be quantitatively quite important. At this point in model

**Table 3.25. Third Plan Targets and Initial Output Levels on a Thirty-Two-Sector Basis
(Rs. crores, 1959-60 prices)**

Sector	X(0) 1960-61	X(S) 1965-66
1. Construction, urban and industrial	1201.0	1,980.0
2. Construction, rural	416.0	436.0
3. Electrical Equipment	126.0	362.0
4. Transport Equipment	201.0	417.0
5. Nonelectrical Equipment	343.5	888.0
6. Iron and Steel	269.0	909.0
7. Iron Ore	7.8	22.0
8. Cement	52.6	88.0
9. Other Metals	32.0	80.0
10. Other Minerals	45.4	77.0
11. Plantations	196.0	250.0
12. Leather and Leather Products	189.0	220.0
13. Animal Husbandry and Fishery	1130.0	1,323.0
14. Food Industries	1323.0	1,733.0
15. Food Grains	3974.3	4.846.0
16. Cotton and Other Textiles	800.0	1,093.0
17. Jute Textiles	130.0	165.0
18. Other Agriculture	2097.0	2571.0
19. Chemical Fertilizers	20.7	166.0
20. Glass, Wooden, and Nonmetallic mineral products	398.0	620.0
21. Forestry Products	180.0	262.0
22. Motor Transport	325.0	580.0
23. Petroleum Products	237.1	659.0
24. Crude Oil	3.2	46.0
25. Rubber Products	67.5	127.0
26. Synthetic Rubber	–	17.0
27. Chemicals	284.0	742.0
28. Railways	454.0	640.0
29. Electricity	103.4	286.0
30. Coal	109.0	206.0
31. Housing	579.8	712.0 *
32. Others and Margin	5854.6	8694.0†

*Constant per cent of projected national income.

†Constant per cent of the sum of domestic output in all sectors.

development, it would be most convenient to introduce this as an exogenous effect, but due to lack of specific information no adjustment of this sort has been attempted.

For the Third Plan period the output levels for the pre-Plan year are taken from the modified input-output table for 1960-61, Table 3.3. The projected growth rates are those implied by the Third Plan targets. The Third Plan targets for the thirty-sector classification of the I.S.I. input-output Table 3.2 were taken from estimates by M. R. Saluja.[7] The targets for Housing and Others and Margin were projected separately. The targets for all thirty-two sectors are shown in Table 3.25. Table 3.26 lists the output levels X(0) and growth rates α_0 and α_5 which are used in the model solutions for the Third Plan period.

[7]M. R. Saluja, "Methods and Sources for Output Levels, 1960-61 and 1965-66," Report No. 5, *Studies in the Structure of the Indian Economy,* Indian Statistical Institute, Planning Unit, Aug. 3, 1964.

Table 3.26. Third Plan Targets, Initial Output Levels, and Projected Growth Rates on an Eleven-Sector Basis (Rs. crores, 1959-60 prices)

	Output,1960-61 X(0)	Initial Growth Rates α_0	Third Plan Targets		96% Level Third Plan Targets	
			Output,1965-66 X(5)	Postterminal Growth Rates, α_5	Output,1965-66 X(5)	Postterminal Growth Rates, α_5
1 AG.PL.	7577.0000	.0452	9452.0000	.045214	9070.9199	.036647
2 M.M.	462.0000	.2287	1794.0000	.228736	1244.2399	.219137
3 EQIPMT	670.5000	.1998	1667.0000	.199796	1600.3159	.190040
4 CHEMIC	612.5000	.2346	1757.0000	.234619	1686.7199	.224581
5 CMGLWD	450.6000	.0945	708.0000	.094582	679.6799	.085682
6 FOODCL	2442.0000	.0563	3211.0000	.056280	3082.5599	.047691
7 ELECTR	103.0000	.2266	286.0000	.226608	274.5599	.216634
8 TRANS	779.0000	.0938	1220.0000	.093867	1171.1999	.084972
9 CONSTR	1617.0000	.0836	2416.0000	.083621	2319.3599	.074810
10 HOUS.	579.8000	.0419	712.0000	.041934	683.5199	.033462
11 OTHMAR	5854.6000	.0823	8694.0000	.082292	8346.1599	.073490

The pre-Plan and target output levels for the Fourth Plan period are estimated from the P.P.D. *Notes*. There, sectoral output levels are furnished only for the organized part of each sector. Therefore, in order to provide comprehensive sectoral data, it has been necessary to estimate the output of the unorganized portion of the sectors. It will be seen that the character of the Fourth Plan Target Model solutions is to some extent dependent on the manner in which this is done; two alternatives are provided. In both cases it is assumed, for lack of any other basis on which to proceed, that in each industry the ratios of the output of the organized and unorganized portions of each sector were unchanged since 1960-61, the last year for which comprehensive data was available.

The P.P.D. *Notes* provide sectoral output levels for 1960-61 for the organized part of each sector. From these and the output levels for 1960-61 of Table 3.3, coverage adjustment ratios are obtained which are then applied to the P.P.D. *Notes* sectoral output levels of 1965-66 and 1970-71. This implies that output in both parts of each sector has grown at the same rate. This is a patently unsatisfactory method, but no alternative procedure available to us seemed an improvement. Moreover, it provides some justification for continuing to use the same capital-output ratios and other technical coefficients. The computations to obtain a comprehensive coverage are first carried out on a thirty-two-sector basis, and the results are then aggregated to the eleven sectors in which most of the solutions are calculated. It has been brought to our attention that this disaggregation may give a disporportionately large influence to the unorganized part of the fastest-growing organized sectors. When the adjustment for coverage is carried out in the same manner on an eleven-sector basis, this effect is reduced, and, as a result, the pre-Plan year output levels are also reduced.

Terminal year output levels for the Fourth Plan Target Model calculations are also estimated from the P.P.D. *Notes* 1970-71 output levels with the adjustments for coverage made as described above. Once again adjustments are made on a thirty-two-sector basis as well as on an eleven-sector basis, and two sets of output levels are obtained. With these pre-Plan and final year output levels for each sector, growth rates are calculated which are then used to project the capital stocks and the capital-in-process at the beginning of the Fourth Plan period on the

Table 3.27. Fourth Plan Targets, Initial Output Levels, and Projected Growth Rates, Adjusted on a Thirty-Two-Sector Basis and Aggregated to Eleven Sectors (Rs. crores, 1959-60 prices)

32 SECTORS			11 SECTORS				
Sector	1965-66 X(0)	1970-71 X(5)	Sector	Output 1965-66 X(0)	Initial Growth Rates α_0	Output Targets 1970-71 X(5)	Postterminal Growth Rates α_5
1. Construction, urban and industrial	2894	5546	1 AG.PL.	8628.0000	.0600	11533.0000	.0600
2. Construction, rural			2 M.M.	1166.5999	.1700	2554.1999	.1700
3. Electrical Equipment	367	959	3 EQIPMT	2275.0000	.2040	5756.0000	.2040
4. Transport Equipment	400	778	4 CHEMIC	1614.2999	.1720	3567.2999	.1720
5. Nonelectrical Equipment	1508	4019	5 CMGLWD	832.8999	.1480	1600.0000	.1480
6. Iron and Steel	804	1861	6 FOODCL	2898.0000	.1090	4235.5999	.1090
7. Iron Ore	19.7	44.2	7 ELECTR	249.0000	.1500	500.0000	.1500
8. Cement	78.9	151	8 TRANS	1255.0000	.1230	2240.0000	.1230
9. Other Metals	85.8	224	9 CONSTR	2894.0000	.1390	5546.0000	.1390
10. Other Minerals	73.1	135	10 HOUS.	700.0000	.0720	988.0000	.0720
11. Plantations	251	282	11 OTHMAR	8338.0000	.1190	14640.0000	.1190
12. Leather and Leather Products	220	379					
13. Animal Husbandry and Fishery	1288	1865					
14. Food Industries	1521	2104					
15. Food Grains	4411	6001					
16. Cotton and Other Textiles	992	2168					
17. Jute Textiles	165	200					
18. Other Agriculture	2453	3104					
19. Chemical Fertilizers	64.6	338					
20. Glass, Wooden, and Non-metallic Mineral Products	724	1449					
21. Forestry Products	225	281					
22. Motor Transport	592	1164					
23. Petroleum Products	552	1266					
24. Crude Oil	42.7	85.3					
25. Rubber Products	155	292					
26. Synthetic Rubber	9	30					
27. Chemicals	761	1556					
28. Railways	663	1076					
29. Electricity, total	249	500					
30. Coal	184	290					
31. Housing	700	988					
32. Others and Margin	8338	14640					

same assumptions used previously. Table 3.27 shows the two sets of initial and terminal outputs and the intra-Plan growth rates with the coverage adjustment made at the level of thirty-two sectors. Table 3.28 presents the same data with the adjustment on the eleven-sector basis.

To complete the specification of postterminal conditions for the Target Models, the sectoral growth rates must be determined for the three post-Plan periods. Lacking information on this subject for the Third Plan period we simply projected the previously derived intra-Plan growth rates. On the other hand, the P.P.D. *Notes* specify growth rates for the Fifth Plan period, which are lower in all sectors than the projected Fourth Plan growth rates. These are shown in Table 3.29. Again solutions are calculated for two versions, one with the intra-Fourth Plan growth rates projected for the postterminal period and the other with the Fifth Plan growth rates of the P.P.D. *Notes*. The latter not only imply a sharp discontinuity in growth rates at the end of the Plan, but also a lower over-all growth rate for the Fifth Plan as compared to the Fourth Plan. Consequently, for most runs we have used the Fourth Plan growth rates.

Table 3.28. Fourth Plan Targets, Initial Output Levels, and Projected Growth Rates, Aggregated to Eleven Sectors and Then Adjusted (Rs. crores, 1959-60 prices)

	Output 1965-66 $X(0)$	Initial Growth Rates α_0	Output Targets 1970-71 $X(5)$	Postterminal Growth Rates α_5
1 AG.PL.	8628.C000	.0600	11533.0000	.0600
2 M.M.	1104.6000	.1700	2384.2999	.1700
3 EQIPMT	1809.0000	.1900	4242.1999	.1900
4 CHEMIC	1519.6000	.1600	3229.5000	.1600
5 CMGLWD	756.C000	.1400	1485.0000	.1400
6 FOODCL	2947.0000	.0800	4350.0000	.0800
7 ELECTR	226.8000	.1400	431.6999	.1400
8 TRANS	1252.0000	.1200	2239.0000	.1200
9 CONSTR	2894.0000	.1400	5546.00C0	.1400
10 HOUS.	700.0000	.0700	965.0000	.0700
11 OTHMAR	8354.0000	.1100	13942.0000	.1100

Table 3.29. Alternative Postterminal Fourth Plan Growth Rates

SECTOR	Postterminal Growth Rates α_5
1 AG.PL.	.C490
2 M.M.	.1050
3 EQ1PMT	.C910
4 CHEMIC	.1140
5 CMGLWD	.0830
6 FOODCL	.0750
7 ELECTR	.1180
8 TRANS	.C96C
9 CONSTR	.0810
10 HOUS.	.C600
11 OTHMAR	.1100

3.5 Review of Data Sources

The data presented have been assembled and adjusted primarily for the methodological purpose of developing a set of techniques to assist in making economic policy. However, we shall attempt to draw some practical insights from the model solutions and expect that others will evaluate them in the same way, since we claim that the data are "realistic" in the sense that they are within the realm of observed experience for some country, if not always for India itself.

The data used might tentatively be grouped into three categories: (1) technical parameters and quantities, (2) behavioral parameters, and (3) policy parameters and quantities. The intermediate flow, capital-output, and inventory coefficients fall into the first category, which also includes estimates of initial productive capacities. Consumption proportions are examples of the second category, while policy quantities and parameters include plan targets and postterminal consumption growth rates, net foreign capital inflows and, to some extent, import coefficients. Import coefficients are to some extent technically determined, but not uniquely so, as they respond to market forces and direct government controls. Moreover, what is true of import coefficients is, in fact, true of nearly all the "technical" data. The so-called technical input-output coefficients are not determined by technical factors alone, but by market influences and government policies working outside the market, e.g., those policies which determine the size of new plants in a particular sector by means of investment licensing procedures. While the range of potential variation of some technical coefficients, as in electricity generation, may in fact be narrow, in other sectors, such as Transport, or Food, Clothing, and Leather, the potential variation can be substantial. Yet even where variations are possible, important changes may not be easily achieved but may come only with considerable cost and effort, which draw attention and emphasis from other activities.

These considerations, as well as the more obvious limitations of our sources, contribute to the uncertainty as to whether we have been able to establish the "true values" of the data. Some of the uncertainty is associated with our essential ignorance of the future; some results from difficulties in judging the will, determination, and ability of policy-makers; and some is due to ignorance of current or past values of parameters, which are either used directly or which form the basis for prediction. Thus, while closer contact with data sources and improved data gathering, collection, and processing would improve the quality of the information, it could not succeed in dispelling all of the uncertainties.

One of the features of the models is that they require explicit attention to many empirical issues not raised by other planning methods, and in this sense, their demands for data are greater than those of less detailed planning procedures. We regard this as a virtue rather than a weakness, since in India there are actually, or potentially, reasonably satisfactory means of satisfying most of the data requirements. Furthermore, it is misleading to think that less sophisticated techniques require fewer data, when in fact, they only conceal or assume away the requirements. For example, aggregate capital-output ratios are only weighted averages of sectoral ratios and finally of plant ratios. Planning procedures making use of the aggregate and not the more detailed ratios do this only by sacrificing sectoral detail and insights.

Because of our enlarged data requirements, we were not able to rely on a single Indian source in developing the necessary information, nor even, in most cases, to use a set of information from a single source without augmenting or modifying it. A brief review will emphasize this aspect of the data preparation and assist in a summary judgment as to the data quality.

The a, b, and p matrices were, for the most part, based on recent Indian estimates. The a matrix was modified to isolate a Housing sector and then aggregated. The b and p matrices were augmented to provide information for these additional sectors and Agriculture, using information about India and from other countries. Thus these coefficients can only be considered as representative of a current range of values. In Agriculture, for example, while a capital-output ratio of 1.5 was used in most trials, the currently effective ratio may range from a value not much less than 1.0 to somewhat over 2.0.

The aggregate values of the s coefficients were first estimated from Indian sources for the most part. The Indian estimates were reduced drastically, however, to make them more comparable with data for other countries. Again they represent a range and are likely to be at the low end of the range with some possible exceptions where alternatives are investigated explicitly. The distribution of the aggregate s coefficients was based on the input-output table. This procedure is plausible but not founded on empirical study.

Likewise the lag proportions matrices were based on a plausible assumption and on some generalized knowledge, but on no specific study; again the consequences of alternative assumptions were investigated. The import coefficients were based on the I.S.G. matrix mentioned earlier but modified on the basis of rough judgments as to the degree to which additional imports would be accepted in particular sectors. Depreciation was projected by means of calculations using macrodata for India. Exports and government consumption were simply extrapolations of past levels and growth rates. Consumption proportions were based on the modified I.S.I. table.

The pre-Plan output levels were taken from Indian data, but to obtain initial capital stocks it was necessary to assume full use of capacity and of some sectoral growth rates. These were backward extrapolations of proposed Plan growth rates and were used to project initial capital-in-process. For the Fourth Plan period, both initial and target year output levels had to be computed from incomplete data and were therefore adjusted for coverage. The adjustment procedure was uniform for all sectors and a rough approximation at best.

There are many places in which judgments on the current and future plausibility of the numbers were necessary. In general we attempted to make these judgments in the direction that would favor Indian economic growth opportunities. For example, the inventory coefficients are usually much lower than some authoritative estimates suggest, and the fixed-capital gestation periods are limited to three years despite considerable evidence of longer gestation processes. On the other hand, our estimate of capacities available at the beginning of the plan may be conservative, due to our inability to estimate initial excess capacities. Probably offsetting this somewhat is our estimate of unfinished capital-in-process at the beginning of the plans. This is calculated by assuming that there has been a perfect scheduling of the necessary investment for new plans before the plans ever start, although the process of plan-making in India does not, in fact, appear to be so foresighted. The background of the data suggests great need for caution in interpreting results, which we shall try to observe and which we recommend to the reader.

4. Target and Transit Model Solutions for the Third Plan and a Proposed Fourth Plan

There is no toy
Called easy joy
But man must strain
To body's pain
Even Vishnu embraces his bride
With arms that had to churn the Milky Way.

The Panchatantra

There are good reasons for the conventional concentration of attention in less developed areas on short-term economic plans of, say, four to eight years. The time span is long enough to complete most types of major industrial, agricultural, and utility projects, and also to begin to judge the results of schemes that do not involve long time lags. Fluctuations in agricultural output due to natural causes can normally be expected to average out over four to eight years. The political future is often reasonably clear, since terms of office usually have more or less the same length. It is also desirable to have a reexamination of premises and appraisal of results at intervals long enough to permit evaluation, but not so long as to permit compounding of errors. Altogether there is much to be said for using a period for detailed economic policy that is longer than two or three years but shorter than ten years.

However, there are also dangers in short-term planning. Sometimes so intense an obsession with the present and near future may arise that the essential dependence of short-term plans on long-term plans is ignored. Economic policies need not be made only seriatim within the order imposed by the progression of time; myopia does not lead to economic efficiency. Short-term plans and policies must be given a context and direction by long-term plans.

The preoccupation of policy-makers with short-term plans has been the inspiration for the construction of the models described in Chapter 2. These models are now applied in this chapter to examine the Indian Third and Fourth Five Year Plan periods. Solutions to the Target Model are calculated using Plan targets for a number of specifications of parameters and constraints. The purpose is to explore the effects of different policies and the sensitivity of the results to alternative estimates of production conditions, export prospects, and foreign economic assistance. In illustrating the use of the Target Model to judge the consistency and feasibility of the Plans, criteria and constraints that we believe to be reasonable representations of reality are applied. However, the caveat must be registered again that these are not necessarily the criteria and constraints implicit in the Plans themselves. For purposes of comparison, Transit Model solutions are found for the Fourth Plan period also.

A five-year model can provide only a limited test of a long-run rationale, but it is a test imposing the necessary condition that the Five Year Plan targets be feasible. If so, the model solution will indicate an "optimum" way of achieving them. If not, a long-run analysis of the targets is beside the point, for there is no way of transferring resources from the future to the present.

Feasibility of a set of targets, however, cannot be finally decided by a formal test using the Target Model or any other model. It remains essentially a matter of judgment, to which calculations using models can only contribute. For example, attempts to find solutions to the Target Model with a specific set of targets might indicate "technical infeasibility," i.e., that with the given set of relationships, constraints and parameters, there is no way of achieving the targets. Yet such a result is not decisive. In the real world, constraints and parameters depend in part upon the policies actually pursued and can be altered by "greater organizational efforts" or by "more intense mobilization of resources." Such feedback effects of the targets chosen on other constraints, however important, are difficult to quantify and embody in formal models. As a result, the Target Model, like other less sophisticated systems, can only provide a test of consistency of the various specifications, and "technical infeasibility" simply means inconsistency. On the other hand, finding a solution to the Target Model is no guarantee that the Plan targets are practically or operationally feasible and socially acceptable. The one test of operational feasibility that we apply is the comparison of the savings and investment proposed in the Plans with the requirements as estimated by the Target Model solutions. This test is both economically important and relatively straightforward. Even if solutions are technically feasible, the Plan targets will not be achieved if they are not consistent with the public and private savings programs. There are other tests, such as availability of managerial skills, which may be equally important, but, partly because they cannot be so easily quantified, they are more subtle and difficult to judge and will not be dealt with here. The formal structure of the Target Model omits many other economic and political conditions that may be quite important, and, in a complete evaluation of any solution, these omitted conditions must be made explicit. For example, the question must be raised and resolved as to whether governmental and private market organizations can and will implement the Plan.

In order to present the results of the alternative solutions to the Target Model in an expeditious manner, much of the discussion will be conducted in terms of "Reference Solutions," one for the Third Plan period and one for the Fourth Plan period. The Reference Solutions are to be interpreted neither as our best guess about the solution most applicable to the Plan periods, nor as representative of the results of trying to achieve the targets. They serve as a means of explaining the characteristics of the model solutions and as a standard against which to judge the results of changes in constraints and parameters. Full details of the solutions are presented only for the Reference Solution; for the variations, only the highlights are described.

4.1 Target Model Solutions for the Third Plan

Though the over-all growth rate of output implied in the Third Five Year Plan was about 5 per cent, the growth rates planned for specific sectors varied substantially from this figure. Table 3.25 indicates the 1960-61 gross output levels, the projected 1965-66 levels, and the implied average annual growth rates for the thirty-sector detail of the I.S.I. input-output table; Table 3.26 presents the same information for the eleven-sector detail in which all the solutions are calculated. When initial output levels are quite low, as for example in the case of Chemical Fertilizers, growth rates can be misleading indicators of the relative emphasis of the Plan. Yet the over-all impression is clear. With the exception of Chemical Fertilizers, the highest growth rates were planned for the capital producing sectors, for their most important suppliers, and for several major import substituting sectors. The sectors supplying consumer goods on the whole had lower growth rates projected for them. The rationalization of this relative emphasis has been based on several related arguments. Capital is necessary to provide the means with which to increase output in the consumer goods sectors, and the well-known accelerator effect accounts for the more rapid growth of the capital goods producing sectors themselves. It is also claimed that the improvement in the individual standard of living would be made not only greater but also more satisfying for the country as a whole by postponing any more rapid growth in consumption until sometime after the Plan period. Capital is also necessary to create import substituting industries in order to reduce the country's reliance on foreign aid. With given export prospects, the need for foreign exchange, and therefore for import substitution, is also implicit in the decision about the rate of investment.

The next step is the solution of the Target Model with the targets of Table 3.26 as constraints.

4.1.1 Assumptions for the Target Model Reference Solution of the Third Plan

The assumed parameters and data for the Reference Solution are as follows:

1. The technical coefficient matrices a, b, s, p', p'', p''', r', r'', and r''' are assumed constant throughout the Plan period and are the reference values presented in Chapter 3.
2. The consumption coefficients c(t), noncompetitive import coefficients m', and competitive import ceilings m'' are also assumed constant throughout the Plan period.
3. Requirements of $\overline{E}$, $\overline{G}$, and $\overline{D}$ are specified at the levels shown in tables of Chapter 3.
4. Net foreign capital inflow is fixed at a constant value of Rs. 500 crores per year.
5. The discount rate w for consumption is fixed at 0.10, i.e., 10.0 per cent.
6. The minimum growth rate of consumption $\rho(t)$ is set at 0.025, i.e., 2.5 per cent for all the periods, which is roughly equal to the population growth rate. However, $\overline{C(0)}$ in Restraints 2.01 of Table A.1 is set at zero. This permits the optimization procedure to reduce C(1), the level of consumption in the first period, as far as necessary in order to meet the consumption growth constraints of later years and produce a solution. Thus it becomes possible to find a solution with levels of aggregate consumption so low as to be clearly unacceptable, whereas if the

constraint were maintained, possibly only a showing of technical infeasibility would result. This is an obvious example of a case in which the feasibility issue cannot be decided solely on the basis of the existence of a feasible solution of the model, but requires a political evaluation of the result.[1]

7.   The initial outputs $\overline{X(0)}$, the terminal year output targets $\overline{X(5)}$, and the implied growth rates are those from Table 3.26.

With the parameters and constraints as specified, no feasible solution can be found that is consistent with the Third Plan targets. In other words, even with a maximand reduced to zero, i.e., with absolutely no diversion of resources to producing consumption, there is no set of allocations of available resources that can create enough capital to reach the target levels of output. This failure to find a solution for the Third Plan targets provides a useful contrast between the real world and the operation of the Target Model. In reality, if Plan targets are technically infeasible, the economic system will not break down and fail to produce; however, it will violate a constraint by, for example, underachieving with respect to one or more of the targets, or by means of a foreign exchange crisis met by emergency foreign capital assistance. In a solution to the model, however, the constraints must be met, and if they cannot be, there is simply no solution at all.

Without a solution, there are no shadow prices to indicate the relative significance of the various constraints and no adjustments permitting a solution. By means of experiments with changes in inventory coefficients, capital coefficients, and lag structures, a feasible solution for the Third Plan targets was obtained, when all these were reduced to what we consider optimistic values. However, this solution is unsatisfactory for studying the sensitivity of the solutions to parametric changes, as most of the variations with less obviously optimistic parameters would lead to infeasible solutions. The solutions that will be used as a Reference Solution are obtained by reducing the targets to the 96 per cent level of targets. The particular changes in parameters are described when the results of the various runs are presented in Section 4.1.3.

In solutions with the 96 per cent level of targets, the growth rates α_0 for estimating initial capacity and initial capital-in-process are still those from Table 3.26 and correspond to the 100 per cent level of targets. However, the growth rates used for projecting postterminal capital requirements in these solutions always correspond to $X(0)$ and to the particular level of targets $X(5)$ in the solution.

4.1.2 Reference Solution for the Third Plan[2]

A complete description of the Reference Solution is given in Tables 4.1 through 4.20 and, in Appendix B, Tables B.1 through B.30. These indicate the kind of detailed information that is obtained in a solution and will be used to describe the operation of the model. In this section the comments on the solution are intended

---

[1]Since a solution, even if politically unacceptable, yields much more information about the structure of the system than a finding of technical infeasibility, it is desirable to avoid the latter result if possible.

[2]As already noted, this solution is for the 96 per cent level of the Third Plan targets.

only to underscore some of the more interesting features of the results. An appraisal of the implications of the Third Plan targets cannot be made until the parametric variations are also described. The linear programming solution explicitly evaluates only the unknowns of the model: gross domestic outputs $X(t)$, for $t = 1$ to 5; competitive imports $M''(t)$, $t = 1$ to 5; available capital stocks $K(t)$, $t = 2$ to 5; restored capacity $R(t)$, $t = 2$ to 8; new capital $Z(t)$, $t = 1$ to 8; and aggregate private consummation $C(t)$, $t = 1$ to 5; and the shadow prices. The remaining details in Tables 4.1 through 4.23 are implicit in the values of these variables and in the equations of the model and are generated from them.

The sectoral output levels and the growth rates of outputs in each year are shown in Table 4.1. As would be expected from the targets, the fastest-growing sectors are nearly always the capital goods sectors and their major suppliers. Agriculture, Food, Clothing, and Leather, and Housing, the major consumer goods producing sectors, are among the slowest-growing. In no sector do the outputs in different years grow either linearly or exponentially, and the growth rates fluctuate from year to year. This is to be expected since the composition of targets is quite different from the composition of initial capacities. The growth rates in the fifth year are not "actual" growth rates but relate only to the full-capacity output levels for the sixth year, which may or may not be internally consistent. The growth rates for the sixth and seventh years are the postterminal growth rates α_r implied by $\overline{X(5)}$ and $\overline{X(0)}$. Since the output of Housing is used only for private consumption, it grows at the same rate as aggregate private consumption. The sudden increase in the growth rate in Others and Margin between the fifth and the sixth years is due to the fact that we set the target output in this sector at the 1960-61 proportion of the sum of the gross domestic output targets in the remaining sectors. Since Others and Margin is primarily a consumption sector, the same proportion in 1966-67 as in 1960-61 may be inappropriate since the proportion of investment goods and consumer goods in the economy change over the years.

Table 4.1. **Gross Domestic Outputs and Sectoral Growth Rates, Third Plan Target Model Reference Solution (Rs. crores, 1959-60 prices)**

SECTOR	1961-62	%	1962-63	%	1963-64	%	1964-65	%	1965-66	%
AG.PL.	7762.35	4.77	8133.22	4.44	8494.50	6.12	9014.76	4.31	9403.33	0.0
M.M.	567.65	17.54	667.24	25.67	838.57	12.08	1013.24	14.87	1163.91	30.33
EQIMT	804.46	19.10	958.14	19.20	1142.42	32.25	1510.93	22.60	1852.46	2.80
CHEMIC	634.44	15.86	735.10	12.45	826.69	16.76	965.28	28.23	1237.82	66.86
CMGLWD	493.18	5.22	518.94	13.84	590.79	13.85	672.64	9.35	735.56	0.31
FOODCL	2384.86	3.73	2473.83	3.43	2558.69	6.15	2716.16	4.65	2842.62	13.61
ELECTR	110.03	8.10	118.95	10.04	130.90	13.27	148.28	11.57	165.45	101.89
TRANS	3809.51	7.06	866.74	9.26	947.01	11.27	1068.11	10.85	1184.00	7.32
CONSTR	1748.04	1.76	1778.84	14.98	2045.46	15.07	2353.74	11.29	2619.55	−4.84
HOUS.	589.34	2.50	604.07	2.50	619.18	6.35	658.53	3.71	683.02	3.43
OTHMAR	5307.16	3.38	5486.99	3.87	5699.61	8.24	6169.60	5.46	6506.88	37.69
SUM	21211.08		22342.10		23893.87		26291.32		28394.65	

	1966-67	%	1967-68	%	1968-69*	
	9403.33	3.66	9747.94	3.66	10105.17	
	1516.89	21.91	1849.30	21.91	2254.55	
	1904.44	19.00	2266.36	19.00	2697.06	
	2065.52	22.46	2529.40	22.46	3097.45	
	737.91	7.52	801.14	7.52	869.78	
	3229.57	4.77	3383.59	4.77	3544.95	
	334.03	21.66	406.40	21.66	494.44	
	1270.71	8.50	1378.69	8.50	1495.84	
	2492.87	7.48	2679.36	7.48	2879.80	
	706.39	3.35	730.02	3.35	754.45	
	8959.51	7.35	6917.94	7.35	10324.76	
	32621.23		35390.18		38518.31	

*Calculated simply by dividing capital stocks by capital-output ratios. No test either of static or of dynamic consistency has been applied.

The shadow prices of outputs that indicate the value to the maximand of an additional unit of output are shown in Table 4.2. These are the shadow prices associated with the production accounting relationships. The shadow prices of output help indicate the priorities in the resource allocations that take place in the solution. The highest shadow prices, and therefore the greatest stringencies, are for the most part in the capital forming sectors, Construction and Equipment, and in their major supplying sectors, Mining and Metals, and Cement and Nonmetals. The shadow prices in the major consumer goods producing sectors, Agriculture, Food, Clothing, and Leather, Housing, and Margin, are relatively low. This occurs, even though the optimization mechanism is directed toward maximizing the production of consumption goods. This is because the maximization must be consistent with the targets and with the various other constraints. Thus the low shadow prices of consumption goods are an indication of the strains put on the system by the targets and other constraints. The strikingly high shadow price of Cement and Nonmetals in the third year will be explained later.

The sectoral levels of private consumption in each year are shown in Table 4.3. These levels are calculated from the fixed-consumption coefficients and the aggregate private consumption in each period as determined by the solution. The level of private consumption in the first year is Rs. 13,050 crores, which, compared with the actual level of Rs. 12,605 crores in the pre-Plan year 1960-61, implies growth of 3.5 per cent. From the third to the fourth year, private consumption grows by 6.4 per cent and from the fourth to the fifth year by 3.7 per cent.

The consumption growth constraints have nonzero shadow prices in the second and the third years. These indicate that, were it not for the consumption growth constraints, more consumption would have been made available in the solution in the first and second years than was actually the case. It was not, because the required additional consumption in the third year could not subsequently have been provided. This might be interpreted as a tendency to concentrate consumption in the first year. On the other hand, the fact that consumption growth constraints are not binding in the fourth and the fifth year indicates that the solution does not tend to concentrate all the consumption at the beginning of the Plan. This apparently contradictory behavior in the first two years is due to the initial specifications of capital-in-process. These are part of the initial conditions that, in this case, limit the capital stocks available in the third period at levels such that they cannot generate more consumption and also the investment necessary to meet the prescribed targets.

Tables 4.4, 4.5, 4.6, and 4.7 disclose the availability and intensity of use of capital stock and provide a great deal of insight into the solution. From Table 4.4 it is seen that maximum increment in capital stock occurs at the end of the Plan period, between the fifth and the sixth years. If the solution showed unconstrained flip-flop behavior, consumption would be concentrated in the last year, and consumption in the early Plan years would be held down in order to provide as much capital as possible by the last Plan year. This capital would then be used to produce private consumption in the fifth year. This doesn't happen here for several reasons, including the existence of three-year lags in investments, which require that investments be started by the second year in order to mature in the fifth year, and because the maximum capital stocks in the first three years are externally specified.

Table 4.2. Shadow Prices of Gross Domestic Outputs, Third Plan Target Model Reference
Solution (Rs. crores)

SECTOR	1961-62	1962-63	1963-64	1964-65	1965-66
AC.PL.	.23738	.18433	.03993	.75262	.79609
M.M.	6.34600	2.30298	6.35539	3.36769	2.50165
EQIPMT	23.02660	2.77326	3.90819	2.77116	1.77718
CHEMIC	3.41063	2.33654	3.54514	2.36426	1.64859
CMGLWD	23.61532	1.15420	117.04334	3.16950	1.23822
FCODCL	.46769	.36433	2.91174	.72012	1.07341
ELECTR	1.04077	.90147	2.94272	.93219	2.11189
TRANS	.93262	.61848	23.48197	.65137	2.68050
CONSTR	6.57441	1.63456	23.94160	5.35714	1.45928
HCUS.	.39451	.03565	1.94364	4.12837	.64001
OTHMAR	.04306	.03035	.44603	.04650	.14365

Table 4.3. Private Consumption, Third Plan Target Model Reference Solution
(Rs. crores, 1959-60 prices)

SECTOR	1961-62	1962-63	1963-64	1964-65	1965-66
AG.PL.	5603.87006	5743.96704	5887.56598	6261.78003	6494.60217
M.M.	6.26408	6.42068	6.58120	6.99950	7.25975
ECIPMT	191.96788	196.76709	201.68626	214.50545	222.48107
CHEMIC	311.11586	318.89377	326.86610	347.64173	360.56756
CMGLWD	65.38131	67.01585	68.69124	73.05726	75.77363
FOODCL	1840.20334	1886.20850	1933.36363	2056.24832	2132.70267
ELECTR	11.35364	11.63748	11.92842	12.68659	13.15830
TRANS	192.62039	197.43591	202.37180	215.23456	223.23730
CONSTR	0.	0.	0.	0.	0.
HOUS.	589.34531	604.07896	619.18092	658.53609	683.02143
OTHMAR	4238.04010	4343.99127	4452.59088	4735.59784	4911.67426
SUM	13050.16162	13376.41602	13710.82605	14582.28699	15124.47754

SUM OF DISCOUNTED CONSUMPTION =   57827.9047852
SUM OF UNDISCOUNTED CONSUMPTION =   69844.1660156

PRICE ON CONSUMPTION GROWTH CONSTRAINT
1962   .238298   1964   0.
1963   .870248   1965   0.

Table 4.4. Available Capital Stock, Third Plan Target Model Reference Solution
(Rs. crores, 1959-60 prices)

SECTOR	1961-62	1962-63	1963-64	1964-65	1965-66	1966-67	1967-68	1968-69
AG.PL.	11970.21509	12511.26855	13076.77783	13620.55884	14213.05347	14213.05347	14733.91614	15273.86621
M.M.	1371.23802	1684.84007	2025.81474	2447.71649	2811.54465	3664.22021	4467.18536	5446.10980
ECIPMT	728.09795	873.57188	1033.96426	1367.51402	1676.61018	1723.65598	2051.21970	2441.03366
CFEMIC	661.92553	775.26622	723.71132	845.24422	1083.51872	1808.03616	2214.08594	2711.32654
CMGLWD	441.08197	482.76419	528.38538	601.62784	657.86394	659.96281	716.50981	777.90181
FCODCL	1420.23839	1442.09811	1408.82649	1501.07823	1565.12172	1778.16893	1862.97130	1951.81804
ELECTR	790.74816	969.93169	1077.68796	1035.54233	1035.54236	2090.71658	2543.63708	3094.67584
TRANS	1893.17212	2070.75156	2104.11496	2501.28839	2630.67178	2823.34747	3063.25427	3323.54654
CCNSTR	268.08372	290.49559	312.95400	360.11098	400.79196	399.12634	409.94231	440.61007
HCUS.	6040.93610	6294.05109	6557.77173	6588.06232	6830.21240	7063.91754	7300.29181	7544.57556
OTHMAR	991.65182	1073.26468	1161.59438	1020.58418	1018.32708	1402.16423	1505.20877	1615.82608
SUM	26577.38770	28468.26270	30011.60205	31889.33057	33923.25635	37626.36865	40868.22119	44621.28809

Table 4.5. Capital Stock Used, Third Plan Target Model Reference Solution
(Rs. crores, 1959-60 prices)

SECTOR	1961-62	1962-63	1963-64	1964-65	1965-66	1966-67	1967-68 TARGET STOCKS	1968-69
AG.PL.	11732.72986	12293.28210	12839.36438	13625.72314	14213.05249	14213.05396	14733.91675	15273.86731
M.M.	1371.23802	1611.78864	2025.66100	2447.59900	2811.54443	3664.22043	4467.18579	5446.11041
EQIPMT	728.09795	867.18808	1033.97513	1367.50471	1676.61021	1723.65605	2051.21985	2441.03397
CHEMIC	555.35185	643.46983	723.63536	844.94914	1083.51874	1808.03624	2214.08606	2711.32681
CMGLWD	441.08197	464.12602	528.38538	601.58808	657.86389	659.96288	716.50983	777.90186
FOODCL	1313.08141	1362.06660	1408.79308	1495.49451	1565.12175	1778.16895	1862.97139	1951.81815
ELECTR	688.72471	744.53965	819.30527	928.07261	1035.54233	2090.71710	2543.63776	3094.67654
TRANS	1798.63223	1925.76819	2104.13187	2373.18280	2630.67181	2823.34857	3063.25546	3323.54773
CONSTR	267.45131	272.16302	312.95614	360.12329	400.79203	381.40924	409.94239	440.61011
HOUS.	5893.45410	6040.79053	6191.81036	6585.36078	6830.21204	7063.92072	7300.29498	7544.57886
OTHMAR	830.57161	858.71466	891.99044	965.54381	1018.32708	1402.16435	1505.20900	1615.82637
SUM	25620.41406	27083.89648	28880.00732	31595.14038	33923.25537	37608.65723	40868.22852	44621.29688

Table 4.6. Idle Capital, Third Plan Target Model Reference Solution (Rs. crores, 1959-60 prices)

SECTOR	1961-62	1962-63	1963-64	1964-65	1965-66	EXCESS OVER TARGET STOCKS 1966-67	1967-68	1968-69
AG.PL.	239.01512	218.42446	235.84876	0.	0.	-.00049	-.00061	-.00110
M.M.	0.	73.03790	0.	0.	0.	-.00021	-.00043	-.00061
EQIPMT	0.	6.35704	0.	0.	0.	-.00008	-.00015	-.00031
CHEMIC	106.63548	131.77221	0.	0.	0.	-.00008	-.00012	-.00027
CMGLWD	0.	18.64527	0.	0.	0.	-.00007	-.00002	-.00005
FOODCL	107.29639	80.08827	0.	0.	0.	-.00002	-.00009	-.00011
ELECTR	102.07161	225.41676	258.36574	106.52858	0.	-.00052	-.00067	-.00070
TRANS	94.67684	145.07639	0.	126.53498	0.	-.00110	-.00119	-.00119
CONSTR	.62410	18.33484	0.	0.	0.	17.71710	-.00009	-.00003
HOUS.	148.15994	253.95572	366.67403	0.	0.	-.00317	-.00317	-.00330
OTHMAR	161.15902	214.62911	269.68377	54.64589	0.	-.00012	-.00023	-.00029
SUM	959.63849	1385.73795	1130.57230	287.70945	0.	17.71125	-.00678	-.00796

Table 4.7. Ratio of Idle Capital to Total Capital, Third Plan Target Model Reference Solution

SECTOR	1961-62	1962-63	1963-64	1964-65	1965-66	1966-67	1967-68	1968-69
AG.PL.	.01997	.01746	.01804	0.	0.	-.00000	-.00000	-.00000
M.M.	0.	.04335	0.	0.	0.	-.00000	-.00000	-.00000
EQIPMT	0.	.00728	0.	0.	0.	-.00000	-.00000	-.00000
CHEMIC	.16110	.16997	0.	0.	0.	-.00000	-.00000	-.00000
CMGLWD	0.	.03862	0.	0.	0.	-.00000	-.00000	-.00000
FOODCL	.07555	.05554	0.	0.	0.	-.00000	-.00000	-.00000
ELECTR	.12908	.23240	.23974	.10287	0.	-.00000	-.00000	-.00000
TRANS	.05001	.07006	0.	.05059	0.	-.00000	-.00000	-.00000
CONSTR	.00233	.06312	0.	0.	0.	.04439	-.00000	-.00000
HOUS.	.02453	.04035	.05591	0.	0.	-.00000	-.00000	-.00000
OTHMAR	.16252	.19998	.23217	.05354	0.	-.00000	-.00000	-.00000
SUM	.03611	.04868	.03767	.00902	0.	.00047	-.00000	-.00000

In Table 4.6 the excess of actual capacity over the targeted capacity in Construction in the sixth year indicates that even more capacity in Construction is required in the fifth year than targeted in order to meet the investment requirements in that year. The capital stocks in the Agriculture and Transport sectors have reached the target levels by the fifth year. Both these capacities are fully required to meet the demand for Agriculture and Transport in the fifth year, and in that year there are no idle capacities. Since capital stocks increase in the sixth year in other consumption goods sectors, this increase implies that the consumption proportions would not be maintained in the sixth year if aggregate private consumption were to grow and if imports in the Agriculture sector were not increased. If the level of investment is also maintained, a transportation shortage would develop if private consumption continued to increase in the post-Plan period.

The idle capacities listed in Table 4.6 in the first years are mainly in the consumption goods sectors. On the other hand, capacities in capital producing sectors, Construction and Equipment, and their major suppliers, Mining and Metals and Cement and Nonmetals, are fully utilized in the first year. The distribution of the excess capacity reflects the lack of balance between the composition of the capital stocks existing at the outset of the Plan and the composition of the targets. The capital stocks at the outset of the Plan, estimated from pre-Plan output levels, are geared primarily to the production of consumer goods. Capital in the Mining and Metals, Equipment, and Construction sectors account for only 8.8 per cent of the total endowment. By the end of the Plan period these sectors were intended to account for over 14 per cent of the total capacity.[3] This change in composition requires that roughly 32 per cent of the total investment over the Plan period go to these three sectors in the Reference Solution.

The idle capital in all the sectors in the second year, as shown in Tables 4.6 and 4.7 is striking since it appears to be wasteful. This capacity could not be used in producing more consumption in the second year, because the consumption growth constraint would in turn require a higher level of consumption in the third year. As explained above, more consumption in the third year could not be provided while at the same time producing the investment required to realize the targets. The third-year bottleneck cannot be broken, because the maximum capital stocks in that year are specified by initial conditions. On the other hand, the excess capacity in the second year cannot be used in the creation of capital goods for investment either. The lag structure of investment in the model is rigidly fixed and requires that investment in each sector be made in three successive years. Since the solution shows no excess capacity in Construction in the third year, if additional investment were made in the second year it could not be complemented with the further investment that would be necessary in the third year to complete it. However, in Table 4.8 it can be seen that the initially available unfinished investment in Construction is not completed in the third year, and it appears as if more Construction capacity could have been provided in the third year. If this were so, it would have then been possible to complement additional investment made in the third year and thus reduce or eliminate excess capacity in the second. But it must also be noted that in the a matrix, Construction needs Cement and Nonmetals as current inputs. The additional outputs of Cement and Nonmetals could not be provided in the third year, since there is then no excess capital in this sector. This also explains why the shadow price of Cement and Nonmetals is so high in the third year. An additional unit of Cement and Nonmetals would have made it possible to use some of the excess capacity in the second year. Still this is not quite a complete explanation of the situation. Why not divert in the third year one unit of Cement and Nonmetals from consumption to the use as an input to the Construction sector? If this were done, fixed consumption coefficients would require that about 200 units of aggregate consumption be sacrificed before 1 unit of Cement and Nonmetals would become available. However, because of the additional consumption generated in later years, the cost of this sacrifice is not 200 but just 117.04 units, the shadow price of Cement and Nonmetals in the third year.

The foregoing tale, with its plot and subplots, demonstrates the interplay of many assumptions and forces within the model. It underlines, for example, the effects of the assumption of three-year lags in rigid sequence and shows how the whole solution is affected by this assumption.[4] This assumption, in turn, would not be so critical, as will be shown, if the targets were lower.

The shadow prices in Table 4.9 are the rental prices of capital in each year. The rental price is zero whenever there is idle capacity in the sector. Thus the rental

---

[3]Since the Plan targets were scaled down by 4 per cent uniformly, the reduction in the level does not affect this comparison.

[4]Solutions T-20 and T-21, described on p. 106, explore the implications of a set of shorter gestation lags.

price of capital can be zero even when the output produced with it has a nonzero shadow price. The shadow prices of the initial capital-in-process are shown in Table 4.10. The new capital capacities maturing at the beginning of each year are shown in Table 4.11. New capital is created in most of the sectors in each period. Among the capital goods sectors, Construction and Equipment and their major suppliers, Cement and Nonmetals, and Mining and Metals, only Mining and Metals has a large increment in capacity in the sixth year. Unless an increase in the demand for Mining and Metals is envisioned, either due to changes in production or consumption coefficients, or due to increase in exports or decrease in imports, the result would be excess capacity in this sector in the sixth year. However, it should be noted that in the Reference Solution no provision is made for any import substitution program and that the Mining and Metals sector may be especially important in such a program.

A large increase in capital stock in Electricity occurs between the fifth and sixth years when the available capital stock doubles. In the solution, this capacity is not created earlier since there is no need for it in the intra-Plan period and the capital-output ratio in Electricity is quite high. The high level of target output in Electricity may reflect programs of rural electrification not reflected in consumption proportions or new industrial demand not prescribed in the technical coefficients in the model. If increases in demand for electricity due to such changes are not foreseen, Electricity would also show excess capacity in the sixth year. In both the Others and Margin, and the Electricity sectors, excess capacities exist in the first four years, and yet new capital is created in the second and third years. This is because the initial capital-in-process created before the plan started must be completed in the second and third years, or else be lost. This cheaper means of creating capital capacity is preferred to the abandonment of this part of the initial endowment and to the creation of completely new capital later. This also explains why capital in Housing is created in the second and third years, even though there is excess capacity in Housing in these years.

The impossibility in the model of interrupting the sequence of investment results in initial capital-in-process being lost in a number of sectors, because it could not be completed due to the shortage in Cement and Nonmetals. This is seen in Table 4.8 where several sectors have ratios less than 1.0 for the third year. This might be taken as indicating the areas in which special efforts would be warranted to modify one or more of the constraints leading to this result. For example, if it were possible to interrupt the sequence of investment in a planned way by starting new investment and then delaying it when particular resource requirements were scarce, the over-all performance of the system would be improved.

The shadow prices of new capital in Table 4.12 correspond to the capital-accounting relationships of Table 2.3. For the first four years, the difference between the shadow price of capital in two successive years is the rental price of capital in the second year. If the rental value is zero, as it is when capital is not fully utilized, the shadow price of that capital remains constant. At the start of the sixth year, i.e., at the end of the fifth year, the shadow price of capital reflects neither the future usefulness, nor the productivity of this capital, but rather the cost in terms of private consumption over the five Plan years which had to be foregone in order to create the amount of capital that the targets stipulated. This

Table 4.8. Ratio of Completed Initial Capital-in-Process to Initially Available Capital-in-Process, Third Plan Target Model Reference Solution

SECTOR	1962-63	1963-64	SECTOR	1962-63	1963-64
AG.PL.	1.000	1.000	ELECTR	1.000	.490
M.M.	1.000	.885	TRANS	1.000	.170
EQIPMT	1.000	.920	CONSTR	1.000	.995
CHEMIC	.730	0.	HOUS.	1.000	1.000
CMGLWD	1.000	1.000	OTHMAR	1.000	1.000
FOODCL	.420	0.			

Table 4.9. Shadow Rental Prices of Capital, Third Plan Target Model Reference Solution (Rs. crores)

SECTOR	1961-62	1962-63	1963-64	1964-65	1965-66
AG.PL.	0.	0.	0.	.34278	.43899
M.M.	1.44197	0.	1.21664	.17845	.56371
EQIPMT	25.79623	0.	1.59974	.16896	.58471
CHEMIC	0.	0.	.17503	.18137	.55719
CMGLWD	24.91092	0.	128.37625	.20170	.51193
FOODCL	0.	0.	2.63892	.11783	.69844
ELECTR	0.	0.	0.	0.	.20823
TRANS	0.	0.	8.43672	0.	.96036
CONSTR	0.	0.	4.14546	.10602	3.71744
HOUS.	0.	0.	0.	.40572	.05842
OTHMAR	0.	0.	0.	0.	.32471

Table 4.10. Shadow Prices of Initial Capital-in-Process, Third Plan Target Model Reference Solution (Rs. crores)

SECTOR	1962-63	1963-64
AG.PL.	6.083212	5.432110
M.M.	.928142	0.
EQIPMT	.944001	0.
CHEMIC	0.	0.
CMGLWD	128.989990	128.101175
FOODCL	0.	0.
ELECTR	.857332	0.
TRANS	1.228992	0.
CONSTR	1.050021	0.
HOUS.	8.524539	7.979734
OTHMAR	2.527952	1.736238

Table 4.11. New Capital, Third Plan Target Model Reference Solution (Rs. crores, 1959-60 prices)

SECTOR	1961-62	1962-63	1963-64	1964-65	1965-66	1966-67	1967-68	1968-69
AG.PL.	0.	541.05370	565.50929	543.78217	592.49355	0.	520.86291	539.95031
M.M.	0.	313.60211	340.97481	421.90172	363.82802	852.67561	802.96523	978.92455
EQIPMT	0.	145.47390	160.39245	333.54976	309.09608	47.04586	327.56376	389.81399
CHEMIC	0.	113.34068	0.	121.53287	238.27448	724.51741	406.04979	497.24069
CMGLWD	0.	41.68220	45.62119	73.24249	56.23608	2.09884	56.54700	61.39200
FOODCL	0.	21.81981	0.	92.25172	64.04341	213.04725	84.80240	88.84677
ELECTR	0.	179.18360	107.75661	0.	0.	1055.17424	452.92059	603.89489
TRANS	0.	262.17208	33.36418	484.35164	217.85467	282.43991	331.05630	352.82700
CONSTR	0.	22.41180	22.45848	47.16137	40.67589	0.	10.81599	30.66780
HOUS.	0.	439.95935	453.42059	222.84833	242.15430	233.70519	437.70098	448.67016
OTHMAR	0.	81.61290	88.32970	0.	0.	383.83718	103.04460	260.29129
SUM	0.	2162.31204	1817.82727	2340.62201	2124.65640	3794.54141	3534.32938	4252.51923

Table 4.12. Shadow Prices of New Capital, Third Plan Target Model Reference Solution (Rs. crores)

SECTOR	1962-63	1963-64	1964-65	1965-66	1966-67	1967-68	1968-69
AG.PL.	9.51687	9.51687	9.51687	9.17409	6.69222	1.63195	.41094
M.M.	7.60161	7.60161	6.38499	6.20655	4.19835	1.23056	.21393
ECIPMT	7.80343	7.80343	6.20371	6.03475	4.04022	1.20728	.20255
CHEMIC	6.61555	6.61555	6.44058	6.25921	4.24692	1.23767	.21744
CMGLWD	135.20402	135.20402	6.82778	6.62609	4.58509	1.28726	.24181
FOODCL	7.86849	7.86849	5.22965	5.11182	3.18964	1.08248	.14126
ELECTR	6.70275	6.70275	6.70275	6.70275	4.89713	1.33313	.26428
TRANS	11.42071	11.42071	2.98402	2.98402	1.22899	.79468	-0.
CONSTR	9.14956	9.14956	5.00412	4.89810	0.	1.05351	.12710
HOUS.	10.71578	10.71578	10.71578	10.31008	7.97973	1.78554	.48638
OTHMAR	7.60653	7.60653	7.60653	7.60653	5.54311	1.42788	.31083

Table 4.13. Restored Capacity, Third Plan Target Model Reference Solution (Rs. crores, 1959-60 prices)

SECTOR	1961-62	1962-63	1963-64	1964-65	1965-66	1966-67	1967-68	1968-69
AG.PL.	0.	277.401	281.641	285.880	290.120	294.360	298.902	303.445
M.M.	0.	71.406	72.497	73.588	74.680	75.771	76.940	78.110
EQIPMT	0.	16.089	16.335	16.580	16.826	17.072	17.336	17.599
CHEMIC	0.	50.779	0.	52.331	53.107	53.883	54.715	55.546
CMGLWD	0.	16.159	16.406	16.653	16.900	17.147	17.411	17.676
FOODCL	0.	32.731	0.	33.732	34.232	34.732	35.268	35.804
ELECTR	0.	48.319	49.058	7.533	50.535	51.274	52.065	0.
TRANS	0.	0.	85.885	0.	0.	0.	0.	0.
CONSTR	0.	1.570	1.594	1.618	1.642	0.	1.691	1.717
HOUS.	0.	0.	0.	0.	195.411	198.267	0.	0.
OTHMAR	0.	136.828	138.919	0.	140.844	145.193	147.433	0.
SUM	0.	651.281	662.334	487.915	874.298	887.699	701.762	509.897

is because the postterminal stream of private consumption is not included in the objective function explicitly, but only through the stipulated requirements of terminal capital stocks. The effect of providing for postterminal consumption, through minimum terminal capital stocks constraints that must be satisfied, is similar to having an objective function with weights of infinity on terminal capacities for values below the targeted levels but with weights of zero once the target level is reached. Consequently, after the stipulated terminal stocks are achieved, further additions to these stocks, which would increase the postterminal stream of private consumption, have a zero value to the objective of the solution. This also helps explain why the shadow price of capital falls with time.

Tables 4.13 and 4.14 show the restored capacities and the ratios of restored capacity to depreciated capacity, respectively. A ratio other than 1.0 indicates decumulation of capital. However, the zeros in the Transport and Housing sectors are misleading, since these two sectors require only construction as capital. In Transport, the special assumption is made that no new construction is required for the Third Plan period and that Housing requires only construction inputs for its capital formation. Consequently, the costs of restoring are the same as those for creating new capital in these sectors. This makes the solution indifferent as to restoring or creating new capacity in Housing and Transport. Capital decumulation, however, does take place in the Others and Margin sector in the fourth and fifth years, in the Chemicals and Food, Clothing, and Leather sectors in the third year, and in Electricity in the fourth year. For the eighth year, zeros do not indicate decumulation, since only the construction component of capital has a

Table 4.14. **Ratio of Restored Capacity to Depreciated Capacity, Third Plan Target Model Reference Solution**

SECTOR	1961-62	1962-63	1963-64	1964-65	1965-66	1966-67	1967-68	1968-69
AG.PL.	0.	1.000	1.000	1.000	1.000	1.000	1.000	1.000
M.M.	0.	1.000	1.000	1.000	1.000	1.000	1.000	1.000
EQIPMT	0.	1.000	1.000	1.000	1.000	1.000	1.000	1.000
CHEMIC	0.	1.000	0.	1.000	1.000	1.000	1.000	1.000
CMGLWD	0.	1.000	1.000	1.000	1.000	1.000	1.000	1.000
FOODCL	0.	1.000	0.	1.000	1.000	1.000	1.000	1.000
ELECTR	0.	1.000	1.000	.151	1.000	1.000	1.000	0.
TRANS	0.	0.	1.000	0.	0.	0.	0.	0.
CONSTR	0.	1.000	1.000	1.000	1.000	0.	1.000	1.000
HOUS.	0.	0.	0.	0.	1.000	1.000	0.	0.
OTHMAR	0.	1.000	1.000	0.	.984	1.000	1.000	0.

Table 4.15. **Shadow Prices of Restorable Capacity, Third Plan Target Model Reference Solution (Rs. crores)**

SECTOR	1962-63	1963-64	1964-65	1965-66	1966-67	1967-68	1968-69
AG.PL.	1.057306	1.320179	5.170472	4.974710	4.706029	1.096219	.234689
M.M.	.172687	.215612	.844352	.812367	.807917	.178995	.038336
EQIPMT	.202553	.252902	.990390	.952874	.947642	.209955	.044965
CHEMIC	.125311	0.	.612697	.589487	.586265	.129885	.027819
CMGLWD	.417264	.521001	2.040456	1.963193	1.952157	.432598	.092622
FOODCL	.167180	0.	.817391	.786423	.782152	.173274	.037114
ELECTR	1.648699	1.847505	0.	.220436	.327321	.128519	0.
TRANS	0.	0.	0.	0.	0.	0.	0.
CONSTR	.431903	.539261	2.111788	2.031791	0.	.447680	.095880
HOUS.	0.	0.	0.	0.	0.	0.	0.
OTHMAR	.202741	.227182	0.	0.	.040209	.015772	0.

three-year lag, only the construction part of the eighth year's new capital is invested during the Plan period, and once again the solution is indifferent as to restoring or creating capacity in these sectors. The shadow prices in Table 4.15 are the values of the undepreciated capital components of restorable capacities. For the Construction and Transport sectors, where there is no undepreciated component left, the nonzero price corresponds to the price of new capital.

In addition to capital, production in most sectors requires imports. Total imports in each sector are listed in Table 4.16, and the allocation between noncompetitive and competitive imports is shown in Tables 4.17 and 4.18. The noncompetitive imports, it will be recalled, are tied to the level of output in the sectors in which they exist. The total amount of imports in each year is limited to the sum in that year of exports and net capital inflow including economic assistance. The noncompetitive imports are nearly 50 per cent of the total in the first year and rise to 85 in the fifth year as output increases.

The noncompetitive import coefficients are assumed constant throughout the Plan period and establish minimum requirements for imports while the competitive import ceilings operate only on the "leftover" foreign exchange. As a result, the limited supplies of foreign exchange could have the effect of reducing the levels of domestic production below what is otherwise feasible. That this has not happened in the Reference Solution is shown by the existence of some competitive imports in all the five years. The distribution of total imports is affected by both the noncompetitive imports coefficients and the competitive import ceilings.

Table 4.16. Total Imports, Third Plan Target Model Reference Solution (Rs. crores, 1959-60 prices)

SECTOR	1961-62	1962-63	1963-64	1964-65	1965-66
AG.PL.	268.32254	260.62337	239.77519	225.95436	195.39632
M.M.	199.85518	203.17592	213.86486	213.56818	205.42150
EQIPMT	394.60483	411.27571	429.82929	471.61966	499.42821
CHEMIC	261.27871	278.50147	290.88176	306.19402	352.91183
CMGLWD	13.78625	12.77186	11.63671	9.38893	6.62630
FOODCL	16.13905	14.63760	12.72395	9.26016	5.20069
ELECTR	0.	0.	0.	0.	0.
TRANS	0.	0.	0.	0.	0.
CONSTR	0.	0.	0.	0.	0.
HOUS.	0.	0.	0.	0.	0.
OTHMAR	0.	0.	9.27352	0.	0.
SUM	1153.98653	1180.98592	1207.98524	1235.98528	1264.98483

Table 4.17. Noncompetitive Imports, Third Plan Target Model Reference Solution (Rs. crores, 1959-60 prices)

SECTOR	1961-62	1962-63	1963-64	1964-65	1965-66
AG.PL.	124.19773	130.13152	135.91211	144.23620	150.45342
M.M.	82.31061	96.75001	121.59333	146.92079	168.76716
EQIPMT	189.04947	225.16405	268.47001	355.07045	435.32920
CHEMIC	165.58916	191.86330	215.76625	251.93836	323.07262
CMGLWD	1.97273	2.07579	2.36319	2.69059	2.94228
FOODQL	.19079	.19791	.20470	.21729	.22741
ELECTR	0.	0.	0.	0.	0.
TRANS	0.	0.	0.	0.	0.
CCNSTR	0.	0.	0.	0.	0.
HOUS.	0.	0.	0.	0.	0.
OTHMAR	0.	0.	0.	0.	0.

Table 4.18. Competitive Imports, Third Plan Target Model Reference Solution (Rs. crores, 1959-60 prices)

SECTOR	1961-62	1962-63	1963-64	1964-65	1965-66
AG.PL.	144.12480	130.49185	103.86307	81.71814	44.94291
M.M.	117.54457	106.42591	92.27154	66.64739	36.65434
EQIPMT	205.55536	186.11166	161.35928	116.54922	64.09901
CHEMIC	95.68955	86.63817	75.11551	54.25566	29.83921
CMGLWD	11.81393	10.69607	9.27352	6.69834	3.68402
FOODCL	15.94826	14.43970	12.51925	9.04286	4.97328
ELECTR	0.	0.	0.	0.	0.
TRANS	0.	0.	0.	0.	0.
CONSTR	0.	0.	0.	0.	0.
HOUS.	0.	0.	0.	0.	0.
OTHMAR	0.	0.	9.27352	0.	0.

Table 4.19. Shadow Prices on Competitive Import Ceilings and on Foreign Trade Balance Constraints, Third Plan Target Model Reference Solution (Rs. crores)

SECTOR	1961-62	1962-63	1963-64	1964-65	1965-66
AG.PL.	0.	0.	0.	0.	0.
M.M.	1.21561	.46141	1.25677	.52040	.33941
EQIPMT	7.93065	.90095	1.34614	.70245	.34142
CHEMIC	.51407	.34866	.56784	.26109	.13810
CMGLWD	.46756	.01940	2.34007	.04834	.00884
FOODCL	.00622	.00486	.07754	-.00088	.00749
ELECTR	0.	0.	0.	0.	0.
TRANS	0.	0.	0.	0.	0.
CONSTR	0.	0.	0.	0.	0.
HOUS.	0.	0.	0.	0.	0.
OTHMAR	0.	0.	.C0812	0.	0.

SHADOW PRICES ON FOREIGN TRADE BALANCE CONSTRAINTS

	1961-62	1962-63	1963-64	1964-65	1965-66
	.23738	.18433	.03998	.75262	.79609

Interpretation of the pattern of imports is facilitated by the use of the shadow prices on the competitive import ceilings and the use of the prices on the foreign exchange balance constraints, which are shown in Table 4.19. These latter shadow prices are higher in the later than in the earlier periods, in spite of the greater stringency of resources in the first periods.[5] This is because the competitive import ceilings force the allocation of foreign exchange to sectors that in early years have lower shadow prices. Furthermore, as explained in Chapter 2, the shadow price on the foreign exchange balance constraint is the value of the least valuable output among the sectors to which noncompetitive imports are made.

In each period in the solution the available foreign exchange that is not used for noncompetitive imports is allocated first to the sector that can import and that has the highest shadow price on its output. In this period, imports continue in this sector until the sector's competitive import ceiling is reached, or the available foreign exchange is exhausted. The allocation of foreign exchange then switches to the sector in which it is next most valuable in the same period and again proceeds until the sector's import ceiling is reached, or the remaining foreign exchange is exhausted. In all periods, Agriculture has the lowest priority for the use of foreign exchange for competitive imports, as is seen from the fact that the price on the Agriculture import ceilings is zero in all years. Agriculture thus receives whatever is left over after the ceilings have been reached in other sectors. In this solution, it is therefore always Agriculture whose shadow price is equal to the foreign exchange balance shadow price.

The highest price on competitive import ceilings in the first year is on Equipment, whereas the output of Cement and Nonmetals has the highest shadow price in the first year. This is because the price on the competitive import ceiling in a particular sector does not reflect the value of an additional unit of competitive imports in that sector but rather the value of an additional unit on the right-hand side of the particular constraint. The shadow price for the competitive imports in Cement and Nonmetals should be 117.00336, which is the shadow price of Cement and Nonmetals, 117.04334, minus the shadow price of foreign exchange in the third year, 0.03998. The competitive import coefficient for Cement and Nonmetals is 0.02, so 50 units of foreign exchange on the right-hand side of its competitive import ceiling are required to have 1 unit of Cement and Nonmetals. From Table 4.19 the price for the constraint on Cement and Nonmetals is 2.34007, and the value of the 50 units becomes $50 \times 2.34007 = 117.0035$, which is the same as the value of an additional unit of competitive imports in Cement and Nonmetals.

Tables B.1 through B.30 in Appendix B at the end of this chapter provide detailed information for the solution on the sectoral patterns of output and for the use of resources in each period: the intermediate flows, production and replacement of fixed capital for various maturities, production for inventory, and the holdings of inventories, imports, exports, and government consumption. These tables amplify the previous exposition and demonstrate the specific workings of the system. The summaries of the sources and the uses of output in each period are particularly enlightening.

---

[5] Imports of the outputs of the Electricity, Transport, Construction, and Housing sectors are not allowed; there are no noncompetitive imports in the Others and Margin sector.

Table 4.20. National Income Accounts, Third Plan Target Model Reference Solution (Rs. crores, 1959-60 prices)

	1961-62	1962-63	1963-64	1964-65	1965-66
CONSUMPTION	13048.660278	13374.876831	13709.248291	14588.266846	15124.476440
INVENTORIES CHANGE	117.897453	373.460052	568.700317	547.170036	716.437073
FIXED INVESTMENT	1932.205078	2072.895813	2455.207550	3093.579376	3799.054840
TOTAL INVESTMENT	2670.669952	3111.110687	3756.389801	4450.548279	5229.743835
GOVERNMENT EXPENDITURE	540.999992	560.999985	581.999985	601.999985	621.999985
VALUE ADDED BY GOVT.	899.753296	933.015884	967.941612	1001.204216	1034.466812
EXPORTS	653.986908	680.986359	707.985817	735.985260	764.984688
IMPORTS	1153.986664	1180.985886	1207.985260	1235.985077	1264.984528
GROSS NATIONAL PRODUCT	16660.083496	17480.003174	18515.579346	20142.018799	21510.686768
REPLACEMENT	620.567459	664.754829	732.481956	809.798920	714.251991
NET NATIONAL PRODUCT	16039.515991	16815.248291	17783.097168	19332.219727	20796.434570
SAVINGS	2170.669952	2611.110687	3256.389801	3950.548279	4729.743835
GROSS NAT. OUTPUT	21209.159668	22341.057129	23894.510742	26302.085449	28394.651855
INTERMEDIATE PRODUCT	5448.827271	5794.068970	6346.870300	7161.272339	7918.433960
CONS./GROSS NAT. PROD.	.783229	.765153	.740417	.724270	.703115
TOTAL INVST/GR.NAT.PR.	.160304	.177981	.202877	.220958	.243123
SAVINGS/GR. NAT. PROD.	.130292	.149377	.175873	.196135	.219879

Finally the national income accounts for each of the five years are summarized in Table 4.20. Since government expenditure in the solution represents only the consumption by government, value added by the government must be added in calculating the national income. This component is assumed to be a fixed proportion of government consumption. Total investment includes inventory change, fixed investment, and replacement. To the extent that restoration is not distinguished from new capacity creation in the solution, replacements are understated and fixed investments are overstated in this table. The net national product is also overstated in the table by the same amount. The total investment requirements for the Plan period add up to Rs. 18,218.72 crores for the 96 per cent level of Third Plan targets. This corresponds to a net investment requirement of about Rs. 13,700 crores, of which Rs. 2322 crores are for inventories and Rs. 11,400 crores for fixed investment. This estimate of total investment depends only on the capital coefficients, inventory coefficients, initial and terminal capital, and capital-in-process. It would change if any one of these changes. It is not dependent on the assumption of any particular lag structure, or of any particular composition of private consumption, or on the assumption of the fixed composition of consumption. For comparison, the estimate of investment requirements for the Third Plan targets in the official documents on a net basis is Rs. 10,400 crores, of which Rs. 9600 crores were for fixed and Rs. 800 crores were for inventory investment.

The domestic savings ratios in Table 4.20 are gross investment over gross national product and are average rates. Even though the savings rates would be considered high by Indian standards, especially in the later years, the solution provides for increases in per capita private consumption in the first, fourth, and fifth years and maintains the per capita consumption levels in the second and third years. Since the savings and investment requirements of the targets have been the focus of considerable discussion in India, we shall return to this issue again.

4.1.3 Alternative Solutions for the Third Plan

A single solution, while it may provide many insights, is not a complete planning exercise or test of a plan. Thorough evaluation of a plan requires exploration not only of sensitivity to changes in technical coefficients and behavioral assumptions, but also of the effects of alternative policy constraints.

As pointed out previously, not all the social and economic policy objectives of a plan can be embodied in one solution or even in one model. Operation of the model requires, however, that the social welfare objectives considered, as well as technical and behavioral parameters, must be specified explicitly. Some of the alternative solutions will explore the significance of changes in these parameters. All the parameters are subject to errors of estimation; this is also true of the initial conditions. In addition, some of these quantities are subject to policy influences and are therefore, to some extent, a matter of choice. The sensitivity tests will include investigation of changes in the international aid and trade conditions of the system as well. The alternative solutions also help in interpretation of the behavior of the model.

Table 4.21 shows some of the major magnitudes obtained from the Third Plan Target Model solutions that were carried out with alternative constraints and parameters.

Third plan targets kept at 100 per cent levels. Solution T-1, the first attempt at a solution with all Third Plan targets was infeasible as reported. In Calculations T-2, T-3, and T-4, the set of lower capital-output ratios and lower inventory coefficients given in the alternative tables of Chapter 3 were tried, but no feasible solution with all Third Plan targets could be found. Infeasibility of solution with 100 per cent of the Third Plan targets means that there is simply not enough capacity to create the additional capital required, even if aggregate consumption is reduced to zero. With three-year investment lags, the maximum capacities in all the sectors are prescribed for the first three years by the initial conditions. Moreover, investments must be started, at the latest, by the third year to meet the target capacity levels at the beginning of the sixth year. Thus, given the targets, the three-year gestation lags, and other constraints, technical feasibility is determined by the initial conditions of capacity and capital-in-process. Though our own estimates of initial conditions are conjectural, in principle they are determined by prior events. Investment lags, on the other hand, are not immutable but may, to some extent, be reduced by special efforts to increase the efficiency of implementation. A solution with shorter investment gestation lags helps in evaluating the significance of such a potential improvement.

In Solution T-5 the set of shorter investment gestation lags shown in Table 3.14 are used along with lower capital and inventory coefficients. In this case, a solution has been obtained with undiscounted consumption of Rs. 71,832 crores. The performance of Solution T-5 is striking when compared with the infeasibility of the prior solutions. In this case the most important changes in the lag structure are in the reduction of the gestation period for Construction from three years to one year, and in the reduction of the three-year lag in Cement and Nonmetals to two years. As a result, a wider range of capacities can be achieved by the end of the Plan period in these sectors. Furthermore, in the sectors with a two-year gestation lag, new investments may be started as late as the third year in order for them to mature in time for production in the fifth year. As a result, critical shortages are relieved more quickly, and substantial additional consumption can be created. The high shadow price of Cement and Nonmetals that was observed in the Reference Solution is eliminated in Solution T-5, and the consumption growth constraints in the second and third years are no longer binding.

The total gross investment associated with Solution T-5, with 100 per cent of targets, is Rs. 19,171 crores, which is even higher than the Reference Solution's

Table 4.21. Alternative Target Model Solutions for Third Plan

Solutions		Private Consumption				Gross National Product		Gross Domestic Savings/GNP		Total Gross Investment
Solutions With 100% Level of Third Plan Targets		Dis-counted Sum	Un-discounted Sum	In First Year	In Fifth Year	In First Year	In Fifth Year	In First Year	In Fifth Year	Over Five Years
T-1	Reference s, b, and lags					INFEASIBLE				
T-2	Reference s and lags; lower capital-output ratios b					INFEASIBLE				
T-3	Reference lags and capital-output ratios; lower inventory co-efficients s					INFEASIBLE				
T-4	Reference lags; lower s and b					INFEASIBLE				
T-5	Shorter lags; lower s and b	59517	71832	13357	15260	16908	22029	.1248	.2320	19171
Solutions With 96% Level of Third Plan Targets										
T-6	Reference Solution: Social discount rate w = 10% $C(t+1) \geqslant 1.025\,C(t)$	57828	69846	13049	15124	16660	21511	.1303	.2199	19218
T-7	Social discount rate w = 0%	69846	69846	13049	15124	16660	21511	.1303	.2199	19218
T-8	Social discount rate w = 20%	49451	69844	13050	15124	16662	21511	.1303	.2199	19218
T-9	$C(t+1) \geqslant C(t)$	58128	70133	13286	15124	16915	21511	.1293	.2199	19223
T-10	$C(t+1) \geqslant 1.05\,C(t)$	57221	69252	12533	15234	16134	21498	.1339	.2143	19212
T-11	Initial capacity in Cement and Nonmetals increased by 5%	58550	70660	13237	15138	16920	21429	.1325	.2163	19167
T-12	Initial capacity in Construction increased by 5%	58055	70101	13119	15125	16131	21509	.1309	.2198	19190
T-13	All initial capacities increased by 10%	66508	80654	14633	18644	18415	23149	.1271	.1230	16909
T-14	All initial capacities reduced by 10%					INFEASIBLE				
T-15	Capital-output ratio in Agriculture increased to 2.5 from 1.5					INFEASIBLE				
T-16	Capital-output ratio in Agriculture decreased to 1.0 from 1.5	59603	72163	13275	16245	16920	22084	.1303	.1894	18629
T-17	Capital-output ratio in Housing reduced to 7.5 from 10.0	58864	71064	13244	15206	16916	21519	.1319	.2164	19002
T-18	Lower b; capital-output ratios in Housing and Agriculture 7.5 and 1.0, respectively	59807	72473	13269	16637	16881	22297	.1286	.1796	18444
T-19	Reference lags, lower s, and lower capital-output ratios in Agriculture and Housing	60841	73713	13377	16540	16893	22301	.1270	.1778	17629
T-20	Shorter lags, lower s, and lower capital-output ratios in Agriculture and Housing	61568	74662	13377	16912	16958	22373	.1262	.1700	17636
T-21	Shorter lags and lower s	59947	72435	13377	15736	16960	21739	.1263	.2000	18261
T-22	NFCI increased by 25% to Rs. 625.0 crores per year	59209	71470	13342	15350	16937	21589	.1272	.2123	19200
T-23	NFCI increased by 50% to Rs. 750.0 crores per year	59735	72177	13377	15777	16912	21717	.1239	.1972	19260
T-24	NFCI increased by 100% to Rs. 1000.0 crores per year	60288	72893	13377	16001	16716	21673	.1136	.1853	19430
T-25	NFCI reduced by 25% to Rs. 375.0 crores per year	52640	63748	11771	14867	15051	21317	.1222	.2249	19143
T-26	NFCI reduced to 0					INFEASIBLE				
T-27	No competitive import ceilings	59173	71522	12989	15618	16233	21179	.1453	.2071	9246
T-28	NFCI increased by 100% to Rs. 1000.0 crores per year; no import ceilings	60725	73495	13377	16247	16671	21710	.1412	.1984	19343
T-29	Intraplan export growth rate reduced by 1% to 3%	57745	69755	13019	15131	16623	21509	.1301	.2195	19218
T-30	Intraplan export growth rate increased by 1% to 5%	57947	69973	13094	15117	16715	21512	.1305	.2203	19219
Solutions with P.P.D. Output Estimates as Targets										
T-31	Reference b, s, and lags	59352	71769	13256	15928	16909	21447	.1308	.1800	17956
T-32	Reference s and lags; lower b	60264	73116	13279	17095	16896	22134	.1288	.1528	17336
T-33	lower b and s; shorter lags	61987	75270	13377	17480	16958	22548	.1262	.1513	17175

Rs. 19,218 crores. Even so, private consumption in solution T-5 is higher in every year than private consumption in the Reference Solution, and the additional freedom provided by the shorter gestation lags is effective in eliminating the bottlenecks much sooner. Idle capacities are reduced to less than 3 per cent of the sum of the sectoral capacities in the first three years and below 1 per cent in the last two years.

The striking performance of Solution T-5 emphasizes the importance of investment lags in the growth process and the need to treat intersectoral and intertemporal relationships explicitly. If there were no investment lags, fixed capital could be constructed and used in the same period in amounts limited only by availability of other nonproducible resources. Associated with each particular set of investment gestation lags and a set of initial capacities is a feasible space of target stocks that can be achieved at the end of T years. Investment gestation lags become crucial only when the stipulated target stocks are close to this feasible surface. This solution provides a good example of the usefulness of the Target Model in determining those characteristics of the economy that are critical for the achievement of a particular set of targets.

Social discount rate varied. Solution T-6 with 96 per cent of Third Plan targets is the Reference Solution with a discount rate of 10 per cent and has been already described. Solutions T-7 and T-8 with social discount rates of 0 per cent and 20 per cent, respectively, indicate the insensitivity of the model solutions to social discount rates over this range. This is to be expected in a linear model that would "flip" the concentration of consumption from one end of the time span to the other only at some critical discount rate. In the present examples, the optimal program is the same for discount rates of 0 per cent and 10 per cent and differs by only one activity from the optimal program for discount rate 20 per cent. This indicates that the critical discount rate is greater than 20 per cent for the Third Plan economy as described by the model parameters. Moreover, given the high levels of investment required by the targets, the social discount rate can be of only marginal importance in the intertemporal allocation of investment, which will be mainly determined by technical production conditions.

Consumption growth rate requirements varied. In Target Model Solutions T-9 and T-10, the constraints on the rate of growth of private consumption are varied. The relaxation of the minimum rate of growth from 2.5 to 0 per cent in Solution T-9 absorbs some of the idle capital present in all sectors in the Reference Solution for the second year. This happens because it is now possible to provide some additional consumption in the first and second years without having to provide even more of it in the third year. However, the consumption growth constraint is still binding between the second and the third years but is no longer binding between the first and the second years.

An annual growth rate of 5 per cent in aggregate consumption provides roughly a 2.5 per cent annual increase in per capita consumption. Imposing this requirement in Solution T-10 reduces the value of the maximand, since the solution can meet the constraint only by lowering the initial level of consumption. The growth constraint now becomes binding for the last four years.[6] Private consumption is lower in the first, second, and fourth years than in the Reference

---

[6]Since $\overline{C(O)} = 0$ in this case also, the constraint is inoperative in the first year.

Solution but higher in the third and the fifth years. The lower consumption in the second year releases Cement and Nonmetals, which are used as inputs to Construction. Investment increases in the second year and idle capacity in Cement and Nonmetals is eliminated, though total idle capacity in the second year is increased.

Initial capacities varied. In Target Model Solutions T-11, T-12, T-13, and T-14, the initial capacities and therefore the total capacities available to the system are adjusted directly to test the effects of possible errors in the measurement of the initial capital endowments. There have been suggestions that substantial excess capacity has existed in Indian industry, and in some sectors, as for example in Construction, capacity is particularly difficult to define and measure. Changes in initial capacities also help in interpreting the shadow prices. These prices on capital and initial endowments indicate the effects on the maximand of marginal changes in the effective capital available to the economy. Their usefulness as indicators of the effects of substantial changes is tested in this next set of solutions. The Target Model Reference Solution indicated that Cement and Nonmetals was the primary bottleneck in the early periods. In Solution T-11 the initial capacity in Cement and Nonmetals is increased by 5 per cent. This increase leads to an increase in fixed capital in Cement and Nonmetals of about Rs. 22.0 crores. An additional unit of capital in the first period is worth the shadow rental price in the first period plus the shadow price of new capital in the second period. Applying shadow prices of the Reference Solution, the additional capital appears to be worth 22.0 X (24.9 + 135.2) or Rs. 3522.2 crores to the maximand. In fact however, the actual increase in the maximand in solution T-11 is 58,550 − 57,828 or Rs. 722 crores.

This result is of some intrinisic interest. If the feasibility surface of the Target Model were, like the maximand and the constraints and relationships which generate it, continuously linear, the calculations using the Reference Solution shadow prices would have provided a good approximation to the results of the change in initial capacities. However, with many sectors of changing importance over a number of time periods, the model generates a feasibility surface broken into many facets, somewhat as if the basic relationships were nonlinear. In the same manner as in a nonlinear model, the shadow prices can be used only for the evaluation of marginal changes.

The additional initial capacity in Solution T-11 eliminates the Cement and Nonmetals bottleneck; no longer is there idle capacity in the second year in Agriculture or in Cement and Nonmetals. The shadow rental price of capital in Cement and Nonmetals in the third year falls to 0.50 from 128.38 in the Reference Solution. Now however, the solution runs into Construction capacity limitations, and the rental price of Construction capital in the third period rises to a maximum of 144.7 from 4.14 in the third period Reference Solution.

In the Reference Solution it seemed that if the shortage in Cement and Nonmetals could be relieved, the over-all performance of the solution would substantially improve. Everything seemed then to hang on one peg. And so it did. In a linear model, the critical constraints at the optimal vertex always dominate the solution. Yet it should be remembered that one is always at a vertex in a linear programming solution. Depending upon the shape of the transformation surface at the vertex, the shifts in prices may be relatively larger or smaller than the shifts in quantities.

Since Construction capacity is intrinsically difficult to estimate, especially when carried on, as in India, with a variety of technologies, initial capacity in Construction is increased by 5 per cent in Solution T-12 to obtain another test of sensitivity. In this case the scarcity in Cement and Nonmetals is still binding, and only a small increase in consumption can be achieved in the first four years.

In Solution T-13 all initial capital availabilities are increased by 10 per cent. This of course is quite a drastic change, even more drastic than a 10 per cent reduction in the targets. It increases the productivity of the system in all directions at the beginning of the planning period. Overall, with the given targets, this change reduces the required rate of growth in capital stocks during the planning period from 7.2 to 5.2 per cent. As a result the total available private consumption increases by about 14 per cent over that of the Reference Solution, and the entire pattern of relative scarcities changes. The targets now become so readily achievable that the system can concentrate more of the available resources on the production of consumer goods in order to increase the value of the maximand. The capital stocks achieved in this solution are even larger than the targets in the Agriculture, Food, Clothing, and Leather, and Housing sectors. In these circumstances, the shadow prices, particularly after the first period, indicate that the relative scarcities are highest in the consumer goods sectors.

The initial capacities are reduced by 10 per cent in T-14, and no feasible solution can be found with the 96 per cent level of targets.

Capital-output ratios varied. In Target Model Solutions T-15 to T-18, capital-output ratios in the Agriculture and Housing sectors are varied. These sectors not only make important contributions to the consumer budget, but their capital-output ratios are relatively large and uncertain. The capital-output ratio in Agriculture, for example, has been variously estimated from 1.0 to 2.5. The capital-output ratio in Housing depends on the character of the housing created as well as the construction methods used.

In Solution T-15, the capital-output ratio in Agriculture is increased to 2.5 from 1.5. This requires additional investment of about Rs. 1500 crores in order to meet the Third Plan targets. No feasible solution can be found for this case.

Next, the capital-output ratio in Agriculture is reduced to 1.0 in Solution T-16. In this case the solution provides more agricultural capacity than demanded by the targets. The change in capital stock in Agriculture from the first to the sixth year is Rs. 1883 crores as compared to Rs. 2243 crores in the Reference Solution, but this capital is now much more productive. The reduction in investment in Agriculture is less than half of what it could have been if only the targeted output capacity had been met. The lowering of investment requirements releases capital goods in the first three years and breaks the Cement and Nonmetals bottleneck. There is no longer excess capacity in all the sectors in the second year. In fact, the prices are smoothed out so effectively that the price of 6.72 for Cement and Nonmetals in the second year is the highest price of any good in any period. All this occurs because demand for investment is reduced by the lowered capital-output ratio in Agriculture, which in turn reduces the strain on Cement and Nonmetals. Once the bottleneck is broken, the solution has enough freedom to provide even more capacity in Agriculture than is targeted and will do so because the value of the objective function is increased as a result.

The capital-output ratio in the Housing sector is the largest in the system. In solution T-17 this ratio is reduced to 7.5 from 10.0. The reduction can be considered as reflecting the uncertainty of estimating the value and quality of housing and consequently of estimating the capital-output ratio. Moreover, Housing is a service the consumption of which might as a matter of policy be given a low priority in an attempt at rapid industrialization. To analyze the effects of different priorities, one could lower the targets in Housing and alter the consumption proportions of the composite consumption. However, since Housing is not used as an intermediate product by any sector, a reduced capital-output ratio in Housing has the same effect.[7] Capital in Housing is all in the form of construction, and lowering its capital-output ratio reduces the demand on Construction and consequently in Cement and Nonmetals. Once again this eliminates some idle capacity. In the second year, capacity in Agriculture is fully used. The consumption growth constraint is now binding only between the fourth and fifth years. The highest shadow price is now that of Cement and Nonmetals in the third year and is 10.71.

In Solution T-18 the capital-output ratios in Housing and in Agriculture are both lowered. The increase in undiscounted consumption over the Reference Solution is Rs. 2627 crores, whereas in solutions T-16 and T-17 the increases are Rs. 2317 crores and Rs. 1218 crores, respectively. This confirms the interpretation that the changes in both Solutions T-16 and T-17 break the same bottlenecks, for otherwise the change in Solution T-18 should be closer to the sum of the changes in Solutions T-16 and T-17.

Inventory coefficients lowered. The alternative, lower inventory coefficients in Agriculture, Food, Clothing, and Leather, and Chemicals, are used along with lower capital-output ratios in Agriculture and Housing in Solution T-19. From the s matrix in Table 3.7 it is seen that lowering the inventory coefficients in the sectors primarily reduces the demand for Agriculture and Chemicals. In Solution T-18 the shadow price of Agriculture in the third year is the highest shadow price of any output and is 4.27, which makes the reduction demand for inventories especially valuable. Therefore, even though the lowered coefficients correspond to a reduction in investment in inventories of Rs. 860 crores for the five years, the increase in undiscounted consumption over Solution T-18 is Rs. 1240 crores.

Investment lags shortened. In addition to the changes in Solution T-19, investment lags are also shortened in Solution T-20. This solution thus has the most optimistic set of technical parameters investigated and results in the highest levels of private consumption. The shorter gestation lags give enough freedom to the solution to virtually eliminate idle capital as early as the third year in which less than 0.5 per cent of capital is unused. However, compared with Solution T-19, the increase in undiscounted private consumption is only Rs. 949 crores. It was pointed out discussing Solution T-5 that the structure of investment lags was important in determining the character of the adjustments and the over-all behavior. However, Solutions T-17, T-18, and T-19 indicate that this lag structure is relatively unimportant when the bottlenecks are broken by lowered demand for investment goods.

In Solution T-21, the shorter set of gestation lags and the lower inventory coefficients are used with the reference capital-output ratios. The sum of

---

[7]Except for the differences in intermediate goods requirements, which are small for Housing.

undiscounted private consumption is Rs. 72,435 crores and is Rs. 2227 crores less than in Solution T-20. This is comparable to the difference of Rs. 2627 crores between Solution T-18 and the Reference Solution, which also differ from each other in the capital-output ratios. Thus a lower demand for investment goods, which results from the lower capital-output ratios for the output of capital producing sectors, is always helpful in these solutions.

Availability of foreign exchange varied. The trial Solutions T-22 to T-30 explore the effects of changes in the availability of foreign exchange due to changes in exports or to net foreign capital inflows, including foreign aid, and of changes in the allocation of imports. In Solution T-22 when the capital inflow is increased by 25 per cent to Rs. 625 crores per year, which amounts to an increase of Rs. 625 crores for the Plan period, the sum of undiscounted private consumption increases by Rs. 1624 crores. Thus the productivity of foreign aid seems to be 1624/625 = 2.6. However, this is not necessarily the real productivity of foreign exchange in the Third Plan period. First, as pointed out in other connections, the model objective function does not make any allowance for increases in the stream of postterminal consumption over and above that provided for by the targets. Thus the additional aid may not be put to the uses that would result if such overfulfillments carried some weight. Second, the additional aid makes it possible for some of the idle capacities existing in the Reference Solution to be utilized. However, part of these idle capacities may be the result of assumptions of fixed composition of consumption or of fixed investment lags. To the extent that these assumptions can be modified in reality, the decrease in idle capital that results when additional foreign exchange becomes available is overstated. Even though idle capacities are not substantial in the Reference Solution, they may be quite important in determining marginal productivity of foreign capital. Finally, the savings rates of the model solutions are substantially higher than those actually observed; therefore, in these solutions the value of foreign exchange is lower than if the savings rates were constrained to lower levels. Nonetheless, the changes made in foreign exchange availability provide useful insights into the effects of additional aid under a variety of alternative circumstances.

For Solution T-22, in which the inflow of foreign capital is increased by 25 per cent, the shadow prices on the foreign exchange balance constraints for the first three years are higher than the corresponding prices in the Reference Solution. This curious behavior is the result of the fact that the shadow prices reflect the value of relaxing only one constraint at a time.[8] However, in Solution T-22 the foreign exchange availability is changed in all five years simultaneously and not just in one year.

In Solution T-24, the inflow of foreign capital is increased by Rs. 500 crores per year to Rs. 1000 crores per year, and as a result, the private consumption over five years increases by Rs. 3037 crores. Compared with Solution T-22, for an additional exchange of Rs. 1875 crores, an increase in private consumption of only Rs. 1413 crores is realized. There are two particularly important reasons why private consumption does not increase by at least as much as the additional exchange. Imports are not permitted in all the sectors whose outputs make up the

[8]Furthermore, the additional foreign exchange creates opportunities for greater increases in consumption than originally existed.

composite consumption good. Moreover, the ceilings on competitive imports force imports in sectoral proportions not consistent with the composition of private consumption. This makes it necessary to supplement imports with domestic production not only in the nonimporting sectors, but also to some degree in most of the importing sectors. In Solution T-24 there is more idle capital in all but the second year than in the Reference Solution. The import ceilings, it will be recalled, simulate diminishing marginal returns to imports in the various sectors and simulate other restrictions on import allocations. If the simulation is an accurate one, the import restrictions, though carrying high shadow prices, will lead to realistic import allocations.

The effects of reduction in the inflow of foreign exchange is much more dramatic, as is seen in Solution T-25 where foreign exchange inflow is set at Rs. 375 crores per year, a reduction of 25 per cent from the Reference Solution. This loss in foreign exchange of Rs. 625 crores over five years leads to a reduction in private consumption of Rs. 6098 crores. In Solution T-26 the foreign capital inflow was reduced to zero, and no feasible solution could be found. In the conditions of the present solutions, aid is more a big stick than a carrot; it is more damaging when withdrawn than it is beneficial when increased. Before this is interpreted as demonstrating India's dependence on aid givers or as a support for import substitution policies, the same qualifications as were made in interpreting the productivity of additional foreign exchange must be recognized. In Solution T-25, where aid is reduced, there are large amounts of idle capacities in the three major consumption sectors, Agriculture, Housing, and Others and Margin, in the first four years. In the real world where consumption and input proportions are not so rigidly fixed, at least some of these idle capacities would have been used to generate additional consumption. However, the fact of these idle capacities is suggestive. The idle capacities in consumer sectors exist because the investment requirements of the targets are so high that in order to reach the targets they exhaust the capacities in Mining and Metals and in Equipment. As a result, there is no capacity left in these two sectors with which to make their proportionate contribution to the composite consumption good.

Import allocations varied. Solution T-27 shows an addition of Rs. 1676 crores in private consumption over the Reference Solution due to the elimination of ceilings on competitive imports. The shadow prices on the foreign exchange balance constraints are higher, since foreign exchange can now be allocated to more profitable uses. Idle capacities are reduced, and in the fourth and fifth years they are completely eliminated. Yet it does not follow from this result that the distribution of imports during the Third Plan Period could have been improved. The distribution of imports enforced in the Reference Solution is not necessarily that which actually prevailed. In addition, a different allocation of imports might be optimal for the 96 per cent level of targets than for the 100 per cent level of targets if the latter were achievable.

In Solution T-28 the ceilings on competitive imports are again removed, and a level of foreign capital inflow of Rs. 1000 crores per year is assumed. The idle capital in this case is greatly reduced, since it is no longer necessary to adjust capacities to imports, but instead competitive imports, at least, can be adjusted to capacity. The additional private consumption generated by the increased foreign exchange inflow in this case should be compared to Solution T-27. For Rs. 1875 crores of additional foreign exchange an increase of Rs. 1875 crores of consumption is obtained in T-28.

Export projections varied. In Solutions T-29 and T-30 the growth rates for the export projections are varied. Beginning with the same level of exports as in the Reference Solution in the first years, exports are projected for subsequent years at 3 per cent and 5 per cent annual growth rates, respectively, in the two solutions, whereas in the Reference Solution they are projected at 4 per cent. The lower export growth rate of Solution T-29 corresponds to a fall of Rs. 47 crores in exports for the five years as compared to the case in the Reference Solution, and as a consequence a decrease of Rs. 91 crores in private consumption occurs. In Solution T-30, for a relative rise in exports of Rs. 76 crores, an increase of Rs. 127 crores in private consumption takes place. Even though producing additional exports requires domestic resources, the foreign exchange earned is more valuable in terms of the objective function. This means that the domestic resources used for exports in fixed proportions are less valuable than the imports increased in not quite so fixed proportions.

Targets based on 1964 estimates of Third Plan achievements. One important and basic test of the model is whether or not a feasible solution can be found for a set of conditions that have actually prevailed. In the present circumstances this test cannot be made rigorously, simply because it is impossible to describe, from the data available, "a set of conditions that have actually prevailed" in the detail necessary. However, an exercise is carried out using some relevant information in order to indicate the problems involved.

As pointed out previously, information is not available on the initial capacities with which the Plan period started at the beginning of 1961 or on the unfinished capital-in-process available at that time. To provide some numbers we made the same assumptions in this test as in the other solutions: that the Third Plan Targets had been fully foreseen and planned for in the last years of the Second Plan and that growth in each sector in the last year of the Second Plan was at the rates foreseen in the Third Plan targets. For terminal conditions it was necessary to rely on the estimates, made in 1964 in the P.P.D. *Notes,* of the levels of output likely to be achieved in 1965-66, the last year of the Third Plan. These estimates were incomplete in several respects however. To estimate the capacities actually available at the end of the Plan from these likely achievements, we extrapolated the growth rates implicit in the likely achievements as compared to the initial conditions. This was also the procedure used in order to estimate the uncompleted capital-in-process intended for the Fourth Plan period. The projections in the P.P.D. *Notes* of 1965-66 output levels were adjusted to an eleven-sector basis from Table 3.26 and used as targets in Solutions T-31, T-32, and T-33. These solutions cannot be considered as simulating the Third Plan period for several reasons. Among the most obvious is that these 1965-66 output levels are not the targets pursued from the beginning of the Plan. They are output levels projected after a variety of revisions and adjustments in the targets, including those made necessary by the conflict with China in 1962. For this reason, if for no other, one would expect the model to perform better than the real world economy in terms of the output and consumption levels achieved.

Table 4.22 shows the national income accounts for Solution T-31 where the reference sets of gestation lags, inventory coefficients, and capital coefficients are

Table 4.22. National Income Accounts for Third Plan Target Model Solution T-31 (Rs. crores, 1959-60 prices)

	1961-62	1962-63	1963-64	1964-65	1965-66
CONSUMPTION	13256.390381	13668.243896	14177.337891	14738.684204	15928.317871
INVENTORIES CHANGE	202.250355	366.767223	443.804562	526.151070	515.829063
FIXED INVESTMENT	1892.778564	2114.158051	2523.078186	2967.386810	3314.911072
TOTAL INVESTMENT	2712.163788	3141.597687	3596.116180	4144.231079	4361.776672
GCVERNMENT EXPENDITURE	540.999992	560.999985	581.999985	601.999985	621.999985
VALUE ADDED BY GOVT.	899.753296	933.015884	967.941612	1001.204216	1034.466812
EXPORTS	653.986908	680.986359	707.985817	735.985260	764.984688
IMPORTS	1153.986603	1190.986084	1207.985413	1235.985016	1264.984360
GROSS NATIONAL PRODUCT	16909.307373	17803.857422	18823.395020	19986.119141	21446.561279
REPLACEMENT	617.134895	660.672424	629.233467	650.693260	531.036606
NET NATIONAL PRODUCT	16292.172363	17143.184814	18194.161377	19335.425781	20915.524658
SAVINGS	2212.163788	2641.597687	3096.116180	3644.231079	3861.776672
GROSS NAT. OUTPUT	21522.492676	22756.053955	24251.706055	25921.120361	27985.071289
INTERMEDIATE PRODUCT	5512.934265	5925.209229	6396.248962	6936.205322	7572.980469
CONS./GROSS NAT. PROD.	.783970	.767712	.753176	.737446	.742698
TOTAL INVST/GR.NAT.PR.	.160395	.176456	.191045	.207355	.203379
SAVINGS/GR. NAT. PRCD.	.130825	.148372	.164482	.182338	.180065

ACTUAL CONSUMPTION IN 1960-61	12604.9*
ACTUAL GROSS NATIONAL PRODUCT IN 1960-61	16037.0*

*From Table 3.2

used. The level of private consumption and the gross national product in the first year are 5 per cent and 5.5 per cent above the respective levels in the year 1960-61. The private consumption and the gross national product in the fifth year are slightly higher than estimated in the P.P.D. *Notes.* The gross savings rate in 1961-62 at 0.1308 is only slightly higher than in 1960-61 at 0.1270 as implied in Table 3.2, the I.S.I. input-output table.

The total investment in the five years, however, is Rs. 17,955 crores. In the solution, the target for Agriculture has been overachieved and about Rs. 450 crores of investment need not have been made to reach the estimated level of output. Subtracting an additional Rs. 4500 crores for replacement, this leaves Rs. 13,000 crores for net investment. This investment is higher than envisioned in the Third Plan, even though the targets are actually lower than the original targets. It is also substantially higher than estimates of the actual investment achieved during the Third Plan period, which range around Rs. 9500 crores. Solution T-31 thus presents an apparent paradox; its estimates of investment requirements are higher than actually realized for the set of target capacities actually achieved. This may be explained, however, by one or more of the following possibilities:

1. The levels of investment calculated in the solution may be in error, because the initial conditions and/or terminal conditions have not been correctly stipulated. It is difficult at this point to know what targets were in fact achieved. The arbitrary adjustments made in order to achieve full coverage of the 1965 outputs and to stipulate the initial and final amounts of capital-in-process should be recalled at this point. In addition, of the total net investment carried out in Solution T-31, Rs. 3484 crores are for the purpose of raising capacities from those producing the likely achievements output in the last year to those existing at the *end* of the last Plan year. An additional Rs. 2295 crores of investment are provided to create the unfinished capital-in-process for the early years of the Fourth Plan. The initial conditions for solution also provide Rs. 1757 crores of unfinished capital at its outset. It seems likely to us that these three figures, and particularly the first two, substantially overestimate what was actually done and the result is an overestimate of the

investment and savings requirements of the likely achievements. The problem is again not intrinsic to the model but due to uncertainty about basic data.

2. The investment calculated in the solution may also be overestimated if the real ratios of fixed capital and inventories to output are lower than the ones used in the solution. If lower ratios were used in a trial solution, even more private consumption could be provided than in Solution T-31, but the investment necessary would be lowered. The value of the maximand would be even further above that actually achieved, though as pointed out, the lower actual level of achievement might be explained by the relative efficiency and foresightedness in the model.

3. The levels of investment calculated for the levels of output expected to be achieved may be closer to a correct representation of reality than the official projections. The "facts" themselves contain elements of conjecture, and the P.P.D. output and investment estimates for 1965-66 are presented only as likely achievements.

4. The accounting used may not be completely comparable to that of the official statistics or the P.P.D. estimates. There is some evidence of noncomparability in the various sources used, and we are not confident that the variances have been entirely eliminated.

Solution T-32 with lower capital coefficients and Solution T-33 with lower inventory and capital coefficients as well as shorter lags indicate even more optimistic performance than does Solution T-31.

4.2 Analysis of Target Model Solutions for the Third Plan

The alternative solutions of the Target Model for the Third Plan period provide a variety of insights from which we shall now try to extract some summary judgments as to the technical and operational feasibility of the Third Plan targets.

On the issue of technical feasibility, as defined above, the results can be summarized as follows: The Third Plan targets were technically *feasible,* if (1) the shorter investment lags, the lower capital coefficients, and the lower inventory coefficients prevailed, and (2) all other coefficients, parameters, and exogenous quantities used were reliable representations of reality. The Third Plan targets were technically *infeasible,* if (1) the three-year investment lags described reality, (2) the reference capital coefficients and the reference inventory coefficients prevailed, and (3) all other coefficients, parameters, and exogenous quantities used were reliable.

The significance of the initial endowments, i.e., the capacities and amounts of capital-in-process, might be overlooked in the customary concern with capital-output ratios and gestation lags. It will be recalled that to establish these, we assumed that the outputs of the pre-Plan year, i.e., the last year of the Second Plan, represented full use of available capacity, that sectoral capacities grew in the pre-Plan year at the average annual rates implicit in the Third Plan targets, and that the capital-in-process started in the last two years of the Second Plan was adequate to maintain these growth rates in the Third Plan period itself.

The existence of excess capacity in Indian industry has been a matter of considerable conjectural discussion, as have been the issues related to the phasing of successive Plans. If in the sectors that were bottlenecks in the solutions there was usable excess capacity, or if our procedures, which were intended to be generous, underestimated the initial capital-in-process the foregoing conclusions would have to be modified. The exact amount by which these initial conditions would have to change in order to affect the outcome of the solutions would again depend on the other coefficients and parameters assumed.

The data available to us do not permit a more definitive judgment on these issues. It is worth noting however, that if our assumptions regarding the initial conditions are warranted, 25 per cent of the total net investment programmed during the Second Plan would have been for the purpose of creating capacity used only during the Third Plan. Based on this and on more general and intuitive impressions, we believe that our errors with respect to initial capacities have in general been in the direction of overestimation.

Even if the issue of technical feasibility is decided favorably, all the problems of operational feasibility remain. We shall not enter into a discussion of the adequacy of the organizational structure to implement the Plan, or the availability of the required skills of all types. Though we would emphasize their importance in a comprehensive evaluation, our technique tells us nothing on such matters. However, it does yield information on another crucial aspect of feasibility: the investment and savings required to realize the targets.

Table 4.23 summarizes four estimates of total investment requirements. Shown first are the official estimates of the Third Five Year Plan document, which, on a net basis, come to Rs. 10,400 crores, of which Rs. 9600 crores are fixed investment, and Rs. 800 crores are inventory investment. We could not find a comprehensive estimate of replacement requirements.[9]

The second estimate in Table 4.23 applies a conventional technique of multiplying projected increments in output in each sector by a sectoral capital-output ratio and summing. This appears to have been a commonly used procedure in preparing the Indian Plans. Line 2.1 is the conventional capital-output ratio calculation of investment requirements. It contains an adjustment to obtain the investment requirement for the actual Plan period. The capacity on hand at the beginning of the Plan period was greater than that which produced the output levels of the pre-Plan period, $X_i(0)$, by the amount of investment maturing during the pre-Plan period. The capacity on hand at the end of the Plan will be greater than that producing the target output levels of the fifth year by the amount of investment that matures only at the end of the last year and is available for production during the last year. The adjustment is made by applying the sectoral growth rates implicit in the Plan to each sector's output levels. Lines 2.2 and 2.3 add the net investment in fixed capital-in-process during the Plan in order to calculate total net investment in fixed capital. With the inventory investment calculated in line 2.5, it adds up to total net investment in line 2.6. When replacement is added, the total gross investment is given in line 2.8.

The third set of estimates in Table 4.23 is taken from two solutions, the Reference Solution for the 96 per cent level of Third Plan targets and Solution

---

[9]An estimate of Rs. 150 crores was made for the industrial sector as a whole as a projection of the replacement carried out in the Second Five Year Plan period. However, this was admittedly less than the replacement requirements estimated for the cotton, jute, and woolen textile industries alone. See *Third Five Year Plan,* Government of India, Planning Commission, p.460.

Table 4.23. Alternative Calculations of Third Plan Investment Requirements (Rs. crores, 1959-60 prices)

		Reference Solution Parameters, 96% of Targets	Third Plan Targets, Lower s, b, Shorter Lags	1965-66 Likely Achievements
1.0	Third Five Year Plan			
1.1	Net Fixed Investment	9,600		
1.2	Inventory Accumulation	800		
1.3	Total Net Investment	10,400		
2.0	Incremental Calculation of Investment Requirements			
2.1	$\Sigma b_i [\overline{X_i(5)}(1 + \alpha_i(5)) - \overline{X_i(0)}(1 + \alpha_i(0))]^{*}$	11,031	11,734	9,616
2.2	Terminal Capital-in-Process	2,732	2,176	2,237
2.3	Initial Capital-in-Process	1,637	1,034	1,637
2.4	Net Fixed Investment	12,126	12,876	10,216
2.5	Inventory Investment $\sum_i s_i [\overline{X_i(5)}(1 + \alpha_i(5)) - \overline{X_i(0)}(1 + \alpha_i(0))]$	2,324	1,614	1,981
2.6	Total Net Investment	14,450	14,490	12,197
2.7	Replacement Investment	4,768	4,752	4,768
2.8	Total Gross Investment	19,218	19,242	16,965
3.0	Investment Estimates of Target Model Solutions	Reference Solution, 96% of Targets		65-66 Likely Achievements Solution T-31
3.1	Net Fixed Investment[†]	12,374		11,691
3.2	Inventory Investment	2,324		2,054
3.3	Total Net Investment	14,698		13,745
3.4	Replacement Investment	4,520		4,209
3.5	Total Gross Investment	19,218		17,954

*The multiplication of $X_i(0)$ and $X_i(5)$ by $[1+\alpha_i(0)]$ and $[1+\alpha_i(5)]$, respectively, is necessary in order to estimate output levels producible at the beginning and end of the Plan period from pre-Plan and fifth year output levels.

†Adjusted for replacement investments in Transport and Housing.

T-31 with the 1965-66 likely achievement estimates. It can be seen that these estimates are roughly the same as those based on the projected increments in output and the use of capital-output ratios. The small differences are due to the fact that replacements are sometimes not made in the solutions, whereas in the calculation on line 2.7 they are all assumed to be made. However, the model solutions provide complete details on the sectoral amounts, timing, and uses of investment.

It may be recalled that the investment estimates of the Target Model are to a considerable degree independent of the optimizing mechanism. The calculation of the investment, required solely to meet the Plan output targets, does not depend on the optimizing mechanism in any way and can be regarded as taking place independently. The distribution of that investment over the planning period will be directed by the optimizing mechanism in a manner permitting the maximum amount of consumption to be produced with the given resources. If at all possible, it will generate additional investment to further increase capacity in order to produce additional consumption goods. In the Reference Solution however, the targets are so high as to allow the solution virtually no opportunity to divert resources to producing even more investment than set by the targets in order to increase consumption goods output within the Plan period. In addition, a solution of the Target Model might call for more investment than a simple incremental calculation, such as that of line 2.3 in Table 4.23, would indicate if the sectoral composition of the targets is unbalanced. That is, the targets may prescribe a level of output for one of the capital producing sectors that is below the actual levels needed if the other sectoral targets are to be achieved. In fact, that appears to be the case in Construction in the Reference Solution. However, the overachievement in Construction is quite small.

The second and third sets of estimates in Table 4.23 show investment requirements that are higher for the 96 per cent level of targets than the planned investment for the 100 per cent level of targets. The differences may arise from discrepancies in any of the elements in the computations. We have mentioned the problems in estimating initial conditions. There are similar problems in estimating terminal conditions. The Plan calculations may have used different capital coefficients, and this in turn may have been due to its projection of increasing returns not embodied in our model and parameters.

The differences may also reflect some lack of comparability in the estimates of the Plan and of the target solutions here, as was suggested by Solution T-31 with the P.P.D. estimates of 1965-66 likely outputs as targets. The 1960-61 gross savings rate in the I.S.I. input-output table, Table 3.2, is 12.8 per cent. The net savings-income rate for the period 1961-63 is estimated by the Reserve Bank[10] at 9.5 per cent. However, the P.P.D. *Notes* give for 1960-61 a gross savings rate of 9.9 per cent.

A comparison of the amounts of investment and saving calculated to be necessary to achieve the Third Plan Targets, or even 96 per cent of them, with the investment and saving actually planned indicates that the Plan was operationally infeasible as the result of an inconsistency between required and planned investment. However, a full answer to the question of operational feasibility, even in the narrow sense considered here, cannot be found in any single solution but requires the interpretation of all the calculations, primarily because of uncertainty as to the "facts." For example, the targets in the model calculations include investment for postterminal growth, while in the Third Plan itself the proposed magnitude of such investment is not explicit. If the objective were only the achievement of the final year's output targets, the model calculations would be quite different and investment requirements would be much lower. In addition, in basing an answer to the question of operational feasibility on the model calculations, it is necessary to assess the significance of errors in estimation of the parameters. Yet, while it is virtually certain that there are such errors in the model's solutions, as in other calculations, it is not an adequate criticism of the solutions to point them out. Their significance must be judged, and the alternative solutions are intended to help in this respect.

There is one potentially significant, contrary indication with respect to the investment and savings implications of the Third Plan targets. This is Solution T-31, for the output levels projected as likely to be achieved in 1965-66, which throws doubt on the Target Model calculations. As we pointed out in the

[10]See *Reserve Bank of India Bulletin,* March 1965, p. 327.

discussion of this solution, it is not difficult to explain the higher levels of consumption that it provides as compared to those achieved in reality. However, if the projected output levels or a close approximation to them have been achieved, and the rough estimates of investment actually carried out are also correct, the investment requirements calculated in the Target Model solution are clearly too high. If that is the case, the calculated investment requirements of the Third Plan targets might also be much too high and the conclusions based on those calculations unwarranted. Yet, as pointed out in the discussion of Solution T-31, there is considerable doubt as to what the achievements actually were, with particular respect to the final year's capacities and the unfinished capital-in-process provided for the beginning of the Fourth Plan. We are also inclined to believe that we have been unduly optimistic with respect to the unfinished capital-in-process available at the beginning of the Third Plan. Adjustments to the initial and terminal conditions could go far toward reconciling the discrepancies left between actual achievements and the model calculations in Solution T-31. Differences between estimated and actual parameters could account for the remainder of the differences.

It is not merely the existence of inconsistencies between the investment calculations of the Plans and those of the Target Model Reference Solution that leads us to doubt the operational feasibility of the Plans, but also the size of the discrepancies. Even substantial adjustments in coefficients, as investigated in the alternative solutions to the Target Model, did not change the general character of the results. Among the lessons to be learned from the solutions is an enhanced appreciation of the difficulties of coming to judgments about a plan when complete specifications are not available and the facts themselves are debatable. Though the Target Model calculations raise doubts as to the technical and operational feasibility of the Third Plan targets, we would stress again the tentative character of the results.

Finally our judgment with respect to the Third Plan should not be misconstrued as a denigration of the Indian development effort. The sacrifices made in India in the name of economic development as measured by average and marginal savings rates have been far beyond those of relatively richer countries. It is just because these sacrifices are so heavy that the efficient use of the resources is imperative.

4.3 Target Model Solutions for a Set of Proposed Fourth Plan Targets

4.3.1 Assumptions for the Fourth Plan Target Model Solutions

A set of targets for the Fourth Five Year Plan was proposed in the P.P.D. *Notes*. These will be the subject of the next set of solutions and analyses. It should be emphasized that the proposals contained in the P.P.D. *Notes* were for discussion and did not represent a final and officially adopted set of targets for the Fourth Plan period. Yet, the P.P.D. *Notes* contain the only set of proposed Fourth Plan targets that was published when this manuscript was prepared and was sufficiently comprehensive to form a basis for analysis.[11]

---

[11]Subsequently the beginning of the Fourth Plan was postponed and a different set of targets has been recommended for the Fourth Plan. The Fourth Plan Period referred to here is the one originally foreseen, 1966-67 to 1970-71.

The analysis of the Fourth Plan targets proceeds along lines similar to the analysis of the Third Plan and, since the results are generally similar in character, can be summarized more briefly. This analysis is even more tentative than that for the Third Plan, however, as neither the initial conditions nor the terminal targets can be as firmly specified as in the Third Plan analysis. Most of the information on initial conditions and targets is taken from the P.P.D. *Notes.* The initial endowments, i.e., the set of capacities and capital-in-process at the beginning of the Fourth Plan period, are more provisional than in the case of the Third Plan, as final estimates for the Third Plan period were not available when the P.P.D. *Notes* were prepared. Furthermore, due to lack of information, our adjustment of the outputs of the organized sectors of the P.P.D. *Notes* in order to obtain a more complete coverage has had some unavoidable arbitrariness in its procedure. This adjustment is carried out on an eleven-sector as well as a thirty-two sector basis. Thus we have two alternative sets of tentative initial and target levels of outputs.

It will again be convenient to conduct the exposition in terms of a Fourth Plan Reference Solution and alternative Fourth Plan solutions with changes in parameters. The following data assumptions are used in the Reference Solution:

1. The technical coefficient matrices a, b, s, p', p'', p''', r', r'', and r''' are assumed constant throughout the Plan period and are those presented in Chapter 3 as the reference values.
2. The consumption coefficient c(t), noncompetitive import coefficients m', and competitive import ceilings m'' are also assumed constant throughout the Plan period.
3. Requirements of $\overline{E}$, $\overline{G}$, and $\overline{D}$ are specified at the levels shown in the tables of Chapter 3.
4. Net foreign capital inflow is fixed at a constant value of Rs. 500 crores per year.
5. A social discount rate of 10 per cent is used for private consumption in the objective function, i.e., w = 0.10.
6. The minimum growth rate of consumption $\rho(t)$ is set at .025, i.e. 2.5 per cent, for all periods. However, C(0) is set at 0.
7. The initial output X(0) and the terminal year output X(5) are based on the projections in the P.P.D. *Notes* for 1965-66 and 1970-71, adjusted for coverage on the eleven-sector basis as established in Table 3.26.[12] The initial and terminal growth rates are the implied growth rates between these X(0) and X(5).

Once again we might point out that the Reference Solution should not be considered as our best guess of the actual Fourth Plan outcome nor as one embodying all the assumptions of the Fourth Plan targets as set out in the P.P.D. *Notes.*

4.3.2 Reference Solution for the Fourth Plan

A feasible solution was obtained for the targets and parameters as described in the preceding section. The Reference Solution is presented in Tables 4.24 through 4.42.

---

[12]These will be referred to as the Fourth Plan targets, recognizing that they are not official in their source and have been further adjusted by us.

The sum of undiscounted private consumption over the five years from 1966-67 through 1970-71 is Rs. 80,311 crores, and the sum of discounted consumption is Rs. 66,664 crores. For comparison, the P.P.D. *Notes'* estimates of undiscounted private consumption for this period is about Rs. 90,000 crores. However, in the Reference Solution there are substantial excess capacities in all the sectors in the third and the fourth years. These excess capacities, resulting from certain rigidities in the production and consumption structure of the model, might in reality be used to provide more consumption if the rigidities are unrealistic or can be overcome.

An over-all guide to the details of the Reference Solution is provided by recognizing that in this case the availability of foreign exchange, rather than domestic capacity, sets a limit to the domestic output that can be produced in the last year of the Plan. In the final Plan year, as shown in Table 4.40, there are no competitive imports, because all the foreign exchange available is required for noncompetitive imports determined by domestic output levels, and these levels are less than domestic capacities. It should be noted that the noncompetitive import coefficients used in the Reference Solution are kept constant at the level of their 1960-61 values. If the import substitution program implied in the P.P.D. *Notes* were successful in changing the noncompetitive import coefficients, the limitations imposed on domestic production by the availability of foreign exchange could be relieved.

In this case, as in the Third Plan, Mining and Metals, Equipment, and Chemicals are planned to be the fastest-growing sectors, while the growth of the predominantly consumer goods sectors is planned at a lower rate. This is seen in Tables 4.24 and 4.27 which present gross domestic outputs and available capital stock, respectively. On the whole, the shadow prices on output in Table 4.25 also reflect this relative emphasis, but we shall return later to this table to explain some of the more striking features of the solution.

From Table 4.26 showing the details of private consumption for the five years, it is seen that the consumption growth constraint is always binding. This is an outcome, not of a flip-flop tendency to concentrate consumption at the beginning of the Plan period, but of the fact that the capacity to produce private consumption in the fifth year is limited by the availability of foreign exchange. The consumption growth constraints, acting backwards, then restrict the private consumption in the first four years. This interpretation is supported by the presence of excess capacities in all the sectors in the third and the fourth years as shown in Table 4.29.

Within the limits of the given availability of foreign exchange in the fifth year, the solution adjusts the composition of the output by altering the amounts of investment and consumption in each period to ameliorate the effects of this scarcity.

Tables 4.27 to 4.31, which summarize the formation, availability, and use of capital, throw considerable light on the forces determining the characteristics of the solution. There is capital formation in all periods, as shown by Table 4.27, but not in all sectors in every period. For example, in Mining and Metals, Equipment, Chemicals, Food, Clothing, and Leather, and Electricity, the capital available in the fourth and fifth periods is the same. There is even decumulation in Housing, and in Others and Margin in these periods, and in Mining and Metals, Food, Clothing, and Leather, and Transport in the sixth period. Tables 4.28, 4.29 and

Table 4.24. Gross Domestic Outputs and Sectoral Growth Rates, Fourth Plan Target Model Reference Solution (Rs. crores, 1959-60 prices)

SECTOR	1966-67	1967-68	1968-69	1969-70	1970-71	1971-72*	1972-73*	1973-74*
AG.PL.	8473.15637	9133.20337	9538.14990	1CC94.07532	11076.66223	12222.18103	12952.54578	13724.55518
M.M.	1292.38196	1512.08888	1662.98289	2C62.35223	2884.70416	2780.94278	3243.56958	3783.15714
EQIPMT	1932.55185	2561.72470	2704.58218	2406.79794	2922.23511	9030.62140	5965.57275	7074.28662
CHEMIC	864.19530	1212.47783	1320.64987	1546.05324	2127.62521	3755.05655	4366.14014	5076.66919
CMGLWD	640.63274	674.64535	906.02741	1C43.59969	1288.37646	1699.68082	1945.39725	2226.63596
FOODCL	3009.38214	3197.04294	3330.53479	3506.13123	3777.44830	4702.30798	5083.14954	5494.83563
ELECTR	169.10184	193.30764	209.45645	226.25267	273.61986	491.00943	558.46715	636.19259
TRANS	1209.75046	1352.72070	1467.87807	1577.20412	1887.16675	2515.03500	2825.10098	3173.39343
CONSTR	2884.93747	2430.43512	3818.61905	4302.35944	5363.02582	6316.49438	7194.03210	8193.48425
HOUS.	705.42956	741.14199	759.67049	778.66241	1028.99472	1097.23334	1169.99722
OTHMAR	6903.98206	7239.41107	7619.84601	7797.17688	8298.23474	15445.82776	17111.86304	18957.60229
SUM	28085.50073	30230.12012	33319.86768	35321.67236	40677.75977	59988.15039	62343.06934	69511.80762

*Calculated simply by dividing capital stocks by capital-output ratios. No test either of static or of dynamic consistency has been applied.

Table 4.25. Shadow Prices of Gross Domestic Outputs, Fourth Plan Target Model Reference Solution (Rs. crores)

SECTOR	1966-67	1967-68	1968-69	1969-70	1970-71
AG.PL.	.05578	.15927	.17956	.18896	2.13333
M.M.	7.15835	64.83441	13.02207	3.C7371	18.05552
EQIPMT	2.08390	4.18406	17.24518	4.19412	19.47141
CHEMIC	.8465C	2.74308	4.44350	2.2445C	19.41205
CMGLWD	.50514	1.46C93	3.19894	1.06922	1.88777
FOODCL	.13555	.43509	.61691	.36086	1.11505
ELECTR	1.01766	2.75591	7.48891	1.6535C	1.47413
TRANS	.45957	2.89C44	1.6C065	.66613	4.48507
CONSTR	.98164	6.71037	3.49707	.98165	2.57174
HOUS.	.04827	.37888	.12886	.C3776	2.29879
OTHMAR	.01995	.11C89	.07548	.C3351	.21078

Table 4.26. Private Consumption, Fourth Plan Target Model Reference Solution (Rs. crores, 1959-60 prices)

SECTOR	1966-67	1967-68	1968-69	1969-70	1970-71
AG.PL.	5926.71014	6074.87805	6226.75000	6382.41876	6541.97937
M.M.	7.18111	7.36064	7.54466	7.73327	7.92661
EQIPMT	369.13977	378.36827	387.82748	397.52317	407.46125
CHEMIC	459.13287	470.61120	482.37648	494.4359C	506.79681
CMGLWD	89.99310	92.24293	94.54900	96.91273	99.33555
FOODCL	2187.64209	2242.33316	2298.39151	2355.85129	2414.74762
ELECTR	15.73733	16.13077	16.53404	16.94739	17.37107
TRANS	267.68745	274.37964	281.23914	288.27011	295.47887
CONSTR	0.	0.	0.	0.	0.
HOUS.	705.42977	723.06553	741.14217	759.67073	778.66251
OTHMAR	5250.31042	5381.56824	5516.10748	5654.C1019	5795.36053
SUM	15278.96375	15660.93811	16052.46155	16453.77295	16865.11768

```
SUM OF   DISCOUNTED CONSUMPTION =    66663.7402344
SUM OF UNDISCOUNTED CONSUMPTION =    80311.2529297


PRICE FOR MONOTONICITY OF CONSUMPTION
    2      .837706
    3     1.269559
    4     1.269901
    5     1.636190
```

Table 4.27. Available Capital Stock, Fourth Plan Target Model Reference Solution (Rs. crores, 1959-60 prices)

SECTOR	1966-67	1967-68	1968-69	1969-70	1970-71	1971-72	1972-73	1973-74
AG.PL.	13807.04980	14635.47253	15513.60083	15613.77722	16722.21533	18451.67959	19554.19604	20722.70190
M.M.	3200.88116	3745.03091	4381.68616	7144.63330	7144.63336	7064.10712	8033.44568	9369.85791
EQIPMT	2055.12762	2445.60172	2910.26608	4521.18671	4521.18671	4802.58284	5695.15253	6753.60815
CHEMIC	1860.79697	2158.52441	2503.88834	2503.88834	2503.88834	3963.95026	4609.02832	5359.08386
CMGLWD	742.79402	846.78518	965.33508	1110.41301	1110.41301	1464.90390	1676.67940	1919.07060
FOODCL	1773.97491	1915.89285	2069.16425	2658.29016	2658.29016	2620.92532	2833.19489	3062.65828
ELECTR	1618.25107	1844.80615	2103.07901	2103.07901	2103.07904	3073.17880	3495.38992	3975.60663
TRANS	3046.46448	3412.04013	3821.48489	3727.56497	5560.87231	5484.08948	6137.72937	6894.41888
CONSTR	504.77147	575.43938	656.00088	829.26928	966.42359	966.42364	1100.68684	1253.60301
HOUS.	7489.99994	8014.29962	8204.57764	7997.13141	7786.62604	10289.94360	10972.32935	11699.96790
OTHMAR	1451.21509	1610.84875	1788.04205	1636.12744	1481.97226	2417.27194	2678.00647	2966.86453
SUM	37551.32520	41204.74072	44917.12354	49845.35938	52559.59814	60578.95459	66785.83691	73977.43750

Table 4.28. Capital Stock Used, Fourth Plan Target Model Reference Solution (Rs. crores, 1959-60 prices)

SECTOR	1966-67	1967-68	1968-69	1969-70	1970-71	1971-72	1972-73	1973-74
AG.PL.	12791.75757	13788.21643	14399.55591	15238.82410	16722.21533	18451.58228	19554.19922	20722.70581
M.M.	3200.88116	3745.03091	4118.75983	5107.88983	7144.63336	6887.64441	8033.44611	9369.85876
EQIPMT	1844.94963	2445.60172	2581.98346	2297.69772	2789.76996	4802.58337	5695.15338	6753.60919
CHEMIC	912.27070	1279.92816	1394.11783	1632.06030	2245.98502	3963.95035	4609.02856	5359.08435
CMGLWD	552.14229	581.45660	780.87790	899.44731	1110.41301	1464.90392	1676.67953	1919.07074
FOODCL	1677.33984	1781.93640	1856.34033	1954.21246	2105.43634	2620.92542	2833.19507	3062.65656
ELECTR	1058.39186	1209.89333	1310.96577	1416.09329	1712.56015	3073.17896	3495.39005	3975.60690
TRANS	2628.26862	2938.88104	3189.06778	3426.58707	4100.00360	5464.08960	6137.72968	6894.41937
CONSTR	441.39556	371.85670	584.24854	658.26171	820.54307	966.42364	1100.68690	1253.60309
HOUS.	7054.29913	7230.65631	7411.42200	7596.70758	7786.62604	10289.94727	10972.33337	11699.97229
OTHMAR	1080.47357	1132.96805	1192.50620	1220.25839	1298.67392	2417.27203	2678.00656	2966.86475
SUM	33242.16895	36506.42383	38819.84424	41448.03857	47836.85840	60402.49951	66785.84570	73977.44824

Table 4.29. Idle Capital, Fourth Plan Target Model Reference Solution (Rs. crores, 1959-60 prices)

SECTOR	1966-67	1967-68	1968-69	1969-70	1970-71	1971-72	1972-73	1973-74
AG.PL.	1015.29223	847.25610	1114.04491	374.95312	0.	-.00269	-.00317	-.00391
M.M.	0.	0.	262.92633	2036.74345	0.	176.46271	-.00043	-.00085
EQIPMT	210.17799	0.	328.28262	2223.48898	1731.41673	-.00073	-.00085	-.00104
CHEMIC	948.52627	878.59624	1109.77051	871.82803	257.90332	-.00009	-.00024	-.00049
CMGLWD	190.65173	265.32858	184.45718	210.96570	0.	-.00002	-.00014	-.00014
FOODCL	96.63507	133.95685	212.82391	704.07769	552.85381	-.00009	-.00018	-.00027
ELECTR	559.85920	634.91283	792.11324	686.98571	390.51889	-.00015	-.00012	-.00027
TRANS	418.19586	473.15908	632.41711	300.57790	1460.86870	-.00012	-.00031	-.00049
CONSTR	63.37591	203.58269	71.75233	171.00757	145.88052	0.	-.00006	-.00008
HOUS.	435.70080	783.64330	793.15562	400.42381	0.	-.00366	-.00403	-.00439
OTHMAR	370.74151	477.88070	595.53585	415.86905	183.29834	-.00009	-.00009	-.00021
SUM	4209.15637	4698.31622	6097.27942	8397.32056	4722.74017	176.45506	-.00963	-.01215

Table 4.30. Ratio of Idle Capital to Total Capital, Fourth Plan Target Model Reference Solution

SECTOR	1966-67	1967-68	1968-69	1969-70	1970-71	1971-72	1972-73	1973-74
AG.PL.	.07353	.05789	.07181	.02401	0.	-.00000	-.00000	-.00000
M.M.	0.	0.	.06001	.28507	0.	.02498	-.00000	-.00000
EQIPMT	.10227	0.	.11280	.49179	.38296	-.00000	-.00000	-.00000
CHEMIC	.50974	.40704	.44322	.34819	.10300	-.00000	-.00000	-.00000
CMGLWD	.25667	.31334	.19108	.18999	0.	-.00000	-.00000	-.00000
FOODCL	.05447	.06992	.10286	.26486	.20797	-.00000	-.00000	-.00000
ELECTR	.34597	.34416	.37664	.32666	.18569	-.00000	-.00000	-.00000
TRANS	.13727	.13867	.16549	.08074	.26270	-.00000	-.00000	-.00000
CONSTR	.12555	.35379	.10938	.20621	.15095	0.	-.00000	-.00000
HOUS.	.05817	.09778	.09667	.05007	0.	-.00000	-.00000	-.00000
OTHMAR	.25547	.29666	.33307	.25418	.12369	-.00000	-.00000	-.00030
SUM	.11475	.11402	.13575	.16847	.08985	.00291	-.00000	-.00000

4.30 recording the availability and use of capital show substantial excess capacities in every period, and, contrary to what one might expect, the absolute and relative amounts of idle capacity actually increase in many sectors in the third and fourth years. These features indicate that with the given conditions, it is preferable in many sectors to concentrate on capital formation at the beginning of the Plan period and have this capital idle in the fourth and fifth years, rather than spread the new capital formation to achieve the targets more uniformly over the Plan years.

The shadow prices of outputs in Table 4.25 reflect these adjustments in the solution to minimize production for fixed investment in the fifth year. The highest shadow price in the entire Plan period is 64.83 for Mining and Metals in the second year, when its capacity is fully utilized. Mining and Metals is one of the major inputs to Construction. An additional unit of output of Mining and Metals in the second year would have made it possible to provide the Construction component of additional investment to mature at the beginning of the fifth year, since Construction has idle capacity in the second year. Furthermore, since there are idle capacities in all the sectors in the third and fourth years and foreign exchange is not an absolute bottleneck, this investment started in the second year could be completed. The importance of Construction in the second year is also indicated by its shadow price, the second highest in that year.

The shadow rental prices in Table 4.31 confirm the earlier interpretation of shadow prices of outputs. So do the idle capitals in Table 4.29. The idle capacities in the third and the fourth years cannot be used in the production of either consumption or investment. The consumption growth constraints would require additional consumption in the fifth year. Investments started in the third or the fourth year have to be supplemented with additional investments in the fifth year. Neither can be provided due to the foreign exchange limitation.

The idle capacities in the first and the second years cannot be used to generate additional investment due to the shortage of capacity in Mining and Metals. The shortages in Mining and Metals cannot be relieved by imports due to the ceilings on competitive imports.

The high shadow prices of the output of Mining and Metals and of Equipment in the third period are striking. Since there are excess capacities in all sectors, there are no bottlenecks to be broken. However, an additional unit of output of either of these in the third year would mean that the domestic production in the third year could be lowered by one unit. This in turn reduces the required investment for inventories in the second year, releasing Mining and Metals for other uses. Other sectors with high requirements of Mining and Metals for inventories also show high shadow prices in the third year.

The high shadow prices for the outputs of the Mining and Metals, Equipment, and Chemicals sectors in the fifth year are due to the high noncompetitive import coefficients in these sectors. If an additional unit of output of these sectors is supplied, domestic production can be lowered in order to release foreign exchange, which could then be diverted towards production of more consumption.

The solution provides more capacity in Mining and Metals than is required by the targets. Furthermore, all this capacity is used in the fifth year. This may indicate a possible shortage in Mining and Metals in the postterminal year,

Table 4.31. Shadow Rental Prices of Capital, Fourth Plan Target Model Reference Solution (Rs. crores)

SECTOR	1966-67	1967-68	1968-69	1969-70	1970-71
AG.PL.	0.	0.	0.	0.	1.00915
M.M.	2.43073	27.13875	0.	0.	1.59037
EQIPMT	0.	1.31123	0.	0.	0.
CHEMIC	0.	0.	0.	0.	0.
CMGLWD	0.	0.	0.	0.	.18952
FOODCL	0.	0.	0.	0.	0.
ELECTR	0.	0.	0.	0.	0.
TRANS	0.	0.	0.	0.	0.
CONSTR	0.	0.	0.	0.	0.
HOUS.	0.	0.	0.	0.	.21383
OTHMAR	0.	0.	0.	0.	0.

Table 4.32. Ratio of Completed Initial Capital-in-Process to Initially Available Capital-in-Process, Fourth Plan Target Model Reference Solution

SECTOR	1967-68	1968-69	SECTOR	1967-68	1968-69
AG.PL.	1.000	1.000	ELECTR	1.000	1.000
M.M.	1.000	1.000	TRANS	1.000	1.000
EQIMPT	1.000	1.000	CONSTR	1.000	1.000
CHEMIC	1.000	1.000	HOUS.	1.000	.339
CMGLWD	1.000	1.000	OTHMAR	1.000	1.000
FOODCL	1.000	1.000			

Table 4.33. Shadow Prices of Initial Capital-in-Process, Fourth Plan Target Model Reference Solution (Rs. crores)

SECTOR	1967-68	1968-69	SECTOR	1967-68	1968-69
AG.PL.	4.209612	2.031869	ELECTR	5.466610	3.402847
M.M.	39.478394	4.318106	TRANS	8.563887	6.712063
EQIPMT	7.718297	4.390698	CONSTR	7.218199	5.263661
CHEMIC	6.032364	3.996973	HOUS.	2.236565	0.
CMGLWD	5.992996	3.946755	OTHMAR	4.743910	2.644100
FOODCL	7.077762	5.110294			

especially since the output of Mining and Metals is used primarily as an input in Construction and Equipment, and since investment in the fifth year is being minimized in the solution. However, the terminal inventory stocks to be provided at the end of the Plan correspond to the target stocks of the sixth year, and since the inventory stocks in the fifth year are small because of the lower domestic outputs, a larger investment in inventories is required in the fifth year than would be the case if foreign exchange were not a bottleneck.

The initial capital-in-process is completed in all sectors except Housing in the third year as shown in Table 4.32. Housing has the lowest shadow price of new capital in the third year in Table 4.35.

Table 4.34 shows the new capital maturing in each year. No capacities are created to mature in the sixth year in Mining and Metals, in Food, Clothing, and Leather, in Transport, or in Construction, and the last three sectors have idle capacities in the fifth year. Once again these allocations indicate that the investment undertaken in the fifth year is being minimized in the solution. Table 4.36 records the restoration of depreciated capacity and Table 4.37 the shadow prices on the restored capacity constraints.

Tables 4.38 through 4.41 show the details of imports. The shadow prices on the competitive import ceilings in the fifth year are nonzero even though there are no

Table 4.34. New Capital, Fourth Plan Target Model Reference Solution (Rs. crores, 1959-60 prices)

SECTOR	1966-67	1967-68	1968-69	1969-70	1970-71	1971-72	1972-73	1973-74
AG.PL.	0.	828.42297	878.12839	1C0.18066	1108.43895	1729.36461	1102.61691	1168.60633
M.M.	0.	544.14977	636.65528	2762.9472C	0.	0.	969.33865	1336.41246
EQIPMT	0.	390.47427	464.66443	1610.92015	0.	281.39599	892.57000	1058.45573
CHEMIC	0.	297.72746	345.36389	0.	0.	1460.06198	645.07816	750.05572
CMGLWC	0.	103.99110	118.54990	145.C7796	0.	354.49096	211.77648	242.39120
FOODCL	0.	141.91798	153.27140	589.12592	0.	0.	212.26959	229.46148
ELECTR	0.	226.55519	258.27288	0.	0.	970.99981	422.21119	480.21679
TRANS	0.	365.57580	409.44479	0.	1928.61255	0.	771.90038	756.68963
CONSTR	0.	70.66799	80.56150	173.2688C	137.15381	0.	134.26320	152.91818
HOUS.	0.	524.29999	190.28027	0.	0.	2717.08701	682.38598	727.63879
OTHMAR	0.	159.63368	177.19330	0.	0.	935.29971	260.73460	288.85815
SUM	0.	3653.41608	3712.38593	5381.52057	3174.20526	8447.79993	6305.14386	7191.60205

Table 4.35. Shadow Prices of New Capital, Fourth Plan Target Model Reference Solution (Rs. crores)

SECTOR	1967-68	1968-69	1969-70	1970-71	1971-72	1972-73	1973-74
AG.PL.	4.62992	4.62992	4.62992	4.62992	1.27384	1.62351	.72343
M.M.	34.14440	7.00566	7.00566	7.00566	0.	5.04521	.37007
EQIPMT	8.39209	7.08086	7.08086	7.08086	1.56811	5.15399	.35876
CHEMIC	6.67655	6.67655	6.67655	6.67655	1.53379	4.74131	.40145
CMGLWC	6.61904	6.61904	6.61904	6.61904	1.51251	4.48985	.42717
FOODCL	7.82891	7.82891	7.82891	7.82891	1.35045	6.23080	.24766
ELECTR	6.06607	6.06607	6.06607	6.06607	1.48183	4.11849	.46574
TRANS	9.49316	9.49316	9.49316	9.49316	.86494	8.62822	-0.
CONSTR	7.98556	7.98556	7.98556	7.98556	1.30385	6.45771	.22400
HOUS.	2.56375	2.56375	2.56375	2.56375	1.16557	.32718	.85716
OTHMAR	5.28621	5.28621	5.28621	5.28621	1.41537	3.32306	.54778

Table 4.36. Restored Capacity, Fourth Plan Target Model Reference Solution (Rs. crores, 1959-60 prices)

SECTOR	1966-67	1967-68	1968-69	1969-70	1970-71	1971-72	1972-73	1973-74
AG.PL.	0.	297.172	301.688	306.205	310.721	315.538	320.356	325.173
M.M.	0.	75.839	76.992	78.144	79.297	0.	81.756	82.985
EQIPMT	0.	17.396	17.661	17.925	18.189	18.471	18.753	19.035
CHEMIC	0.	56.900	57.765	58.630	59.495	60.417	61.339	62.262
CMGLWC	0.	17.458	17.724	17.989	18.254	18.537	18.820	19.103
FOODCL	0.	35.190	35.725	36.260	36.794	0.	37.935	38.506
ELECTR	0.	52.065	52.856	53.647	54.439	55.283	56.127	56.971
TRANS	0.	91.149	92.535	0.	0.	0.	0.	99.738
CONSTR	0.	1.691	1.717	1.743	1.768	1.796	1.823	1.851
HOUS.	0.	201.327	204.386	0.	0.	0.	217.033	220.297
OTHMAR	0.	147.433	149.674	0.	0.	156.545	158.935	161.325
SUM	0.	993.622	1008.723	570.543	578.958	626.588	972.878	1087.246

Table 4.37. Shadow Prices of Restorable Capacity, Fourth Plan Target Model Reference Solution (Rs. crores)

SECTOR	1967-68	1968-69	1969-70	1970-71	1971-72	1972-73	1973-74
AG.PL.	.156884	1.229322	1.788217	1.788226	1.126775	.567878	.411015
M.M.	.021412	.167791	.244077	.244114	0.	.077440	.056120
EQIPMT	.031293	.249220	.356708	.356753	.224700	.113201	.082010
CHEMIC	.030576	.239597	.230461	.230489	.219569	.110630	.080123
CMGLWC	.062964	.493383	.717694	.717714	.452206	.227890	.164967
FOODCL	.024307	.190462	.277084	.277130	0.	.087903	.063712
ELECTR	.149352	.449864	1.239630	1.239650	1.690261	1.399730	0.
TRANS	0.	0.	0.	0.	0.	0.	0.
CONSTR	.064472	.509223	.734921	.739019	.090121	.233202	.168971
HOUS.	0.	0.	0.	0.	0.	0.	0.
OTHMAR	.018362	.059293	0.	0.	.208544	.171593	0.

competitive imports. When all the exchange is used up for noncompetitive imports, the import ceilings are binding for all the sectors as the ceilings now take the form of $[m']^{-1}M'(5) \leqslant 0$. The shadow price associated with the balance of trade constraint for the fifth year is the same as the shadow price of Others and Margin, which has the lowest shadow price among all the sectors in which imports are permitted.[13]

As pointed out in the preceding discussion, the ceilings imposed by noncompetitive import requirements in the final year affect not only the output of that year but also the output pattern throughout the Plan period. The noncompetitive imports that would be required in the sixth year if all the targeted capacities could be fully utilized, amount to Rs. 2768.24 crores. This is Rs. 925.0 crores or 50 per cent more than the previous year. While there is no guarantee that such full utilization would be possible, it again suggests the importance of achieving the import substitution program of the P.P.D. *Notes* and changing the noncompetitive import coefficients accordingly. These coefficients are changed in an alternative run described in the next section. However, it should also be kept in mind that the need for noncompetitive imports is itself a function of the size and composition of the targets.

Table 4.42 shows the national income accounts for the Reference Solution. Achievement of the gross national product of Rs. 30,725 crores in the fifth year represents an exponential growth rate of 8.5 per cent over the gross national product in the first year of Rs. 22,172 crores. The total gross investment required is Rs. 35,037 crores. Just as they have been understated in the Third Plan Reference Solution, the replacement requirements are also understated in Table 4.42 and the net investment requirements overstated to the extent that restoration and new capital creation are undifferentiated in the solution. The replacement requirements amount to about Rs. 5000 crores. The net investment required over the Fourth Plan period is then Rs. 30,000 crores. The inventory change in the first year is negative and inventories are decumulated. This happens because the initial inventories correspond to full capacity outputs, whereas there is substantial idle capital in the first year in the solution. However, the terminal inventories have to correspond to the target stocks. Consequently, the decumulation in the first year has to be made up subsequently, and the total requirements over the Plan years of investment toward inventories remain unchanged at Rs. 4762 crores.

If the idle capacities in the Reference Solution could be employed by suitable variation of the coefficients, the gross savings rates in Table 4.42 would be reduced because of additional income generated. The calculations of investment requirements, however, are not affected by idle capacities since they depend on the initial and the terminal capitals completed and in process, and on the aggregate inventory-output and capital-output coefficients.

---

[13]The negative shadow prices for competitive import ceilings on Others and Margin in the first and the second years are due to numerical round-off in the computer solution. By setting the tolerance limit in the program more stringently, the negative prices could have been eliminated. These negative prices lead to a slight distortion in the allocation of competitive imports in these years and the model solution imports Others and Margin. Since these imports are small and would otherwise have been allocated to Agriculture, and since there are idle capacities in both the sectors in both the years, the effect of correcting the tolerance would have been small. Consequently, the computer p.ogram was not rerun.

Table 4.38. Total Imports, Fourth Plan Target Model Reference Solution (Rs. crores, 1959-60 prices)

SECTOR	1966-67	1967-68	1968-69	1969-70	1970-71
AG.PL.	235.59195	198.81580	208.75449	229.30808	177.22659
M.M.	276.25404	266.05731	286.92229	354.33942	418.28210
EQIPMT	609.54073	683.85479	715.65141	662.30013	686.72524
CHEMIC	297.89218	354.55906	381.96571	448.53664	555.31017
CMGLWD	11.49305	7.40257	8.22603	9.73211	5.15351
FOODCL	12.29695	6.60615	6.47904	7.78340	.30220
ELECTR	0.	0.	0.	0.	0.
TRANS	0.	0.	0.	0.	0.
CONSTR	0.	0.	0.	0.	0.
HOUS.	0.	0.	0.	0.	0.
OTHMAR	8.93052	4.70399	0.	0.	0.
SUM	1451.99937	1521.99963	1607.99898	1711.99976	1842.99979

Table 4.39. Noncompetitive Imports, Fourth Plan Target Model Reference Solution (Rs. crores, 1959-60 prices)

SECTOR	1966-67	1967-68	1968-69	1969-70	1970-71
AG.PL.	135.57050	146.13125	152.61040	161.50520	177.22659
M.M.	187.39538	219.25260	241.13252	299.04107	418.28210
EQIPMT	454.14968	602.00530	635.57681	565.59751	686.72524
CHEMIC	225.55497	316.45671	344.68961	403.51989	555.31017
CMGLWD	2.56253	2.69858	3.62411	4.17440	5.15351
FOODCL	.24075	.25576	.26644	.28049	.30220
ELECTR	0.	0.	0.	0.	0.
TRANS	0.	0.	0.	0.	0.
CONSTR	0.	0.	0.	0.	0.
HOUS.	0.	0.	0.	0.	0.
OTHMAR	0.	0.	0.	0.	0.

Table 4.40. Competitive Imports, Fourth Plan Target Model Reference Solution (Rs. crores, 1959-60 prices)

SECTOR	1966-67	1967-68	1968-69	1969-70	1970-71
AG.PL.	100.02145	52.68455	56.14409	67.80288	0.
M.M.	88.85866	46.80471	45.78978	55.29835	0.
EQIPMT	155.39105	81.84949	80.07460	96.70263	0.
CHEMIC	72.33720	38.10235	37.27610	45.01675	0.
CMGLWD	8.93052	4.70399	4.60192	5.55771	0.
FOODCL	12.05620	6.35039	6.21259	7.50290	0.
ELECTR	0.	0.	0.	0.	0.
TRANS	0.	0.	0.	0.	0.
CONSTR	0.	0.	0.	0.	0.
HOUS.	0.	0.	0.	0.	0.
OTHMAR	8.93052	4.70399	0.	0.	0.

Table 4.41. Shadow Prices on Competitive Import Ceilings and on Foreign Trade Balance Constraints, Fourth Plan Target Model Reference Solution (Rs. crores)

SECTOR	1966-67	1967-68	1968-69	1969-70	1970-71
AG.PL.	0.	0.	0.	0.	.57869
M.M.	1.41341	12.87035	2.55566	.57406	3.55110
EQIPMT	.70579	1.40063	5.93884	1.39380	6.70270
CHEMIC	.12810	.41858	.69076	.33300	3.11060
CMGLWD	.00899	.02603	.06039	.01760	.03354
FOODCL	.00215	.00745	.01181	.00464	84.76132
ELECTR	0.	0.	0.	0.	0.
TRANS	0.	0.	0.	0.	0.
CONSTR	0.	0.	0.	0.	0.
HOUS.	0.	0.	0.	0.	0.
OTHMAR	-.00072	-.00097	0.	0.	0.

SHADOW PRICE ON FOREIGN TRADE BALANCE CONSTRAINTS

	1966-67	1967-68	1968-69	1969-70	1970-71
	0.05578	0.15927	0.17956	0.18896	0.21078

Table 4.42. National Income Accounts, Fourth Plan Target Model Reference Solution (Rs. crores, 1959-60 prices)

	1966-67	1967-68	1968-69	1969-70	1970-71
CONSUMPTION	15278.963745	15660.938110	16052.461548	16453.772949	16865.117676
INVENTORIES CHANGE	-209.808346	510.595775	451.292912	1327.700165	2683.526031
FIXED INVESTMENT	3756.554962	4174.466492	5836.097107	5704.343323	7031.820862
TOTAL INVESTMENT	4442.285461	5419.695374	6879.455139	7729.392090	10556.546143
GOVERNMENT EXPENDITURE	1107.999985	1176.999969	1253.999969	1336.999969	1427.999969
VALUE ADDED BY GOVT.	1842.747971	1957.503922	2085.564911	2223.604706	2374.949524
EXPORTS	951.999977	1021.999977	1107.999969	1211.999969	1342.999954
IMPORTS	1451.999374	1521.999634	1607.998962	1711.999756	1842.999786
GROSS NATIONAL PRODUCT	22171.996826	23715.136963	25771.481689	27243.769287	30724.612793
REPLACEMENT	895.538857	734.633148	592.065125	697.348633	841.199394
NET NATIONAL PRODUCT	21276.457764	22980.503662	25179.416504	26546.420654	29883.413330
SAVINGS	3942.285461	4919.695374	6379.455139	7229.392090	10056.546143
GROSS NAT. OUTPUT	28085.500732	30230.120117	33319.867676	35321.672363	40677.759766
INTERMEDIATE PRODUCT	7756.251709	8472.487305	9633.951660	10301.510132	12328.101807
CONS./GROSS NAT. PROD.	.689111	.660377	.622877	.603946	.548912
TOTAL INVST/GR.NAT.PR.	.200356	.228533	.266941	.283712	.343586
SAVINGS/GR. NAT. PROD.	.177805	.207450	.247539	.265359	.327312

4.3.3 Alternative Fourth Plan Target Model Solutions

The Fourth Plan Reference Solution, though in general similar to the Reference Solution for the Third Plan targets, differs in many details. It cannot be assumed that the alternative solutions with variations in parameters for the Third Plan targets provide exact predictions of the effects of similar variations in the Fourth Plan context.

The first calculation is one outside the model structure, in which it is arbitrarily assumed that all the idle capacity of the Reference Solution can be utilized by whatever variation of input proportions is necessary. The additional output thus generated is allocated to consumption and to other uses in the proportions of the fifth period of the Reference Solution to allow for uses of the additional output as intermediate inputs, for inventory accumulation, etc. The total additional output of consumption goods that is generated in this way is Rs. 15,500 crores and provides a rough and generous adjustment to offset the rigidities in the assumptions of fixed production and consumption proportions. This amount, added to the undiscounted consumption of Rs. 80,311 crores of the Reference Solution, provides a total consumption of Rs. 95,811 crores, which is higher than the Rs. 90,000 crores estimated in the P.P.D. *Notes.*

Consumption growth constraints varied. Turning to the alternative calculations, shown in Table 4.43, the Solution F-1.1 demonstrates the effect of increasing the minimum annual growth rate of private consumption from 2.5 to 5.0 per cent. This growth rate of consumption is achieved by depressing the level of consumption in the early years. Interestingly, the shadow prices on the consumption growth constraints in all the years are lower in this case than the corresponding shadow prices in the Reference Solution, even though the constraints are made more stringent. This is possible because several constraints are modified simultaneously, and because the constraint planes $C(t + 1) - (1.0 + \rho(t))C(t) = 0$ do not move parallel to themselves but instead change their slopes when the consumption growth rate is changed.

Availability of foreign exchange varied. In Solutions F-1.2, F-1.3, and F-1.4, net foreign capital inflow is increased. An increase of 25 per cent to Rs. 625 crores per year in Solution F-1.2 is not sufficient to relieve the noncompetitive import bottleneck in the fifth year, though aggregate consumption rises by 12 per

Table 4.43. Alternative Target Model Solutions for Fourth Plan

Solutions	Private Consumption				Gross National Product		Gross Domestic Savings/GNP		Total Gross Investment
	Dis-counted Sum	Un-discounted Sum	In First Year	In Fifth Year	In First Year	In Fifth Year	In First Year	In Fifth Year	Over Five Years
F-1.0 Reference Solution: reference s, b, and lags; social discount rate w = 10%; C (t + 1) ⩾ 1.025 C(t); net foreign capital inflow (NFCI) = Rs. 500 Crores per year; constant m'(t); X(0) and X(5) extended for cover-age on 11-sector basis	66664	80311	15279	16865	22172	30725	.1778	.3273	35027
F-1.1 C (t + 1) ⩾ 1.05 C(t)	64737	78348	14179	17235	21082	30906	.1874	.3193	34961
F-1.2 NFCI increased by 25% to Rs. 625 crores per year	74197	90197	16132	21434	23441	33646	.1859	.2499	35060
F-1.3 NFCI increased by 50% to Rs. 750 crores per year	75101	91448	16201	22449	23551	34340	.1868	.2355	35262
F-1.4 NFCI increased to Rs. 625 crores in the fourth year and to Rs. 750 crores in the fifth year	74230	90349	16043	21969	23407	34229	.1885	.2470	35211
F-2.0 Decreasing noncompetitive import coefficient m'(t) to reflect import substitution; NFCI = Rs. 500 crores	73661	89420	16011	20547	23363	33523	.1883	.2736	34972
F-2.1 NFCI decreased by 25% to Rs. 375 crores per year	68069	82559	15110	19813	21981	33077	.1783	.2860	34950
F-2.2 NFCI decreased by 50% to Rs. 250 crores per year	60613	73466	12982	19559	19554	32987	.1852	.2918	34981
F-3.0 Lower inventory coefficients s; m'(t) constant	73395	88733	16157	19118	23163	31847	.1751	.2803	33189
F-4.0 Lower inventory coefficients s; capital coefficient in Agriculture decreased to 1.0	75713	91997	16153	20877	23314	32659	.1806	.2443	31567
F-5.0 Lower inventory coefficients s; capital coefficient in Agriculture increased to 2.5 from 1.51	62291	75043	14277	15759	21272	30195	.1901	.3522	36511
F-6.0 Lower inventory coefficients s; lower capital coefficients b; constant m'(t); C (t + 1) ⩾ 1.025 C(t); social discount rate w = 10%	76443	93024	16154	21431	23289	32892	.1797	.2328	30943
F-6.1 NFCI up by 25% to Rs. 625.0 crores per year	79706	97721	16174	24890	23548	35626	.1878	.1946	32058
F-6.2 NFCI up by 50% to Rs. 750.0 crores per year	80355	98610	16223	25370	23343	35911	.1786	.1876	32365
F-6.3 NFCI up by 100% to Rs. 1000.0 crores per year	81085	99584	16223	25725	23025	35879	.1673	.1770	32858
F-6.4 NFCI reduced by 25% to Rs. 375 crores per year	68192	82152	15629	17252	22342	29656	.1684	.2900	30808

cent. However, in F-1.3 when net foreign capital inflow is increased by 50 per cent to Rs. 750 crores per year, the bottleneck is broken, as seen from the fact that there are some competitive imports in the fifth year. In Solution F-1.4 the net foreign capital inflow is increased only in the fourth and the fifth years, and the over-all performance is even better than that of Solution F-1.2 in which there is a larger total inflow of foreign capital. Once the import bottleneck is broken, the major consumption goods sectors show higher shadow prices than the investment goods sectors in the fifth year.

Alternative import substitution and foreign aid projections. In order to investigate directly the significance of import substitution, Solutions F-2.0, F-2.1,

Solutions	Private Consumption				Gross National Product		Gross Domestic Savings/GNP		Total Gross Investment
	Dis-counted Sum	Un-discounted Sum	In First Year	In Fifth Year	In First Year	In Fifth Year	In First Year	In Fifth Year	Over Five Years
F-6.5 NFCI reduced by 100% to Rs. 0.0 per year	16637	20043	3813	4209	10272	17519	.3415	.5427	30785
F-7.0 Shorter lags; coverage extended on 11-sector basis; lower s and b; C (t + 1) ⩾ 1.025 C(t); social discount rate w = 10%	80241	97986	16039	22525	23579	33263	.1947	.2085	30694
F-7.1 NFCI up by 25% to Rs. 625.0 crores per year	83067	101951	16061	24631	23693	35370	.1976	.1961	31704
F-7.2 NFCI up by 50% to Rs. 750.0 crores per year	84446	103927	16157	26157	23765	36701	.1960	.1837	32873
F-7.3 NFCI doubled to Rs. 1000.0 crores per year	85809	105871	16214	28459	23742	38285	.1927	.1573	34734
F-7.4 NFCI reduced by 25% to Rs. 375.0 crores per year	75463	91501	16128	20028	23255	31069	.1796	.2330	30265
F-7.5 NFCI reduced by 100% to Rs. 0.0 per year	29488	35525	6759	7460	13657	18713	.2891	.3981	30255
F-8.0 Fourth Plan; coverage extended on 32-sector basis; C (t + 1) ⩾ 1.05 C(t) social discount rate w = 10%	36350	43992	7962	9677	13487	25988	.1864	.4813	39170
F-8.1 Social discount rate w = 0%	42992	43992	7962	9677	13487	25988	.1864	.4813	39170
F-8.2 Social Discount rate w = 20%	31024	43992	7962	9677	13487	25988	.1864	.4813	39170
F-8.3 NFCI up by 25% to Rs. 625.0 crores per year	55476	67140	12151	14769	18822	30163	.1947	.3843	39178
F-8.4 NFCI up by 50% to Rs. 750.0 crores per year	70826	85717	15513	18856	22959	33110	.1958	.3156	39028
F-8.5 NFCI doubled to Rs. 1000.0 crores per year	73907	89850	15840	21578	23159	34917	.1886	.2731	39216
F-8.6 NFCI reduced by 25% to Rs. 375.0 crores per year	16913	20469	3704	4503	8065	21711	.1669	.6175	39158
F-8.7 NFCI cut off to 0.0	INFEASIBLE								
F-8.8 Export projection rate reduced by 1.0% to 6.0% per year	34588	41860	7576	9208	12982	25584	.1843	.4914	39167
F-8.9 Export projection rate increased by 1.0% to 8.0% per year	38044	46043	8333	10128	13973	26379	.1882	.4719	39166
F-8.10 Targets lowered by 10% to 90% level	74863	91341	15730	23190	23465	32698	.2026	.1745	29292
F-8.11 Initial capacity increased by 10%	81513	99187	17317	23678	25553	33615	.2068	.1825	32368
F-8.12 C (t + 1) ⩾ 1.025 C(t)	37421	45082	8577	9467	14200	25844	.1840	.4865	39170
F-8.13 C (t + 1) ⩾ 1.0 C(t)	38572	46250	9250	9250	14919	25696	.1822	.4920	39169
F-8.14 K/0 in Housing reduced to 7.5	38761	46911	8490	10319	14099	26296	.1886	.4630	38441
F-8.15 No ceilings on competitive imports	51519	62352	11284	13716	17305	28639	.1774	.3882	39048
F-8.16 No ceilings on competitive imports; NFCI doubled to Rs. 1000.0 crores per year	76184	92545	16253	21735	23632	35049	.1874	.2714	39150
F-8.17 Postterminal growth rate α_T from Fifth Plan C (t + 1) ⩾ 1.025 C(t)	72083	87148	16058	18861	23603	31265	.1947	.2260	34478

and F-2.2 are carried out with decreasing coefficients for noncompetitive imports as shown in Table 3.16 and with alternative amounts of net foreign capital inflows. In Solution F-2.0, with net foreign capital inflows kept at Rs. 500 crores per year but with lower noncompetitive import coefficients, the noncompetitive imports are no longer binding. Mining and Metals still has the highest shadow price, but it is reduced to 12.96 in the third year from the second year high of 64.83 in the Reference Solution. However, capacity in Agriculture is now used in all the periods and, in fact, restricts aggregate consumption in the first four years. The consumption growth constraint is not binding in any year, and a growth rate over the Plan period of nearly 7 per cent is obtained for private consumption.

Solution F-2.0 is in general similar to solution F-1.4, and the difference in undiscounted private consumption is only Rs. 929 crores, of which Rs. 375 crores may be accounted for by difference in foreign capital inflows. In Solutions F-2.1 and F-2.2, the lower import coefficients are kept, but net foreign capital inflows are lowered by 25 and 50 per cent, respectively. These solutions indicate that the targets are technically feasible, even when net inflows are reduced substantially, when the import coefficients are reduced. There are even considerable amounts of idle capacity in these solutions; this could generate additional consumption if the composition of private consumption and/or input proportions were varied. All these solutions show high shadow prices for Mining and Metals in almost all years. Furthermore, these solutions provide more capital in Mining and Metals in the sixth year than is targeted. Since Mining and Metals is a major supplier to both the capital producing sectors, Equipment and Construction, the implication is that the production of the investment necessary to meet the targets requires more Mining and Metals than planned.

In Solution F-2.2 idle capital exists in all sectors in the fourth year, and the consumption growth constraint is not binding between the fourth and the fifth years. The capacities in the fourth year could not be used for producing additional private consumption, because the corresponding inventories in the form of Mining and Metals could not be produced in the third year.

Inventory coefficients and capital-output ratios varied. Solution F-3.0 shows the effects of using the alternative, lower inventory coefficients. As a result, the total investment required for inventories decreases from Rs. 4762 crores to Rs. 3124 crores. This reduction of Rs. 1638 crores in investment requirements alters the solution significantly. Much more consumption is produced. Though non-competitive imports are still a bottleneck in the fifth year, they are not as significant a limitation as in the Reference Solution, as indicated by the fact that consumption growth constraint is binding only between the fourth and the fifth years. The shadow prices on Mining and Metals are reduced, and capacity in excess of the target amount is no longer created in Mining and Metals, even though the inventory requirements in the form of Mining and Metals are not smaller than in the Reference Solution.

Inventories in the model serve as shock absorbers to fluctuations of demand and supply but only to a limited degree because of the fixed coefficients. The reduction in inventory coefficients may be regarded as the result of increased efficiency in distribution. The rather substantial increase in consumption that results indicates still another way of alleviating the bottlenecks associated with a particular set of targets.

When the capital-output ratio is decreased in Agriculture from 1.5 to 1.0 and used with the set of lower inventory coefficients in Solution F-4.0, the total investment requirements are reduced by Rs. 1622 crores. The targets now can be attained easily, and the solution reaches target capacities in four sectors by the fifth year. In this solution, Food, Clothing, and Leather rather than Mining and Metals now has the highest shadow price. The shadow prices in this case reflect mainly the problems of increasing the objective function.

When the capital-output ratio in Agriculture is raised to 2.5 in Solution F-5.0 as a way of indicating the difficulties of expanding output in that sector, private consumption is reduced by 15 per cent as compared to Solution F-3.0. The consumption growth constraints are now binding in all the years. The noncompetitive import coefficients are a bottleneck in the fifth year, and more than 15 per cent of the capacity is idle in each of the first four years. Idle capacity in the fifth year is 9.5 per cent of the total capital stock. The shadow price of Mining and Metals is high in all years and is 73.8 in the third year. Again, more capacity is created in Mining and Metals than is required by the targets.

The Solutions F-3.0, F-4.0, and F-5.0 demonstrate the sensitivity of the model solutions to changes in investment coefficients and, therefore, to total investment requirements. This sensitivity is accentuated by the assumptions of fixed coefficients and fixed composition. However, to the extent that the coefficients cannot be varied from year to year without cost, the results are an indication of the strains and scarcities that may be generated with different investment requirements.

In Solution F-6.0, in addition to lowering the capital coefficient in Agriculture, we reduced the capital-output ratio in Housing. This has a small effect, and private consumption increases only by Rs. 1027 crores over that in F-4.0, in which only the capital coefficient in Agriculture is reduced. Capital in Housing consists entirely of Construction, and Construction is not a bottleneck in these solutions. Noncompetitive imports are binding in the fifth year, as in the Reference Solution.

Foreign exchange availability and investment coefficients changed. Solutions F-6.1 through F-6.5 explore the effects of different availabilities of foreign exchange when the set of lower inventory and capital coefficients prevail. The import bottleneck is broken in Solution F-6.2 when net foreign capital inflow is increased to Rs. 750 crores a year. Solution F-6.2 can be compared with Solution F-1.3 to estimate the effect of lower inventory and capital coefficients, when the noncompetitive import bottlenecks in the last period are broken by additional foreign aid. The private consumption goes up from Rs. 91,448 crores in F-1.3 to Rs. 98,610 crores in F-6.2, an increase of Rs. 7162 crores, whereas the difference in total investment requirements is Rs. 2897 crores.

Solution F-6.3, in which net foreign capital inflow is doubled, shows an increase of Rs. 974 crores in private consumption over Solution F-6.2, even though the additional foreign exchange amounts to Rs. 1250 crores. As was pointed out for the Third Plan target solutions, this is an outcome of the competitive import ceilings, fixed composition of consumption, and the lack of incentive to the model solution to provide more capacity than called for by the targets. These conditions lead to a waste of resources, and in the solution in the first year Mining and Metals is produced domestically and is also imported and thrown away at the same time since there is no use for it. In this way, the solution saves on production of inventories in the first period by reducing the increment of output of the second period over that of the first period. This is desirable whenever the saving on inventories is greater than the cost of producing them.[14]

With the lower capital and inventory coefficients, the targets are still feasible, when net foreign capital inflow is reduced to zero in F-6.5. Noncompetitive imports are now a bottleneck to domestic production in the second, third, and fifth years. There are idle capacities in all sectors in the third, fourth, and fifth years, and on an average 55 per cent of the capital stock is idle in each year.

---

[14] The solution in a sense is transforming current inputs $a_i x_i$ into inventories $s_i x_i$. If at least one coefficient of column s_i is greater than the corresponding element of column a_i, $s_i x_i$ may be preferred.

Investment gestation lags reduced. Solution F-7.0 has shorter lags in addition to the lower coefficients of Solution F-6.0, and Solutions F-7.1 through F-7.3 indicate the effects of varying net foreign capital inflow with these conditions. The effect of shorter investment lags can be appreciated when Solution F-7 is compared to Solution F-6.0. Solution F-7.0 provides Rs. 4962 crores of additional consumption, produces more gross national product, and generates more total investment.

Targets adjusted on a thirty-two-sector basis. Adjusting the P.P.D. targets for the organized sector to cover the unorganized sector on a thirty-two-sector level of disaggregation results in higher targets and initial conditions. These are used in solutions F-8.0 through F-8.17. With these conditions larger amounts of investment are required than in Solutions F-1.0 through F-7.0, even though the initial capacities are also higher.

The general characteristics of Solution F-8.0 are similar to those of the Reference Solution. Noncompetitive imports exhaust all the foreign exchange available in the fifth year and limit the total domestic output. The larger investment demand in the fifth year required to meet the targets restricts still further the private consumption in that year. The consumption growth constraints, which require a minimum growth rate of 5 per cent, bind the consumption in the first four years to even lower levels. Investment goods and especially Mining and Metals are in even shorter supply and have higher shadow prices. The highest shadow price is 78.78 for Mining and Metals in the second year. Substantial excess capacities exist in all years, all sectors have idle capital in the fourth year, and only Construction capacity is fully used in the first and third years.

Solutions F-8.1 through F-8.17 show effects of various changes in parameters. Increased availability of foreign exchange has a greater effect under these conditions, because the larger investment requirements create more severe scarcities. When ceilings on the distribution of competitive imports are removed in Solution F-8.15, the performance of the economy improves dramatically since imports can now be concentrated to relieve the shortages in Mining and Metals.

In Solution F-8.17 the growth rates implied by the P.P.D. *Notes* targets for the Fifth Plan are used as postterminal growth rates α_T. These growth rates are uniformly lower than the Fourth Plan growth rates. Furthermore, the stipulated minimum growth rate of consumption is reduced to 2.5 per cent in this solution. The lower postterminal growth rates reduce the level of required terminal capital stock from Rs. 64,187 crores to Rs. 62,241 crores. The terminal amounts of capital-in-process as well as terminal inventories are also lowered, and the required gross investment falls to Rs. 34,478 crores as compared to Rs. 39,170 crores in Solution F-8.0. This reduction of Rs. 4692 crores in the investment demand is sufficient to break many bottlenecks, and the private consumption goes up from Rs. 45,082 crores in Solution F-8.12 to Rs. 87,148 crores in Solution F-8.17.

4.4 Analysis of Target Model Solutions for a Proposed Fourth Plan

The Fourth Plan targets that have been analyzed are obtained by extending the projections made in the P.P.D. *Notes* for the organized sector to include the unorganized sector. They are therefore not the targets of the *Notes* themselves.

The distinction must be kept in mind, since it creates an additional conjectural step in coming to judgments on the feasibility of the latter targets.

The solutions to the Target Model indicate that the targets are technically feasible under a wide variety of assumptions in regard to coefficients and other data. This suggests to us that the P.P.D. targets themselves would be technically feasible, since the adjustments made are not uniformly, and we think not extremely, favorable or unfavorable.

The sectoral detail of the Target Model solutions is also useful in exploring issues of feasibility. For example, in all solutions where the reference set of inventory coefficients is used, more capacity is created in Mining and Metals than called for by the targets. These coefficients may, in fact, be much too low, at least for the industrial sectors.[15] It would seem then that provided no substantial amount of excess capacity in Mining and Metals exists in 1965-66, and provided our adjustments of targets for coverage have not distorted the demand for Mining and Metals, a shortage in Mining and Metals would develop unless the target for Mining and Metals were to be increased.

Furthermore, if noncompetitive import coefficients remain at their 1960-61 levels, imports of intermediate goods would form a bottleneck in the fifth year, i.e., in 1970-71, unless net foreign capital inflow were increased in that year. The noncompetitive import coefficients will stay at their 1960-61 levels if the import substitution program is not adequate or successful in meeting the increased demand for intermediate goods that is likely to accompany rapid and varied growth of industries.

The issues related to operational feasibility are more difficult to resolve. We shall again concentrate on the question of investment and savings and refer to the total gross investment estimates presented in the last column of Table 4.43 and in Table 4.44. Table 4.44 presents the P.P.D. *Notes* estimates and our incremental calculations under various assumptions. For the most part, the solutions indicate substantially higher levels of investment requirements for the adjusted targets than projected in the P.P.D. *Notes* for the targets there. With the same levels of net foreign capital inflow, this would mean higher levels of domestic saving. The average and marginal savings rates implied in the solution are at levels that would imply relatively large changes from recent Indian experience. Yet the changes in savings that have taken place in recent years would also have to be regarded as relatively large. Thus, one could not conclude that the implied savings and investment rates would necessarily be unachievable, particularly since the solutions also indicate the potential of relatively high rates of growth for per capita consumption. Yet the savings and investment rates that have actually figured in Fourth Plan discussions are less than those implied by the most optimistic solutions found in column 4, Table 4.44. It is unlikely that the calculated required rates could be achieved without explicit government policies being prepared and vigorously pursued, and that would require a clear view of the need for such policies.

To move to judgments about the P.P.D. targets themselves requires an assessment of the adjustments made and the other assumptions about initial

[15] *Economic Weekly,* Dec. 11, 1965, reports that twenty-two large public enterprises carried inventories amounting to the output of a year or more. This means an inventory coefficient of at least 1.0, closer to A. K. Sen's estimates. See Table 3.6.

Table 4.44. Alternative Calculations of Fourth Plan Investment Requirements (Rs. crores, 1959-60 prices)

1.0 P.P.D. Notes Estimates in Current Prices

1.1 Net Fixed Investment	20,760
1.2 Inventory Investment	1,400
1.3 Total Net Investment	22,160
1.4 Replacement*	4,000
1.5 Total Gross Investment	26,160

2.0 Incremental Calculations for Adjusted
P.P.D. Targets in 1959-60 Prices

	$\overline{X}(0)$ and $\overline{X}(5)$ Adjusted on Eleven-Sector Basis				$\overline{X}(0)$ and $\overline{X}(5)$ Adjusted on Thirty-Two-Sector Basis			
	1	2	3	4	5	6	7	8
	Reference Parameters	Reference Parameters Fifth Plan $\alpha(5)$	Lower s Lower b	Lower s Lower b Fifth Plan $\alpha(5)$	Reference Parameters	Reference Parameters Fifth Plan $\alpha(5)$	Lower s Lower b	Lower s Lower b Fifth Plan $\alpha(5)$
2.1 $\sum b_i [\overline{X_i}(5)(1+\alpha_i(5)) - \overline{X_i}(0)(1+\alpha(0))]$	22,915	21,373	20,635	19,183	25,487	23,541	23,147	21,293
2.2 Terminal Capital-in-Process	5,082	3,607	4,546	3,168	5,735	3,855	5,192	3,412
2.3 Initial Capital-in-Process	2,948	2,948	2,551	2,551	3,226	3,226	2,825	2,826
2.4 Net Fixed Investment	25,049	22,032	22,630	19,800	27,996	24,170	25,514	21,879
2.5 Inventory Investment								
$\sum s_i [\overline{X_i}(5)(1+\alpha_i(5)) - \overline{X_i}(0)(1+\alpha_i(0))]$	4,766	4,388	3,129	2,830	5,428	4,926	3,738	3,328
2.6 Total Net Investment	29,815	26,420	25,759	22,630	33,424	29,096	29,252	25,207
2.7 Replacement Investment	5,138	5,138	5,138	5,138	5,138	5,138	5,138	5,138
2.8 Total Gross Investment	34,953	31,558	30,897	27,768	38,562	34,234	34,390	30,345

*Interpolated from P.P.D. Notes, Table 7, p. 11.

conditions. There are many of these, each one of which is of considerable importance in affecting the outcome.

1. Our technique of setting initial conditions by assuming a conscious phasing of the Third and Fourth Plans again seems to us to be somewhat optimistic. There is relatively little evidence that such phasing was done, yet the potential achievements of the first years of the Plan and, therefore, of the entire Plan are crucially dependent on the amount and composition of the capital-in-process started in the previous Plan period.
2. If there were significant amounts of excess capacity in industry that could be utilized, it would help offset inadequacies in phasing.
3. The adjustment to extend the coverage of the explicit P.P.D. targets when carried out on an eleven-sector basis implies much lower aggregate targets than when done on a thirty-two-sector basis.
4. The Fifth Plan growth rates of the P.P.D. *Notes* imply lower growth rates in all sectors and discontinuities in the growth rates of many. However, even with these conditions imposed, the adjusted targets still require much more investment than projected by the P.P.D. *Notes* with our reference set of parameters and coefficients.[16] If these parameters can be

---

[16]Not all of which are those used by the P.P.D.

made more favorable, including, for example, achieving a lower effective capital-output ratio in Agriculture, the Target Model calculations of investment requirements can be brought into general alignment with the P.P.D. *Notes* estimates. In summary, in our judgment the operational feasibility of the P.P.D. Fourth Plan output targets, in the special sense of consistency of these targets with the investment and savings program, requires relatively optimistic projections of the productivity of capital and the ability to direct resources into the organized sectors.

4.5 Transit Model Solutions

The procedure of the Transit Model for setting targets which guarantee the attainment of stipulated postterminal growth rates makes it an open-ended model as compared to the Target Model, in which both initial and terminal conditions are stipulated. This procedure reflects the future into the model in an explicit manner, and this endows the model with a kind of foresight. This foresight is restricted however. Beyond the postterminal periods, which must enter the Plan calculations due to gestation lags, the procedure cannot provide for changing the composition of consumption, except in a predetermined manner, or for varying the rate of growth of consumption. As in the Target Model, the targets enter the system as constraints rather than as part of the objective function. This is equivalent to an objective function that has infinite weights on terminal capital stocks up to the point of their satisfying the target constraints and beyond that no weight at all. Though this limitation might be overcome by repeated trials with different terminal conditions, the shortness of the period over which optimal adjustment can occur remains a major deficiency corrected only in the long-term Guidepath Models. The Transit Model solutions are worthy of attention however, as contrasts to the Target Model solutions. By generating and adjusting to targets whose level and composition are substantially different from those for the Third and Fourth Plan periods, the Transit Model provides additional insights into the Target Model solutions and the operation of the Indian economy. We shall present Transit Model solutions only for the Fourth Plan period, since the quality of the solutions for the Third Plan period is generally similar. At the risk of being repetitious, we again warn that no one of the Transit Model solutions can be accepted as necessarily representing the best of all possible paths for India to take.

To carry out the Transit Model computations, initial capacities and capital-in-process must be specified. These initial conditions are taken from those specified for the Target Solutions. That is, it is again assumed that in the pre-Plan period preparations were made to achieve those targets actually specified in the Plans. This starts the solutions in the direction of the Plan targets, but now the solution of the model determines if that direction is to be followed. In place of the specified target outputs, only postterminal growth rates are specified in each of the sectors for private consumption, government consumption, exports, and imports. The stipulated annual postterminal growth rates are as follows: (1) private consumption, 5.0 per cent; (2) government consumption, 2.5 per cent; (3) exports, 4.0 per cent; (4) imports, 3.0 per cent. The fixed and inventory investments necessary to maintain these rates are determined by Eqs. 14.0 and

Table 4.45. Alternative Transit Model Solutions for Fourth Plan

Solutions[*]		Private Consumption				Gross National Product		Gross Domestic Savings/GNP		Total Gross Investment
		Dis-counted Sum	Undis-counted Sum	In First Year	In Fifth Year	In First Year	In Fifth Year	In First Year	In Fifth Year	Over Five Years
R-1	Reference Solution; $C(t+1) \geqslant 1.025\,C(t)$	77,112	94,246							
R-2	$C(t+1) \geqslant C(t)$	77,586	94,926	16,253	24,133	21,685	31,092	.1144	.1015	19,904
R-3	$C(t+1) \geqslant 1.05\,C(t)$	76,383	93,124	16,143	23,544	21,675	30,086	.1191	.0911	18,491
The following variations are with $C(t+1) \geqslant 1.05\,C(t)$										
R-4	Social discount rate w = 0%	76,339	93,201	16,022	24,146	21,642	30,935	.1234	.0965	19,837
R-5	Social discount rate w = 20%	64,855	92,790	16,253	21,866	21,522	27,850	.1077	.0783	14,787
R-6	All initial capacities increased by 10%		84,212	102,704	17,769	26,124	23,592	32,**883**	.1218	.0899	20,201
R-7	All initial capacities decreased by 10%		68,615	83,637	14,516	21,078	19,709	27,435	.1138	.0931	16,816
R-8	Postterminal consumption growth rate ϕ reduced to 2.5%	77,031	94,070	16,144	24,472	21,478	29,861	.1110	.0531	16,664
R-9	Postterminal consumption growth rate ϕ increased to 7.5%	75,644	91,939	16,193	21,698	22,048	29,369	.1317	.1317	18,965
R-10	No competitive import ceilings	79,458	97,028	16,253	23,506	22,038	24,279	.1286	.0957	18,308
R-11	Net foreign capital inflow (NFCI) increased by 25%	75,801	93,623	16,241	23,627	21,574	30,042	.1104	.0869	18,396
R-12	NFCI increased by 50%	77,191	94,154	16,275	24,015	21,473	30,403	.1047	.0850	18,980
R-13	NFCI increased by 100%	77,895	95,128	16,275	24,405	21,062	30,694	.0872	.0810	19,301
R-14	NFCI reduced by 25%	76,024	92,712	16,046	23,558	21,728	30,264	.1257	.0959	18,600
R-15	NFCI reduced to 0	74,779	91,236	15,746	23,374	22,069	30,506	.1528	.1091	19,156
R-16	Intra-Plan and postterminal export growth rate = 6%	76,434	93,196	16,146	23,606	21,620	30,046	.1167	.0878	18,281
R-17	Intra-Plan and postterminal export growth rate = 8%	76,432	93,198	16,142	23,633	21,616	29,980	.1167	.0849	18,242
R-18	NFCI increased by 100%; no competitive import ceilings	81,629	99,973	16,253	24,536	21,444	30,999	.0917	.0858	19,625
R-19	Capital-output ratio in Housing lowered to 7.5 from 10.0.	76,571	93,421	16,123	23,928	21,708	30,183	.1213	.0813	18,159
R-20	Capital-output ratio in Agriculture raised to 2.5 from 1.5	75,627	91,793	16,253	20,772	21,690	27,562	.1146	.1084	16,446
R-21	Extreme case: K/O in Agriculture = 2.5; initial capacities reduced by 10%; export rate = 6%; NFCI reduced by 25%; postterminal growth rate of consumption increased to 7.5 %	66,616	80,730	14,466	17,992	20,246	26,836	.1397	.1879	19,775

[*]Unless otherwise indicated the following assumptions are made in all solutions:
1. Social discount rate w = 10%.
2. Minimum intra-Plan growth rate required for aggregate consumption p = 5%; i.e. $C(t+1) \geqslant 1.05\,C(t)$.
3. Intra-Plan growth rate for exports ξ = 7%.
4. Level of aggregate consumption of the initial period is left unconstrained.
5. Postterminal growth rates for private consumption, government consumption, exports, and imports are 5%, 2.5%, 4%, and 3%, respectively.
6. Net foreign capital inflow from all sources including foreign aid is Rs. 500 crores annually.
7. Other parameters are as specified for the Fourth Plan Target Model.

Table 4.46. Gross Domestic Outputs, Fourth Plan Transit Model Reference Solution (Rs. crores, 1959-60 prices)

SECTOR	1966-67	1967-68	1968-69	1969-70	1970-71	1971-72	1972-73	1973-74
AG.PL.	9145.67957	9634.41956	10276.08472	11906.95056	13582.47058	14296.55212	15038.31531	15818.65833
M.M.	1364.92195	1046.83937	970.58666	1084.94011	1224.43541	1317.23434	1400.58926	1489.20770
EQIPMT	1316.27910	1233.22746	969.13441	798.06700	1116.86339	1685.67824	1778.79140	1877.30621
CHEMIC	777.83463	1109.76054	1210.64719	1337.42223	1506.14810	1609.86496	1710.17082	1816.34261
CMGLWD	748.28090	846.18726	837.61243	769.01888	771.76611	842.80833	882.99776	925.27739
FOODCL	3164.30640	3339.34592	3506.43259	4050.64838	4709.83698	4960.32587	5224.53571	5503.01776
ELECTR	125.70409	173.04614	185.57793	211.59070	234.19975	247.11302	260.73820	275.12480
TRANS	1212.73180	1237.54668	1242.13950	1367.17403	1583.13579	1719.33456	1811.70154	1909.10393
CONSTR	3296.26523	3754.44937	3804.15015	3215.07938	2905.86349	3271.60709	3418.02222	3571.86218
HOUS.	750.39993	769.15997	789.38799	928.36067	1115.02299	1170.77425	1229.31296	1290.77858
OTHMAR	7125.73894	7331.70782	7468.85681	8490.09253	10037.06201	10706.95911	11252.42676	11826.01941
SUM	29028.19165	30535.68823	31259.60962	34159.34326	38786.90371	41828.25049	44007.60059	46302.69727

15.0 in Table 2.2 simultaneously as part of the optimum solution for the Plan period.[17]

The salient features of the solutions to the Transit Model that were computed for the Fourth Plan period are shown in Table 4.45. A glance at the table and comparison with Table 4.43 indicates that the values of consumption made available in these solutions are uniformly higher than in the Target Model solutions with comparable specifications of parameters. The levels of gross national product achieved in the fifth year are roughly comparable, but the amount of gross investment undertaken during the Plan period in the Transit Model solutions is usually only somewhat more than half that undertaken in the Target Model solutions. The latter observation goes far toward explaining the higher values of the maximand in the Transit Model solutions.

It is again convenient to carry out the presentation mainly in terms of a Reference Solution and variations on it.[18] Table 4.46 shows the sectoral outputs in each year for the Reference Solution. In the Transit Model case, total output grows less rapidly, but in Agriculture, Food, Clothing, and Leather, and Housing, the major consumer goods sectors, output growth is faster than in the Target Model Reference Solution. The rates of growth in the Electricity and Transport sectors are about the same in the two Reference Solutions, but the rates of growth in the capital goods sectors and their major suppliers, Mining and Metals, Equipment, Chemicals, and Cement and Nonmetals are much higher in the Target Model Reference Solution. Interestingly, in the Transit Model solution, output in the first two of these sectors actually declines during the Plan period. This happens after the inherited capital-in-process, which needs only the last dose of investment, is finished up in most sectors. The endowed capital-in-process, which requires two years to finish, is not completed in the capital goods and closely related sectors, and the total demand for their output falls, even though demand for capacity in other sectors and for inventories is increasing.

The shadow prices of output in Table 4.47 are lower and generally more uniform than in the Target Model Reference Solution. They are higher in the consumer goods sectors rather than in the capital goods sectors and their major suppliers. This indicates a greater degree of correspondence among the objective function, the initial endowments, and the terminal targets internally generated in the Transit Model.

Consumption as shown in Table 4.48 starts from a higher level, and after being constrained by the consumption growth requirements until the third period, grows by 17 per cent and 20 per cent in the fourth and fifth periods.

---

[17]There are slight discrepancies in the specification of initial conditions and in the a and s matrices used in the Transit Model solutions for the Fourth Plan period as compared to those used for the Target Model solutions. As a result differences in the maximands are not precise measures of the effects of the alternative terminal conditions, though these remain the most important source of the contrasts in the solutions. This qualification reinforces the caveat that the quantitative differences observed in the solutions should not be interpreted as precise forecasts. In addition, the initial conditions for the Transit Model were taken from those for the Fourth Plan Target Model solutions when the P.P.D. targets were adjusted on a thirty-two-sector basis.

[18]In the Transit Model Reference Solution the minimum intra-Plan annual consumption growth rate is 2.5 per cent and the discount rate is 10 per cent.

Table 4.47. Shadow Prices of Output, Fourth Plan Transit Model Reference Solution (Rs. crores)

SECTOR	1966-67	1967-68	1968-69	1969-70	1970-71
AG.PL.	.00089	0.	4.62623	1.16126	.39329
M.M.	0.	.00032	.22901	.14644	.09126
EQIPMT	.00089	.00076	.31396	.22891	.14274
CHEMIC	.00050	.00045	.21194	.41559	.25930
CMGLWD	.00080	.00070	.21147	.55970	.20443
FOODCL	.00089	.00065	.99115	1.69837	.51068
ELECTR	.00048	.00043	.02230	.05086	.03790
TRANS	.00023	.00021	.05218	.09204	.06170
CONSTR	.24281	.21488	.20552	.18461	.08723
HOUS.	15.03633	.00026	.01074	.20699	.43067
OTHMAR	.00638	.00563	.13567	.07300	.02837

Table 4.48. Private Consumption, Fourth Plan Transit Model Reference Solution (Rs. crores, 1959-60 prices)

SECTOR	1966-67	1967-68	1968-69	1969-70	1970-71	1971-72	1972-73	1973-74
AG.PL.	6304.52185	6462.13525	6623.68848	7799.67621	9367.93298	9836.32959	10328.14600	10844.55310
M.M.	7.63889	7.82986	8.02561	9.45050	11.35068	11.91821	12.51412	13.13983
EQIPMT	392.67143	402.48824	412.55043	485.79576	583.47321	612.64687	643.27921	675.44316
CHEMIC	488.40134	500.61140	513.12668	604.22858	725.71896	762.00491	800.10515	840.11039
CMGLWD	95.72991	98.12317	100.57624	118.43282	142.24575	149.35803	156.82593	164.66723
FOODCL	2327.09833	2385.27591	2444.90775	2878.98334	3457.85162	3630.74417	3812.28137	4002.89539
ELECTR	16.74055	17.15906	17.58804	20.71066	24.87489	26.11864	27.42457	28.79580
TRANS	284.75180	291.87061	299.16737	352.28236	423.11469	444.27042	466.48394	489.80812
CONSTR	0.	0.	0.	0.	0.	0.	0.	C.
HOUS.	750.39900	769.15902	788.38799	928.36053	1115.02312	1170.77426	1229.31297	1290.77859
OTHMAR	5585.00342	5724.62885	5867.74445	6909.51978	8298.79553	8713.73523	9149.42200	9606.89294
SUM	16252.95605	16659.28101	17075.76270	20107.43994	24150.38086	25357.89990	26625.79468	27957.08398

```
SUM OF   DISCOUNTED CONSUMPTION =    77111.9902344
SUM OF UNDISCOUNTED CONSUMPTION =    94245.8085938


PRICE FOR MONOTONICITY OF CONSUMPTION
   2     .295668
   3    1.173345
   4    0.
   5    0.
```

Table 4.49. Available Capital Stock, Fourth Plan Transit Model Reference Solution (Rs. crores, 1959-60 prices)

SECTOR	1966-67	1967-68	1968-69	1969-70	1970-71	1971-72	1972-73	1973-74
AG.PL.	13807.04980	14635.47253	15513.60083	18861.26416	20505.18408	21583.20898	22703.04248	23881.11133
M.M.	3380.54318	3865.60303	3788.61142	3710.46719	3631.17038	3550.64417	3468.88855	3688.36752
EQIPMT	2614.93555	1902.24326	1884.58255	1866.65746	1848.46797	1829.99648	1811.24297	1792.20744
CHEMIC	1997.20926	2192.95782	2045.19275	1986.56274	1927.06804	1866.65091	1805.31137	1917.38727
CMGLWD	794.41072	852.34685	834.62314	816.63414	798.37984	779.84249	761.02213	797.45558
FOODCL	1791.32140	1986.57536	2203.11203	2661.91626	2625.12183	2764.74304	2912.01035	3067.21518
ELECTR	1792.23599	1904.29068	1851.43457	1797.78717	1743.34856	1688.06593	1631.93930	1721.97919
TRANS	3061.94406	3438.56314	3861.50638	3927.46140	3832.15619	3735.37338	3935.03592	4147.66449
CONSTR	504.32869	574.43024	582.03452	553.73256	551.96416	550.16830	548.34503	546.49434
HOUS.	7503.99994	8044.28766	8623.47607	9283.60657	11150.23035	11707.74170	12293.12244	12907.77368
OTHMAR	1460.17970	1633.94107	1828.37996	1724.95549	1570.80029	1675.65147	1761.00826	1850.77565
SUM	38708.15820	40940.71045	43016.55322	47191.04346	50183.88965	51732.08545	53631.96631	56318.42578

The higher levels of consumption and related lower levels of saving lead to lower levels of capital accumulation as compared with the Target Model Reference Solution as shown in Table 4.49. Since both models start with the same capital endowment, they end with substantially different final capacities. In the Transit Model Reference Solution, the capital on hand at the end of the Plan period is Rs. 51,732 crores. In the Target Model case, the corresponding total is Rs. 60,579 crores, a difference of 17 per cent, which is about the same as the percentage difference in the total amounts of consumption made available. In examining Table 4.49, it is useful to recall that in setting initial conditions we assumed that the Indian economy had in the pre-Plan period actually been directed toward achievement of the next Plan's goals. Thus, even in the Transit Model, the particular orientation of the adjusted targets based on the P.P.D. *Notes* has an effect. Through the third period, the pattern of new capital is affected by the initial endowments of capital-in-process and the relative merits of completing these components. In the fourth and fifth periods however, the optimizing mechanism has full control over the pattern of investment subject to terminal conditions. The big increases in capacity in these periods in the major consumer goods producing sectors confirms the indications of the shadow prices that the system is concentrating on increasing output in these sectors.

Table 4.50, which indicates the proportions of idle capacity in each sector in each period, shows a strikingly different pattern from the Target Model solutions. In this case, the idle capacity is concentrated in the capital goods sectors and their major suppliers. The shift in emphasis in the targets has created a new pattern of relative scarcities. With this new emphasis, the idle capacities are so great in the Equipment, Chemicals, Cement and Nonmetals, Electricity, and Transport sectors as to prevail throughout the Plan periods. This difference in relative scarcities is also apparent in the shadow rentals on capital services and in the shadow prices of capital in Tables 4.51 and 4.52, in which the highest values are now in the consumer goods sectors, rather than in the capital goods sectors as in the Target Model.

The uses of foreign exchange for imports and the shadow prices on the competitive import ceilings in Tables 4.53, 4.54, and 4.55 also reflect the new emphasis. All of the relatively small shadow prices, including those on the foreign exchange balance, indicate that in this solution there are fewer major bottlenecks to increasing the value of the maximand, since the open-ended system has a greater freedom to adjust to the constraints, including the one on uses of imports. Because the gross national product in the last year is lower in the Transit Model case, the noncompetitive import requirements are not an absolute limit to total output in the last period as they are in the Target Model case.

The national income accounts in Table 4.56 indicate an uneven rate of growth of gross national product as well as of consumption. The gross savings rates rise from 12.1 per cent in the first period to 17.1 per cent in the third period and then fall to 9.7 per cent in the last period. This is an indication that postterminal conditions imposed in the Reference Solution by stipulation of growth rates guaranteeing a less than 5 per cent rate of increase in gross national product are relatively easy to achieve. The total investment requirements of the Transit Model Reference Solution are shown in Table 4.57. The net investment requirements at Rs. 17,805 crores are substantially less than the Rs. 29,815 crores estimated in the Fourth Plan Target Model Reference Solution.

Table 4.50. Ratio of Idle Capital to Total Capital, Fourth Plan Transit Model Reference Solution

SECTOR	1966-67	1967-68	1968-69	1969-70	1970-71	1971-72	1972-73	1973-74
AG.PL.	0.	0.	0.	.04695	0.	-.00000	-.00000	-.00000
M.M.	0.	.32928	.36550	.27580	.16484	.08117	.00000	.00000
EQIPMT	.51945	.38109	.50907	.59164	.42318	.12062	.06243	-.00000
CHEMIC	.58887	.44293	.37512	.28931	.17495	.08959	.00000	.00000
CMGLWD	.18818	.14436	.13504	.18838	.16686	.06854	-.00001	-.00002
FOODCL	.01543	.06309	.11290	.15185	0.	.00000	.00000	-.00000
ELECTR	.56101	.43124	.37264	.26336	.15919	.08377	.00000	-.00000
TRANS	.13952	.21809	.30114	.24371	.10247	-.00000	-.00000	.00000
CONSTR	0.	0.	0.	.11165	.19452	-.09018	.04630	-.00000
HOUS.	0.	.04384	.08577	0.	0.	-.00000	-.00000	-.00000
OTHMAR	.23627	.29776	.36070	.22972	0.	.00001	.00000	.00000
SUM	.11598	.13649	.15633	.12789	.05238	.01780	.00258	-.00000

Table 4.51. Shadow Rental Prices of Capital, Fourth Plan Transit Model Reference Solution (Rs. crores)

SECTOR	1966-67	1967-68	1968-69	1969-70	1970-71
AG.PL.	.00052	-.00022	3.83963	0.	.04871
M.M.	-.00016	0.	0.	0.	0.
EQIPMT	0.	0.	0.	0.	0.
CHEMIC	0.	0.	0.	0.	0.
CMGLWD	0.	0.	0.	0.	0.
FOODCL	-0.	0.	0.	0.	.00162
ELECTR	0.	0.	0.	0.	0.
TRANS	0.	0.	0.	0.	-0.
CONSTR	1.58198	1.39997	.04092	0.	0.
HOUS.	1.50360	0.	0.	.01940	.04255
OTHMAR	0.	0.	0.	0.	.02843

Table 4.52. Shadow Prices of New Capital, Fourth Plan Transit Model Reference Solution (Rs. crores)

SECTOR	1966-67	1967-68	1968-69	1969-70	1970-71	1971-72	1972-73	1973-74
AG.PL.	—	4.04899	4.04921	.20958	.20958	.07429	.06205	.02454
M.M.		.03537	.03537	.03537	.03537	0.	.02282	.01255
EQIPMT		0.	-0.	-0.	-0.	0.	0.	-0.
CHEMIC		.03831	.03831	.03831	.03831	0.	.02469	.01362
CMGLWD		.04071	.04071	.04071	.04071	0.	.02622	.01449
FOODCL		.16869	.16869	.16869	.16869	.09481	.06386	.00840
ELECTR		.04432	.04432	.04432	.04432	0.	.02852	.01580
TRANS		.14739	.14739	.14739	.14739	.08260	.06479	-0.
CONSTR		1.44089	.04092	0.	-0.	0.	0.	-0.
HOUS.		.22105	.22105	.22105	.20165	.06850	.06153	.02907
OTHMAR		.19157	.19157	.19157	.19157	.08185	.06271	.01858

Table 4.53. Noncompetitive Imports, Fourth Plan Transit Model Reference Solution (Rs. crores, 1959-60 prices)

SECTOR	1966-67	1967-68	1968-69	1969-70	1970-71	1971-72	1972-73	1973-74
AG.PL.	146.33087	155.11071	164.41735	190.51121	217.31953	228.74483	240.61304	253.09853
M.M.	197.91368	151.79171	140.73507	157.31631	177.54313	190.99898	203.08544	215.93512
EQIPMT	309.32558	289.80845	227.74658	187.54574	262.46289	396.13438	418.01598	441.16696
CHEMIC	203.01484	289.64750	315.97891	349.06720	393.10465	420.17475	446.35458	474.06542
CMGLWD	2.99312	3.38475	3.35045	3.07608	3.08706	3.37123	3.53199	3.70111
FOODCL	.25314	.26715	.28051	.32405	.37679	.39683	.41796	.44024
ELECTR	0.	0.	0.	0.	0.	0.	0.	0.
TRANS	0.	0.	0.	0.	0.	0.	0.	0.
CONSTR	0.	0.	0.	0.	0.	0.	0.	0.
HOUS.	0.	0.	0.	0.	0.	0.	0.	0.
OTHMAR	0.	0.	0.	0.	0.	0.	0.	0.

Table 4.54. Competitive Imports, Fourth Plan Transit Model Reference Solution (Rs. crores, 1959-60 prices)

SECTOR	1966-67	1967-68	1968-69	1969-70	1970-71	1971-72	1972-73	1973-74
AG.PL.	145.69935	190.22885	227.40272	248.07188	237.52081	239.74071	241.92705	243.91775
M.M.	117.84152	77.10266	150.34262	117.03050	157.03201	153.61341	151.86531	149.66415
EQIPMT	193.02053	219.93233	262.91077	286.80737	229.62978	110.72107	104.04512	96.55596
CHEMIC	95.93128	102.38226	79.32650	133.51376	127.83510	116.39318	106.31037	95.17947
CMGLWD	11.84362	12.63979	15.10981	16.48318	15.78210	16.06401	16.48631	16.91774
FOODCL	15.98889	17.06371	20.39825	22.25229	21.30584	21.93628	22.58513	23.25295
ELECTR	0.	0.	0.	0.	0.	0.	0.	0.
TRANS	0.	0.	0.	0.	0.	0.	0.	0.
CONSTR	0.	0.	0.	0.	0.	0.	0.	0.
HOUS.	0.	0.	0.	0.	0.	0.	0.	0.
OTHMAR	11.84362	12.63979	0.	0.	0.	0.	0.	0.

Table 4.55. Shadow Prices on Competitive Import Ceilings and on Foreign Trade Balance Constraints, Fourth Plan Transit Model Reference Solution (Rs. crores, 1959-60 prices)

SECTOR	1966-67	1967-68	1968-69	1969-70	1970-71
AG.PL.	0.	-.00010	1.32870	.30546	.15448
M.M.	-.00019	0.	.00340	0.	.00932
EQIPMT	-0.	.00015	.03551	.02870	0.
CHEMIC	-.00006	.00002	0.	.04360	.04840
CMGLWD	-.00000	.00001	-.00001	.00826	.00278
FOODCL	-0.	.00001	.02104	.04190	.01949
ÉLECTR	0.	0.	0.	0.	0.
TRANS	0.	0.	0.	0.	0.
CONSTR	0.	0.	0.	0.	0.
HOUS.	0.	0.	0.	0.	0.
OTHMAR	.00011	.00011	0.	0.	0.

SHADOW PRICES ON FOREIGN EXCHANGE BALANCE CONSTRAINTS

	0.00083	0.00032	0.21194	0.14644	0.35298

Table 4.56. National Income Accounts, Fourth Plan Transit Model Reference Solution (Rs. crores, 1959-60 prices)

	1966-67	1967-68	1968-69	1969-70	1970-71
CONSUMPTION	16252.956055	16659.281006	17075.762695	20107.439941	24150.380859
INVENTORIES CHANGE	-825.075676	226.638762	822.250969	1138.377365	716.552345
FIXED INVESTMENT	3588.856293	3830.237549	3517.401703	2505.401123	2283.562683
TOTAL INVESTMENT	3145.265656	4439.966309	4712.729553	4061.800079	3487.182190
GOVERNMENT EXPENDITURE	1107.999985	1176.999969	1253.999969	1336.999969	1427.999969
VALUE ADDED BY GOVT.	1842.747971	1957.503922	2085.564911	2223.604706	2374.949524
EXPORTS	951.999977	1021.999977	1107.999969	1211.999969	1342.999954
IMPORTS	1452.000000	1521.999619	1607.999512	1711.999542	1842.999664
GROSS NATIONAL PRODUCT	21848.968994	23733.750977	24628.056885	27229.844238	30940.512207
REPLACEMENT	381.485046	383.090050	373.076942	418.021610	487.067188
NET NATIONAL PRODUCT	21467.483887	23350.660889	24254.979736	26811.822510	30453.444824
SAVINGS	2645.265656	3939.966309	4212.729553	3561.800079	2987.182190
GROSS NAT. OUTPUT	29028.191650	30535.688232	31259.609619	34159.343262	38786.803711
INTERMEDIATE PRODUCT	8021.913208	8462.842041	8547.022705	8980.503052	10045.956909
CONS./GROSS NAT. PROD.	.743877	.701924	.693346	.738434	.780542
TOTAL INVST/GR.NAT.PR.	.143955	.187074	.191356	.149167	.112706
SAVINGS/GR. NAT. PROD.	.121071	.166007	.171054	.130805	.096546

Table 4.57. Investment Requirements, Fourth Plan Transit Model Reference Solution (Rs. crores, 1959-60 prices)

1.	Total Net Fixed Investment	15,726
2.	Inventory Investment	2,079
3.	Total Net Investment during the Fourth Plan Period	17,805
4.	Replacement	2,079
5.	Total Gross Investment during the Fourth Plan Period	19,884

Turning back to the alternative solutions for the Fourth Plan Transit Model as summarized in Table 4.45, changes in the social discount rate have only a small effect, as do changes in the consumption growth restraints.[19] A 10 per cent increase in the initial endowments has a significant effect, as would be expected, but not as large as in the corresponding Target Model solution, for, as pointed out already, the Transit Model is not subject to the bottlenecks that the P.P.D. targets create.

Reducing the required postterminal growth rate for consumption to 2.5 per cent from 5 per cent in solution R-8 brings only a small change in the value of consumption goods produced and leaves more slack in the system. Increasing the required postterminal growth rate to 7.5 per cent in R-9 reduces the amount of undiscounted consumption available in the Plan period by about Rs. 2500 crores. However, the total capital stock on hand at the end of the Plan period goes up by only Rs. 500 crores compared to the Reference Solution, since the level of consumption in the fifth year is lower in this case.

Since the import ceiling constraints and the foreign exchange constraints are not major limitations, as indicated by the shadow prices, their relaxation does not lead to substantial changes in the character of the solutions, compared to the effects of such changes in the Target Model solutions. This is seen in Solutions R-10 through R-18 in Table 4.45. Removal of the competitive import ceilings gives the model some added flexibility, and the allocation of imports is now concentrated in one or two of the major consumer goods sectors in each period. The effect on the maximand is relatively minor but noticeable, as is also the effect on savings and investment.

Increasing the foreign capital available increases the maximand, but the effect is much smaller in the Transit Model solution than in the corresponding Target Model solution F-1.2, in which foreign exchange availability constitutes a ceiling to output in the last period. The additional foreign capital substitutes for domestic savings in this case, and the domestic savings rate falls by 0.5 per cent to 1 per cent in each period in the case of Solution R-11 with 25 per cent additional foreign capital. With still more foreign capital, the domestic savings rate falls further.

Reducing the foreign capital inflow forces a reduction in the consumption made available and the output levels achieved. By the fifth period, with 25 per cent less foreign capital in Solution R-14, gross national product is about 2.5 per cent below that of the Reference Solution. The elimination of foreign capital reduces the consumption available by about 3 per cent; the level of gross national product in the final Plan year falls by 2 per cent. The ability of the Transit Model solutions to adjust to reductions in foreign capital inflows is striking and naturally raises some questions when compared to the reality of foreign exchange stringency in India. The Transit Model solutions do not represent the real world but an alternative set of targets, so correspondence with actual events cannot be expected. Still the question remains as to how the Transit Model achieves its relative independence of foreign capital inflows. The answer is in the different patterns of outputs and targets of the Indian Plans, as compared to those

---

[19]For this set of solutions the minimum intra-Plan annual consumption growth rate was set at 5.0 per cent. However, this qualifies only slightly the comparisons made.

generated by the Transit Model solutions. The analysis suggests that the immediate effect of the attempt to create import substituting industries reflected in the Plan Targets is the source of foreign exchange stringency. The analysis is deficient however, in that it does not indicate the subsequent effect of successful import substitution programs.

In Solutions R-16 and R-17 the intra-Plan export growth rate is changed, up and down, by 1 per cent. The effects are relatively small, as could be expected. A smaller amount of exports increases the availability of resources for domestic use and vice versa.

In Solution R-18, net foreign capital inflows are increased by 100 per cent and the competitive import ceilings are removed. Under these conditions, the additional foreign exchange is much more productive than when the ceilings are maintained.

Lowering the capital-output ratios in Agriculture and Housing has a smaller effect in the Transit, as compared to the corresponding Target Model solution, because of the greater scarcity of capital in the latter case. But even in the Transit Model, an unfavorable combination of specifications, as in Solution R-21, can lead to a drastic reduction in available consumption.

4.6 Evaluation of the Transit Model Solutions

As a guide to policy-making the Transit Model suffers from its short-run character which allows the model solutions only limited flexibility in determining the intertemporal pattern of consumption and investment and, therefore, the relative weights to be placed on the consumer and capital goods sectors. The overlapping constraints of the initial endowments and terminal conditions further restrict the freedom of the optimizing mechanism.

The Transit Models do provide additional understanding of the operation of the Indian economy and the Target Model solutions. They indicate the effects of the forces acting on the economy that arise from the expansion of consumer demands within the framework of domestic capital resources and foreign exchange resources without a long-range vision of future goals. There appears to be a closer correspondence between the savings rates actually achieved in the Indian economy and those of the Transit Model solutions than in the Target Models. On the other hand, the Transit Model solutions are not good descriptions of what has happened in India, nor necessarily what will happen, because the targets which they generate are so much different from those of the Plans. By comparison with Target Model solutions, Transit Model solutions indicate the direction of the adjustment of the economy if inadequate saving and investment force scaling down of the Plan targets and adjustment of their composition.

APPENDIX B

Table B.1. Interindustry Flow, Period 1, Third Plan Target Model Reference Solution (Rs. crores, 1959-60 prices)

	1 AG.PL.	2 M.M.	3 EQIPMT	4 CHEMIC	5 CMGLWD	6 FOODCL	7 ELECTR	8 TRANS	9 CONSTR	10 HOUS.	11 OTHMAR	12 SUM
AG.PL.	619.425	.123	13.799	32.211	64.575	1204.409	0.	0.	74.485	0.	183.133	2192.159
M.M.	1.024	118.102	185.878	15.733	25.423	9.763	14.422	32.938	255.055	3.023	3.609	664.969
EQIPMT	0.	11.521	29.400	10.048	1.315	6.934	0.	0.	28.106	0.	0.	87.325
CHEMIC	77.000	11.273	29.514	125.942	39.734	67.184	3.098	149.526	14.593	0.	15.071	532.935
CMGLWD	3.322	6.304	4.360	6.918	12.389	7.006	0.	0.	385.704	8.827	0.	434.831
FCODCL	60.329	1.058	1.800	21.544	8.977	134.850	0.	C.	0.	0.	4.192	232.749
ELECTR	8.204	13.161	10.197	10.045	11.056	31.830	0.	3.533	0.	0.	5.731	93.756
TRANS	54.632	82.287	58.745	62.080	34.729	117.273	12.979	33.949	46.001	3.966	110.219	616.860
CCNSTR	0.	0.	0.	0.	0.	0.	0.	0.	0.	0.	0.	0.
HCUS.	0.	0.	0.	0.	0.	0.	0.	0.	-0.	0.	C.	0.
OTHMAR	38.069	15.959	108.378	20.252	43.859	132.000	7.520	13.427	187.503	26.276	0.	593.243

Table B.2. Investment Maturing in 1 Year, Period 1, Third Plan Target Model Reference Solution (Rs. crores, 1959-60 prices)

	1 AG.PL.	2 M.M.	3 EQIPMT	4 CHEMIC	5 CMGLWD	6 FOODCL	7 ELECTR	8 TRANS	9 CONSTR	10 HOUS.	11 OTHMAR	12 SUM
AG.PL.	0.	0.	0.	0.	0.	0.	0.	0.	0.	0.	0.	0.
M.M.	0.	0.	0.	0.	0.	0.	0.	0.	0.	0.	0.	0.
EQIPMT	37.170	77.742	37.561	27.734	9.274	6.851	36.213	116.011	7.324	0.	13.034	368.916
CHEMIC	0.	0.	0.	0.	0.	0.	0.	0.	0.	0.	0.	0.
CMGLWD	0.	0.	0.	0.	0.	0.	0.	0.	C.	0.	0.	0.
FCODCL	0.	0.	0.	0.	0.	0.	0.	0.	0.	0.	0.	0.
ELECTR	0.	0.	0.	0.	0.	0.	0.	0.	0.	0.	0.	0.
TRANS	0.	0.	0.	0.	0.	0.	0.	0.	0.	0.	0.	0.
CONSTR	152.361	45.974	20.192	16.888	6.907	2.112	32.450	0.	1.952	146.638	17.384	442.857
HCUS.	0.	0.	0.	0.	0.	0.	0.	0.	0.	0.	0.	0.
OTHMAR	4.815	10.098	4.888	3.604	1.205	.890	4.713	15.075	.953	0.	1.698	47.938

Table B.3. Investment Maturing in 2 Years, Period 1, Third Plan Target Model Reference Solution (Rs. crores, 1959-60 prices)

	1 AG.PL.	2 M.M.	3 EQIPMT	4 CHEMIC	5 CMGLWD	6 FOODCL	7 ELECTR	8 TRANS	9 CONSTR	10 HOUS.	11 OTHMAR	12 SUM
AG.PL.	0.	0.	0.	0.	0.	0.	0.	0.	0.	0.	0.	0.
M.M.	0.	0.	0.	0.	0.	0.	0.	0.	0.	0.	0.	0.
EQIPMT	38.850	84.528	41.413	0.	10.151	0.	21.778	14.764	7.339	0.	14.106	232.929
CHEMIC	0.	0.	0.	0.	0.	0.	0.	0.	0.	0.	0.	0.
CMGLWD	0.	0.	0.	0.	0.	0.	0.	0.	0.	0.	0.	0.
FCODCL	0.	0.	0.	0.	0.	0.	0.	0.	0.	0.	0.	0.
ELECTR	0.	0.	0.	0.	0.	0.	0.	0.	0.	0.	0.	0.
TRANS	0.	0.	0.	0.	0.	0.	0.	0.	0.	0.	0.	0.
CONSTR	159.247	49.987	22.262	0.	7.559	0.	19.515	0.	1.956	151.125	18.814	430.466
HCUS.	0.	0.	0.	0.	0.	0.	0.	0.	0.	0.	0.	0.
OTHMAR	5.033	10.979	5.389	0.	1.318	0.	2.834	1.918	.954	0.	1.837	30.264

Table B.4. Investment Maturing in 3 Years, Period 1, Third Plan Target Model Reference
Solution (Rs. crores, 1959-60 prices)

	1 AG.PL.	2 M.M.	3 EQIPMT	4 CHEMIC	5 CMGLWD	6 FOODCL	7 ELECTR	8 TRANS	9 CONSTR	10 HOUS.	11 OTHMAR	12 SUM
AG.PL.	0.	0.	0.	0.	0.	0.	0.	0.	0.	0.	0.	0.
M.M.	0.	0.	0.	0.	0.	0.	0.	0.	0.	0.	0.	0.
EQIPMT	0.	0.	0.	0.	0.	0.	0.	0.	0.	0.	0.	0.
CHEMIC	0.	0.	0.	0.	0.	0.	0.	0.	0.	0.	0.	0.
CMGLWD	0.	0.	0.	0.	0.	0.	0.	0.	0.	0.	0.	0.
FOODCL	0.	0.	0.	0.	0.	0.	0.	0.	0.	0.	0.	0.
ELECTR	0.	0.	0.	0.	0.	0.	0.	0.	0.	0.	0.	0.
TRANS	0.	0.	0.	0.	0.	0.	0.	0.	0.	0.	0.	0.
CONSTR	153.129	61.851	46.297	18.108	12.136	8.930	0.	0.	4.108	74.275	0.	378.834
HOUS.	0.	0.	0.	0.	0.	0.	0.	0.	0.	0.	0.	0.
OTHMAR	0.	0.	0.	0.	0.	0.	0.	0.	0.	0.	0.	0.

Table B.5. Stock Held, Period 1, Third Plan Target Model Reference Solution
(Rs. crores, 1959-60 prices)

	1 AG.PL.	2 M.M.	3 EQIPMT	4 CHEMIC	5 CMGLWD	6 FOODCL	7 ELECTR	8 TRANS	9 CONSTR	10 HOUS.	11 OTHMAR	12 SUM
AG.PL.	2521.475	.072	18.350	23.322	49.896	768.465	0.	0.	11.768	0.	44.729	3438.085
M.M.	4.482	92.188	207.588	14.083	19.116	6.018	13.416	10.072	40.174	0.	.874	408.012
EQIPMT	0.	24.915	37.203	41.086	1.016	4.380	0.	0.	4.475	0.	0.	113.075
CHEMIC	320.977	8.157	37.355	298.102	30.687	45.920	2.882	7.308	1.913	0.	3.675	756.976
CMGLWD	15.411	7.839	5.654	5.588	9.573	4.181	0.	0.	60.992	0.	0.	109.238
FOODCL	249.448	2.950	2.501	17.229	6.568	102.676	0.	0.	0.	0.	1.027	382.399
ELECTR	0.	0.	0.	0.	0.	0.	0.	0.	0.	0.	0.	0.
TRANS	0.	0.	0.	0.	0.	0.	0.	0.	0.	0.	0.	0.
CONSTR	0.	0.	0.	0.	0.	0.	0.	0.	0.	0.	0.	0.
HOUS.	0.	0.	0.	0.	0.	0.	0.	0.	0.	0.	0.	0.
OTHMAR	0.	0.	0.	0.	0.	0.	0.	0.	0.	0.	0.	0.

Table B.6. Summary of Flow, Period 1, Third Plan Target Model Reference Solution
(Rs. crores, 1959-60 prices)

	X	M	AX	SΔX	R1+R2+R3	Z1	Z2	Z3	E	G	CONS	CHECK
AG.PL.	7761.35	268.31	2192.16	36.09	0.	0.	0.	0.	198.19	0.	5603.23	.00
M.M.	567.66	199.86	664.97	56.20	0.	0.	0.	0.	40.09	0.	6.26	.00
EQIPMT	804.47	394.62	87.33	10.28	205.76	368.92	232.93	c.	4.34	97.60	191.95	.00
CHEMIC	634.37	261.27	532.94	8.13	0.	0.	0.	c.	15.09	28.40	311.08	.00
CMGLWD	493.18	13.79	434.83	3.97	0.	0.	0.	0.	2.79	0.	65.37	.00
FCODCL	2384.61	16.14	232.75	3.23	0.	0.	0.	0.	215.66	109.12	1839.99	-.00
ELECTR	110.03	0.	93.76	-c.	0.	c.	0.	0.	0.	4.92	11.35	-.00
TRANS	809.46	0.	616.86	-0.	0.	0.	0.	c.	0.	0.	192.60	-.00
CCNSTR	1748.10	0.	0.	-0.	387.74	442.86	430.47	378.83	0.	108.20	0.	-.00
HCUS.	589.28	0.	0.	-0.	0.	0.	0.	0.	c.	0.	589.28	-.00
OTHMAR	5306.66	0.	593.24	-0.	27.07	47.94	30.26	c.	177.84	192.76	4237.55	-.00

Table B.7. Interindustry Flow, Period 2, Third Plan Target Model Reference Solution (Rs. crores, 1959-60 prices)

	1 AG.PL.	2 M.M.	3 EQIPMT	4 CHEMIC	5 CMGLWD	6 FOODCL	7 ELECTR	8 TRANS	9 CONSTR	10 HOUS.	11 OTHMAR	12 SUM
AG.PL.	649.081	.144	16.436	37.327	67.947	1249.384	0.	0.	75.794	0.	189.339	2285.452
M.M.	1.074	138.821	221.394	18.232	26.750	10.127	15.591	35.267	259.538	3.099	3.731	733.623
EQIPMT	0.	13.542	35.017	11.645	1.384	7.193	0.	0.	28.600	0.	0.	97.382
CHEMIC	80.687	13.250	35.153	145.947	41.809	69.693	3.350	160.100	14.850	0.	15.582	580.420
CMGLWD	3.481	7.410	5.193	8.017	13.036	7.268	0.	0.	392.484	9.048	0.	445.937
FOODCL	63.217	1.243	2.143	24.967	9.446	139.885	0.	0.	0.	0.	4.334	245.236
ELECTR	8.597	15.469	12.145	11.641	11.633	33.018	0.	3.783	0.	0.	5.925	102.212
TRANS	57.248	96.723	69.969	71.941	36.543	121.652	14.032	36.349	46.810	4.065	113.954	669.286
CCNSTR	0.	0.	0.	0.	0.	0.	0.	0.	0.	0.	0.	0.
HCUS.	0.	0.	0.	0.	0.	0.	0.	0.	0.	0.	0.	0.
OTHMAR	39.892	18.759	129.086	23.468	46.150	136.929	8.129	14.377	190.799	26.933	0.	634.522

Table B.8. Investment Maturing in 1 Year, Period 2, Third Plan Target Model Reference Solution (Rs. crores, 1959-60 prices)

	1 AG.PL.	2 M.M.	3 EQIPMT	4 CHEMIC	5 CMGLWD	6 FOODCL	7 ELECTR	8 TRANS	9 CONSTR	10 HOUS.	11 OTHMAR	12 SUM
AG.PL.	0.	0.	0.	0.	0.	0.	0.	0.	0.	0.	0.	0.
M.M.	0.	0.	0.	0.	0.	0.	0.	0.	0.	0.	0.	0.
EQIPMT	38.850	84.528	41.413	0.	10.151	0.	21.778	14.764	7.339	0.	14.106	232.929
CHEMIC	0.	0.	0.	0.	0.	0.	0.	C.	0.	0.	0.	0.
CMGLWD	0.	0.	0.	0.	0.	0.	0.	0.	0.	0.	0.	0.
FCODCL	0.	0.	0.	0.	0.	0.	0.	0.	0.	0.	0.	0.
ELECTR	0.	0.	0.	0.	0.	0.	0.	C.	0.	0.	0.	0.
TRANS	0.	0.	0.	0.	0.	0.	0.	0.	0.	0.	0.	0.
CCNSTR	159.247	49.987	22.262	0.	7.559	0.	19.515	0.	1.956	151.125	18.814	430.466
HCUS.	0.	0.	0.	0.	0.	0.	0.	0.	0.	0.	0.	0.
OTHMAR	5.033	10.979	5.389	0.	1.318	0.	2.834	1.918	.954	0.	1.837	30.264

Table B.9. Investment Maturing in 2 Years, Period 2, Third Plan Target Model Reference Solution (Rs. crores, 1959-60 prices)

	1 AG.PL.	2 M.M.	3 EQIPMT	4 CHEMIC	5 CMGLWD	6 FOODCL	7 ELECTR	8 TRANS	9 CONSTR	10 HOUS.	11 OTHMAR	12 SUM
AG.PL.	0.	0.	0.	0.	0.	C.	0.	0.	C.	0.	0.	0.
M.M.	0.	0.	0.	0.	0.	0.	0.	0.	C.	0.	0.	0.
EQIPMT	37.358	104.589	86.123	29.739	16.296	28.967	0.	214.326	15.412	0.	0.	532.810
CHEMIC	0.	0.	0.	0.	0.	0.	0.	0.	C.	0.	0.	0.
CMGLWD	0.	0.	0.	0.	0.	C.	0.	0.	C.	0.	0.	0.
FOODCL	0.	0.	0.	0.	0.	0.	0.	0.	C.	0.	0.	0.
ELECTR	0.	0.	0.	0.	0.	0.	0.	0.	0.	0.	0.	0.
TRANS	0.	0.	0.	0.	0.	0.	0.	0.	C.	0.	0.	0.
CCNSTR	153.129	61.851	46.297	18.108	12.136	8.930	0.	0.	4.108	74.275	0.	378.834
HCUS.	0.	0.	0.	0.	0.	0.	0.	0.	0.	0.	0.	0.
OTHMAR	4.840	13.585	11.207	3.865	2.117	3.764	0.	27.850	2.004	0.	0.	69.232

Table B.10. Investment Maturing in 3 Years, Period 2, Third Plan Target Model Reference Solution (Rs. crores, 1959-60 prices)

	1 AG.PL.	2 M.M.	3 EQIPMT	4 CHEMIC	5 CMGLWD	6 FOODCL	7 ELECTR	8 TRANS	9 CONSTR	10 HOUS.	11 OTHMAR	12 SUM
AG.PL.	0.	0.	0.	0.	0.	0.	0.	0.	0.	0.	0.	0.
M.M.	0.	0.	0.	0.	0.	0.	0.	0.	0.	0.	0.	0.
EQIPMT	0.	0.	0.	0.	0.	0.	0.	0.	0.	0.	0.	0.
CHEMIC	0.	0.	0.	0.	0.	0.	0.	0.	0.	0.	0.	0.
CMGLWD	0.	0.	0.	0.	0.	0.	0.	0.	0.	0.	0.	0.
FCODCL	0.	0.	0.	0.	0.	0.	0.	0.	0.	0.	0.	0.
ELECTR	0.	0.	0.	0.	0.	0.	0.	0.	0.	0.	0.	0.
TRANS	0.	0.	0.	0.	0.	0.	0.	0.	0.	0.	0.	0.
CCNSTR	166.846	53.337	42.903	35.503	9.318	6.199	0.	0.	3.543	80.710	0.	398.359
HCUS.	0.	0.	0.	0.	0.	0.	0.	0.	0.	0.	0.	0.
OTHMAR	0.	0.	0.	0.	0.	0.	0.	0.	0.	0.	0.	0.

Table B.11. Stock Held, Period 2, Third Plan Target Model Reference Solution (Rs. crores, 1959-60 prices)

	1 AG.PL.	2 M.M.	3 EQIPMT	4 CHEMIC	5 CMGLWD	6 FOODCL	7 ELECTR	8 TRANS	9 CONSTR	10 HOUS.	11 OTHMAR	12 SUM
AG.PL.	2589.436	.085	21.866	22.673	52.502	736.936	0.	0.	11.947	0.	38.729	3474.173
M.M.	4.603	108.362	247.252	13.690	20.115	5.771	12.631	10.245	40.785	0.	.757	464.211
EQIPMT	0.	29.286	44.311	39.942	1.070	4.200	0.	0.	4.543	0.	0.	123.352
CHEMIC	329.628	9.588	44.493	289.801	32.290	44.036	2.714	7.434	1.942	0.	3.182	765.107
CMGLWD	15.827	9.214	6.734	5.433	10.073	4.010	0.	0.	61.919	0.	0.	113.209
FCODCL	256.171	3.467	2.979	16.749	6.911	98.464	0.	0.	0.	0.	.889	385.630
ELECTR	0.	0.	0.	0.	0.	0.	0.	0.	0.	0.	0.	0.
TRANS	0.	0.	0.	0.	0.	0.	0.	0.	0.	0.	0.	0.
CCNSTR	0.	0.	0.	0.	0.	0.	0.	0.	0.	0.	0.	0.
HCUS.	0.	0.	0.	0.	0.	0.	0.	0.	0.	0.	0.	0.
OTHMAR	0.	0.	0.	0.	0.	0.	0.	0.	0.	0.	0.	0.

Table B.12. Summary of Flow, Period 2, Third Plan Target Model Reference Solution (Rs. crores, 1959-60 prices)

	X	M	AX	SΔX	R1+R2+R3	Z1	Z2	Z3	E	G	CONS	CHECK
AG.PL.	8132.93	260.62	2285.45	158.42	0.	0.	0.	0.	206.37	0.	5743.31	-.00
M.M.	667.25	203.17	733.62	88.63	0.	0.	0.	0.	41.75	0.	6.42	.10
EQIPMT	958.17	411.28	97.38	22.00	181.87	232.93	532.81	0.	4.52	101.20	196.74	.00
CHEMIC	735.14	278.51	580.42	69.20	0.	0.	0.	0.	15.71	29.45	318.86	.00
CMGLWD	518.94	12.77	445.94	15.86	0.	0.	0.	0.	2.91	0.	67.01	.00
FCODCL	2473.66	14.64	245.24	19.35	0.	0.	0.	0.	224.56	113.15	1885.99	-.00
ELECTR	118.95	0.	102.21	0.	0.	0.	0.	0.	0.	5.11	11.64	.00
TRANS	866.70	0.	669.29	0.	0.	0.	0.	0.	0.	0.	197.41	-.00
CCNSTR	1778.83	0.	0.	0.	458.97	430.47	378.83	398.36	0.	112.20	0.	.00
HOUS.	604.01	0.	0.	0.	0.	0.	0.	0.	0.	0.	604.01	-.00
OTHMAR	5486.49	0.	634.52	0.	23.92	30.26	69.23	0.	185.18	199.88	4343.49	-.00

Table B.13. Interindustry Flow, Period 3, Third Plan Target Model Reference Solution (Rs. crores, 1959-60 prices)

	1 AG.PL.	2 M.M.	3 EQIPMT	4 CHEMIC	5 CMGLWD	6 FOODCL	7 ELECTR	8 TRANS	9 CONSTR	10 HOUS.	11 OTHMAR	12 SUM
AG.PL.	678.021	.181	19.596	41.980	77.356	1292.367	0.	0.	87.155	0.	196.676	2393.332
M.M.	1.121	174.480	263.964	20.505	30.454	10.476	17.158	38.535	298.439	3.176	3.875	862.183
EQIPMT	0.	17.021	41.751	13.096	1.576	7.441	0.	0.	32.887	0.	0.	113.771
CHEMIC	84.284	16.654	41.913	164.140	47.598	72.090	3.686	174.936	17.075	0.	16.185	638.562
CMGLWD	3.636	9.314	6.192	9.017	14.841	7.518	0.	0.	451.312	9.274	0.	511.104
FOODCL	66.036	1.562	2.556	28.079	10.754	144.698	0.	0.	0.	0.	4.502	258.187
ELECTR	8.980	19.443	14.480	13.092	13.244	34.154	0.	4.134	0.	0.	6.155	113.682
TRANS	59.800	121.567	83.422	80.909	41.603	125.837	15.442	39.718	53.826	4.167	118.370	744.662
CONSTR	0.	0.	0.	0.	0.	0.	0.	0.	0.	0.	0.	0.
HOUS.	0.	0.	0.	0.	0.	0.	0.	0.	0.	0.	0.	0.
OTHMAR	41.671	23.577	153.907	26.394	52.540	141.640	8.946	15.709	219.397	27.606	0.	711.388

Table B.14. Investment Maturing in 1 Year, Period 3, Third Plan Target Model Reference Solution (Rs. crores, 1959-60 prices)

	1 AG.PL.	2 M.M.	3 EQIPMT	4 CHEMIC	5 CMGLWD	6 FOODCL	7 ELECTR	8 TRANS	9 CONSTR	10 HOUS.	11 OTHMAR	12 SUM
AG.PL.	0.	0.	0.	0.	0.	0.	0.	0.	0.	0.	0.	0.
M.M.	0.	0.	0.	0.	0.	0.	0.	0.	0.	0.	0.	0.
EQIPMT	37.358	104.589	86.123	29.739	16.296	28.967	0.	214.326	15.412	0.	0.	532.810
CHEMIC	0.	0.	0.	0.	0.	0.	0.	0.	0.	0.	0.	0.
CMGLWD	0.	0.	0.	0.	0.	0.	0.	0.	0.	0.	0.	0.
FOODCL	0.	0.	0.	0.	0.	0.	0.	0.	0.	0.	0.	0.
ELECTR	0.	0.	0.	0.	0.	0.	0.	0.	0.	0.	0.	0.
TRANS	0.	0.	0.	0.	0.	0.	0.	0.	0.	0.	0.	0.
CONSTR	153.129	61.851	46.297	18.108	12.136	8.930	0.	0.	4.108	74.275	0.	378.834
HOUS.	0.	0.	0.	0.	0.	0.	0.	0.	0.	0.	0.	0.
OTHMAR	4.840	13.585	11.207	3.865	2.117	3.764	0.	27.850	2.004	0.	0.	69.232

Table B.15. Investment Maturing in 2 Years, Period 3, Third Plan Target Model Reference Solution (Rs. crores, 1959-60 prices)

	1 AG.PL.	2 M.M.	3 EQIPMT	4 CHEMIC	5 CMGLWD	6 FOODCL	7 ELECTR	8 TRANS	9 CONSTR	10 HOUS.	11 OTHMAR	12 SUM
AG.PL.	0.	0.	0.	0.	0.	0.	0.	0.	0.	0.	0.	0.
M.M.	0.	0.	0.	0.	0.	0.	0.	0.	0.	0.	0.	0.
EQIPMT	40.704	90.193	79.809	58.306	12.513	20.110	0.	96.401	13.293	0.	0.	411.327
CHEMIC	0.	0.	0.	0.	0.	0.	0.	0.	0.	0.	0.	0.
CMGLWD	0.	0.	0.	0.	0.	0.	0.	0.	0.	0.	0.	0.
FOODCL	0.	0.	0.	0.	0.	0.	0.	0.	0.	0.	0.	0.
ELECTR	0.	0.	0.	0.	0.	0.	0.	0.	0.	0.	0.	0.
TRANS	0.	0.	0.	0.	0.	0.	0.	0.	0.	0.	0.	0.
CONSTR	166.846	53.337	42.903	35.503	9.318	6.199	0.	0.	3.543	80.710	0.	398.359
HOUS.	0.	0.	0.	0.	0.	0.	0.	0.	0.	0.	0.	0.
OTHMAR	5.273	11.715	10.386	7.577	1.625	2.613	0.	12.527	1.729	0.	0.	53.445

Table B.16. Investment Maturing in 3 Years, Period 3, Third Plan Target Model Reference Solution (Rs. crores, 1959-60 prices)

	1 AG.PL.	2 M.M.	3 EQIPMT	4 CHEMIC	5 CMGLWD	6 FOODCL	7 ELECTR	8 TRANS	9 CONSTR	10 HOUS.	11 OTHMAR	12 SUM
AG.PL.	0.	0.	0.	0.	0.	0.	0.	0.	0.	0.	0.	0.
M.M.	0.	0.	0.	0.	0.	0.	0.	0.	0.	0.	0.	0.
EQIPMT	0.	0.	0.	0.	0.	0.	0.	0.	0.	0.	0.	0.
CHEMIC	0.	0.	0.	0.	0.	0.	0.	0.	0.	0.	0.	0.
CMGLWD	0.	0.	0.	0.	0.	0.	0.	0.	0.	0.	0.	0.
FOODCL	0.	0.	0.	0.	0.	0.	0.	0.	0.	0.	0.	0.
ELECTR	0.	0.	0.	0.	0.	0.	0.	0.	0.	0.	0.	0.
TRANS	0.	0.	0.	0.	0.	0.	0.	0.	0.	0.	0.	0.
CONSTR	0.	125.002	6.530	107.953	.348	20.623	191.092	0.	0.	77.894	81.757	611.199
HOUS.	0.	0.	0.	0.	0.	0.	0.	0.	0.	0.	0.	0.
OTHMAR	0.	0.	0.	0.	0.	0.	0.	0.	0.	0.	0.	0.

Table B.17. Stock Held, Period 3, Third Plan Target Model Reference Solution (Rs. crores, 1959-60 prices)

	1 AG.PL.	2 M.M.	3 EQIPMT	4 CHEMIC	5 CMGLWD	6 FOODCL	7 ELECTR	8 TRANS	9 CONSTR	10 HOUS.	11 OTHMAR	12 SUM
AG.PL.	2704.887	.107	26.070	25.499	59.772	762.290	0.	0.	13.737	0.	40.230	3632.592
M.M.	4.808	136.196	294.794	15.397	22.900	5.970	13.900	11.195	46.898	0.	.786	552.844
EQIPMT	0.	36.809	52.831	44.921	1.218	4.345	0.	0.	5.224	0.	0.	145.347
CHEMIC	344.324	12.050	53.048	325.927	36.761	45.551	2.986	8.123	2.234	0.	3.305	834.310
CMGLWD	16.532	11.581	8.029	6.110	11.467	4.148	0.	0.	71.200	0.	0.	129.067
FOODCL	267.593	4.358	3.552	18.837	7.868	101.851	0.	0.	0.	0.	.923	404.982
ELECTR	0.	0.	0.	0.	0.	0.	0.	0.	0.	0.	0.	0.
TRANS	0.	0.	0.	0.	0.	0.	0.	0.	0.	0.	0.	0.
CCNSTR	0.	0.	0.	0.	0.	0.	0.	0.	0.	0.	0.	0.
HCUS.	0.	0.	0.	0.	0.	0.	0.	0.	0.	0.	0.	0.
OTHMAR	0.	0.	0.	0.	0.	0.	0.	0.	0.	0.	0.	0.

Table B.18. Summary of Flow, Period 3, Third Plan Target Model Reference Solution (Rs. crores, 1959-60 prices)

	X	M	AX	SΔX	R1+R2+R3	Z1	Z2	Z3	E	G	CONS	CHECK
AG.PL.	8495.54	239.78	2393.33	240.55	0.	0.	0.	0.	214.55	0.	5886.89	.00
M.M.	838.64	213.87	862.18	140.34	0.	0.	0.	0.	43.40	0.	6.58	.00
EQIPMT	1142.41	429.81	113.77	33.49	169.47	532.81	411.33	0.	4.69	104.99	201.66	.00
CHEMIC	826.78	290.90	638.56	105.39	0.	0.	0.	0.	16.33	30.55	326.83	.00
CMGLWD	590.80	11.64	511.10	19.62	0.	0.	0.	0.	3.02	0.	68.68	.00
FOODCL	2558.76	12.72	258.19	29.30	0.	0.	0.	0.	233.46	117.39	1933.14	.00
ELECTR	130.91	0.	113.68	0.	0.	0.	0.	0.	0.	5.30	11.93	-.00
TRANS	947.01	0.	744.66	0.	0.	0.	0.	0.	0.	0.	202.35	.00
CCNSTR	2045.45	0.	0.	0.	540.66	378.83	398.36	611.20	0.	116.40	0.	-.00
HCUS.	619.11	0.	0.	0.	0.	0.	0.	0.	0.	0.	619.11	-.00
OTHMAR	5699.11	9.27	711.39	0.	22.35	69.23	53.44	0.	192.52	207.37	4452.08	.00

Table B.19. Interindustry Flow, Period 4, Third Plan Target Model Reference Solution (Rs. crores, 1959-60 prices)

	1 AG.PL.	2 M.M.	3 EQIPMT	4 CHEMIC	5 CMGLWD	6 FOODCL	7 ELECTR	8 TRANS	9 CONSTR	10 HOUS.	11 OTHMAR	12 SUM
AG.PL.	719.186	.219	25.917	49.030	88.079	1376.993	0.	0.	100.289	0.	213.000	2572.713
M.M.	1.189	210.817	349.117	23.948	34.676	11.162	19.455	43.491	343.414	3.380	4.197	1044.845
EQIPMT	0.	20.566	55.219	15.295	1.794	7.928	0.	0.	37.843	0.	0.	138.645
CHEMIC	89.402	20.122	55.434	191.704	54.196	76.811	4.180	197.436	19.649	0.	17.529	726.462
CMGLWD	3.857	11.254	8.189	10.531	16.898	8.010	0.	0.	519.324	9.869	0.	587.932
FOODCL	70.045	1.888	3.380	32.794	12.244	154.173	0.	0.	0.	0.	4.876	279.400
ELECTR	9.525	23.492	19.151	15.291	15.080	36.391	0.	4.665	0.	0.	6.666	130.261
TRANS	63.431	146.885	110.334	94.496	47.370	134.077	17.509	44.826	61.937	4.434	128.195	853.495
CONSTR	0.	0.	0.	0.	0.	0.	0.	0.	0.	0.	0.	0.
HOUS.	0.	0.	0.	0.	0.	0.	0.	0.	0.	0.	0.	0.
OTHMAR	44.201	28.488	203.556	30.826	59.823	150.915	10.144	17.730	252.460	29.376	0.	827.518

Table B.20. Investment Maturing in 1 Year, Period 4, Third Plan Target Model Reference Solution (Rs. crores, 1959-60 prices)

	1 AG.PL.	2 M.M.	3 EQIPMT	4 CHEMIC	5 CMGLWD	6 FOODCL	7 ELECTR	8 TRANS	9 CONSTR	10 HOUS.	11 OTHMAR	12 SUM
AG.PL.	0.	0.	0.	0.	0.	0.	0.	0.	0.	0.	0.	0.
M.M.	0.	0.	0.	0.	0.	0.	0.	0.	0.	0.	0.	0.
ECIPMT	40.704	90.193	79.809	58.306	12.513	20.110	C.	96.401	13.293	0.	0.	411.327
CHEMIC	0.	0.	0.	0.	0.	C.	0.	0.	0.	0.	0.	0.
CMGLWD	0.	0.	0.	0.	0.	0.	0.	0.	0.	0.	0.	0.
FOODCL	0.	0.	0.	0.	0.	0.	0.	0.	C.	0.	0.	0.
ELECTR	0.	0.	0.	0.	0.	0.	0.	0.	0.	0.	0.	0.
TRANS	0.	0.	0.	0.	0.	C.	0.	0.	0.	0.	0.	0.
CONSTR	166.846	53.337	42.903	35.503	9.318	6.199	0.	0.	3.543	80.710	0.	398.359
HCUS.	0.	0.	0.	0.	0.	C.	0.	0.	C.	0.	0.	0.
OTHMAR	5.273	11.715	10.386	7.577	1.625	2.613	0.	12.527	1.729	0.	0.	53.445

Table B.21. Investment Maturing in 2 Years, Period 4, Third Plan Target Model Reference Solution (Rs. crores, 1959-60 prices)

	1 AG.PL.	2 M.M.	3 EQIPMT	4 CHEMIC	5 CMGLWD	6 FOODCL	7 ELECTR	8 TRANS	9 CONSTR	10 HOUS.	11 OTHMAR	12 SUM
AG.PL.	0.	0.	0.	0.	0.	0.	C.	0.	0.	0.	0.	0.
M.M.	0.	0.	0.	0.	0.	0.	0.	0.	0.	0.	0.	0.
EQIPMT	0.	211.378	12.147	177.289	.467	66.897	213.251	124.980	0.	0.	61.299	867.708
CHEMIC	0.	0.	0.	0.	0.	0.	0.	0.	0.	0.	0.	0.
CMGLWD	0.	0.	0.	0.	0.	0.	0.	0.	0.	0.	0.	0.
FOODCL	0.	0.	0.	0.	0.	0.	0.	0.	0.	0.	0.	0.
ELECTR	0.	0.	0.	0.	0.	0.	0.	0.	0.	0.	0.	0.
TRANS	0.	0.	0.	0.	0.	0.	C.	0.	0.	0.	0.	0.
CCNSTR	0.	125.002	6.530	107.953	.348	20.623	191.092	0.	0.	77.894	81.757	611.199
HOUS.	0.	0.	0.	0.	0.	0.	0.	0.	0.	0.	0.	0.
OTHMAR	0.	27.456	1.581	23.040	.061	8.692	27.751	16.240	0.	0.	7.984	112.805

Table B.22. Investment Maturing in 3 Years, Period 4, Third Plan Target Model Reference Solution (Rs. crores, 1959-60 prices)

	1 AG.PL.	2 M.M.	3 EQIPMT	4 CHEMIC	5 CMGLWD	6 FOODCL	7 ELECTR	8 TRANS	9 CONSTR	10 HOUS.	11 OTHMAR	12 SUM
AG.PL.	0.	0.	0.	0.	0.	0.	0.	0.	0.	0.	0.	0.
M.M.	0.	0.	0.	0.	0.	0.	0.	0.	0.	0.	0.	0.
EQIPMT	0.	0.	0.	0.	0.	0.	0.	0.	0.	0.	0.	0.
CHEMIC	0.	0.	0.	0.	0.	0.	0.	0.	0.	0.	0.	0.
CMGLWD	0.	0.	0.	0.	0.	0.	0.	0.	0.	0.	0.	0.
FCODCL	0.	0.	0.	0.	0.	0.	0.	0.	0.	0.	0.	0.
ELECTR	0.	0.	0.	0.	0.	0.	0.	0.	0.	0.	0.	0.
TRANS	0.	0.	0.	0.	0.	0.	0.	0.	0.	0.	0.	0.
CONSTR	146.675	117.715	45.466	60.501	9.370	8.209	82.024	0.	.942	145.886	21.948	638.736
HOUS.	0.	0.	0.	0.	0.	0.	0.	0.	0.	0.	0.	0.
OTHMAR	0.	0.	0.	0.	0.	0.	0.	0.	0.	0.	0.	0.

Table B.23. Stock Held, Period 4, Third Plan Target Model Reference Solution (Rs. crores, 1959-60 prices)

	1 AG.PL.	2 M.M.	3 EQIPMT	4 CHEMIC	5 CMGLWD	6 FOODCL	7 ELECTR	8 TRANS	9 CONSTR	10 HOUS.	11 OTHMAR	12 SUM
AG.PL.	2869.113	.129	34.480	29.782	68.057	812.205	0.	0.	15.807	0.	43.569	3873.143
M.M.	5.100	164.560	389.893	17.983	26.074	6.360	15.761	12.634	53.966	0.	.852	693.184
ECIPMT	0.	44.475	69.874	52.465	1.386	4.629	0.	0.	6.011	0.	0.	178.840
CHEMIC	365.230	14.560	70.161	380.660	41.857	48.534	3.386	9.167	2.570	0.	3.580	939.705
CMGLWD	17.536	13.993	10.619	7.136	13.057	4.419	0.	0.	81.930	0.	0.	148.690
FCODCL	283.839	5.265	4.698	22.001	8.959	108.521	0.	0.	0.	0.	1.000	434.282
ELECTR	0.	0.	0.	0.	0.	0.	0.	0.	0.	0.	0.	0.
TRANS	0.	0.	0.	0.	0.	0.	0.	0.	0.	0.	0.	0.
CCNSTR	0.	0.	0.	0.	0.	0.	0.	0.	0.	0.	0.	0.
HCUS.	0.	0.	0.	0.	0.	0.	0.	0.	0.	0.	0.	0.
OTHMAR	0.	0.	0.	0.	0.	0.	0.	0.	0.	0.	0.	0.

Table B.24. Summary of Flow, Period 4, Third Plan Target Model Reference Solution (Rs. crores, 1959-60 prices)

	X	M	AX	SΔX	R1+R2+R3	Z1	Z2	Z3	E	G	CONS	CHECK
AG.PL.	9011.35	234.93	2572.71	186.18	0.	0.	0.	0.	223.04	0.	6264.35	-.00
M.M.	1013.30	213.57	1044.85	129.90	0.	0.	0.	0.	45.12	0.	7.00	.00
ECIPMT	1510.95	471.61	138.65	38.20	198.60	411.33	867.71	0.	4.88	108.60	214.59	.00
CHEMIC	965.62	306.27	726.46	149.06	0.	0.	0.	0.	16.98	31.60	347.78	.00
CMGLWD	672.69	9.39	587.93	17.92	0.	0.	0.	0.	3.14	0.	73.09	-.00
FCODCL	2726.31	.22	279.40	25.92	0.	0.	0.	0.	242.70	121.42	2057.09	.00
ELECTR	148.43	0.	130.26	0.	0.	0.	0.	0.	0.	5.48	12.69	-.00
TRANS	1068.82	0.	853.50	0.	0.	0.	0.	0.	0.	0.	215.32	-.00
CCNSTR	2353.70	0.	0.	0.	585.00	398.36	611.20	638.74	0.	120.40	0.	-.00
HOUS.	658.81	0.	0.	0.	0.	0.	0.	0.	0.	0.	658.81	.00
OTHMAR	6172.13	0.	827.52	0.	26.20	53.44	112.80	0.	200.13	214.49	4737.54	-.00

Table B.25. Interindustry Flow, Period 5, Third Plan Target Model Reference Solution (Rs. crores, 1959-60 prices)

	1 AG.PL.	2 M.M.	3 EQIPHT	4 CHEMIC	5 CMGLWD	6 FOODCL	7 ELECTR	8 TRANS	9 CONSTR	10 HOUS.	11 OTHMAR	12 SUM
AG.PL.	750.471	.251	31.775	62.852	96.312	1435.742	0.	0.	111.617	0.	224.553	2713.573
M.M.	1.241	242.153	428.027	30.699	37.917	11.638	21.686	48.178	382.204	3.504	4.425	1211.672
EQIPHT	0.	23.623	67.700	19.607	1.962	8.266	0.	0.	42.117	0.	0.	163.275
CHEMIC	93.291	23.113	67.963	245.746	59.262	80.088	4.659	218.713	21.868	0.	18.480	833.182
CMGLWD	4.025	12.926	10.040	13.500	18.478	8.352	0.	0.	577.985	10.232	0.	655.536
FOODCL	73.092	2.168	4.144	42.039	13.389	160.751	0.	0.	0.	0.	5.140	300.723
ELECTR	9.939	26.984	23.480	19.601	16.489	37.943	0.	5.168	0.	0.	7.027	146.633
TRANS	66.190	168.718	135.273	121.135	51.798	139.798	19.517	49.657	68.934	4.597	135.148	960.763
CONSTR	0.	0.	0.	0.	0.	0.	0.	0.	0.	0.	0.	0.
HCUS.	0.	0.	0.	0.	0.	0.	0.	0.	0.	0.	0.	0.
OTHMAR	46.123	32.722	249.566	39.516	65.415	157.354	11.307	19.640	280.976	30.456	0.	933.076

Table B.26. Investment Maturing in 1 Year, Period 5, Third Plan Target Model Reference Solution (Rs. crores, 1959-60 prices)

	1 AG.PL.	2 M.M.	3 EQIPHT	4 CHEMIC	5 CMGLWD	6 FOODCL	7 ELECTR	8 TRANS	9 CONSTR	10 HOUS.	11 OTHMAR	12 SUM
AG.PL.	0.	0.	0.	0.	0.	0.	0.	0.	0.	0.	0.	0.
M.M.	0.	0.	0.	0.	0.	0.	0.	0.	0.	0.	0.	0.
EQIPHT	0.	211.378	12.147	177.289	.467	66.897	213.251	124.980	0.	0.	61.299	867.708
CHEMIC	0.	0.	0.	0.	0.	0.	0.	0.	0.	0.	0.	0.
CMGLWD	0.	0.	0.	0.	0.	0.	0.	0.	0.	0.	0.	0.
FCODCL	0.	0.	0.	0.	0.	0.	0.	0.	0.	0.	0.	0.
ELECTR	0.	0.	0.	0.	0.	0.	0.	0.	0.	0.	0.	0.
TRANS	0.	0.	0.	0.	0.	0.	0.	0.	0.	0.	0.	0.
CCNSTR	0.	125.002	6.530	107.953	.348	20.623	191.092	0.	0.	77.894	81.757	611.199
HOUS.	0.	0.	0.	0.	0.	0.	0.	0.	0.	0.	0.	0.
OTHMAR	0.	27.456	1.581	23.040	.061	8.692	27.751	16.240	0.	0.	7.984	112.805

Table B.27. Investment Maturing in 2 Years, Period 5, Third Plan Target Model Reference Solution (Rs. crores, 1959-60 prices)

	1 AG.PL.	2 M.M.	3 EQIPHT	4 CHEMIC	5 CMGLWD	6 FOODCL	7 ELECTR	8 TRANS	9 CONSTR	10 HOUS.	11 OTHMAR	12 SUM
AG.PL.	0.	0.	0.	0.	0.	0.	0.	0.	0.	0.	0.	0.
M.M.	0.	0.	0.	0.	0.	0.	0.	0.	0.	0.	0.	0.
EGIPHT	35.783	199.055	84.577	99.360	12.582	26.628	91.535	146.492	3.535	0.	16.456	716.004
CHEMIC	0.	0.	0.	0.	0.	0.	0.	0.	0.	0.	0.	0.
CMGLWD	0.	0.	0.	0.	0.	0.	0.	0.	0.	0.	0.	0.
FCODCL	0.	0.	0.	0.	0.	0.	0.	0.	0.	0.	0.	0.
ELECTR	0.	0.	0.	0.	0.	0.	0.	0.	0.	0.	0.	0.
TRANS	0.	0.	0.	0.	0.	0.	0.	0.	0.	0.	0.	0.
CCNSTR	146.675	117.715	45.466	60.501	9.370	8.209	82.024	0.	.942	145.886	21.948	638.736
HCUS.	0.	0.	0.	0.	0.	0.	0.	0.	0.	0.	0.	0.
OTHMAR	4.636	25.855	11.006	12.912	1.634	3.460	11.912	19.036	.460	0.	2.143	93.054

Table B.28. **Investment Maturing in 3 Years, Period 5, Third Plan Target Model Reference Solution (Rs. crores, 1959-60 prices)**

	1 AG.PL.	2 M.M.	3 EQIPMT	4 CHEMIC	5 CMGLWD	6 FOODCL	7 ELECTR	8 TRANS	9 CONSTR	10 HOUS.	11 OTHMAR	12 SUM
AG.PL.	0.	0.	0.	0.	0.	0.	0.	0.	0.	0.	0.	0.
M.M.	0.	0.	0.	0.	0.	0.	0.	0.	0.	0.	0.	0.
EQIPMT	0.	0.	0.	0.	0.	0.	0.	0.	0.	0.	0.	0.
CHEMIC	0.	0.	0.	0.	0.	0.	0.	0.	0.	0.	0.	0.
CMGLWD	0.	0.	0.	0.	0.	0.	0.	0.	0.	0.	0.	0.
FCODCL	0.	0.	0.	0.	0.	0.	0.	0.	0.	0.	0.	0.
ELECTR	0.	0.	0.	0.	0.	0.	0.	0.	0.	0.	0.	0.
TRANS	0.	0.	0.	0.	0.	0.	0.	0.	0.	0.	0.	0.
CCNSTR	152.050	143.510	54.106	74.089	10.173	8.600	109.365	0.	2.671	149.542	55.442	759.549
HCUS.	0.	0.	0.	0.	0.	0.	0.	0.	0.	0.	0.	0.
OTHMAR	0.	0.	0.	0.	0.	0.	0.	0.	0.	0.	0.	0.

Table B.29. **Stock Held, Period 5, Third Plan Target Model Reference Solution (Rs. crores, 1959-60 prices)**

	1 AG.PL.	2 M.M.	3 EQIPMT	4 CHEMIC	5 CMGLWD	6 FOODCL	7 ELECTR	8 TRANS	9 CONSTR	10 HOUS.	11 OTHMAR	12 SUM
AG.PL.	2993.920	.148	42.273	38.177	74.419	846.858	0.	0.	17.593	0.	45.932	4059.320
M.M.	5.322	189.020	478.019	23.052	28.511	6.632	17.569	13.996	60.061	0.	.898	823.081
EQIPMT	0.	51.085	85.667	67.255	1.516	4.827	0.	0.	6.690	0.	0.	217.040
CHEMIC	381.117	16.724	86.019	487.968	45.769	50.604	3.775	10.155	2.861	0.	3.774	1088.767
CMGLWD	18.299	16.072	13.019	9.148	14.277	4.608	0.	0.	91.184	0.	0.	166.608
FCODCL	296.186	6.048	5.759	28.203	9.796	113.151	0.	0.	0.	0.	1.054	460.197
ELECTR	0.	0.	0.	0.	0.	0.	0.	0.	0.	0.	0.	0.
TRANS	0.	0.	0.	0.	0.	0.	0.	0.	0.	0.	0.	0.
CCNSTR	0.	0.	0.	0.	0.	0.	0.	0.	0.	0.	0.	0.
HCUS.	0.	0.	0.	0.	0.	0.	0.	0.	0.	0.	0.	0.
OTHMAR	0.	0.	0.	0.	0.	0.	0.	0.	0.	0.	0.	0.

Table B.30. **Summary of Flow, Period 5, Third Plan Target Model Reference Solution (Rs. crores, 1959-60 prices)**

	X	M	AX	SΔX	R1+R2+R3	Z1	Z2	Z3	E	G	CONS	CHECK
AG.PL.	9403.34	195.40	2713.57	158.73	0.	0.	0.	0.	231.83	0.	6494.60	.00
M.M.	1163.91	205.42	1211.67	103.51	0.	0.	0.	0.	46.89	0.	7.26	-.00
EQIPMT	1852.46	499.43	163.28	63.21	201.94	867.71	716.00	0.	5.07	112.21	222.48	-.00
CHEMIC	1237.83	352.91	833.18	346.68	0.	0.	0.	0.	17.65	32.65	360.57	-.00
CMGLWD	735.57	6.63	655.54	7.62	0.	0.	0.	0.	3.27	0.	75.77	-.00
FCODCL	2842.63	5.20	300.72	36.68	0.	0.	0.	0.	252.26	125.46	2132.70	.00
ELECTR	165.45	0.	146.63	0.	0.	0.	0.	0.	0.	5.66	13.16	.00
TRANS	1184.00	0.	960.76	0.	0.	0.	0.	0.	0.	0.	223.24	.00
CCNSTR	2619.56	0.	0.	0.	485.68	611.20	638.74	759.55	0.	124.40	0.	-.00
HCUS.	.683.02	0.	0.	0.	0.	0.	0.	0.	0.	0.	683.02	.00
OTHMAR	6506.88	0.	933.08	0.	26.64	112.80	93.05	0.	208.02	221.62	4911.67	-.00

5. Guidepath and Guidepost Models

The fool who does not know
His own resource, his foe,
His duty, time and place,
Who sets a reckless pace,
Will by the wayside fall,
Will reap no fruit at all.

The Panchatantra

5.1 Introduction

Planning involves decisions about the distant as well as the near future, and concentration on short-period planning inevitably omits relevant considerations. In principle the planning horizon should be infinite, but in practice it must be truncated. Still, economic decisions are made in a more and more satisfactory manner as the time horizon is pushed out further and further until there are no further advantages to be gained from exercising foresight vis-à-vis the immediate economic issues.

A long-term model for making economic policy would always be preferable to a short-term model if the uncertainties associated with technical and behavioral coefficients did not increase with time for coefficients further in the future. When such increasing uncertainties are not accounted for in making optimal plans, it is conceivable that a shorter plan might turn out to be better than a longer one. The optimum horizon cannot be known a priori, but in development planning it seems certainly to be more than the conventional five years. The short-term models were presented first because of the conventional interest in short-term plans and particularly because of their usefulness in analyzing the Five Year Plan targets and other aspects of Indian economic policy. The basic justification for short-term planning models, however, is their computational convenience, since the cost of calculations rises rapidly as systems are expanded to cover more and more time periods.

Because of the greater computational costs of the long-term planning models, compromises must be made in their structure in order to solve them. The type of compromise most frequently made has been the aggregation of the economy portrayed to one or two sectors. This has characterized many of the theoretical models developed to provide qualitative insights into the growth process. But aggregation imposes the assumption of full substitutability among all the commodities drawn into each sector. While not a disadvantage with respect to some issues, that assumption is a handicap to understanding when outputs and inputs are, to an important extent, specific in their uses. On the other hand, if, because of the absence of any other basis for decision, proportions among the outputs and inputs of different sectors are held constant, the sectors can just as well be aggregated, and no knowledge is added by carrying them along separately. However, the various sectors contribute to the production of consumption and investment goods in different proportions. This, in turn, means that changes in the relative proportions of these goods over time will lead to changes in the relative weight of these sectors in the whole economy. It is not known in advance whether aggregation of sectors, on balance, overstates or understates the potential achievements of a system. Aggregation permits full substitution within sectors and thus may overstate production potential. On the other hand, if as the result of aggregation the average input requirements imposed on a particularly fast-growing part of the economy are higher than if that sector were treated separately, the effect is to penalize growth.

Another device often used in growth models is the aggregation of time periods, as this provides another means of reducing the computational burden of models with long time horizons. When discrete time periods are used in planning, their length should be chosen so that the time shape of events within the period has no effect on the outcome. In many of the economically more advanced countries, a year may be too long for this to hold true, but it is still used in large part because it coincides with the conventional accounting period. In India the relative importance of the agricultural sectors may provide more justification for annual accounting.

The aggregation of time periods has effects analogous to those of the aggregation of sectors; it implies complete substitution within the period. This provides an additional degree of freedom in breaking bottlenecks, which is not in fact present, and which may be particularly significant for countries like India, starting their development with an industrial composition substantially different from that toward which they are aiming. On the other hand, there may be compensating disadvantages in time aggregation since it forces a kind of synchronization among sectors in each aggregated time period which in actuality need not be present.

While the computational burden associated with long-term models requires simplification of structure, some elaboration is desirable if the models are to provide guidance for short-term planning. For short-term plans it can often be assumed, for example, that consumption or input proportions will not change substantially within the plan period. However, even in five-year plans it may be important to use different parameters in reflecting postterminal conditions into the planning period. Furthermore, where a prediction can be made of a change in technology, as in the foreseen displacement of a traditional with a modern technology, a long-term model ought to provide a basis for determining the values of the technical parameters to be used in a short-term model.

It is not possible on the basis of qualitative arguments alone to predict the quantitative effects of the various types of compromises in model structure, since they will depend to a considerable degree on the particular economy studied and the parameter values used. As our primary purpose, especially in conjunction with the long-term models, is to develop techniques of planning, we shall not be exhaustive in our own calculations. No twenty- to thirty-year detailed programs are publicly available for India which we can subject to the type of testing performed on the Third and Fourth Five Year Plans. We can and will, however, indicate some alternative long-run development policies and their implications. We shall also demonstrate a technique for linking an explicit long-term plan to a short-term five-year plan.

5.2 Structure of the Guidepath Model

The long-term model that we call the Guidepath Model is created by modifications and additions to the structure of the Basic Model core, although some definitions will be modified and variables and relationships added. The entire model will be described in this chapter. The description will be brief, except where there have been significant modifications. The major structural changes in the long-term as compared to the short-term models are (1) a greater degree of aggregation over time, (2) the provision for change in consumption proportions through the use of expenditure elasticities, and (3) the inclusion of a mechanism for shifting from a traditional to a modern technology in the agricultural sector. Inasmuch as the savings rate is of major importance in determining the character of the solutions, the long-term model will be solved in two versions, the Guidepath-I and Guidepath-II formulations, which are distinguished by the explicit specification of a savings constraint in the latter case.

The time period is changed from one year to three years partly because of the rationalization that events within such a relatively short period are unimportant for long-term planning of fifteen to thirty years. This rationalization has more justification for the later years of a long-term plan than for the early years, in which imbalances and bottlenecks of various types may be of considerable importance. One way of dealing with this situation would be to change the length of the unit time period over the planning horizon. This approach has some complexities in programming, which we avoid by making detailed short-term plans using the long-term plans as a guide. The three-year period is chosen in order to collapse the gestation lag. Most of the relationships will not have to change as a

Table 5.1. Additional Variables and Parameters for the Guidepath Models

$X_1(t)$	output of the Incremental Agriculture activity in period t
$X_{12}(t)$	output of the Traditional Agriculture activity in period t
η	diagonal matrix for expenditure elasticities of consumption of each sector's output
$\lambda(t)$	population growth rate between periods t and $t-1$
τ	growth rate of cultivable land available to Agriculture
y_1, y_{12}	yields of output per unit of land in Incremental and Traditional Agriculture, respectively
$P(t)$	population in period (t)
U	activity aggregation matrix
$*$	variables marked by asterisks, e.g. $\overset{*}{X}$, apply only to first eleven activities

result of this modification, but the magnitude of those parameters that have time dimensions will have to change. The capital-output ratios, for example, which have a time dimension will be divided by three. Extending the unit period may have a retarding effect on growth, as it effectively lengthens the gestation lag in some sectors. Offsetting this is the assumption that resources and production in any one of the three years of the unit period are perfectly substitutable.

Table 5.1 lists the additional parameters and changes in definitions of variables for the Guidepath Models, and Table 5.2 presents the complete set of relationships. Maximand 1.0 in Table 5.2 is the same as in the Basic Model, but the unit period is now three years, so C(t) is the sum of private consumption in three years; w is the discounting factor applied to C(t) and is similarly adjusted so that it reflects the three-year period. Provision is again made in Eq. 2.0 for a growth constraint on total consumption.

Since in this model there are two activities producing agricultural goods, the accounting must be adjusted to reflect this. Both activities deliver agricultural output to fulfill the various requirements for it. The total agricultural output is obtained by summing the outputs of both the activities. This is indicated by use of the activity aggregation matrix [U] in the distribution Eq. 3.0. The matrix [U] is a rectangular matrix with rows equal to the number of sectors and columns equal to the number of activities. Element U_{ij} = 1.0, if the jth activity contributes to the ith sector; otherwise, U_{ij} = 0. We find it convenient to make the first activity "Incremental Agriculture" and the twelfth activity "Traditional Agriculture" for reasons to be explained subsequently. Then the [U] matrix, which has eleven rows and twelve columns, is shown below:

$$U = \begin{bmatrix} 1 & 0 & . & . & . & 1 \\ 0 & 1 & & & & 0 \\ . & & . & & & . \\ . & & & . & & . \\ . & & & & . & . \\ 0 & 0 & . & . & 1 & 0 \end{bmatrix}$$

Each of the activities in Agriculture has a different technical coefficient, and the matrices a(t) of intermediate inputs, s(t) of inventory output coefficients, and p of capital proportions are therefore all rectangular. The intermediate requirements for output are shown in Eq. 3.1. The relationships for inventory requirements in Eqs. 3.2 and 3.3 are like the analogous relationships in the Basic Model.

The proportions in which each sector contributes to aggregate private consumption are determined by consumption-expenditure elasticities η_i and initial proportions. The consumption-expenditure elasticity η_i for sector i is defined as follows:

$$\eta_i = \frac{F_i(t)/P(t) - \overline{F_i(0)}/\overline{P(0)}}{\overline{F_i(0)}/\overline{P(0)}} \bigg/ \frac{F(t)/P(t) - \overline{F(0)}/\overline{P(0)}}{\overline{F(0)}/\overline{P(0)}}$$

where P(t) is the population in period t. P(t) is obtained from the initial population P(0) and the projected growth rates of population $\lambda(t)$ as

$$P(t) = P(0)[1 + \lambda(1)][1 + \lambda(2)] \cdots [1 + \lambda(t)] = P(0) \prod_{t=1}^{t} [1 + \lambda(t)]$$

Table 5.2. Guidepath-I and Guidepath-II Models

1. Objective Function

   (1.0)   Maximize: $W = \sum\limits_{t=1}^{T} \cdot \dfrac{C(t)}{(1 + W)^{t-1}}$

   Subject to:

2. Consumption Growth Constraints

   (2.0) $C(t + 1) \geqslant (1 + \rho(t))C(t),$ for $t = 0, \cdots, T - 1,$
   Initial consumption:
   (2.1) $C(0) = \overline{C(0)},$

3. Distribution Relationships

   (3.0) $J(t) + H(t) + N(t) + Q(t) + F(t) + G(t) + E(t) \leqslant M(t) + UX(t),$ for $t = 1, \cdots, T,$

   where $U = \begin{bmatrix} 1 & 0 & \cdot & 0 & 1 \\ 0 & 1 & \cdot & \cdot & 0 \\ \cdot & \cdot & \cdot & \cdot & \cdot \\ 0 & \cdot & \cdot & 1 & 0 \end{bmatrix}$

   Intermediate products:
   (3.1) $J(t) = a(t)X(t),$ for $t = 1, \cdots, T,$
   Inventory requirements:
   (3.2) $H(t) = s(t)\{X(t + 1) - X(t)\},$ for $t = 2, \cdots, T,$
   (3.3) $H(1) = s(1)\{X(2) - (1 + \alpha_0)\overline{X(0)}\},$ for $t = 1,$
   Private consumption:

   (3.4) $F(t) = \eta cC(t) + \left\{ \prod\limits_{t=1}^{t} [1 + \lambda(t)] \right\} (I - \eta)c\overline{C(0)},$ for $t = 1, \cdots, T,$

   Government consumption:
   (3.5) $G(t) = \overline{G(t)},$ for $t = 1, \cdots, T,$
   Exports:
   (3.6) $E(t) = \overline{E(t)},$ for $t = 1, \cdots, T,$

4. Capacity Restraints
   (4.0) $b(t)X(t) \leqslant K(t),$ for $t = 1, \cdots, T,$

5. Capital Accounting Relationships

   Investment requirements:
   (5.0) $N(t) = pZ(t + 1),$ for $t = 1, \cdots, T,$
   Depreciated capital:
   (5.1) $D(t) = \overline{D(t)},$ for $t = 2, \cdots, T + 1,$
   Depreciated capacity:
   (5.2) $V(t) = dD(t),$ for $t = 2, \cdots, T + 1,$
   Restoration requirements:
   (5.3) $Q(t) = r(t)d(t)^{-1}R(t),$ for $t = 1, \cdots, T,$
   Capital accounting:
   (5.4) $K(t + 1) \leqslant K(t) + Z(t + 1) + R(t + 1) - V(t + 1),$ for $t = 1, \cdots, T,$

6. Restoration ceilings
   (6.0) $R(t) \leqslant V(t),$ for $t = 2, \cdots, T + 1,$

7. Balance of Payments Constraints
   (7.0) $uM(t) \leqslant \overline{A(t)} + uE(t),$ for $t = 1, \cdots, T,$

8. Imports
   Import composition:
   (8.0) $M(t) = M'(t) + M''(t),$ for $t = 1, \cdots, T,$
   Noncompetitive imports:
   (8.1) $M'(t) = m'(t)X(t),$ for $t = 1, \cdots, T,$
   Competitive import ceilings:
   (8.2) $M''(t) \leqslant m''(t)[\overline{A(t)} + uE(t) - uM'(t)],$ for $t = 1, \cdots, T,$

Table 5.2. (cont.)

9. Relationships Between Incremental and Traditional Agriculture Activities

   (9.0) $\quad X_{12}(t) - [1 + \tau] X_{12}(t - 1) \leqslant 0, \quad$ for $t = 1, \cdots, T,$

   (9.1) $\quad X_1(t) - \dfrac{y_1}{y_{12}} X_{12}(t) \leqslant 0, \quad$ for $t = 1, \cdots, T,$

10. Initial Capital Restraints

    (10.0) $\quad K(1) = b(1)(I + \alpha_0)\overline{X(0)},$

11. Terminal Requirements in General

    (11.0) $\quad K(T + 1) \geqslant \overline{K(T + 1)}.$

12. Derivation of Terminal Conditions from Postterminal Growth Requirements

    Postterminal growth rates of demands and imports:

    (12.0) $\quad C(t) = \overline{C(T)}(1 + \phi)^{t-T},$

    (12.1) $\quad G(t) = \overline{G(T)}(1 + \gamma)^{t-T},$

    (12.2) $\quad E(t) = \overline{E(T)}(1 + \epsilon)^{t-T},$

    (12.3) $\quad D(t) = \overline{D(T)}(1 + \delta)^{t-T},$

    (12.4) $\quad M(t) = \overline{M(T)}(1 + \mu)^{t-T},$

    (12.5) $\quad X_{12}(t) = \overline{X_{12}(T)}(1 + \tau)^{t-T},$

    (12.6) $\quad F(t) = \eta c C(T)(1 + \phi)^{t-T} + \left\{ \prod_{t=1}^{t}[1 + \lambda(t)] \right\}(I - \eta)c\overline{C(0)}.$

    This implies

    (12.7) $\quad \overset{*}{X}(t) + X_{12}(t) = \overset{*}{a}(T)\overset{*}{X}(t) + [\overset{*}{s}(T) + \overset{*}{b}(T)\overset{*}{p}]\,\overset{*}{X}(t + 1) - \overset{*}{X}(t)$

    $\quad\quad + [a_{12}(T) + (s_{12}(T) + b_{12}(T)p_{12})\tau]\overline{X_{12}(T)}(1 + \tau)^{t-T}$

    $\quad\quad + \eta c C(T)(1 + \phi)^{t-T} + \prod_{t=1}^{T}(1 + \lambda(t))\,(I - \eta)c\overline{C(0)}(1 + \lambda(T))^{t-T}$

    $\quad\quad + \overline{G(T)}(1 + \gamma)^{t-T} + \overline{E(T)}(1 + \epsilon)^{t-T} + \overline{D(T)}(1 + \delta)^{t-T}$

    $\quad\quad - M''(T)(1 + \mu)^{t-T} - \overset{*}{m}'(T)\overset{*}{X}(T)(1 + \mu)^{t-T} - m'_{12}(T)\overline{X_{12}(T)}(1 + \mu)^{t-T},$

    $\quad\quad\quad\quad\quad\quad\quad\quad\quad\quad\quad\quad\quad\quad\quad\quad\quad\quad\quad\quad\quad\quad\quad$ for $t > T.$

    Define:

    $\quad q_\xi \equiv [I - \overset{*}{a}(T) - (\overset{*}{b}(T)p + \overset{*}{s}(T))\xi], \quad$ for $\xi \equiv \tau, \lambda(T), \phi, \gamma, \epsilon, \delta, \mu.$

13. Particular Solution of (12.7)

    (13.0) $\quad \overset{*}{X}(T + 1) = [\overset{*}{q}_\tau]^{-1}[-I + a_{12}(T) + (s_{12}(T) + b_{12}(T)p_{12})\tau]\overline{X_{12}(T)}(1 + \tau)$

    $\quad\quad + [\overset{*}{q}_\phi]^{-1}\eta c C(T)(1 + \phi)$

    $\quad\quad + [\overset{*}{q}_{\lambda(T)}]^{-1}\prod_{t=1}^{T}(1 + \lambda(t))\,(I - \eta)c\overline{C(0)}(1 + \lambda(T))$

    $\quad\quad + [\overset{*}{q}_\gamma]^{-1}\overline{E(T)}(1 + \gamma)$

    $\quad\quad + [\overset{*}{q}_\epsilon]^{-1}\overline{E(T)}(1 + \epsilon)$

    $\quad\quad + [\overset{*}{q}_\delta]^{-1}\overline{D(T)}(1 + \delta)$

    $\quad\quad - [\overset{*}{q}_\mu]^{-1}M''(T)(1 + \mu)$

    $\quad\quad - [\overset{*}{q}_\mu]^{-1}m'(T)\overset{*}{X}(T)(1 + \mu)$

    $\quad\quad - [\overset{*}{q}_\mu]^{-1}m'_{12}(T)\overline{X_{12}(T)}(1 + \mu), \quad$ for $t = t + 1, T + 2, T + 3.$

14. Terminal Capital Stocks

    (14.0) $\quad \overset{*}{K}(T + 1) \geqslant \overset{*}{b}(T)\overset{*}{X}(T + 1)$

    $\quad\quad\quad K_{12}(T + 1) \geqslant b_{12}(T)\overline{X_{12}(T + 1)}$

15. Terminal inventories

    (15.0) $\quad s(T)X(T + 1) \geqslant \overset{*}{s}(T)\overset{*}{X}(T + 1) + s_{12}(T)\overline{X_{12}(T + 1)}.$

16. Consumption or Savings Constraint for the Guidepath-II Model

    (16.0) $\quad C(t) + \mu G(T) \geqslant \beta_0 + \beta_1\mu[(I - A)X(t) - \overline{D}(t)], \quad$ for $t = 1, \cdots, T.$

With F(0) = cC(0), where c is the vector of initial consumption proportions, the sectoral private consumptions in period t can be written as in Eq. 3.4:

$$(3.4) \quad F(t) = \eta cC(t) + \left\{ \prod_{t=1}^{t} [1 + \lambda(t)] \right\} (I - \eta)c\overline{C(0)}, \qquad \text{for } t = 1, \cdots T,$$

where η is the diagonal matrix of sectoral consumption-expenditure elasticities. With this formulation, the proportions of sectoral to aggregate consumption will vary with the growth of total consumption. However, it should be realized that this still does not provide freedom to substitute one good for the other in consumption in any one period.

The demands for government consumption and exports, Eqs. 3.5 and 3.6, are provided as data. The form of the capital accounting relationships, Eqs. 5.0 through 5.4 does not change, except that with the aggregation of the time period, there is only a one-period gestation lag. Consequently there is only one p matrix and one r matrix.

Depreciation and replacement are treated as in the short-run model. When the planning period exceeds the lifetime of the shortest-lived component of capital, the model should have some provision for recording amounts invested during the plan period for depreciation purposes. This procedure has not been followed, since it would have required additional accounting, and the long-term model's computation requirements are already heavy. In the present case, the length of the planning period is only slightly longer than the life of the shortest-lived component, so the external specification of depreciation for the entire plan period is kept. This requires a guess about the rate of investment in the various sectors during the early part of the plan period.

The gross investments made since the beginning of the First Plan in 1951 are substantially different in composition from the assumed steady state prior to 1951. These investments come up for replacement during the long-term plan period. Consequently the replacement proportions matrix r(t) and the depreciated-capacity transformation matrix d(t) are different in each period, so they now have a time notation in Eq. 5.3.

The balance of payments constraints remain unchanged, and imports in any period may not exceed the available foreign exchange in that period. Although there is no provision endogenous to the model for changing the proportions of noncompetitive imports to output, this is done by changing the specification of the m′ coefficients from period to period. The models have been solved without limitations on the degree of specialization of competitive imports by setting all the m″ coefficients equal to one in Eq. 8.2.

The Guidepath Models also provide for a shift from traditional to modern technology in the agricultural sector. This sector is by far the largest in the Indian economy and provides the largest component of the consumer's budget. Intensive efforts are under way to change its technology, and while in the short run these may have only a marginal effect, in the long run they must be successful if India is to maintain a viable economy. Satisfactory treatment of the requirements for agricultural expansion are therefore particularly crucial in projecting long-run development in India. Agricultural development is a complex of social reorganization, additional inputs, and technological change. If it is successful, more capital inputs and more of some, though less of other, current inputs will be required. The consequence will be an increase in land and labor productivity. However, the produced factors which appear in the model and are inputs into the traditional technology may cost less than the inputs required by the modern technology. In this case, if there are not other constraints, the traditional technology would be preferred over modern methods. However, the scarcity of land imposes a limit on the output of the traditional sector. In order to satisfy increasing demands for agricultural products, a shift to the modern technology with higher land productivity would be required. The current input vectors for the alternative technologies, the capital coefficients, and the two productivities of land must be specified. In addition, a constraint embodying the limits on output imposed by the available land when used with the two technologies must be added.

For the purpose of determining the terminal levels of capital stocks in Agriculture, it is necessary to specify the level of output in one of the two agricultural activities in the terminal period. In order to do this, it is convenient to consider the agricultural sector as composed of "traditional" and "incremental" activities rather than "traditional" and "modern" activities. In this approach, the process of modernization is not one in which the modern sector displaces the traditional sector on existing land. Rather, it is as if incremental inputs to supplement the traditional inputs are applied to the same piece of land. The land then yields both traditional and incremental output.[1] In this formulation, the traditional sector continues to operate throughout the planning period on all the land that is cultivable. The available cultivable land is assumed to increase by 0.5 per cent a year due to reclamation efforts. The maximum available cultivable land for each period is thus known, and during the planning period the traditional activity is limited by this ceiling in each period. Restraints 9.0 reflect these ceilings.

$$(9.0) \quad X_{12}(t) - [1 - \tau] X_{12}(t - 1) \leqslant 0, \quad \text{for } t = 1, \cdots, T,$$

where X_{12} is output of the Traditional Agriculture activity, and τ is the specified growth rate of cultivable land available to Agriculture. The incremental activity cannot be operated on any land that is not cultivated by the traditional activity. Thus the incremental activity in each period is confined to the land actually cultivated by the traditional activity in that period. The restraints 9.1 stipulate this requirement.

$$(9.1) \quad X_1(t) - \frac{y_1}{y_{12}} X_{12}(t) \leqslant 0, \quad \text{for } t = 1, \cdots, T,$$

where y_1 and y_{12} are the yields of output per unit of land in Incremental and Traditional Agriculture. An explicit specification of these constraints is necessary because the incremental inputs, without the necessary traditional inputs which they supplement, may be less costly than the traditional inputs. It should be noted that since y_{12}, the yield of Traditional Agriculture, is a specified constant,

---

[1]The Incremental Agriculture sector can be conceived of as the additional output that the extension worker on the village level gets by applying additional inputs to the same piece of land on which the farmer has applied the traditional inputs to get his traditional output.

the yield in Incremental Agriculture must increase with the growth of this activity to reflect the growing over-all productivity of the agricultural sector. [2]

For the postterminal years it is assumed that Traditional Agriculture uses all the cultivable land available, and thus the terminal level of output of Traditional Agriculture is fixed. It may happen that the model solution indicates idle land capacity in the terminal year, in which case the assumption of full use of land in postterminal years would not be optimal. An iterative procedure would then be required to stipulate the terminal level of Traditional Agriculture. However, in the solutions to be presented this was not necessary. The input coefficients for the newly defined traditional sector are the same as those for the traditional sector conventionally defined. The input coefficients in the incremental sector are derived as follows. Consider a unit of land in Modern Agriculture. The vector of inputs applied to the land is $a_M y_M$ where a_M is the vector of input coefficients for Modern Agriculture and produces output y_M. Alternatively, if the unit of land is viewed as employed in Incremental and Traditional Agriculture, their inputs $a_1 y_1 + a_{12} y_{12}$ would produce the same output; i.e. $y_1 + y_{12} = y_M$. Total inputs must be the same in either interpretation, so

$$a_1 y_1 + a_{12} y_{12} = a_M y_M, \text{ i.e., } a_1 = \frac{a_M y_M - a_{12} y_{12}}{y_M - y_{12}} = \frac{a_M y_M - a_T y_T}{y_M - y_T}$$

The capital coefficent b_1 is similarly derived, and

$$b_1 = \frac{b_M y_M - b_T b_T}{y_M - y_T}$$

Since the time aggregation has reduced the investment lag to one period, there is no initial capital-in-process, and only the initial capital capacities need be specified in order to start the model solution. This is shown in Eq. 10.0.

Terminal conditions are determined from the specified postterminal growth rates, as in the Transit Model.

In Eqs. 12.0 through 12.6, not only the postterminal growth rates for demands and imports, but also the level and the growth rate of the output of the Traditional Agriculture activity, are specified. In the distribution Eq. 12.7 for the postterminal years, $\overset{*}{a}(T)$, $\overset{*}{s}(T)$, $b^*(T)$, $\overset{*}{p}(T)$ and $\overset{*}{m}'(T)$ are the square matrices for the first eleven activities. The twelfth columns for the Traditional Agriculture activity have been separated from each of these matrices and are denoted by $a_{12}(T)$, $s_{12}(T)$, $b_{12}(T)$, $p_{12}(T)$, and $m'_{12}(T)$. Similarily $X(t)$ is partitioned into $\overset{*}{X}(t)$ and $X_{12}(t)$. For the postterminal period in Eq. 12.7, all the coefficients are assumed to remain constant at their terminal period values.

The particular solution in Eq. 13.0 gives the output levels of the first eleven activities for the postterminal period from which the terminal capital and inventory stocks are derived in Relationships 14.0 and 15.0.

Relationships 1.0 through 15.0 complete the description of the Guidepath-I Model.

---

[2]The yield in Incremental Agriculture is $\dfrac{(L_T y_T + L_M y_M - L y_T)}{L}$, where L_T and L_M, are the land in the Traditional and Modern Agriculture sectors, respectively, L is total land, and y_T and y_M are the yields of Traditional and Modern Agriculture.

The Guidepath-II Model embodies an additional constraint in the form of a behavioral relation of private and public consumption to national income. This is shown in Eq. 16.0.

$$(16.0) \quad C(t) + \mu G(t) \geqslant \beta_0 + \beta_1 \mu [(I - A)X(t) - \bar{D}(t)], \quad \text{for } t = 1, \cdots, T.$$

The additional Constraints 16.0 constitute limits on the maximum net savings rates that can be realized in each period. This reflects an institutional limitation on the ability to raise savings. The coefficients β_0 and β_1 in Eq. 16.0 may be altered by economic policy and can be considered policy parameters. If Eq. 16.0 were formulated as a strict equality, β_1 would be the marginal propensity to consume. As pointed out previously, specification of these minimum levels of saving in this equation would not be required if there were reason to believe that the objective function was a good representation of the social welfare function.

5.3 Guidepost Models

These models are really versions of the Target Model. They are given a new name since their terminal conditions are based on solutions to the long-term Guidepath Model, and since the structural changes of the Guidepath Models are retained even though the Guidepost Models are short-run models. Compared to the Target and Transit Model solutions the Guidepost solutions are compatible with an explicit long-term optimizing path. They provide a more detailed working-out of the first years of the Guidepath solution.

In this case the procedure for establishing terminal conditions is based on the stocks in the third three-year period of the Guidepath solution. These are interpolated to determine conditions for the Guidepost Model that provide the same capital stocks in the postterminal years as provided by the Guidepath solution for the same years.

5.4 Additional Data and Assumptions for the Guidepath and Guidepost Models

Long-term planning calls for additional data intrinsically more difficult to provide than the data required for short-term planning. Technological change can be expected to modify current and capital flow coefficients. Income elasticities will change with time and income. New products may be introduced. Yet there are no generally accepted techniques and empirical materials with which to predict such changes. In general, parameters appropriate to different time periods can be embodied in the model, if they are known. The obstacles to better specification are as much empirical as theoretical. For example, although the method to provide for a change in technology in the agricultural sector could be used in other sectors, the data available to us did not warrant it.

For the 1960-61 input-output matrix used previously, another matrix was substituted for the period after 1971-72. This is based on a modification of the 1959-60 matrix projected for 1970-71 by Manne and Rudhra.[3] After some investigation of the possibility of substituting matrices for other countries for

[3] A. Manne and A. Rudhra, *Studies in the Structure of the Indian Economy*, Indian Statistical Institute, 1964.

later periods, the attempt was dropped. If it could have succeeded, it would have required far more time and resources than have been available to us in order to establish comparability. The same conclusion was reached after trying to find alternative estimates of capital coefficients. The input requirements for Modern Agriculture are, however, taken from the input vector of a Japanese input-output matrix.[4] The capital-output ratio of 2.5 is used for Modern Agriculture in all but one solution in which a ratio of 4 is used. The composition of capital in this activity is also obtained from Japanese data.

The inventory coefficients are reduced by 1.0 per cent every year, i.e., by 3.03 per cent every 3-year period, in the Guidepath Models to reflect a common conjecture as to their behavior.

The depreciation and replacement requirements for the longer period are estimated from the estimates of investments made during the First, Second, and Third Plans. Likewise, procedures similar to those previously employed were used to project the government and export vectors. In the former case, the sectoral composition of government demand is held constant, and the total is projected at the rate of 6.0 per cent per year, i.e., 19.10 per cent per period. Exports of each sector are projected at different rates, representing a judgment as to the sector's potential. The numbers used could only be called guesses based on judgment of recent years' achievements and on the projections of potential shares of total markets made by B. Balassa.[5]

The noncompetitive import coefficients are reduced from period to period to reflect growing self-reliance. No restraints on the use of foreign exchange for competitive imports are introduced in the Guidepath and Guidepost Models.

Estimates of expenditure elasticities are required for the models. There is an abundance of data for India, stemming mainly from the National Sample Surveys conducted by the Indian Statistical Institute, though extensive analysis of this data has not yet been fully successful in establishing comparability. Moreover, the goods categories for which the elasticities have been estimated do not conform in general to the sectoral classifications of the input-output tables.

New research on this subject has been beyond the scope of the project, so the estimates used in the computations reported here are no more than personal judgments based on existing analyses of Indian data and international comparisons.[6] There is clearly material and scope for further analysis reorganizing and reestimating consumption-expenditure relationships in categories more useful for policy purposes.

The ratio of consumption and net national product in the last year of the Third Plan as projected by the Perspective Planning Division is used along with alternative marginal savings rates to determine the parameters of the consumption-income constraint when it is enforced in the Guidepath-II model.

---

[4] An unpublished paper by S. Ichimura and S. Miyano, "A Dynamic Input-Output Model of the Japanese Economy."

[5] B. Balassa, *Trade Prospects for Developing Countries,* Richard D. Irwin, Homewood, Ill., 1964.

[6] For purposes of comparison we used the study by H. Houthakker, "An International Comparison of Household Expenditure Patterns, Commemorating the Centenary of Engel's Law," *Econometrica, 25,* 1957, pp. 532-551.

In most cases, net foreign capital inflow is set at Rs. 500 crores per year until 1977, after which it is set at zero. This reflects, in a rough way, a frequently stated Indian goal of self-sufficiency by the Fifth Plan. In alternative solutions this stipulation is changed, and the net foreign capital inflow is increased or the period of availability is extended.

The first solutions to the Guidepath-I Model cover a span of eighteen years in six periods each of three-years' duration. A solution for thirty years in ten three-year periods will also be presented. The data inputs are shown in Tables C.1 through C.11, which may be found in Appendix C at the end of this chapter.

The postterminal growth rates which are used to determine the terminal conditions unless otherwise specified are as follows:

Private consumption	12.5 per cent per year	or	42.382 per cent per three-year period.
Government consumption	6.0 per cent per year	or	19.102 per cent per three-year period.
Exports	5.5 per cent per year	or	17.424 per cent per three-year period.
Imports	5.5 per cent per year	or	17.424 per cent per three-year period.
Replacement requirements	same as that for private consumption.		

In addition, the availability of land for use in both Traditional and Incremental Agriculture is assumed to grow at 0.5 per cent per year. In alternative runs, when the postterminal growth rate of private consumption is changed, the rate for replacement requirements is also changed by the same amount.

5.5 Guidepath-I Model Solutions

5.5.1 General Characteristics of the Solutions

The Guidepath Models may be regarded as multisectoral versions of finite horizon, linear models of capital accumulation and growth with the addition of a number of exogenously specified demands on the system. As such, the general quality of the solutions may be predicted from the simpler models which have already been worked out in a number of variations.

The long planning period and the reduction in intertemporal dependence that results from collapsing the gestation lag provides the Guidepath Models with more freedom to choose a time pattern of output than is available to the Target and Transit Models. Otherwise, the discussion in Chapter 2 of the characteristics of the optimizing process and the role of the shadow prices applies here as well.

Depending on the rate at which consumption is discounted and on the productivity of investment, there will be a tendency to concentrate consumption at the beginning or end of the planning period. The flip-flop tendency, which is quite marked in the simpler, linear models, will be moderated in the Guidepath solutions by a number of features of the Models. First of all, there are many sectors, each with different initial capacities and with changing input requirements and demands for consumption and investment. The provision of two activities in the agricultural sector with different input requirements makes the aggregate output of that sector respond in a nonlinear fashion to total inputs to the sector. The composition of consumption demand, export demand, and depreciation change over time, as do import and inventory coefficients and the availability of net foreign capital inflows. Unlike single-sector models in which capital can be consumed or used for further production, the capital stocks in the Guidepath Models are durable and cannot be used up all at once even if that were to be desired. In addition, the terminal conditions guaranteeing postterminal growth from the endogenously determined consumption levels of the final Plan period tend to depress the level of consumption in that period. These create effective, over-all nonlinearities in the model even though the relationships in each sector are linear.

All these elements act to create many facets in the feasibility hypersurface, so that it more closely approximates a smooth, convex transformation function. Increments in consumption gained in a future period are not linearly related to the current sacrifices in consumption necessary to gain the increments. As a result, the solutions to the Guidepath Models cannot be expected to take on a simple flip-flop pattern, through this remains an underlying tendency. Yet, though the nonlinearities avoid the extremes of the flip-flop pattern, they will not necessarily provide a desirable pattern of consumption. One of the objectives of the alternative solutions will be to find methods of achieving the consumption patterns desired.

Each solution to the Guidepath Model illustrates an alternative potential path of development that corresponds to a particular specification of parameters. In order to find an acceptable solution, it is necessary to carry out a series of iterations. The iterative approach is required partly because of the linearities in the model and partly because of difficulties in specifying all its parameters precisely. Out of the many solutions found, we shall present only a few in order to illustrate certain properties of the model and to demonstrate the significance of alternative time preferences and policies.

The process of finding acceptable solutions is illustrated in Table 5.3 and Fig. 5.1 in which are plotted the time paths of consumption generated in alternative solutions of the Guidepath-I Model with six three-year periods. Case G-1 is a solution in which the only requirement on the consumption pattern in the intra-Plan period is that aggregate consumption not fall from the level of the preceding period. Furthermore, the discount rate w is set at zero in G-1. It can be seen that it displays the flip-flop tendency; consumption is at a minimum in the early periods and then rises rapidly in the later periods. The period in which the biggest increase comes and the subsequent pattern of consumption production depends in part on the effective aggregate capital-output ratio and in part on the postterminal growth requirements imposed. Consumption in the last period is at the same level as in the fifth period in this solution, because a higher level would only increase the investment requirements for postterminal growth. Since the effective, aggregate capital-output ratio is less than 1.0 in the Guidepath solution because of its three-year periods, the big increase in private consumption might be expected to occur in the last period. However, the postterminal capital requirements depend upon the level of private consumption in the terminal

Table 5.3. Values of Private Consumption in Alternative Guidepath-I Solutions (Rs. crores, 1959-60 prices)

Solution*	Period						
	1 1965–69	2 1969–72	3 1972–75	4 1975–78	5 1978–81	6 1981–84	7 1984–87
G-1 Minimum growth rate of consumption in period t, $\rho(t) = 0\%$; postterminal growth rate of consumption $\phi = 12.5\%$ per year	51,051	51,051	51,051	127,935	149,215	149,215	212,456
G-2 C(6) has a weight of 4.0 in objective function; $\rho(t) = 0\%$; $\phi = 12.5\%$ per year	51,051	51,051	51,051	66,151	110,758	185,866	264,487
G-3 Social discount rate w = 10% $\phi = 12.5\%$; no monotonicity requirements	51,474	52,590	42,328	131,447	199,486	116,953	166,424
G-4 Social discount rate w = 20% $\phi = 12.5\%$; no monotonicity requirements	52,291	67,927	92,927	112,074	123,737	40,135	57,112
G-5 Social discount rate w = 30% $\phi = 12.5\%$; no monotonicity requirements	52,539	68,705	101,219	102,330	103,996	27,315	38,891
G-6 $\rho(t) = 5\%, 6\%, 7\%, 8\%, 9\%$, per year successively; $\phi = 12.5\%$ per year	51,051	59,097	70,386	88,497	121,455	157,287	223,948
G-7 $\rho(t) = 6\%, 7\%, 8\%, 9\%, 10\%$ per year successively; $\phi = 0\%$ per year	51,051	60,803	74,486	93,831	124,493	165,701	220,547
G-8 10-period plan; $\rho(t) = 0\%$; $\phi = 12.5\%$	51,440	51,440	51,440	51,440	51,440	51,440	442,218
	8 1987–90	9 1990–93	10 1993–96	11 1996–99			
	742,148	742,148	742,148	1,056,077			
G-9 10-period plan; $\rho(t) = 5\%, 6\%, 7\%, 8\%, 9\%,$ 10%, 11%, 12% 12.5%, successively; $\phi = 12.5\%$	51,051	59,098	70,387	86,226	108,620	173,238	280,194
	8 1987–90	9 1990–93	10 1993–96	11 1996–99			
	383,201	538,367	766,538	1,091,411			
G-10.0 Reference Solution; $\phi = 12.5\%$ per year; $\rho = 5\%, 6\%, 7\%, 8\%$ and 9% per year in successive periods; X(0) adjusted on 11-sector basis	51,051	59,098	70,386	86,226	143,291	185,564	264,210
G-10.1 Net foreign capital inflow (NFCI) doubled to Rs. 1000 crores per year for 4 periods, then zero	51,051	59,098	70,388	115,924	157,572	204,059	290,543
G-10.2 NFCI continued at Rs. 500 crores per year for 6 periods	51,051	59,098	70,386	86,226	145,482	188,402	268,251
G-11.0 $\phi = 12.5\%$ per year; $\rho = $ 5%, 6%, 7%, 8% and 9% per year in successive periods; X(0) adjusted on 32-sector basis	51,051	59,098	70,386	86,226	156,922	203,217	289,344
G-11.1 NFCI doubled to Rs. 1000 crores per year for 4 periods, then zero	51,051	59,098	70,386	127,877	161,088	208,613	297,027
G-11.2 NFCI continued at Rs. 500 crores per year for 6 periods	51,051	59,098	70,386	86,226	159,115	206,057	293,388

Table 5.3. (cont.)

Solution	Period						
	1	2	3	4	5	6	7
	1965-69	1969-72	1972-75	1975-78	1978-81	1981-84	1985-87
G-12.0 ϕ = 12.5% per year; ρ = 3%, 6%, 7%, 8%, 9% per year in successive periods; X(0) on 11-sector basis; K/0 in Modern Agriculture changes from 2.5 to 4.0	51,051	55,785	66,441	81,392	109,406	141,683	201,731

*Unless otherwise indicated all solutions had the following constraints:
  1. Postterminal annual growth rates of   2. Net foreign capital inflow set at Rs. 500 crores per year for the first 12 years,
     Government consumption, 6.0%   i.e., 4 periods, then at zero.
     Exports, 5.5%
     Imports, 5.5%
     Replacement at ϕ, the same rate as consumption

Figure 5.1. Consumption in Guidepath-I Solutions.

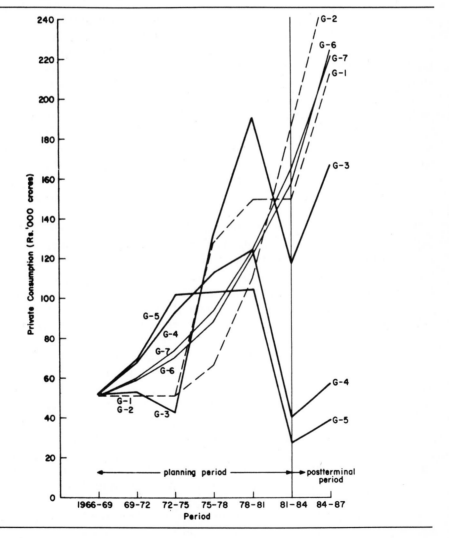

period. To satisfy these requirements at lowest cost to the maximand, the model solution if not constrained would be depressed to that level at which no additional capital needs to be provided for the postterminal periods. Hence in Case G-1, the jump in consumption occurs in the fourth period rather than in the sixth period.

The postterminal consumption stream can be introduced explicitly in the objective function by adding a second term in the maximand:

$$W = \sum_{t=1}^{T} \frac{C(t)}{(1+w)^t} + C(T) \sum_{t=T+1}^{\infty} \frac{(1+\phi)^{t-T}}{(1+w)^{t-T}}$$

This is used in Solution G-2 in which a weight of 4.0 is given to the terminal period consumption C(6), and intra-Plan consumption is not discounted. The objective function becomes

$$W = C(1) + \cdots + C(T) \left\{ 1 + \left(\frac{1+\phi}{1+\sigma}\right)^{t-T} + \left(\frac{1+\phi}{1+\sigma}\right)^{t-T+1} \cdots \right\},$$

where the required postterminal rate of growth of consumption ϕ equals 0.4238 per cent per period, and where the discount rate for the postterminal consumption σ equals 0.908 per cent per period. In Solution G-2 a 26 per cent higher level of consumption is reached in the sixth period than in Solution G-1. More extreme flip-flop behavior in the form of still greater concentration of consumption in the last period is prevented by the lack of foreign exchange required for noncompetitive imports. In Solution G-2 all the available foreign exchange is used for noncompetitive imports in all periods but the first. This happens in spite of the fact that the noncompetitive import coefficients are reduced every two periods in order to reflect import substitution. The import requirements in the terminal period are 2.14 per cent of the gross national product compared to 5.37 per cent of the gross national product in the first period.

Social discount rates on consumption of 10, 20, and 30 per cent per year are applied, respectively, in Solutions G-3, G-4, and G-5, which do not include postterminal consumption explicitly in the objective function, but all of which require postterminal consumption growth of 12.5 per cent per year. The intra-Plan consumption growth constraints are removed in these solutions so not even monotonicity is required. Removal of this requirement permits the flip-flop tendency to show itself more clearly if it exists. It is most obvious in Solution G-3 in which consumption declines absolutely in the third period in order to accumulate capital in the capital producing sectors at a high rate. The payoff to this accumulation comes in the fourth and fifth periods. Consumption in the last period is now lowered in order to reduce the diversion of resources to postterminal growth. The higher discount rates in Solutions G-4 and G-5 offset the flip-flop shown in Solution G-3 and lead to consumption patterns in which a much higher proportion of total consumption is provided in the first three periods. The effective nonlinearities in the model prevent a full reversal of the pattern of consumption in Solution G-3, and the pattern is one of smooth growth until the weight of the postterminal conditions leads to a reduction of the consumption produced in the last Plan period.

The concentration of consumption at the end, or at the beginning, of a planning period is a feature of linear models rather than an essential economic property of growth. Such behavior violates the general sense of an acceptable time shape of consumption and forces drastic changes on the system in resource allocations in particular years. It may even be difficult to reproduce in practice the characteristics of the solution. In order that the Guidepath Models be useful for planning, it is therefore necessary to find methods of altering the shape of the time path of aggregate consumption to conform, within the limits of economic feasibility, to social preferences. The first device used for this purpose is simply that of setting constraints on that path. In Solution G-6 private consumption is constrained to grow in successive periods at minimum rates of 5, 6, 7, 8, and 9 per cent per year, and a postterminal growth requirement of 12.5 per cent per year of consumption is also imposed. This solution is plotted in Fig. 5.1. The effect of the progressively higher consumption growth requirements in raising the levels in the early years and smoothing the over-all path is apparent. Solution G-7 in Fig. 5.1 has consumption growth constraints in successive periods of 6, 7, 8, 9, and 10 per cent per year and a postterminal consumption growth requirement of 10 per cent per year.

Table 5.3 and Fig. 5.1 also illustrate the over-all effects of the added constraints. The level of consumption reached in the final period in Solution G-1, without intra-Plan consumption growth constraints but with a 12.5 per cent per year postterminal growth requirement, is less than the final levels reached in Solutions G-6 and G-7 with the same postterminal growth constraint but with intra-Plan consumption growth requirements of 5 per cent and higher. The value of the maximand in Solution G-1 is higher, of course, as the intra-Plan growth constraints force a higher level of consumption in the early Plan years at the sacrifice of aggregate consumption over the entire Plan period.

In order to test further the significance of changes in the length of the planning period, a few trials were made with the Guidepath-I Model covering ten three-year periods, i.e., thirty years.

Figure 5.2 gives the time path of consumption generated in various solutions of the Guidepath-I Model with ten periods. In Solution G-8 the intra-Plan requirement on consumption is merely that consumption in any period may not fall below the level attained in the preceding period; the postterminal requirement is that consumption be able to grow at 12.5 per cent per year. Again the solution exhibits the flip-flop tendency; increases in consumption are delayed until the latter portion of the planning period when consumption is increased very rapidly. Also, as in the analogous six-period Solution G-1, the postterminal consumption growth requirement is responsible for the constancy of consumption in the last three periods, since this pattern requires a smaller diversion of resources to meet the postterminal requirements than one with higher terminal consumption levels. The effect of imposing intra-Plan consumption growth requirements between successive periods of 5, 6, 7, 8, 9, 10, 11, 12, and 12.5 per cent per year, while keeping the 12.5 per cent per year postterminal consumption growth requirement, is shown in Fig. 5.2 as Solution G-9. For purposes of comparison, the Solution G-6, which has similar intra-Plan consumption growth requirements for six periods is also plotted in Fig. 5.2. The close correspondence of the over-all results for the first four periods is quite evident. The national income accounts for Solutions G-6 and G-9 are presented in Tables 5.4 and 5.5, respectively.

In the first four periods the consumption growth constraints are binding in both solutions, and the rates of saving and investing are as high as possible given these

Figure 5.2. Consumption in Thirty-Year Guidepath-I Solutions.

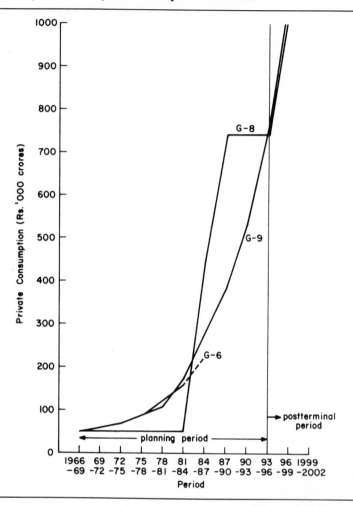

Table 5.4. National Income Accounts for Guidepath-I Solution G-6
(Rs. crores, 1959-60 prices)

	1966-69	1969-72	1972-75	1975-78	1978-81	1981-84
CONSUMPTION	51051.3	59093.0	70386.3	88496.5	121455.1	157236.8
INVENTORIES CHANGE	243.1	2291.8	2396.4	3638.5	4820.0	7892.4
FIXED INVESTMENT	16320.4	17722.6	31208.5	45811.6	62359.0	94949.8
TOTAL INVESTMENT	19410.1	23176.4	36579.8	53768.0	71888.4	109410.4
GOVERNMENT EXPENDITURE	3539.0	4123.0	5017.7	5976.1	7117.5	8476.9
VALUE ADDED BY GOVT.	5865.8	6857.1	8345.1	9939.0	11837.3	14098.2
EXPORTS	3087.6	3709.2	4626.4	5691.2	6762.7	8112.8
IMPORTS	4587.6	5209.2	6126.4	7191.2	6762.7	8112.8
GROSS NATIONAL PRODUCT	78356.2	91754.5	118828.9	156679.6	212293.3	288272.3
REPLACEMENT	2846.6	3162.0	2974.9	4317.9	4709.4	5568.2
NET NATIONAL PRODUCT	75509.6	88592.4	115853.9	152361.7	207588.9	282704.1
SAVINGS	17910.1	21676.4	35079.8	52268.0	71888.4	108410.4
GROSS NATIONAL OUTPUT	101732.3	120437.3	171187.0	231859.3	319285.5	443778.4
INTERMEDIATE PRODUCT	29231.9	35539.9	60703.2	85118.7	118924.5	169604.3
CONS./GROSS NAT. PROD.	0.65129	0.64409	0.59233	0.56482	0.57210	0.54562
TOTAL INVST/GR.NAT.PR.	0.24762	0.25259	0.30784	0.34317	0.33862	0.37607
SAVINGS/GR. NAT. PROD.	0.22849	0.23624	0.29521	0.33360	0.33862	0.37607
MARGINAL SAVINGS RATE		.2817	.4250	.4540	.3527	.4807

Table 5.5. National Income Accounts for Guidepath-I Solution G-9 (Rs. crores, 1959-60 prices)

	1966-69	1969-72	1972-75	1975-78	1978-81	1981-84	1984-87	1987-90	1990-93	1993-96
CONSUMPTION	51051.3	59098.2	70386.6	86226.4	108620.2	173237.8	280193.7	383201.2	538367.1	766537.8
INVENTORIES CHANGE	240.9	2289.6	2266.4	3890.2	5563.3	8678.3	11981.1	20567.9	-11627.3	48436.4
FIXED INVESTMENT	16939.8	17698.0	30961.7	45050.8	74972.0	95589.8	151740.9	242424.8	508840.4	0.
TOTAL INVESTMENT	19414.0	23149.6	36203.1	53258.8	84511.5	109504.6	169126.1	269232.4	505225.5	48436.4
GOVERNMENT EXPENDITURE	3539.0	4123.0	5017.7	5976.1	7117.5	8476.9	10049.3	11967.4	14067.4	16348.7
VALUE ADDED BY GOVT.	5885.8	6857.1	8345.1	9939.0	11837.3	14098.2	16713.3	19903.3	23395.9	27190.0
EXPORTS	3087.6	3709.2	4626.4	5691.2	6762.7	8112.8	9777.2	11440.6	13351.3	15612.7
IMPORTS	4587.6	5209.2	6126.4	7191.2	6762.7	8112.8	9777.2	11440.6	13351.3	15612.7
GROSS NATIONAL PRODUCT	78390.1	91727.9	118452.4	153900.3	212086.5	305317.5	476082.3	684304.3	1081055.8	858512.9
REPLACEMENT	2233.3	3162.0	2974.9	4317.9	3976.2	5236.6	5404.0	6239.7	8012.3	0.
NET NATIONAL PRODUCT	76156.7	88565.8	115477.5	149582.4	208110.3	300080.9	470678.3	678064.7	1073043.5	858512.9
SAVINGS	17914.0	21649.6	34703.1	51758.8	84511.5	109504.6	169126.1	269232.4	505225.5	48436.4
GROSS NATIONAL OUTPUT	101738.6	120391.9	170614.8	227910.7	325869.7	466057.0	690612.9	1010893.0	1642291.3	1153167.3
INTERMEDIATE PRODUCT	29234.3	35521.1	60507.5	83949.4	125620.5	174837.7	231243.9	346492.0	584631.4	321844.4
CONS./GROSS NAT. PROD.	0.65125	0.64428	0.59422	0.56027	0.51215	0.56740	0.58854	0.55999	0.49800	0.89287
TOTAL INVST/GR.NAT.PR.	0.24766	0.25237	0.30563	0.34606	0.39848	0.35866	0.35525	0.39344	0.46734	0.05642
SAVINGS/GR. NAT. PROD.	0.22852	0.23602	0.29297	0.33631	0.39848	0.35866	0.35525	0.39344	0.46734	0.05642

constraints. The differences in the fifth and sixth periods reflect the influences of terminal conditions. In the six-period solution, the 12.5 per cent postterminal growth requirement is reflected into the sixth period, and some part of the adjustment to these postterminal requirements is started even in the fourth and fifth periods. However, in the ten-period case, the policy of delaying rapid changes in consumption is continued until the sixth period when the big increase occurs, whereas in the six-period case the biggest increase in consumption comes in the fifth period. As the over-all results suggest, the sectoral uses and allocations of resources in the six- and ten-period solutions are quite similar in the first three periods and after that diverge in their relative emphasis on consumption and capital goods production. Thus, the edge effects of terminating the Guidepath-I solutions extend up to two or three periods into the Plan period. This type of knowledge provides a basis for choice of the length of the Plan period. It should be noted that with a different set of parameters, the edge effects could extend all the way to the first period, so this result should not be generalized but requires investigation with alternative parameters for specific cases.

In the national income accounts for Solution G-9 in Table 5.5, there is a substantial amount of disinvestment in inventories in the ninth period, and there is no fixed investment in the tenth period. This is the result of the ceiling on total output of Agriculture imposed by the full use of the limited amount of land. Even when all available land is modernized, the maximum level of consumption in the tenth period is still restricted by the maximum available output of Agriculture.

Since investment goods production requires output of Agriculture as an intermediate input, all investments for the terminal targets are made in the ninth period to maximize consumption in the tenth. Consequently, the outputs of the investment goods sectors are higher in the ninth than in the tenth period. This in turn leads to disinvestment in inventory in the ninth period.

5.5.2 Details of the Solutions

Solutions G-10, G-11, and G-12 are computed with the data as given in Section 5.5. They differ slightly from Solutions G-1 through G-9 in initial capacities, noncompetitive import coefficients, and in the input-output matrix from the third period onward; the two sets are thus not strictly comparable.[7] Solution G-10, in which the same consumption growth requirements are imposed as in solution G-6, is used as a Reference Solution. Tables 5.6 to 5.14 present various features of the Guidepath-I Reference Solution. The national income accounts are shown in Table 5.6. The rate of growth of gross national product in different periods ranges from 7.8 to 12.7 per cent. This is mainly the result of the high rates of investment, which are also shown. Net foreign capital inflows contribute to this investment, but domestic savings are far and away the largest source. This is reflected in the unusually high *average* savings rates created by the even more unusually high *marginal* domestic savings rates shown in Table 5.6. The savings rate information helps to dispel some of the possible wonder at the growth performances reflected in the Guidepath Model solutions. Not only are resources allocated optimally, but output is plowed back into investment for further growth at increasingly high rates.

It should be noted that since labor and raw materials are always assumed in the model, to be in adequate supply, no restraints on growth arising from their scarcity are considered. To the extent that these assumptions are true at all, they are likely to be so only for the first few periods.

The composition of output in each time period in the Reference Solution is shown in Table 5.7. It will be noticed that it reflects a growing "industrialization." Table 5.8 presents the annual growth rates of the individual sectors from the first to the postterminal period. Mining and Metals, Electricity, and Chemicals have markedly the highest growth rates. Equipment, Cement and Nonmetals, Transport, and Construction, with roughly similar growth rates, rank next. Finally, the slowest-growing group includes Others and Margin, Food, Clothing, and Leather, Housing, and Agriculture. However, it will be noticed that Incremental Agriculture continues to grow rapidly, even after it has achieved a position dominating Traditional Agriculture by the fifth period or fifteenth year. The outputs for the seventh period, that is, the first postterminal period, are those required by the terminal conditions. The output of Incremental Agriculture is slightly more than three times the output of Traditional Agriculture. This is inconsistent with the assumption of a land productivity ratio of 3.0 between the

---

[7]In Solutions G-10, G-11, and G-12 the initial capacities are based on the adjusted estimated outputs of 1965-66, so that these solutions may be compatible with the Fourth Plan period solutions of Chapter 4. Solutions G-1 through G-9 have small discrepancies which make them less comparable.

Table 5.6. National Income Accounts, Guidepath-I Reference Solution
(Rs. crores, 1959-60 prices)

	1966-69	1969-72	1972-75	1975-78	1978-81	1981-84
CONSUMPTION	51051.3	59098.0	70386.3	96226.0	143290.3	185564.4
INVENTORIES CHANGE	1031.7	2089.6	3091.1	4632.5	5744.4	9238.7
FIXED INVESTMENT	16412.5	26599.4	36794.2	62506.9	73355.4	111956.4
TOTAL INVESTMENT	17780.4	31321.6	42860.2	70756.1	83076.0	125996.6
GOVERNMENT EXPENDITURE	3539.0	4123.0	5017.7	5976.1	7117.5	8476.9
VALUE ADDED BY GOVT.	5835.8	6857.1	8345.1	9939.0	11837.3	14098.2
EXPORTS	3087.6	3709.2	4626.4	5691.2	6762.7	8112.8
IMPORTS	4587.6	5209.2	6126.4	7191.2	6762.7	8112.8
GROSS NATIONAL PRODUCT	76756.5	99899.7	125109.2	171397.2	245321.6	334136.1
REPLACEMENT	2286.2	2632.6	2974.9	3616.7	3976.2	4801.5
NET NATIONAL PRODUCT	74470.3	97267.0	122134.3	167730.4	241345.4	329334.6
SAVINGS	16280.4	29821.6	41350.2	69256.1	83076.0	125996.6
GROSS NATIONAL OUTPUT	96569.0	134614.7	181872.1	260401.5	369916.4	516244.1
INTERMEDIATE PRODUCT	27934.5	41572.1	65108.0	98943.3	136432.1	196206.2
CONS./GROSS NAT. PROD.	0.66511	0.59157	0.56260	0.50308	0.58409	0.55536
TOTAL INVST/GR.NAT.PR.	0.23165	0.31353	0.34259	0.41282	0.33864	0.37708
SAVINGS/GR. NAT. PROD.	0.21210	0.29852	0.33059	0.40407	0.33864	0.37708

MARGINAL GROSS SAVINGS RATES	0.585	0.457	0.603	0.167	0.483	
ANNUAL RATE OF GROWTH OF GNP	9.2%	7.8%	11.0%	12.7%	10.9%	

Table 5.7. Gross Domestic Outputs, Guidepath-I Reference Solution
(Rs. crores, 1959-60 prices)

ACTIVITY	1966-69	1969-72	1972-75	1975-78	1978-81	1981-84	1984-87
INCAGR	0.	4168.48	9658.55	18651.67	42352.90	62961.80	98834.39
M.M.	-4573.61	8923.57	17775.23	27812.92	38603.70	57020.90	81507.84
EQIPMT	7620.75	13407.56	20389.92	31292.81	42959.62	62995.84	89282.52
CHEMIC	3944.11	6062.62	9161.96	14084.69	22054.52	32259.16	47752.91
CMGLWD	2466.24	3915.23	5449.98	9080.03	10876.25	16295.89	23415.44
FCCDCL	10332.52	12279.68	14950.76	18853.48	29295.54	38078.75	53547.02
ELECTR	614.26	912.12	1941.51	2890.95	4142.40	5945.70	8509.97
TRANS	4359.74	6376.80	9521.25	13964.91	20248.59	28788.77	41253.62
CCNSTR	10074.98	16713.76	22440.13	40162.25	43689.69	66998.56	96385.37
HOUS.	2338.10	2686.47	3170.44	3841.76	6226.79	7997.95	11281.27
OTHMAR	23524.75	29613.24	37411.73	49313.01	78554.72	105522.72	151118.10
TRADAG	29116.18	29555.11	30000.65	30452.91	30911.99	31377.99	31851.01

Table 5.8. Annual Sectoral Growth Rates of Output, Guidepath-I Reference Solution
(in per cent)

	Annual Growth Rate Between Periods					
Sector	1-2	2-3	3-4	4-5	5-6	6-7
1. AG.PL.	5.1	5.5	7.4	14.3	8.8	11.5
2. M.M.	25.0	26.0	16.1	11.5	13.9	12.7
3. EQIPMT	21.0	15.0	15.3	11.1	13.6	12.3
4. CHEMIC	15.4	14.8	15.4	16.1	13.5	14.0
5. CMGLWD	16.8	11.6	18.5	6.2	14.4	12.8
6. FOODCL	5.9	6.8	8.0	15.8	9.2	12.0
7. ELECTR	14.1	29.0	14.2	12.7	12.8	12.7
8. TRANS	13.5	14.3	13.6	13.2	12.4	12.7
9. CONSTR	18.5	10.3	21.2	2.8	15.3	12.9
10. HOUS.	4.7	5.7	6.6	17.5	8.7	12.2
11. OTHMAR	8.0	8.1	9.6	16.8	10.3	12.7

Table 5.9. Shadow Prices of Output, Guidepath-I Reference Solution (Rs. crores)

SECTOR	1966-69	1969-72	1972-75	1975-78	1978-81	1981-84
AG.PL.	0.	7.64	3.46	1.83	0.94	0.49
M.M.	45.22	11.82	5.29	2.80	1.45	0.75
ECIPMT	19.58	9.41	4.99	2.57	1.33	0.69
CHEMIC	14.56	7.97	3.60	1.84	0.94	0.52
CMGLWD	4.92	5.70	2.73	1.42	0.74	0.38
FOODCL	45.22	6.47	3.33	1.73	0.89	0.46
ELECTR	6.92	15.61	7.12	3.83	1.99	1.03
TRANS	4.85	11.28	5.3	2.84	1.47	0.77
CCNSTR	6.68	3.68	1.95	1.02	0.53	0.27
HCUS.	0.35	10.25	5.91	3.16	1.67	0.86
OTHMAR	0.22	0.79	0.39	0.21	0.11	0.86

Table 5.10. Imports and Shadow Prices on Foreign Trade Balance Constraints, Guidepath-I Reference Solution (Rs. crores, 1959-60 prices)

NCN-COMPETITIVE IMPORTS

ACTIVITY	1966-69	1969-72	1972-75	1975-78	1978-84	1981-84	1984-87
INCAGR	0.	50.02	77.27	93.93	42.35	62.96	93.83
M.M.	663.17	936.97	1294.27	1390.65	1158.11	1140.42	1630.16
ECIPMT	1790.88	2346.32	2344.84	2503.42	2147.98	2519.83	3571.30
CHEMIC	1029.41	1321.65	1603.34	2112.70	2756.81	3225.92	4775.29
CMGLWD	9.86	11.75	10.90	13.62	10.83	16.30	23.42
FOODCL	0.83	0.74	0.60	0.57	0.59	0.57	0.80
ELECTR	0.	0.	0.	0.	0.	0.	0.
TRANS	0.	0.	0.	0.	0.	0.	0.
CCNSTR	0.	0.	0.	0.	0.	0.	0.
HCUS.	0.	0.	0.	0.	0.	0.	0.
OTHMAR	0.	0.	0.	0.	0.	0.	0.
TRADAG	465.85	354.66	240.01	137.04	30.91	31.33	31.05

COMPETITIVE IMPORTS

SECTOR	1966-69	1969-72	1972-75	1975-78	1978-81	1981-84	1984-87
AG.PL.	0.	0.	0.	0.	0.	0.	-19.91
M.M.	495.21	187.10	605.17	949.31	615.03	1115.46	1018.78
ECIPMT	0.	0.	0.	0.	0.	0.	-612.41
CHEMIC	0.	0.	0.	0.	0.	0.	-987.29
CMGLWD	0.	0.	0.	0.	0.	0.	-4.28
FOODCL	132.35	0.	0.	0.	0.	0.	-0.13
ELECTR	0.	0.	0.	0.	0.	0.	0.
TRANS	0.	0.	0.	0.	0.	0.	0.
CCNSTR	0.	0.	0.	0.	0.	0.	0.
HCUS.	0.	0.	0.	0.	0.	0.	0.
OTHMAR	0.	0.	0.	0.	0.	0.	0.

SHADOW PRICES ON FOREIGN TRADE BALANCE CONSTRAINTS

45.22	11.82	5.29	2.80	1.45	1.90

Table 5.11. Private Consumption and Shadow Prices on Consumption Growth Constraints, Guidepath-I Reference Solution (Rs. crores, 1959-60 prices)

SECTOR	1966-69	1969-72	1972-75	1975-78	1978-81	1981-84	1984-87
AG.PL.	19405.01	22040.18	25637.43	30521.24	47413.19	60017.53	83219.81
M.M.	23.61	26.92	31.47	37.69	59.43	75.62	105.52
ECIPMT	1332.50	1648.02	2115.45	2812.15	5497.18	7463.63	11183.52
CHEMIC	1571.07	1858.06	2269.93	2863.08	5065.32	6688.31	9730.66
CMGLWD	307.94	364.19	444.92	561.18	992.84	1310.95	1907.27
FOODCL	7309.52	8461.65	10077.91	12345.84	20516.37	26569.11	37829.63
ELECTR	53.01	61.81	74.27	91.92	156.27	203.84	292.60
TRANS	908.79	1067.33	1293.34	1616.40	2805.64	3683.34	5325.15
CCNSTR	0.	0.	0.	0.	0.	0.	0.
HCUS.	2338.10	2686.47	3170.44	3841.75	6226.79	7997.95	11281.27
OTHMAR	17801.72	20883.32	25271.12	31534.73	54557.75	71554.12	103334.89
SUM	51051.26	59097.96	70386.26	86225.98	143290.76	185564.40	264210.30

SUM OF DISCOUNTED CONSUMPTION = 595616.6328125
SUM OF UNDISCOUNTED CONSUMPTION = 595616.6328125

SHADOW PRICES ON CONSUMPTION GROWTH CONSTRAINTS

14.25	6.04	1.74	0.26	0.0	0.27

two activities.[8] The lack of cultivable land will make the outputs of the seventh period unachievable unless technological progress makes Modern Agriculture more productive by then.

The shadow prices on output for each period of the Guidepath Reference Solution are shown in Table 5.9. The tendency for the prices to decrease over time is a result of the greater contribution to the maximand, which is made by output in the early as compared to the later periods, in part because the postterminal consumption is not explicitly included in the objective function but only in the terminal stock requirements.

It will be recalled that in these solutions the constraints on the use of foreign exchange for competitive imports are made inoperative. Table 5.10 shows noncompetitive and competitive imports by sectors.[9] It also includes the shadow price on the foreign exchange balance constraint.

The existence of competitive imports in each period indicates that the availability of foreign exchange does not set an absolute limit to output. The usefulness of foreign exchange is reflected here in the shadow price on the balance of payments constraints. Without the constraints on competitive imports that were imposed in the Target and Transit Models, the shadow prices on the foreign exchange balance reflect the value of the output of the sector in which competitive imports are made.

Table 5.11 presents the sectoral consumptions in each period. These now reflect the consumption-expenditure elasticities specified for each sector. Although Agriculture continues to provide the largest single component of consumption, its share is reduced from 38 to 32 per cent over the planning period. By comparison, the share of Equipment in total consumption is increased from 2.6 to 3.9 per cent.

The shadow prices on the consumption growth constraints are also shown in Table 5.11. The relatively high prices in the initial period reflect the tendency in the model solution to concentrate consumption toward the end of the period. Between the fourth and fifth periods, consumption is increased by more than the required amount, so the constraint is not binding.

The available capital stocks and the new capital capacity that becomes effective in each period are shown in Tables 5.12 and 5.13, respectively; the shadow prices of new capital are given in Table 5.14.[10] The rapid growth of the capital stocks is the result of the high rates of saving and investment. It might be noted that the pattern of accumulation varies considerably from period to period, though the relative prices on new capital do not change substantially. The changes in the investment pattern can be associated with the consumption growth path. In the early periods when consumption grows relatively slowly, the emphasis is on investment in the capital goods producing sectors and their major suppliers. In the fifth period when consumption grows more rapidly, the emphasis switches to accumulation in the consumption producing sectors. The industrial sectors (Mining and Metals, Equipment, Chemicals, Cement and Nonmetals, and Electricity) had

---

[8]This is possible in the postterminal period in the model, since Inequalities 9.1 cannot be included in deriving Eq. 13.0 for postterminal output.

[9]Since competitive imports for the postterminal period $M''(T + 1)$ do not enter the model explicitly, the linear programming solution does not prevent competitive imports from being negative, though, of course, total imports in a sector must be nonnegative.

[10]All the new capital available at the beginning of the first period is already included in the specified total initial endowment.

Table 5.12. Available Capital, Guidepath-I Reference Solution (Rs. crores, 1959-60 prices)

ACTIVITY	1966-69	1969-72	1972-75	1975-78	1978-81	1981-84	1984-87
INCAGR	0.	3932.42	9111.59	17595.42	39954.46	59396.27	93237.26
M.M.	3775.83	7367.12	14674.37	22961.79	31870.44	47075.31	67291.32
EQIPMT	2470.31	4266.55	6438.48	9958.00	13670.61	20046.54	28411.51
CHEMIC	2174.42	2133.32	3223.91	4956.12	7760.54	11351.35	16803.34
CMGLWD	851.64	1124.81	1565.72	2608.60	3124.64	4681.65	6726.96
FOODCL	1919.68	2281.44	2777.70	3502.79	5442.82	7074.65	9948.42
ELECTR	1855.39	1902.97	4050.57	6031.39	8642.30	12404.52	17754.36
TRANS	6827.87	9201.72	13739.16	20151.42	29218.72	41542.20	59528.94
CONSTR	578.74	852.40	1144.45	2048.27	2228.17	3416.93	4915.74
HOUS.	8026.53	8954.90	10568.14	12805.85	20755.98	26659.84	37604.16
OTHMAR	1616.81	1544.92	1951.77	2572.66	4098.20	5505.12	7883.76
TRADAG	14652.14	14873.02	15097.23	15324.82	15555.84	15790.34	16028.38
SUM	44749.39	58435.58	84393.59	120517.12	182322.71	254944.71	366134.14

Table 5.13. New Capital, Guidepath-I Reference Solution (Rs. crores, 1959-60 prices)

ACTIVITY	1966-69	1969-72	1972-75	1975-78	1978-81	1981-84	1984-87
INCAGR	0.	3932.42	5179.17	8483.83	22359.04	19441.81	33840.99
M.M.	0.	3591.24	7307.76	3286.91	8908.66	15204.67	20216.01
EQIPMT	0.	1796.25	2221.93	3469.52	3712.61	6375.92	8364.98
CHEMIC	0.	0.	1090.60	1732.21	2804.42	3590.81	5451.99
CMGLWD	0.	273.17	440.92	1042.88	516.04	1557.01	2045.31
FOODCL	0.	361.77	496.23	725.09	1940.03	1631.83	2873.76
ELECTR	0.	47.59	2147.60	1980.82	2610.90	3762.22	5349.84
TRANS	0.	2373.85	4537.44	6412.26	9267.30	12323.48	17986.74
CONSTR	0.	273.66	292.05	903.83	179.90	1188.75	1498.81
HOUS.	0.	1541.63	2254.53	2908.28	8651.33	6637.10	11711.04
OTHMAR	0.	0.	406.85	620.89	1525.54	1406.92	2378.64
TRADAG	0.	220.88	224.21	227.59	231.02	234.50	238.04
SUM	0.	14412.46	26599.29	35794.09	62506.77	73355.23	111956.15

Table 5.14. Shadow Prices of New Capital, Guidepath-I Reference Solution (Rs. crores)

ACTIVITY	1966-69	1969-72	1972-75	1975-78	1978-81	1981-84	1984-87
INCAGR	0.	11.39	5.78	3.06	1.59	0.82	0.43
M.M.	0.	12.74	6.38	3.37	1.75	0.90	0.47
EQIPMT	0.	12.88	6.44	3.41	1.76	0.91	0.47
CHEMIC	0.	11.59	6.20	3.28	1.70	0.88	0.46
CMGLWD	0.	12.03	6.06	3.21	1.66	0.86	0.45
FOODCL	0.	14.27	7.05	3.73	1.93	1.00	0.52
ELECTR	0.	11.55	5.85	3.09	1.60	0.83	0.43
TRANS	0.	12.03	6.06	3.21	1.66	0.86	0.45
CONSTR	0.	14.56	7.13	3.80	1.97	1.02	0.53
HOUS.	0.	6.69	3.68	1.95	1.02	0.53	0.27
OTHMAR	0.	10.19	5.39	2.85	1.48	0.77	0.40
TRADAG	0.	8.35	4.42	2.34	1.22	0.63	0.33

Table 5.15. National Income Accounts for Guidepath-I Solution G-10.1
(Rs. crores, 1959-60 prices)

	1966-69	1969-72	1972-75	1975-78	1978-81	1981-84
CONSUMPTION	51051.3	59098.0	70386.3	115924.3	157572.5	204059.5
INVENTORIES CHANGE	1425.7	2646.1	3813.6	4506.4	6292.3	10113.1
FIXED INVESTMENT	16797.2	32144.5	49560.6	60249.5	80343.6	122682.0
TOTAL INVESTMENT	20594.8	37423.2	56349.1	68372.6	90612.1	137596.6
GOVERNMENT EXPENDITURE	3539.0	4123.0	5017.7	5976.1	7117.5	8476.9
VALUE ADDED BY GOVT.	5885.8	6857.1	8345.1	9939.0	11837.3	14098.2
EXPORTS	3087.6	3709.2	4626.4	5691.2	6762.7	8112.8
IMPORTS	6087.6	6709.2	7626.4	8691.2	6762.7	8112.8
GROSS NATIONAL PRODUCT	78070.9	104501.2	137098.2	197212.0	267139.4	364231.2
REPLACEMENT	2371.9	2632.6	2974.9	3616.7	3976.2	4801.5
NET NATIONAL PRODUCT	75699.0	101868.6	134123.2	193595.3	263163.2	359429.7
SAVINGS	19094.8	35723.2	54849.1	66872.6	90612.1	137596.6
GROSS NATIONAL OUTPUT	101000.4	142663.0	205168.2	294571.3	404818.8	565080.8
INTERMEDIATE PRODUCT	28815.3	45018.9	76415.1	107298.3	149516.7	214947.8
CONS./GROSS NAT. PROD.	0.65391	0.56552	0.51340	0.58782	0.58985	0.56025
TOTAL INVST/GR.NAT.PR.	0.26330	0.35811	0.41101	0.34670	0.33919	0.37777
SAVINGS/GR. NAT. PROD.	0.24458	0.34376	0.40007	0.33909	0.33919	0.37777

24.9 per cent of the capital at the outset; their total share by the third period rises to 35.6 per cent; and their share in the sixth period is 37.4 per cent. In this solution there was idle capacity only in the first period which reflects the lack of balance in the initial conditions as compared to the proportions that are most advantageous in this particular solution. The initial imbalance is eliminated in the second and following periods.

In judging the significance of the patterns of accumulation and use of capital, many of the qualifications applied to the Target and Transit Models because of their short time horizon do not apply. The time period now is sufficiently long that policies and goals of the postplanning period, such as import substitution and self-sufficiency, have less weight than in the shorter models, to the extent that the longer-term model adequately reflects such goals in its constraints and parameters. In addition, while the treatment of changing technology in Agriculture and the change in consumption proportions is still quite simple, the Guidepath Models meet some of the possible objections to the rigid treatment of these aspects of planning in the Target and Transit Models.

The Guidepath-I Model for six periods is solved with several variations in parameters. In Table 5.15 the period-by-period national income accounts are shown for Solution G-10.1, in which net foreign capital inflow is doubled for the same twelve years for which it was available in the previous solutions. Comparison with Table 5.5 indicates that the additional foreign exchange is used to carry out additional investment in the early periods and consumption is kept virtually unchanged in the first nine years. The additional foreign exchange makes it possible to break some bottlenecks, as shown by the fact that investment increases by much more than the additional foreign exchange in the first three periods. Whereas in the Reference Solution the capacities in the Agriculture, Food, Clothing, and Leather, and Mining and Metals sectors were fully utilized in the first period, now the idle capacities in this period in the Equipment and the Construction sectors are also eliminated. The total effect on the maximand of the change in foreign aid availability of Rs. 6000 crores is to raise the value of consumption available over the entire planning period by Rs. 60,375 crores, or over 10 per cent. The entire amount of that change comes in the last nine years. However, alternative patterns of saving and investment would be possible with the additional net foreign capital inflow. By changing the consumption growth constraints, for example, some part of the additionally available consumption could be shifted forward in time if that were desired, with resultant reduction in the maximand.

Table 5.16 shows the national income accounts for the Solution G-10.2 with net foreign aid extended over the entire planning period at the rate of Rs. 1500 crores per period, the same rate as in the Reference Solution. The effect on the solution is to increase the maximand by Rs. 5029 crores, i.e., by less than 1.0 per cent, as compared to the Reference Solution; as would now be expected, the increase comes entirely in the last two periods. Again, however, with modification of the consumption growth constraints, some part of consumption increase could be shifted forward in time. The effects of additional net foreign capital are only partly due to the difference in the net increments. Providing additional net foreign aid in the early plan years is much more valuable than providing the same amount of aid over a longer period. Resources "now" are always worth more than

Table 5.16. National Income Accounts for Guidepath-I Solution G-10.2
(Rs. crores, 1959-60 prices)

	1966-69	1969-72	1972-75	1975-78	1978-81	1981-84
CONSUMPTION	51051.3	59098.0	70386.3	86226.0	145482.0	188402.1
INVENTORIES CHANGE	1081.8	2090.6	3093.4	4728.8	5809.3	9346.9
FIXED INVESTMENT	14412.4	26598.8	36801.8	62603.1	74169.2	113079.6
TOTAL INVESTMENT	17780.6	31322.0	42870.2	70948.6	83954.7	127228.0
GOVERNMENT EXPENDITURE	3539.0	4123.0	5017.7	5976.1	7117.5	8476.9
VALUE ADDED BY GOVT.	5995.8	6857.1	8345.1	9939.0	11837.3	14098.2
EXPORTS	3087.6	3709.2	4626.4	5691.2	6762.7	3112.8
IMPORTS	4587.6	5209.2	6126.4	7191.2	8262.7	9612.8
GROSS NATIONAL PRODUCT	76756.6	99900.1	125119.3	171589.7	246891.5	336705.2
REPLACEMENT	2286.4	2632.6	2974.9	3616.7	3976.2	4801.5
NET NATIONAL PRODUCT	74470.3	97267.4	122144.3	167973.0	242915.3	331903.7
SAVINGS	16280.6	29822.0	41370.2	69448.6	83954.7	127228.0
GROSS NAT. OUTPUT	98855.4	134615.4	181888.7	260686.4	371893.1	519806.1
INTERMEDIATE PRODUCT	27984.6	41572.4	65114.5	99035.7	136838.9	197199.1
CONS./GROSS NAT. PROD.	0.66511	0.59157	0.56255	0.50251	0.58925	0.55955
TOTAL INVST/GR.NAT.PR.	0.23165	0.31353	0.34263	0.41348	0.34005	0.37786
SAVINGS/GR. NAT. PROD.	0.21211	0.29852	0.33065	0.40474	0.34005	0.37786

resources "later." This effect is accentuated by the bottlenecks, resulting from the imbalance in the composition of the initial endowments, which can be broken with additional aid in early Plan years.

Solutions G-11 are similar to Solutions G-10, but with initial capacities based on 1965-66 outputs adjusted for coverage on a thirty-two-sector basis. In Solutions G-11, the initial capital is greater than in Solution G-10 by Rs. 1580 crores. This leads to a difference of Rs. 17,653 crores in consumption in the sixth period. In Solution G-12.0 the capital-output ratio in Modern Agriculture is set at 4.0 which corresponds to the Japanese ratio, as compared to 2.5 in the Reference Solution G-10.0. With the consumption growth constraints of Solution G-10.0, a feasible solution did not exist. When the intra-Plan growth rate in the first period is reduced from 5 to 3 per cent per year, a feasible solution is obtained. The increased difficulty of modernizing Agriculture due to the higher capital-output ratio substantially reduces the total consumption provided. Consumption in the terminal period in this case is only 70 per cent of the consumption in the Reference Solution G-10.0. Even then, the capital stock in Incremental Agriculture is higher in G-12.0 than in G-10.0. The total terminal stock is also higher, and the sectoral composition of capacities is different.

5.6 Guidepath-II Model Solutions

As pointed out in discussion of the Guidepath-I solutions, one of their striking characteristics is the high savings rates which they generate. These are both required by, and the source of, the high growth rates. The savings rates are not imposed on the solutions but are the outcome of optimization in the model solutions. In the Guidepath-II model a savings constraint is added setting a limit in each period on the maximum rate of savings.[11] It provides another way, though indirect, of imposing on the solution the preferences of society, and another explicit policy variable.

---

[11]The base year is taken as 1965-66, for which net national product (NNP) and net domestic savings are estimated at Rs. 19,570 crores and Rs. 2080 crores, respectively. The minimum consumption for a three-year period is then

$$C(t) + \overline{G(t)} \geqslant 5520 + 0.80 \text{ NNP}(t) \quad \text{when marginal savings rate} \leqslant .20.$$

and

$$C(t) + \overline{G(T)} \geqslant 11{,}385 + 0.70 \text{ NNP}(t) \quad \text{when marginal savings rate} \leqslant .30.$$

**Table 5.17. Values of Private Consumption in Guidepath-II Solutions
(Rs. crores, 1959-60 prices)**

Solution*		Period						
		1	2	3	4	5	6	7
		1966-69	1969-72	1972-73	1975-78	1978-81	1981-84	1984-85
S-1.0	X(0) on 11-sector basis; postterminal growth rate of consumption ϕ = 6% per year; minimum growth rate of consumption in period t, $\rho(t)$ = 5% per year; marginal savings rate < 20%	52732	64668	74861	87064	101284	117248	139644
S-1.1	Net foreign capital inflow (NFCI) doubled for 4 periods, then zero	52732	68558	79365	93832	110974	128467	153006
S-1.2	NFCI continued for 6 periods	52732	64686	74882	87172	104450	120914	144010
S-2.0	X(0) on 11 sector-basis; ϕ = 8% per year; $\rho(t)$ = 5% per year; Marginal savings rate <30%	52732	65203	75481	87378	108339	125416	157988
S-2.1	NFCI doubled for 4 periods, then zero	52732	67385	78006	94179	120530	139528	175765
S-2.2	NFCI continued	52732	65203	75481	87378	111173	128696	162120
S-3.0	X(0) on 32-sector basis; ϕ = 8% per year; ρ = 5% per year; Marginal savings rate <30%	52954	66501	76983	89709	113230	131078	165120
S-3.1	NFCI doubled for 4 periods, then zero	52954	68939	79806	97041	124941	144635	182198
S-3.2	NFCI continued	52954	66501	76983	89901	115924	134197	169050

*Unless otherwise indicated all solutions had the following constraints:
1. Postterminal annual growth rates of
   Government consumption, 6.0%
   Exports, 5.5%
   Imports, 5.5%
   Replacement at ϕ, the same rate as consumption
2. Net foreign capital inflow set at Rs. 500 crores per year for the first 12 years
   i.e., 4 periods, then at zero

Finding an acceptable solution to the Guidepath-II Model or a menu of reasonable alternatives is again an iterative process. As a first step, the potential growth rate of the system with a savings constraint was estimated by a rough, macroeconomic calculation, using an aggregate capital-output ratio. From this it appears that with a marginal net savings rate of 20 per cent, it might be possible for the system to maintain a growth rate of 8 per cent per year. This rate is therefore set as the required postterminal growth rate for consumption in the first solution for the Guidepath-II Model. The minimum required intra-Plan growth rate of consumption is set at zero, so that only monotonic behavior is required. A feasible solution is obtained under these conditions. However, in this solution the investments required for the postterminal period are spread over the last two periods, and the savings constraints are binding in these periods. This indicates the impossibility of indefinitely maintaining the required 8 per cent per year postterminal growth of consumption with a marginal net savings rate of 20 per cent.

In Solution S-1.0 in Table 5.17, still using the 20 per cent marginal savings rate, the postterminal consumption growth requirement is reduced to 6 per cent per year, and a 5 per cent per year intra-Plan growth requirement is imposed. This

In the constraints embodied in the solutions, the value added by government, which is assumed to be 1.66 $\overline{G(t)}$ and is external to the model, was inadvertently omitted from the net national product. This has the effect of lowering the required consumption and, thus, of raising the permissible savings. The constraints are actually

$$C(t) + \overline{G(t)} \geqslant 5520 + 0.80 \, [NNP(t) - 1.66 \, \overline{G(t)}].$$

and

$$C(t) + \overline{G(t)} \geqslant 11,385 + 0.70 \, [NNP(t) - 1.66 \, \overline{G(t)}].$$

also gives a feasible solution, but again one whose character indicates that the postterminal growth requirement is too high in the sense that it cannot be indefinitely maintained. This is shown in the model solution by the fact that some investment necessary to fulfill postterminal requirements is carried out prior to the last Plan period, even though the capital formed remains idle until the end of the Plan. This demonstrates the inability to produce in the last Plan period alone the investment requirements for 6 per cent postterminal growth in consumption, when the marginal savings rate is constrained to 20 per cent. The amounts involved are relatively small however, and the investment for postterminal growth is all carried out in the last period, when the postterminal consumption growth requirement is reduced to 5 per cent per year.

When a solution is attempted with the required intra-Plan and postterminal consumption growth rates both set at 5 per cent per year, but the marginal net savings rate reduced to 15 per cent, it is found to be infeasible. On the other hand, when the marginal net savings rate is raised to 30 per cent with a required 5 per cent per year intra-Plan consumption growth rate and an 8 per cent per year postterminal rate, the solution is feasible. This is Solution S-2.0 in Fig. 5.3. These solutions, with some further variations, are also tabulated in Table 5.17. Table 5.18 presents the national income accounts for the Guidepath-II Solution S-1.0, which will serve as a Reference Solution. It has 5 per cent per year intra-Plan and 6 per cent per year postterminal consumption growth requirements and a maximum marginal savings rate of 20 per cent. The other postterminal growth requirements are the same as in the Guidepath-I Reference Solution. The Guidepath-I and Guidepath-II Reference Solutions have interesting contrasts as shown in Fig. 5.4. The 21 to 38 per cent average savings rates of the Guidepath-I Reference Solution cannot be realized in Solution S-1.0, the marginal savings rate of which is constrained at a lower level. In the Guidepath-II Reference Solution, the savings constraints are binding in all periods and limit the rate of change of net domestic savings from the 10.6 per cent average rate which was obtained in the pre-Plan period. Subsequently, the average net savings rate never rises about 15.3 per cent, which corresponds to 17.7 per cent on a gross basis. The average gross savings rate actually achieved goes up from 14.0 per cent at the outset to 17.7 per cent in the last period.

Most of the characteristic features distinguishing the Guidepath-II Reference Solution from the Guidepath-I Reference Solution follow from the savings constraint. With less domestic saving, the rate of investment must be lower and in some years is less than half that of the Guidepath-I Reference Solution. In the Guidepath-II Reference Solution, the levels of consumption are higher in the first nine years and lower in the last nine, and the postterminal achievement of the solution is lower. Though the level of savings is lower, consumption is maintained by the consumption growth constraints. As a result, fewer resources can be devoted to creating capacity in the capital goods sectors. Eventually less capacity can be created in the consumer goods sectors. The total value of consumption produced in this Guidepath-II Reference Solution is Rs. 497,858 crores over the eighteen years, and is 16.6 per cent less than the Rs. 595,616 crores produced in the Guidepath-I Reference Solution. Although the Guidepath-II Reference Solution has higher consumption levels in the first half of the planning period than has the Guidepath-I Reference Solution, the gross national product is uniformly lower.

Figure 5.3. Consumption in Guidepath-II Solutions.

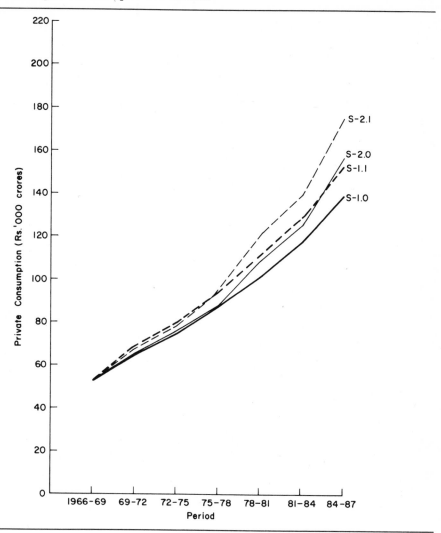

Table 5.18. National Income Accounts, Guidepath-II Reference Solution
(Rs. crores, 1959-60 prices)

	1966-69	1969-72	1972-78	1975-78	1978-81	1981-84
CONSUMPTION	52732.5	64568.1	74861.4	87063.9	101293.7	117248.5
INVENTORIES CHANGE	256.9	1021.5	1046.5	1141.6	1372.2	1988.8
FIXED INVESTMENT	8410.9	10778.1	14093.8	16718.3	19561.2	23308.9
TOTAL INVESTMENT	11674.7	15071.7	18115.3	22177.8	24909.5	30099.2
GOVERNMENT EXPENDITURE	3539.0	4123.0	5017.7	5976.1	7117.5	8476.9
VALUE ADDED BY GOVT.	5885.8	6857.1	8345.1	9939.0	11837.3	14098.2
EXPORTS	3087.6	3709.2	4626.4	5691.2	6762.7	8112.8
IMPORTS	4587.6	5209.2	6126.4	7191.2	6762.7	8112.8
GROSS NATIONAL PRODUCT	72332.0	89219.8	104839.5	123656.8	145148.0	169922.8
REPLACEMENT	3006.8	3272.1	2974.9	4317.9	3976.2	4801.5
NET NATIONAL PRODUCT	69325.2	85947.7	101864.5	119338.9	141171.9	165121.3
SAVINGS	10174.7	13571.7	16615.3	20677.8	24909.5	30099.2
GROSS NAT. OUTPUT	91075.9	114115.4	138495.6	165056.7	194832.0	229674.5
INTERMEDIATE PRODUCT	24629.7	31752.7	42001.2	51338.9	61521.3	73849.9
CONS./GROSS NAT. PROD.	0.72903	0.72482	0.71406	0.70408	0.69780	0.69001
TOTAL INVST/GR.NAT.PR.	0.16140	0.16893	0.17279	0.17935	0.17161	0.17713
SAVINGS/GR. NAT. PROD.	0.14067	0.15212	0.15848	0.16722	0.17161	0.17713

Figure 5.4. Consumption in Alternative Guidepaths.

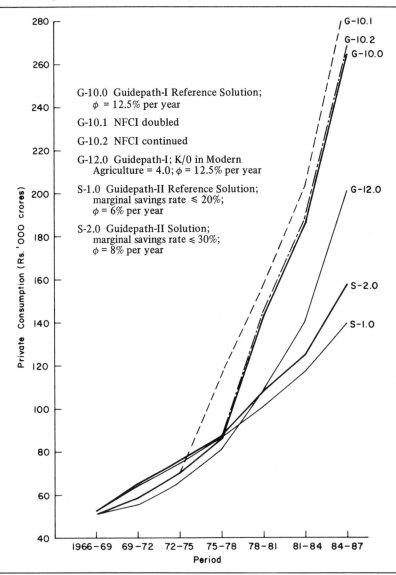

G-10.0 Guidepath-I Reference Solution;
$\phi = 12.5\%$ per year

G-10.1 NFCI doubled

G-10.2 NFCI continued

G-12.0 Guidepath-I; K/0 in Modern
Agriculture = 4.0; $\phi = 12.5\%$ per year

S-1.0 Guidepath-II Reference Solution;
marginal savings rate $\leq 20\%$;
$\phi = 6\%$ per year

S-2.0 Guidepath-II Solution;
marginal savings rate $\leq 30\%$;
$\phi = 8\%$ per year

Some of the detailed sectoral implications of the Guidepath-II Reference Solution are shown in Tables 5.19 through 5.25. Table 5.19, which presents the gross domestic outputs by sector, indicates again a growing industrialization of the economy, but, in comparison with the Guidepath-I Reference Solution, at a substantially slower rate. The use of foreign exchange for noncompetitive and competitive imports and the shadow prices associated with the foreign exchange balance constraint for the Guidepath-II Reference Solution are shown in Table 5.21.

Table 5.19. Gross Domestic Outputs, Guidepath-II Reference Solution (Rs. crores, 1959-60 prices)

ACTIVITY	1966-69	1969-72	1972-75	1975-78	1978-81	1981-84	1984-87
INCAGR	0.	4442.98	9912.21	15416.71	21732.28	28991.05	39033.53
M.M.	3414.95	4573.61	5913.61	7133.03	9813.59	11769.15	14264.96
EQIPMT	4566.43	7632.67	9984.92	12973.86	15527.59	19708.10	22798.00
CHEMIC	3665.25	5477.16	7229.40	9224.05	11627.32	14651.37	18067.03
CMGLWD	2144.82	2403.36	3037.85	3680.28	4278.31	5033.81	6431.74
FOODCL	10332.51	13043.61	15360.87	18031.07	21029.98	24487.56	29296.00
ELECTR	537.47	712.03	1195.46	1465.66	1801.39	2184.87	2633.32
TRANS	3876.13	5089.93	6291.12	7607.08	9238.89	11060.31	13342.09
CONSTR	8928.80	8972.53	11302.33	13601.27	15330.50	17460.47	23120.92
HOUS.	2407.96	2917.92	3356.40	3876.57	4481.27	5159.22	6105.20
OTHMAR	22085.42	29294.56	34910.67	41594.20	49059.10	57790.75	69637.54
TRADAG	29116.18	29555.11	30000.65	30452.91	30911.99	31377.99	31851.01

Table 5.20. Shadow Prices on Output and on Savings Constraints, Guidepath-II Reference Solution (Rs. crores)

SECTOR	1966-69	1969-72	1972-75	1975-78	1978-81	1981-84
AG.PL.	7.55	7.55	4.87	2.39	1.85	1.72
M.M.	7.55	7.55	6.39	3.35	2.20	1.83
EQIPMT	7.55	7.55	5.67	3.18	2.15	1.84
CHEMIC	7.55	7.55	4.41	2.46	1.89	1.90
CMGLWD	7.55	7.55	3.57	2.05	1.77	1.71
FOODCL	7.55	7.55	4.16	2.39	1.86	1.72
ELECTR	7.55	7.55	10.03	4.22	2.38	1.88
TRANS	7.55	7.55	7.11	3.34	2.15	1.84
CONSTR	7.55	7.55	2.33	1.67	1.67	1.67
HOUS.	77.07	7.55	17.70	2.98	1.38	1.57
OTHMAR	7.55	7.55	0.71	0.88	1.42	1.58

SHADOW PRICES ON SAVINGS CONSTRAINTS

	7.55	7.55	0.14	0.69	1.37	1.57

Table 5.21. Imports and Shadow Prices on Foreign Trade Balance Constraints, Guidepath-II Reference Solution (Rs. crores, 1959-60 prices)

NONCOMPETITIVE IMPORTS

ACTIVITY	1966-69	1969-72	1972-75	1975-78	1978-81	1981-84	1984-87
INCAGR	0.	53.32	79.30	69.38	21.73	28.99	39.03
M.M.	495.17	480.23	413.95	356.65	294.41	235.38	285.30
EQIPMT	1073.11	1335.72	1148.27	1037.91	776.38	788.32	911.92
CHEMIC	956.63	1194.02	1265.14	1383.61	1453.41	1465.14	1608.70
CMGLWD	8.58	7.21	6.08	5.52	4.28	5.03	6.43
FOODCL	0.83	0.78	0.61	0.54	0.42	0.37	0.44
ELECTR	0.	0.	0.	0.	0.	0.	0.
TRANS	0.	0.	0.	0.	0.	0.	0.
CONSTR	0.	0.	0.	0.	0.	0.	0.
HOUS.	0.	0.	0.	0.	0.	0.	0.
OTHMAR	0.	0.	0.	0.	0.	0.	0.
TRADAG	465.86	354.66	240.01	137.04	30.91	31.38	31.85

COMPETITIVE IMPORTS

SECTOR	1966-69	1969-72	1972-75	1975-78	1978-81	1981-84	1984-87
AG.PL.	196.73	1077.10	0.	0.	0.	0.	0.00
M.M.	0.	706.18	2973.03	4200.60	4181.11	5558.21	6517.77
EQIPMT	0.	0.	0.	0.	0.	0.	13.76
CHEMIC	0.	0.	0.	0.	0.	0.	-88.28
CMGLWD	0.	0.	0.	0.	0.	0.	-0.52
FOODCL	347.31	0.	0.	0.	0.	0.	-0.01
ELECTR	0.	0.	0.	0.	0.	0.	0.
TRANS	0.	0.	0.	0.	0.	0.	0.
CONSTR	0.	0.	0.	0.	0.	0.	0.
HOUS.	0.	0.	0.	0.	0.	0.	0.
OTHMAR	1043.35	0.	0.	0.	0.	0.	0.

SHADOW PRICES ON FOREIGN TRADE BALANCE CONSTRAINTS

	7.55	7.55	6.39	3.35	2.20	6.11	

In the first period, the output of all sectors but Housing have the same shadow price, which is the same as the shadow price associated with the foreign trade balance. The only obstacle to increasing investment in this period is the inability to provide the additional consumption required by the maximum savings constraint. This can be seen from the existence of excess capacity in all sectors but Housing, Food, Clothing, and Leather, and Agriculture. However, Housing is not an input to any sector and cannot be imported while Food, Clothing, and Leather, and Agriculture can be imported. That foreign exchange is available for such imports is seen from the fact that competitive imports are made in Others and Margin, even though there is excess capacity in the sector, again because Others and Margin contributes most to net national product per unit of output.

The correspondence of the prices of all outputs, except Housing, imports, and savings, is due to the fact that violation of the constraints by external provision of an additional unit of any output, other than Housing, or of a unit of foreign exchange, helps to relieve the same constraint, namely the savings constraint. Neither imports nor an externally provided unit of output add to the net national product. With an additional external unit of output, domestic production can be reduced by one unit, which reduces net national product without changing total availabilities. With a lower net national product, less consumption is required, and, since total availability is the same, more savings become possible.

An additional unit of Housing on the other hand, is more valuable than any other type of output. Since Housing contributes only 5 per cent of the composite consumption good, 20 units of aggregate consumption can be provided if the other, complementary components of consumption can be made available. This can be done, because, as pointed out above, the complementary requirements can be met from excess capacity or imports. By permitting more consumption, an additional unit of Housing would also raise net national product and, therefore, the maximum possible savings. In the second period, the shadow prices of output of all the sectors are the same as the shadow price associated with the savings constraint for the period. From the third period onwards, other constraints become more significant, and the savings constraint though still binding is no longer so completely dominant.

In the first period, competitive imports are concentrated in consumer goods sectors, as domestic capacity in these sectors is fully utilized, and there is excess capacity in all other sectors. After the first period, Mining and Metals continues to be the sector toward which foreign exchange is directed after noncompetitive imports requirements have been satisfied. The shadow prices associated with the foreign exchange balance indicate a somewhat lesser foreign exchange scarcity in the first periods, as compared to the case in the Guidepath-I Reference Solution, and a slightly greater scarcity in the latter periods.

Table 5.22 presents the sectoral distribution of consumption in each period and the shadow prices associated with the consumption growth constraints and the savings constraints. The higher levels of aggregate consumption in the first periods lead to an earlier shifting of the composition of consumption away from agricultural products relative to the Guidepath-I Reference Solution. This is an interesting result indicating that the larger the role of growth of consumption, the greater the impetus toward industrialization from the consumption side. The shifting toward industrial products slows down in the latter periods, as aggregate

Table 5.22. Private Consumption and Shadow Prices on Consumption Growth Constraints, Guidepath-II Reference Solution (Rs. crores, 1959-60 prices)

SECTOR	1966-69	1969-72	1972-75	1975-78	1978-81	1981-84	1984-87
AG.PL.	19894.13	23660.67	26939.35	30765.00	35192.28	40142.74	46980.62
M.M.	24.24	29.01	33.15	38.01	43.63	49.93	58.67
EQIPMT	1413.74	1917.17	2331.68	2852.63	3467.39	4162.61	5164.52
CHEMIC	1636.75	2075.66	2444.75	2895.81	3424.32	4019.55	4864.51
CMGLWD	320.81	406.84	479.19	567.60	671.19	787.86	953.48
FOODCL	7550.24	9259.17	10718.65	12465.80	14521.80	16787.65	19994.36
ELECTR	54.91	68.12	79.34	92.87	108.67	126.44	151.47
TRANS	944.14	1184.44	1387.43	1634.01	1922.48	2247.07	2706.29
CONSTR	0.	0.	0.	0.	0.	0.	0.
HOUS.	2407.96	2917.92	3356.40	3876.57	4481.27	5159.22	6105.20
OTHMAR	18485.60	23149.06	27091.45	31875.55	37470.66	43765.49	52665.79
SUM	52732.52	64668.07	74861.38	87063.85	101283.70	117248.55	139644.89

```
SUM OF   DISCOUNTED CONSUMPTION =   497858.0390625
SUM CF  UNDISCOUNTED CONSUMPTION =   497858.0390625

SHADOW PRICES ON CONSUMPTION GROWTH CONSTRAINTS
         0.        0.        2.495        0.        0.        0.888
```

Table 5.23. Available Capital Stock, Guidepath-II Reference Solution (Rs. crores, 1959-60 prices)

ACTIVITY	1966-69	1969-72	1972-75	1975-78	1978-81	1981-84	1984-87
INCAGR	0.	4191.38	9350.88	14543.67	20501.58	27349.28	36823.05
M.M.	3775.88	3775.88	4882.16	5888.89	8101.90	9716.38	11776.85
EQIPMT	2470.31	2470.31	3177.40	4128.54	4941.19	6271.51	7254.80
CHEMIC	2174.42	2174.42	2543.88	3245.76	4091.42	5155.52	6364.50
CMGLWD	851.64	851.64	872.74	1057.31	1229.12	1446.16	1847.76
FOODCL	1919.68	2423.37	2853.90	3349.99	3907.16	4549.54	5442.90
ELECTR	1855.38	1855.38	2494.10	3057.80	3758.24	4558.30	5493.88
TRANS	6827.87	7344.77	9078.09	10977.01	13331.72	15960.02	19252.61
CONSTR	578.74	578.74	576.42	693.67	781.86	890.48	1179.18
HOUS.	8026.53	11004.61	11187.99	12921.90	15318.14	18203.00	20350.70
OTHMAR	1616.81	1616.81	1821.29	2169.97	2559.41	3014.94	3632.99
TRADAG	14652.14	14873.02	15097.23	15324.82	15555.84	15790.35	16028.38
SUM	44749.39	53160.32	63936.08	77359.31	94077.57	112905.50	135447.61

Table 5.24. Ratio of Idle Capital to Total Capital, Guidepath-II Reference Solution

ACTIVITY	1966-69	1969-72	1972-75	1975-78	1978-81	1981-84	1984-87
INCAGR	0.	0.	0.	0.	0.	0.	-0.00
M.M.	0.25	0.	0.	0.	0.	0.	-0.00
EQIPMT	0.41	0.02	0.	0.	0.	0.	0.00
CHEMIC	0.41	0.11	0.	0.	0.	0.	0.00
CMGLWD	0.28	0.19	0.	0.	0.	0.	-0.00
FOODCL	0.	0.	0.	0.	0.	0.	0.00
ELECTR	0.40	0.20	0.	0.	0.	0.	-0.00
TRANS	0.18	0.	0.	0.	0.	0.	-0.00
CONSTR	0.21	0.21	0.	0.	0.	0.	0.00
HOUS.	0.	0.12	0.	0.	0.02	0.06	0.00
OTHMAR	0.29	0.05	0.	0.	0.	0.	-0.00
TRADAG	0.	0.	0.	0.	0.	0.	-0.00
SUM	0.13	0.04	0.	0.	0.00	0.01	0.00

Table 5.25. New Capital, Guidepath-II Reference Solution (Rs. crores, 1959-60 prices)

ACTIVITY	1966-69	1969-72	1972-75	1975-78	1978-81	1981-84	1984-87
INCAGR	0.	4191.38	5153.51	5192.78	5957.91	6847.71	9473.76
M.M.	0.	0.	1106.28	1006.72	2213.01	1614.48	2060.47
EQIPMT	0.	0.	707.10	951.14	812.65	1330.32	983.29
CHEMIC	0.	0.	369.46	701.88	845.66	1064.10	1208.97
CMGLWD	0.	0.	21.11	184.56	171.31	217.05	401.60
FOODCL	0.	503.70	430.52	496.10	557.17	642.38	893.36
ELECTR	0.	0.	638.72	563.70	700.44	800.07	935.56
TRANS	0.	516.90	1733.32	1898.93	2354.71	2628.30	3292.59
CONSTR	0.	0.	0.	117.25	88.19	108.63	288.70
HOUS.	0.	2978.08	183.38	2404.48	2396.24	3618.00	2914.43
OTHMAR	0.	0.	204.48	348.68	389.44	455.53	618.04
TRADAG	0.	220.88	224.21	227.59	231.02	234.50	238.04
SUM	0.	8410.94	10778.08	14093.80	16718.25	19561.16	23308.83

consumption grows more slowly. The consumption growth constraint is binding only between the second and third periods and the fifth and sixth periods.

The total availability of capital and its use is shown in Tables 5.23 and 5.24. These tables also reflect the relatively greater emphasis on consumer goods rather than capital goods in the Guidepath-II Reference Solution as compared with the Guidepath-I Reference Solution. However, the productive capacity in all sectors grows more slowly in the Guidepath-II as compared to the Guidepath-I Reference Solution. As shown by the ratios of idle to total capacity in Table 5.24, substantial idle capacities exist in the capital goods sectors and their major suppliers in the first two periods, before the proportions in which capacity is originally available can be adjusted to requirements. For these periods the consumer goods sectors are the bottlenecks. This suggests a lack of correspondence between the investment policies prior to the beginning of the Guidepath-II solution and the optimal policies as determined by that solution. In the Guidepath-I Reference Solution by comparison, idle capacities were eliminated by the second period.

Table 5.25, which lists the new capacity by period and by sector, confirms the previous contrasts in the solutions. Agriculture, Housing, and Food, Clothing, and Leather account for over 50 per cent of the total capacity in all periods, whereas in the Guidepath-I Reference Solution, their total proportion was a third or less, except at the very end of the planning period when consumption rose rapidly. The total new capital formation in the Guidepath-II Model Reference Solution varies from 27 to 60 per cent of that of the Guidepath-I Reference Solution in corresponding periods.

Differences among the Guidepath-II solutions with various constraints are illustrated in Table 5.17. Their qualitative features are by now predictable. For example, the effect of increasing the maximum marginal net savings rate to 30 per cent in Solution S-2.0 relieves the savings constraint somewhat, and, as a result, the total and final levels of consumption rise. The postterminal growth requirement of 8 per cent in this solution as compared to 6 per cent in the Guidepath-II Reference Solution offsets this effect somewhat. As can be seen in Fig. 5.3, in every period the consumption provided in Solution S-2.0 is equal to or higher than that provided in the Reference Solution S-1.0, in which the maximum marginal savings rate is 20 per cent. This result is possible only in a multisectoral model. If only one good were produced, a higher savings rate would lead to lower consumption in at least one period of a solution of dynamic model, as compared to a solution with a lower savings rate. If there are many sectors, the initial composition of capacities may not be in balance with a particular rate of savings, so that a lower savings rate, rather than leading to more consumption, would only lead to more idle capacity than if the savings rate were higher.[12]

The comparative effects of increasing new foreign capital availabilities are not so obvious. It might be thought, for example, that such an increase would always benefit most the solution with the tightest domestic saving constraint. In fact

---

[12]The existence of relationships between the composition of output and the savings rate has been remarked on many times though not often in the context of a multisector model for planning development. In the context of a simpler, two-sector model, a similar point has been made by Marvin Frankel, "Producer Goods, Consumer Goods, and Acceleration of Growth," *The Economic Journal, 71,* 1961, pp. 1-19.

however, when the specified net foreign capital inflow is doubled over four periods, the value of the maximand goes up more when the marginal savings rate is 30 per cent than when it is 20 per cent. The higher marginal savings rate permits a greater plowback of increments of output into investment, which will in turn yield even more consumption in the future. Aid is more effective in raising output when it is possible to raise domestic savings rapidly than when it is not. To achieve the same results, more foreign aid is required by the country that must respect a tight savings constraint than by a country that is not limited in forcing savings. The effect is the reverse when the net foreign capital inflow is extended at the same rate for six periods. This is because the higher postterminal growth rate stipulated in the solution with the marginal savings rate of 30 per cent absorbs a larger amount of the additional foreign exchange.

5.7 Guidepost Model Solutions

Once a long-run guidepath is selected, the next step is to check its short-run feasibility and, if that is demonstrated, to determine the year-by-year allocations necessary. For this task we use the Guidepost Model in which year-by-year accounting and gestation lags of up to three years are provided. Prior to the Guidepost solution, it cannot be known whether a short-run plan using as targets the capital stocks interpolated from an intermediate point in a Guidepath solution can do better or worse with respect to its maximand than a Guidepath Model solution itself over the same years. As pointed out previously, the time aggregation in the Guidepath Model not only provides some unwarranted flexibility but also creates undue rigidity, and the net effect cannot be predicted from qualitative considerations alone.

The Guidepost Model can be used in a variety of ways to test and detail a Guidepath solution, depending on what short-run constraints and targets it is desired to enforce. In the applications to be described, emphasis has been placed on achieving targets so that the minimum intra-Plan consumption growth rates are reduced to 2.5 per cent per year. When the targets are taken from a Guidepath-II solution, the savings constraints of that solution are also enforced for every year. This yearly specification of savings constraints makes it more difficult for a Guidepost model solution to achieve the targets. In order to fit the Guidepath results most conveniently, the planning period is set at six years.

The third-period capital stocks in the Guidepath Model solutions correspond to the stocks in the period covering 1972-73, 1973-74, and 1974-75. This capital stock is taken to be the target capital stock in the Guidepost Model for the year 1973-74, which is the eighth year starting from 1966-67. The capital stocks for the seventh and ninth years are projected from the initial stocks of 1966-67 and from the growth rates implied by the eighth-year targets. In projecting the targets for Incremental Agriculture, the initial capacity of which is zero, the growth rate between the third and fourth period in the Guidepath solution is used. To project the initial capital-in-process however, the intra-Plan growth rates of the Fourth Plan Target Model solutions are used. This establishes comparability with the initial conditions of the Target and Transit Model solutions for the Fourth Plan period as well as the Guidepath solution. Thus the maximum potential capacity in the second year of a Guidepost solution, 1967-68, is the same as the capacity in the first three-year period, 1966-69, of the corresponding Guidepath solution.

Table 5.26. National Income Accounts for Guidepost Solution P-1 (Rs. crores, 1959-60 prices)

	1966-67	1967-68	1968-69	1969-70	1970-71	1971-72
CONSUMPTION	15761.5	16155.5	16559.4	19128.0	21063.7	21769.0
INVENTORIES CHANGE	-41.5	225.4	558.7	683.7	410.1	830.6
FIXED INVESTMENT	4143.1	5449.2	6161.1	6638.2	8170.1	9099.3
TOTAL INVESTMENT	4885.7	6398.7	7360.0	8103.6	9549.4	11054.0
GOVERNMENT EXPENDITURE	1108.0	1177.0	1254.0	1293.0	1372.0	1458.0
VALUE ADDED BY GOVT.	1842.7	1957.5	2085.6	2150.4	2281.8	2424.8
EXPORTS	976.9	1026.6	1084.0	1151.5	1232.0	1325.7
IMPORTS	1476.9	1526.6	1584.0	1651.5	1732.0	1825.7
GROSS NATIONAL PRODUCT	23098.0	25188.8	26759.0	30175.1	33766.9	36205.8
REPLACEMENT	784.1	724.2	640.2	781.6	969.1	1124.0
NET NATIONAL PRODUCT	22313.9	24464.6	26118.8	29393.4	32797.7	35081.8
SAVINGS	4385.7	5898.7	6860.0	7603.6	9049.4	10554.0
GROSS NATIONAL OUTPUT	9657.2	9705.5	9754.0	9705.5	9754.0	9754.0
INTERMEDIATE PRODUCT	8842.4	9454.0	10306.5	11782.8	13658.5	15137.9
CONS./GROSS NAT. PROD.	0.68238	0.64138	0.61884	0.63350	0.62380	0.60126
TOTAL INVST/GR.NAT.PR.	0.21152	0.25403	0.27505	0.26855	0.28280	0.30531
SAVINGS/GR. NAT. PROD.	0.18988	0.23418	0.25636	0.25198	0.26800	0.29150

Table 5.27. National Income Accounts for Guidepost Solution P-2 (Rs. crores, 1959-60 prices)

	1966-67	1967-68	1968-69	1969-70	1970-71	1971-72
CONSUMPTION	15775.2	16169.6	16573.3	18535.2	19669.7	20300.8
INVENTORIES CHANGE	44.0	226.2	454.3	603.4	449.1	714.2
FIXED INVESTMENT	4143.1	5431.2	6295.8	6801.0	8478.7	9778.4
TOTAL INVESTMENT	4883.2	6370.0	7369.6	8165.3	9897.9	11517.5
GOVERNMENT EXPENDITURE	1108.0	1177.0	1254.0	1293.0	1372.0	1458.0
VALUE ADDED BY GOVT.	1842.7	1957.5	2085.6	2150.4	2281.8	2424.8
EXPORTS	976.9	1026.6	1084.0	1151.5	1232.0	1325.7
IMPORTS	1476.9	1526.6	1584.0	1651.5	1732.0	1825.7
GROSS NATIONAL PRODUCT	23109.2	25174.1	26783.0	29643.9	32721.4	35301.1
REPLACEMENT	784.1	712.6	619.4	760.9	970.0	1124.9
NET NATIONAL PRODUCT	22325.1	24461.5	26163.6	28883.1	31751.4	34176.2
SAVINGS	4383.2	5870.0	6865.6	7665.3	9397.9	11117.5
GROSS NATIONAL OUTPUT	29772.3	32666.5	35019.9	30107.2	43862.7	47882.8
INTERMEDIATE PRODUCT	8505.8	9449.9	10322.5	11613.7	13423.1	15006.5
CONS./GROSS NAT. PROD.	0.68264	0.64231	0.61882	0.62526	0.60113	0.57507
TOTAL INVST/GR.NAT.PR.	0.21131	0.25304	0.27516	0.27545	0.30249	0.32910
SAVINGS/GR. NAT. PROD.	0.18967	0.23318	0.25649	0.25858	0.28721	0.31493

Table 5.28. National Income Accounts for Guidepost Solution P-3 (Rs. crores, 1959-60 prices)

	1966-67	1967-68	1968-69	1969-70	1970-71	1971-72
CONSUMPTION	16304.8	17530.9	18414.3	20997.8	22067.9	23181.5
INVENTORIES CHANGE	-332.4	114.3	289.5	573.9	273.9	389.9
FIXED INVESTMENT	3858.7	3343.2	3322.3	2609.3	3876.7	4028.3
TOTAL INVESTMENT	4272.4	4079.0	4136.1	3911.1	5118.6	5559.9
GOVERNMENT EXPENDITURE	1108.0	1177.0	1254.0	1293.0	1372.0	1458.0
VALUE ADDED BY GOVT.	1842.7	1957.5	2085.6	2150.4	2281.8	2424.8
EXPORTS	976.9	1026.6	1084.0	1151.5	1232.0	1325.7
IMPORTS	1476.9	1526.6	1584.0	1651.5	1732.0	1825.7
GROSS NATIONAL PRODUCT	23027.9	24244.4	25389.9	27852.3	30340.3	32124.3
REPLACEMENT	746.1	621.5	524.3	727.9	968.0	1141.7
NET NATIONAL PRODUCT	22281.8	23622.9	24865.7	27124.4	29372.4	30982.6
SAVINGS	3772.4	3579.0	3636.1	3411.1	4618.6	5059.9
GROSS NATIONAL OUTPUT	28987.2	30596.5	32059.1	34781.2	38994.8	41387.0
INTERMEDIATE PRODUCT	7802.0	8309.6	8754.8	9079.3	10936.3	11687.5
CONS./GROSS NAT. PROD.	0.70804	0.72309	0.72526	0.75390	0.72735	0.72162
TOTAL INVST/GR.NAT.PR.	0.18553	0.16824	0.16290	0.14042	0.16871	0.17307
SAVINGS/GR. NAT. PROD.	0.16382	0.14762	0.14321	0.12247	0.15223	0.15751

The Guidepost Model has little freedom or scope for choice left to it once all the above targets, conditions, and constraints are set. As in the Target Model, the initial conditions determine the maximum capital stocks for the first three years, and the terminal conditions determine these stocks for the last three years of the Guidepost Plan period. The minimum consumption level for the first year is set, and while the solution may provide more than this, it is not allowed to provide less. If the Guidepost solution is feasible, its general character is predetermined by the Guidepath solution on which it is based, and it will contain few surprises.

Feasible solutions have been found for the Guidepost Model corresponding to the Guidepath Model Solutions G-10.0 and G-12.0. However, the Guidepost solution corresponding to Guidepath Solution S-1.0 is infeasible. The maximum, marginal net savings rate of 20 per cent here is too low to allow completion of the initially endowed capital-in-process in the Guidepost solution. By comparison, in the Guidepath solution, it is assumed in computing the initial capital capacity endowment that the initial capital-in-process has been completed. When the marginal savings rate in the first two years is allowed to rise to 24 and 22 per cent,[13] the Guidepost Solution P-3 is found. Alternatively, corresponding solutions could have been found by proportional reductions in the targets or by relaxing the consumption growth or other constraints. Tables 5.26, 5.27, and 5.28 present the annual national income accounts for these Guidepost solutions P-1, P-2, and P-3, respectively.

In the Guidepost solutions, as in other cases, the rate of growth of national product is neither a simple linear nor an exponential function. However, if such a pattern were desired, for example, to provide for smooth growth in employment, it could be imposed as a constraint, though relaxation of some other constraint might become necessary to achieve such a guidepath. The savings and investment rates of the corresponding Guidepath and Guidepost solutions are more or less the same over comparable periods, as are the sectoral resource allocations lying behind the aggregate results.

Table 5.29 summarizes some of the major aspects of the Guidepost and corresponding Guidepath solutions. As shown in this table, the Guidepost solutions for targets taken from the two Guidepath-I solutions perform better, in terms of the consumption produced, than the Guidepath solutions themselves over the same period. However, the differences are slight, and in these two cases the time aggregation in the Guidepath Models does not seem to have significant effects. That was not the case with the Guidepath-II solution, but this can be ascribed to inconsistencies in the implied marginal savings rates necessary to complete the assumed initial capital-in-process and the constrained savings rate of the Guidepost solution.

5.8 Comparison of the Guidepath Model Solutions with the Target Model Solutions for a Proposed Fourth Plan

Since the capital stocks generated by a Guidepath Model solution for its early years are consistent with an explicit, optimum long-run growth path, it is interesting to compare these stocks with those called for by the adjusted Fourth Plan targets. Table 5.30 presents capital stocks for 1971-72 interpolated from

---

[13]Even then not all the initial capital-in-process that could have been completed in the third year is completed, and Solution P-3 has lower initial capacities than would correspond to S-1.0.

Table 5.29. Values of Private Consumption in Guidepost Solutions (Rs. crores, 1959-60 prices)

Solution	Sum of Undiscounted Consumption Over 6 years	Private Consumption		Gross National Product		Gross Dom. Savings Gross Nat. Prod.		Total Gross Investment Over Six Years
		In First Year	In Sixth Year	In First Year	In Sixth Year	In First Year	In Sixth Year	
P-1. Corresponds to G-10.0, the Guidepath-I Reference Solution	110437 (110149)*	15762	21769	23098	36206	.1899	.2915	47351
P-2. Corresponds to G-12.0, K/0 = 4.0 in Modern Agriculture	107024 (106836)*	15775	20301	23109	35301	.1897	.3149	48303
P-3. Corresponds to 5-1.0, the Guidepath-II Reference Solution	118497 (117400)*	16305	23182	23028	32124	.1638	.1575	27077

*Sum of consumption for the corresponding six years, first two periods, in the Guidepath solution.

Table 5.30. Capital Stocks in 1971-72* Guidepath Solutions and Adjusted Fourth Plan Targets

Sector	Guidepath-I Solutions		Guidepath-II Solutions		Adjusted Fourth Plan Targets
	G-10.0 Reference Solution	G-12.0 K/0 = 4.0 in Modern Agriculture	S-1.0 Marginal Savings ≤ 20%	S-2.0 Marginal Savings ≤ 30%	
1. Modern Agriculture	5203 (.079)†	6285 (.096)	5483 (.098)	6519 (.113)	5840‡
12. Traditional Agriculture	14937 (.227)	14947 (.227)	14947 (.266)	14947 (.259)	14947‡ } (18451)
2. Mining and Metals	9269 (.141)	9391 (.143)	4114 (.073)	4456 (.077)	6888
3. Equipment	4907 (.075)	4935 (.075)	2686 (.048)	2987 (.052)	4803
4. Chemicals	2448 (.037)	2303 (.035)	2291 (.041)	2327 (.040)	3964
5. Cement and Nonmetals	1256 (.019)	1279 (.019)	859 (.015)	886 (.015)	1465
6. Food, Clothing, and Leather	2436 (.037)	2315 (.035)	2560 (.046)	2585 (.045)	2621
7. Electricity	2448 (.037)	2406 (.037)	2047 (.036)	2108 (.037)	3073
8. Transport	10517 (.160)	10305 (.157)	7883 (.148)	8291 (.144)	10898‡(5464)
9. Construction	940 (.014)	980 (.015)	578 (.010)	599 (.010)	966
10. Housing	9463 (.144)	8980 (.137)	11058 (.197)	10269 (.178)	10290
11. Others and Margin	1670 (.025)	1590 (.024)	1682 (.030)	1662 (.029)	2417
Sum	65505 (1.000)	65715 (1.000)	56189 (1.000)	57637 (1.000)	68172‡(60402)

*Capital stocks for 1971-72 are interpolated log-linearly from the stocks in period 2 (1969-72) and period 3 (1972-75) of the Guidepath solution.

†Numbers in parentheses are ratios of sector stock to total stock.

‡Adjusted for different capital-output ratios.

several Guidepath solutions and the adjusted Fourth Plan target stocks.[14] With similar capital coefficients, the Guidepath-I solution generates higher capital stocks than the Guidepath-II solutions in all but the three major consumer goods sectors, Agriculture, Food, Clothing, and Leather, and Housing. The total capital stock of Guidepath-I Solution G-10.0 is 17 per cent larger than that of Guidepath-II Solution S-1.0, in which the maximum marginal savings rate is 20 per cent. In Solution G-12.0, where the capital-output ratio of Modern Agriculture is raised from 2.5 to 4.0, the capital stock in that sector is higher than in the Guidepath-II solutions, but its effective productive capacity is lower. The differences in the sectoral stocks in the Guidepath-I and II solutions are most striking in Mining and Metals and Equipment, where they are close to 100 per cent, and in Construction, where the difference is about 60 per cent.

The size and composition of the extrapolated Fourth Plan target stocks correspond more closely to those of the Guidepath-I solutions than to stocks generated by the Guidepath-II solutions. The correspondence is far from exact however. In Mining and Metals, the target stock is about 74 per cent of that of the Guidepath-I solutions, though about 60 per cent more than that of the Guidepath-II solutions. In the Equipment sector, the target and Guidepath-I stocks are roughly similar, as they are also in Agriculture, Food, Clothing, and Leather, Transport, Construction, and Housing. In other sectors, the target stocks are moderately to substantially higher than those of the Guidepath-I solutions, and the difference in Chemicals is particularly striking. The over-all levels of the adjusted Fourth Plan target capacities are more similar to those of the Guidepath-I solutions than the Guidepath-II solutions, as would be expected from the implied savings rates. The adjusted Fourth Plan target stocks are higher than those of the Guidepath-II solutions, except in Housing and Agriculture. The over-all difference is about 20 per cent.

The sectoral proportions of capital stocks are also shown in Table 5.30. Comparing the Guidepath-I and II solutions with similar capital-output ratios, it is clear that the Guidepath-II solution, with the higher maximum marginal savings rate of 30 per cent, resembles the Guidepath-I solution slightly more than the solution in which the marginal savings rate is 20 per cent. It is understandable that this should be so, since the savings requirements of the Guidepath-I solutions are much higher than in either of the Guidepath-II solutions. The greater relative emphasis on consumer goods in the Guidepath-II solutions leads to a higher proportion of capital stock in Chemicals than in the Guidepath-I solutions in order to supply the input requirements of Agriculture. The proportions of total stock in Electricity show an unexpected constancy. In general, the higher the rate of savings in the solutions, the higher is the proportion of capital stock in the capital goods producing sectors and their major suppliers. The Guidepath solutions thus provide the means for determining the quantitative implications of alternative savings rates.[15]

[14]The adjusted Fourth Plan capital stocks in Agriculture are further adjusted to provide the same output capacities as would be provided if the two activities of the Guidepath Model had been used. The adjustment adds Rs. 2306 crores to the capital stock in this sector. The Transport output target is multiplied by its long-term capital-output ratio, 4.329, of the Guidepath Models.

[15]The literature on the theory of capital accumulation and growth is rich in illustrations of single-sector models with optimal growth paths having some of the properties of the multisectoral Guidepath Model. Of particular relevance to the discussion of growth in less developed countries is the paper of Richard Goodwin, "The Optimal Growth Path for an Underdeveloped Economy," *The Economic Journal, 71,* 1961, pp. 756-774.

APPENDIX C

Table C.1. Input-Output Coefficients Matrix for Period 1966-77 to 1972-73

	1 INCAGR	2 M.M.	3 EQIPMT	4 CHEMIC	5 CMGLWD	6 FOODCL	7 ELECTR	8 TRANS	9 CONSTR	10 HOUS.	11 OTHMAR	12 TRADAG
AG.PL.	.007	.000	.010	.048	.134	.502	0.	0.	.035	0.	.035	.079
M.M.	.004	.235	.263	.027	.048	.004	.131	.037	.118	.005	.001	.000
ECIPMT	.004	.018	.033	.014	.003	.003	0.	0.	.013	0.	0.	0.
CHEPIC	.095	.023	.030	.198	.082	.029	.028	.202	.006	0.	.003	.010
CMGLWD	.003	.013	.005	.011	.026	.003	0.	0.	.180	.015	0.	.000
FCOCCL	.040	.002	.002	.034	.015	.056	0.	0.	0.	0.	.001	.008
ELECTR	.002	.023	.012	.016	.022	.014	0.	.004	0.	0.	.001	.001
TRANS	.005	.150	.071	.099	.068	.050	.118	.043	.018	.007	.021	.007
CONSTR	0.	0.	0.	0.	0.	0.	0.	0.	0.	0.	0.	0.
HCUS.	0.	0.	0.	0.	0.	0.	0.	0.	0.	0.	0.	0.
OTHMAR	.049	.033	.132	.032	.090	.055	.068	.018	.090	.046	0.	.005
SUM	.209	.498	.558	.479	.488	.715	.346	.304	.459	.071	.061	.110

Table C.2. Input-Output Coefficients Matrix for Periods after 1972-73

	1 INCAGR	2 M.M.	3 EQIPMT	4 CHEMIC	5 CMGLWD	6 FOODCL	7 ELECTR	8 TRANS	9 CONSTR	10 HOUS.	11 OTHMAR	12 TRADAG
AG.PL.	.007	.000	.010	.048	.134	.477	0.	0.	.034	0.	.035	.079
M.M.	.004	.246	.449	.025	.048	.004	.097	.022	.134	.005	.001	.000
ECIPNT	.004	.018	.059	.008	.003	.000	0.	0.	.043	0.	0.	0.
CHEMIC	.095	.022	.046	.161	.082	.026	.032	.196	.011	0.	.003	.010
CMCLWD	.003	.013	.008	.011	.026	.004	0.	0.	.177	.015	0.	.000
FCOCCL	.040	.002	.002	.034	.015	.058	0.	0.	0.	0.	.001	.008
ELECTR	.002	.033	.020	.031	.022	.014	0.	.015	0.	0.	.001	.001
TRANS	.005	.150	.071	.099	.068	.050	.118	.043	.018	.007	.021	.007
CCNSTR	0.	0.	0.	0.	0.	0.	0.	0.	0.	0.	0.	0.
HOUS.	0.	0.	0.	0.	0.	0.	0.	0.	0.	0.	0.	0.
OTHMAR	.049	.033	.132	.032	.090	.065	.068	.018	.090	.045	0.	.005
SUM	.209	.517	.797	.448	.488	.687	.316	.293	.507	.071	.061	.110

Table C.3. Aggregate Capital-Output Coefficients

1	INCAGR	.943370
2	M.M.	.825580
3	ECIPMT	.318220
4	CHEMIC	.351880
5	CMGLWC	.287290
6	FOCDCL	.185790
7	ELECTR	2.086300
8	TRANS	1.443000
9	CCNSTR	.051000
10	HOUS.	3.333333
11	OTHMAR	.052170
12	TRADAG	.503230

Table C.4. Capital Proportions Matrix p

	1 INCAGR	2 M.M.	3 EQIPMT	4 CHEMIC	5 CMGLWD	6 FOODCL
AG.PL.	0.	0.	0.	0.	0.	0.
M.M.	0.	0.	0.	0.	0.	0.
EQIPMT	.368	.503	.515	.471	.444	.629
CHEMIC	0.	0.	0.	0.	0.	0.
CMGLWD	0.	0.	0.	0.	0.	0.
FCODCL	0.	0.	0.	0.	0.	0.
ELECTR	0.	0.	0.	0.	0.	0.
TRANS	0.	0.	0.	0.	0.	0.
CCNSTR	.627	.432	.418	.468	.498	.289
HOUS.	0.	0.	0.	0.	0.	0.
OTHMAR	.005	.065	.067	.061	.058	.082
SUM	1.000	1.000	1.000	1.000	1.000	1.000

	7 ELECTR	8 TRANS	9 CONSTR	10 HOUS.	11 OTHMAR	12 TRADAG
	0.	0.	0.	0.	0.	0.
	0.	0.	0.	0.	0.	0.
	.404	.444	.654	0.	.319	.138
	0.	0.	0.	0.	0.	0.
	0.	0.	0.	0.	0.	0.
	0.	0.	0.	0.	0.	0.
	0.	0.	0.	0.	0.	0.
	0.	0.	0.	0.	0.	0.
	.543	.498	.261	1.000	.639	.844
	0.	0.	0.	0.	0.	0.
	.053	.058	.085	0.	.042	.018
	1.000	1.000	1.000	1.000	1.000	1.000

Table C.5. Aggregate Inventory-Output Coefficients sj(t)

ACTIVITY	'966-69	1969-72	1972-75	1975-78	1978-81	1981-84
INCAGR	.092	.092	.092	.092	.092	.092
M.M.	.079	.076	.074	.072	.070	.068
EQIPMT	.128	.124	.120	.117	.113	.110
CHEMIC	.176	.171	.166	.161	.156	.151
CMGLWD	.079	.076	.074	.072	.070	.068
FOODCL	.120	.116	.113	.109	.106	.103
ELECTR	.043	.042	.040	.039	.038	.037
TRANS	.006	.006	.006	.006	.005	.005
CONSTR	.023	.022	.021	.021	.020	.019
HOUS.	0.	0.	0.	0.	0.	0.
OTHMAR	.003	.003	.002	.002	.002	.002
TRADAG	.131	.127	.123	.120	.116	.113

Table C.6. Depreciated Capital D (Rs. crores, 1959-60 prices)

	INCAGR	M.M.	EQIPMT	CHEMIC	CMGLWD	FOODCL	ELECTR	TRANS	CONSTR	HOUS.	OTHMAR	TRADAC	SUM
1966-69													
Total	0.	216.0	48.0	157.0	43.0	99.4	133.0	780.6	4.2	613.3	440.4	471.6	3,006.8
Proportion													
of EQIPMT	0.	.538	.568	.519	.549	.679	.311	.314	.812	0.	.308	.265	
CONSTR	0.	.391	.357	.413	.379	.231	.648	.644	.080	1.000	.652	.700	
OTHMAR	0.	.071	.075	.068	.072	.090	.041	.041	.109	0.	.041	.035	
1969-72													
Total	0.	229.1	59.5	169.0	50.4	107.1	150.0	843.1	4.7	641.3	497.3	522.3	3,273.9
Proportion													
of EQIPMT	0.	.542	.618	.529	.586	.685	.353	.332	.819	0.	.350	.304	
CONSTR	0.	.386	.301	.402	.337	.225	.601	.624	.073	1.000	.603	.661	
OTHMAR	0.	.071	.081	.069	.077	.090	.046	.044	.108	0.	.046	.035	
1972-75													
Total	0.	241.2	79.5	182.8	62.6	115.8	176.5	925.2	5.6	670.6	487.0	598.8	3,645.5
Proportion													
of EQIPMT	0.	.545	.676	.541	.633	.692	.412	.359	.829	0.	.411	.363	
CONSTR	0.	.384	.235	.389	.284	.217	.534	.594	.064	1.000	.535	.603	
OTHMAR	0.	.072	.089	.071	.083	.091	.054	.047	.107	0.	.054	.035	
1975-78													
Total	0.	445.2	112.3	209.8	77.1	151.4	243.2	1,108.5	6.9	701.2	632.8	629.4	4,317.9
Proportion													
of EQIPMT	0.	.692	.730	.571	.671	.731	.526	.426	.836	0.	.426	.366	
CONSTR	0.	.217	.174	.354	.241	.174	.405	.519	.055	1.000	.519	.599	
OTHMAR	0.	.090	.095	.075	.088	.096	.069	.056	.110	0.	.056	.035	
1978-81													
Total	0.	549.5	129.2	225.1	84.8	169.9	278.9	1,213.9	7.6	733.2	663.5	653.8	4,709.4
Proportion													
of EQIPMT	0.	.722	.745	.579	.682	.741	.558	.446	.837	0.	.427	.362	
CONSTR	0.	.184	.158	.345	.229	.162	.369	.495	.052	1.000	.517	.603	
OTHMAR	0.	.094	.097	.076	.089	.097	.073	.058	.111	0.	.045	.035	
1981-84													
Total	0.	621.2	251.7	332.0	109.3	211.2	428.9	1,268.5	9.5	766.7	819.6	749.6	5,568.2
Proportion													
of EQIPMT	0.	.734	.810	.666	.720	.764	.662	.446	.846	0.	.497	.412	
CONSTR	0.	.170	.085	.245	.186	.136	.251	.496	.043	1.000	.438	.550	
OTHMAR	0.	.096	.105	.089	.094	.100	.086	.058	.110	0.	.065	.038	

Table C.7. Government Consumption G (Rs. crores, 1959-60 prices)

SECTOR	1966-69	1969-72	1972-75	1975-78	1978-81	1981-84
AG.PL.	0.	0.	0.	0.	C.	0.
M.M.	0.	0.	0.	0.	C.	0.
EQIPMT	638.436	743.789	905.193	1078.088	1283.997	1529.233
CHEMIC	185.797	216.457	263.429	313.745	373.669	445.037
CMGLWD	0.	0.	0.	0.	C.	0.
FOODCL	713.816	831.609	1012.070	1205.379	1435.600	1709.791
ELECTR	32.205	37.519	45.661	54.383	64.769	77.140
TRANS	0.	0.	0.	0.	0.	0.
CONSTR	707.800	824.600	1003.540	1195.220	1423.500	1695.380
HOUS.	0.	0.	0.	0.	0.	0.
OTHMAR	1260.946	1469.025	1787.806	2129.284	2535.965	3020.319
SUM	3539.000	4123.000	5017.700	5976.100	7117.500	8476.900

Table C.8. Exports E (Rs. crores, 1959-60 prices)

SECTOR	1966-69	1969-72	1972-75	1975-78	1978-81	1981-84
AG.PL.	696.130	766.680	888.980	1017.760	1121.880	1236.650
M.M.	383.760	609.220	824.830	1074.560	1353.630	1705.200
ECIPMT	183.260	246.700	367.320	539.900	758.520	1065.670
CHEMIC	64.660	176.900	273.470	387.680	530.220	725.130
CMCLWD	7.510	24.920	46.150	76.390	116.190	176.710
FCCDCL	1337.640	1403.080	1632.380	1876.180	2050.150	2240.250
ELECTR	0.	0.	0.	0.	C.	0.
TRANS	0.	0.	0.	0.	0.	0.
CONSTR	0.	0.	0.	0.	0.	0.
HOUS.	0.	0.	0.	0.	C.	0.
OTHMAR	414.610	481.720	593.260	718.770	832.070	963.220
SUM	3087.570	3709.220	4626.390	5691.240	6762.660	8112.830

Table C.9. Noncompetitive Import Coefficients m′

ACTIVITY	1966-69	1969-72	1972-75	1975-78	1978-81	1981-84
1 INCAGR	.016000	.012000	.008000	.004500	.001000	.001000
2 M.M.	.145000	.105000	.070000	.050000	.030000	.020000
3 ECIPMT	.235000	.175000	.115000	.080000	.050000	.040000
4 CHEMIC	.261000	.218000	.175000	.150000	.125000	.100000
5 CMCLWD	.004000	.003000	.002000	.001500	.001000	.001000
6 FCCDCL	.000080	.000060	.000040	.000030	.000020	.000015
7 ELECTR	0.	0.	0.	0.	0.	0.
8 TRANS	0.	0.	0.	0.	0.	0.
9 CONSTR	0.	0.	0.	0.	0.	0.
10 HOUS.	0.	0.	0.	0.	0.	0.
11 CTHMAR	0.	0.	0.	0.	0.	0.
12 TRADAG	.016000	.012000	.008000	.004500	.001000	.001000

Table C.10. Consumption-Expenditure Elasticities η and Initial Consumption Coefficients c (0)

SECTOR	c(0)	η
1 AG.PL.	.388	.7500
2 M.M.	.000	.8000
3 EQIPMT	.024	2.0000
4 CHEMIC	.030	1.3000
5 CMGLWD	.006	1.3000
6 FOODCL	.143	1.0000
7 ELECTR	.001	1.1000
8 TRANS	.018	1.2000
9 CONSTR	0.	0.
10 HOUS.	.046	.9000
11 OTHMAR	:344	1.1837

INITIAL LEVEL OF CONSUMPTION = Rs. 44100 CRORES PER PERIOD

RATE OF GROWTH OF POPULATION

1966-69	1969-72	1972-75	1975-78	1978-81	1981-84
.0646	.0646	.0646	.0534	.0534	.0534

Table C.11. Initial and Terminal Conditions (Rs. crores, 1959-60 prices)

ACTIVITY	K(1)*	K(1)†
INCAGR	0.	0.
M.M.	3775.8811	3987.8173
EQIPMT	2470.3059	3184.6245
CHEMIC	2174.4238	2360.4467
CMGLWD	851.6380	917.7837
FOODCL	1919.6773	1993.6696
ELECTR	1855.3786	2074.5130
TRANS	6827.8694	6882.3491
CONSTR	578.7373	577.6784
HOUS.	8026.5325	8057.2538
OTHMAR	1616.8052	1640.9384
TRADAG	14652.1378	14652.1378

POSTTERMINAL GROWTH RATES

PRIVATE CONSUMPTION	VARIES WITH SOLUTION
GOVERNMENT CONSUMPTION	6.0% PER YEAR (19.1% PER PERIOD)
EXPORTS	5.5% PER YEAR (17.4% PER PERIOD)
IMPORTS	5.5% PER YEAR (17.4% PER PERIOD)
REPLACEMENT	AT THE SAME RATE AS CONSUMPTION
TRADITIONAL AGRICULTURE	0.5% PER YEAR (1.51% PER PERIOD)

OUTPUT LEVEL OF TRADITIONAL AGRICULTURE IN PERIOD T + 1 = 31851 RS. CRORES

*PROJECTED FROM 1965-66 OUTPUT ESTIMATES ADJUSTED ON AN 11-SECTOR BASIS
†PROJECTED FROM 1965-66 OUTPUT ESTIMATES ADJUSTED ON A 32-SECTOR BASIS

6. Summary and Conclusions

Infinite learning does not aid
To virtue those who are afraid;
As men with lamps no sooner find
Lost objects, if those men are blind.

The Panchatantra

The objective of this study has been to develop and test models for understanding and planning the sectoral and temporal allocation of resources for economic development. The analytical technique used in the models is that of linear programming in the context of the theory of capital accumulation and growth. It has been our conviction that the best test of models is in their actual confrontation with practical problems. The models are therefore applied to India in order to examine the implications of the Third Five Year Plan and a proposed Fourth Five Year Plan. They are also used with Indian data to generate long-term plans extending up to thirty years and to construct short-term plans consistent with the long-term ones. Since our purposes have been those of a pilot study, we have not fully elaborated all the features provided in the models. Instead, we have tried to determine the potentialities of the approach by building models that illustrate the major issues.

The process of developing the models and of calculating and explaining their solutions has been a fertile source of insights into the Indian Plans and India's growth potential, into the behavior of linear programming models, and into the process of development in general. We shall now comment on each of these.

6.1 Observations on the Indian Plans

The model solutions provide the basis for an appraisal of the performance of the Indian economy, though our conclusions must remain tentative mainly because of inadequacies in the available data.

The official justifications of the Indian Plans have been couched in terms of long-run objectives, as should be the case for five-year plans. The Target Model used to analyze the Plans cannot and is not intended to examine their long-term rationale but only to investigate the implications *for the plan period itself* of targets previously determined. Such an analysis of the short-run implications of such targets does not require a long-term model. If solutions cannot be found with the plan targets, then that is a definitive result indicating technical infeasibility with the assumed parameters and constraints. Resources cannot be transferred from the future to the present, and short-term plans infeasible due to lack of resources do not become feasible in the long run. However, the results can be changed by modifying the assumptions. Thus, the issue of feasibility always finally depends on a judgment as to whether the parameters and allocations necessary for success will in fact be achieved.

A number of solutions to the Target Model were found using targets specified for the Third and Fourth Plan periods. These alternative solutions indicate the sensitivity of the results to changes in the various quantities and parameters, which must be specified in order to be able to find a solution. They also demonstrate the difficulty of drawing unequivocal conclusions from the solutions. The major problems that arise in using the Target Model to examine the Indian Plans are due to lack of specificity in the Plans themselves. For example, the Plans are formulated in terms of output targets to be reached in the final Plan year, but provide little if any information on the goals of the post-Plan period, even though these goals determine most of the investment activity in the last year of each Plan period. Similarly, there is little information in the Plans as to the amounts of uncompleted capital-in-process at the beginning of the Plan period, which are the main determinants of growth in the early years of each Plan period. Furthermore, many of the production coefficients essential to the Plans have not been made explicit. If the assumptions behind the Plans had been more fully specified, the significance of possible defects in the structure of the Target Model could be assessed with more accuracy than has been possible.

The difficulties in basing judgments on evidence from the models' solutions are not a special feature of the models but are intrinsic to the problems. The models only force a greater awareness of alternative possibilities by being more comprehensive and explicit than less detailed models the structure of which permits a greater degree of ambiguity. Yet many of the qualifications of the present study, which are necessary because of our dependence on secondary data sources, could be overcome in India at least, where the potential exists for better and more comprehensive statistics.

6.1.1 Third Five Year Plan

Analysis of the Third Five Year Plan with the Target Model was first carried out using a reference set of parameters and specified quantities. These embodied our best guesses as to the specifications actually made in the Plan, except where there were obvious omissions. In general, we tried to make these guesses in a manner moderately optimistic with respect to the Plan outcome. Yet, the analysis indicates that the Plan targets were technically infeasible. No solution, i.e., no set of resource allocations, exists that could have achieved the targets. Only with a set of parameters even more optimistic that the reference set could a feasible solution be obtained. These more optimistic parameters require substantial improvements in the efficiency of implementation, as indicated by shorter gestation lags and lower capital and inventory coefficients. Under these latter conditions, consumption levels close to those projected by the Third Plan itself are achieved.

Solutions to a Target Model were also obtained for the Third Plan period by reducing the targets. When the targets in all sectors are reduced by 4 per cent and solutions are found using the reference set of parameters, the investment and domestic savings requirements in the Target solutions are substantially higher than those projected in the Third Plan itself. The difference indicates that even the lower level of output targets could not have been achieved with the amounts of investment and saving projected in the Third Plan.

In an attempt to determine whether the Target Model and the reference parameters contain built-in biases in estimating investment requirements, a solution was found for a set of targets that were the likely achievements of the Third Plan period as estimated in 1964. The investment requirements in this solution were higher than the projected actual levels of investment in the Third Plan period. This suggests the possibility of overestimation of investment requirements by the Target Model. Unfortunately, the solution does not provide the test desired because of uncertainty about initial and terminal conditions. In particular, the overestimation of likely achievements and of terminal investment and capital-in-process is the probable explanation of the divergences.

On balance, though the results are not unequivocal, we believe that they do throw doubt on the operational feasibility of the Third Plan targets, in the sense that adequate provision was not made in the Plan for investment and for domestic savings consistent with the targets. This is not a new criticism of the Third Plan, but the Target Model provides a more comprehensive means of evaluation than other analytical techniques available. In a sense the scope for controversy is broadened, since solution of the Model requires the estimation of many technological and behavioral parameters and economic quantities. In another and more relevant sense, use of the Target Model focuses the controversy, since more of the significant issues are made explicit.

Although, in general, the Third Plan targets have not been achieved, this result, in itself, cannot be taken as "proof" of the infeasibility of the Third Plan targets as implied by the solutions. Several major, unforeseen events partially account for the shortfalls in the Third Plan period. Unfavorable weather hampered agricultural production, and the hostilities with China and Pakistan forced diversions of domestic capacity and foreign exchange resources from their originally intended uses. But it is also true that the savings rates actually achieved in the Third Plan period were substantially less than those which the Target Model solutions indicate as necessary for the fulfillment of the targets. Either the Target Model calculations are wrong, or the targets were unachievable with the savings projected in the Plan.

6.1.2 A Proposed Fourth Five Year Plan

In this series of tests the Plan targets are again uncertain.[1] Targets specified for the organized sectors of the economy had to be extended to cover the unorganized sector as well. Two adjustment procedures were used, one of which leads to higher terminal stocks. The policy issue involved in choosing between the procedures lies in the extent to which the fairly small business firms, of the unorganized sector would attempt or be allowed to expand to keep pace with the larger firms of the organized sector.

Application of the Target Model to both the higher and lower sets of adjusted targets for the Fourth Plan leads to technically feasible solutions under a wide variety of specifications.

On the question of operational feasibility, i.e., consistency of output targets and savings and investment plans, results are less clear than for the Third Plan, but in this case also the Target Model solutions raise doubts. In most of the solutions, the adjusted targets require more investment and domestic saving than were projected in the P.P.D. *Notes.* Yet in one solution of the Target Model, the

---

[1] As already noted, the basis of the targets is the *Notes on Perspective of Development, India: 1960-61 to 1975-76* published in April 1964 by the Perspective Planning Division of the Planning Commission.

calculated levels of investment and saving are more or less equivalent to the proposed levels. In this solution, the adjusted targets embody the lower set of goals for the unorganized sector, and coefficients are used that imply particularly optimistic projections of agricultural output and inventory investment requirements. Furthermore, it is necessary in this case to project sharp reductions in growth rates in many sectors after the Fourth Plan. The latter assumption substantially reduces the amount of investment required in the Fourth Plan for the Fifth Plan period. The various alternative calculations and sensitivity tests led us to conclude that the proposed Fourth Plan Targets, as adjusted, were likely to be operationally infeasible. The fundamental reason for this is relatively simple. The total amount of investment and therefore of domestic savings required by the Plan's adjusted targets, as computed in the comprehensive calculations of the Target Model, is more than that projected in the Plan calculations.

The Fourth Plan Target Model solutions also indicate that the import substitution program is a crucial factor in the Plan. Unless import requirements are reduced, foreign exchange shortages set a limit to the over-all performance of the economy in achieving the targets. This is not a new idea, but the analysis has the advantage of being specific and quantitative, and of relating the foreign exchange requirements to the size and composition of the targets.

The great amount of detail in the Target Model solutions raises many questions of particular relevance to the outcome of the Plans. Only a few examples will be repeated here. Capacity in Construction is often a bottleneck in the early years of the Target Model solutions; this indicates the importance of a careful study of this sector and its requirements for expansion. The significance of foreign exchange allocations is emphasized in the alternative solutions, in which variation of these allocations leads to substantial differences in the results. The output targets in Mining and Metals often appear low in relation to what is required by other targets. For this reason, as well as the sector's high direct and indirect costs, the solutions often indicate the desirability of larger foreign exchange allocations than those permitted by the import constraints intended to reflect current practices. This again suggests the need for more detailed studies.

The Target Model solutions do not indicate exactly how the Indian economy would perform if unachievable targets were pursued. An infinite number of adjustments are possible, and the combination of sectoral outputs which will in fact be produced when targets are infeasible cannot be predicted by the model. That depends on the relative success of the different sectors in exercising entrepreneurship, mobilizing investment, gaining access to foreign exchange, etc.

The Transit Model was also solved for the Fourth Plan period, the terminal capital stock conditions having been determined as part of the solution by the requirement that certain stipulated postterminal growth rates be achievable. In the Transit Model solutions, which were found with a 5 per cent postterminal consumption growth requirement, the over-all levels of investment are much less than in most of the Target Model solutions. The over-all levels of consumption are higher in the Transit Model than in the Target Model solutions. For example, in one solution an average intra-Plan growth rate of consumption of 9.3 per cent was achieved with a 5 per cent postterminal consumption growth rate. In such solutions, accordingly, the emphasis on the capital goods sectors was much less than in the Target Model solutions with the adjusted P.P.D. targets. Other feasible combinations of intraplan and postplan growth rates could also be found with the Transit Model.

Comparison of the Transit with the Target Model solutions helps in understanding the characteristics of the latter. Sensitivity tests on the Transit Model solutions indicate that the results are much less dependent on imports than in the Target Model solutions. This emphasizes the importance of the size and composition of the planned output targets in determining import requirements and, to a considerable extent, the foreign exchange stringency to be expected in a plan.

The short-run analyses of the Target Models cannot reveal the long-run implications of a set of five-year plan targets. Similarly the Transit Model is not a satisfactory method for setting targets the implications of which will last long into the future. These issues require an expressly long-term approach, such as is embodied in the Guidepath Models.

No sufficiently explicit long-term plans, comparable to the Third and Fourth Plan targets, have been available to us for testing with the Guidepath Models. Nonetheless, the Indian Plans are based on some implicit long-run objectives, and a comparison of the character of the Guidepath Model solutions with the adjusted targets proposed for the Fourth Plan provides a basis for conjecture about the long-term path with which those targets are consistent. In the Guidepath-I Model Reference Solution, in which the consumption path is smoothed by being constrained to grow at increasing rates, the average net savings rates range from 18.8 per cent to 36.8 per cent. In the Guidepath-II Model solutions, the marginal net savings rates are constrained to 20 per cent and 30 per cent, and the average rates never rise above 15.6 per cent and 21.4 per cent, respectively. It is interesting to note that the level and sectoral composition of the adjusted Fourth Plan targets are more comparable in corresponding years to the level and composition of the capacity created in the solutions to the Guidepath-I Model than to the capacity in the Guidepath-II Model. Yet, there are interesting contrasts between the Fourth Plan targets and the capacities typically provided in the Guidepath-I solutions for the same period. For example, compared to the Fourth Plan targets, the Guidepath-I solutions provide much more Mining and Metals capacity and much less Chemicals capacity, in spite of the fact that in these solutions imports tend to be concentrated in Mining and Metals. Since total imports provided in the Guidepath solution are roughly equal to those envisaged for the Fourth Plan period, this suggests that a shortage of Mining and Metals would develop if the adjusted targets of the P.P.D. *Notes* were pursued.

6.2 Linear Models and Economic Growth

In the Guidepath Models, our primary objectives have been the development of techniques for generating alternative plan outlines and the illustration of growth paths that might be achieved under various circumstances. The achievement of a more or less smooth growth path in the alternative Guidepath-I solutions is of some methodological interest. It is well known that in an economic system like the Guidepath Model consumption, unless otherwise constrained, will be concentrated at either the beginning or the end of the planning period, depending on the discount rate and the productivity of capital. In such systems, the period in which consumption is concentrated depends on the length of the planning horizon and on the character of the terminal conditions. Though such flip-flop behavior remains an underlying tendency in the Guidepath Models, it is modulated not only by the constraints imposed specifically for that purpose, but also by other essential features of the models. For example, the multisectoral character of the models, with different input requirements for each sector and changing sectoral composition of various demands over time, is a source of effective nonlinearity. The provision of two production technologies in Agriculture, with a gradual shift to the higher-cost activity, creates diminishing returns in this sector. In addition, nonlinearities are also imposed in the specification of requirements for the export sectors, in the depreciation levels, and in the projections of foreign capital inflow, as well as by changes over time in some of the parameters, such as import and inventory coefficients. The result of all these nonlinearities is that the models do not behave like simple linear systems. Even when a large proportion of total consumption is postponed to the end of the plan period, some increase in consumption also takes place in the earlier years, and there is no drastic shift within the single period to a relative emphasis on consumption.

Flip-flop behavior is also effectively controlled in the solutions by the imposition of constraints on the minimum growth rate of consumption in each period of the plan. The intraplan consumption growth constraints, when binding, compel the time path of consumption along a specified path. These constraints combined with the postterminal growth requirements can be used to generate different time shapes of consumption. As a result of these conditions, the flip-flop behavior never takes the extreme form it does in simpler models and, in fact, becomes so controlled that it is often difficult to discover what the tendency is.

Of some practical interest is the fact that the growth rates of gross national product achieved in the Guidepath-I Model solutions are high in comparison with India's or almost any other nation's performance. These rates are generated even though there are diminishing returns in the important Agriculture sector, net foreign capital inflows are eliminated after twelve years, and there are no benefits from external economies or technological change. There are, on the other hand, no labor or natural resource constraints except the land limitation in Agriculture.

Much of the outstanding performance in the Guidepath-I Model solutions is due to the extraordinarily high savings rates generated. In an unconstrained flip-flop solution, everything above minimum consumption would be saved for the final payoff. With steadily increasing intraplan consumption requirements, some of the final jackpot is traded for additional consumption in each plan year. Even so, the Guidepath-I Model solutions have shown that if the savings rates themselves are not constrained, both increasing growth rates of intraplan consumption and relatively high postterminal consumption growth rate requirements can be achieved up to some limit rate of about 10 to 12 per cent.

The differences between the solutions of the Guidepath-II Model for six and ten periods were slight for the first four periods or twelve years. After that, the discrepancies were clearly due to the terminal conditions imposed on the shorter-term model. This similarity in the early periods is an outcome of the imposition of the consumption growth constraints. When such constraints are used, a planning horizon of roughly twenty years appears to be adequate, at least for the parametric variations investigated.

The Guidepost Model solutions provide a year-by-year elaboration of a path towards a set of targets taken from an intermediate point of a Guidepath Model solution in which the time periods are three-year aggregates. The Guidepost Model is therefore like the Target Model in the manner of specifying the terminal conditions. In the Guidepost Model, however, the Targets are taken from an explicit long-term growth path, so the annual resource allocations are also consistent with the path. In the Guidepost solutions presented, it was possible with little, if any, adjustment in the constraints to achieve the stipulated targets, meet the intermediate conditions, and provide about the same annual amounts of consumption as implied by the corresponding Guidepath solution.

Since solutions to the Guidepost Model performed slightly better in terms of consumption than solutions to the corresponding Guidepath Models, the effect of time aggregation in these models appears to be small. The result may not be generalized, however, since it depends upon the particular values of the parameters.

6.3 Suggestions for Improvements in the Models

Though not intended to be applicable only to India, the models presented are more relevant to that country's circumstances than to those of many other countries. Even with respect to India, a variety of further structural generalizations improving the usefulness of the models as planning tools are possible. Most of these have not been embodied for lack of empirical information or because of the increased computational burden that they would impose. For example, one of the most obvious omissions is the complete lack of consideration of labor requirements. To a reasonable approximation, these could be computed using productivity coefficients. In this way, the consistency of manpower plans with the over-all plan could be tested by calculations external to, but based on, the solutions of the optimizing model. It is more difficult to find a satisfactory first approximation for labor supply relationships however. Differentiation of capital by vintages, each with its own input coefficients, would be another improvement in the present structure, but it would require separate accounting for the capital of each vintage. With such accounting, more freedom could be permitted in the capital gestation process. Depreciation could be made a function of the existing stock or of output, if either method is clearly preferable to its exogenous specification. To take into account economies of scale, minimum investment level constraints can be imposed.[2] Many of these and other improvements would be desirable and important in the context of a more disaggregated system. In such a system, it would be possible and desirable to permit some degree of substitution among consumption goods. Similarly, sectoral comparative advantage for exports could be fruitfully investigated by means of greater detail in the industrial classification. On the savings side, if income distribution generated by each sector could be determined, savings relationships appropriate to each income category could then be applied. This list of potential improvements in the models suggests again the limitations of the present structure.

---

[2]This can be done only under limited circumstances. In general, mixed-integer or nonlinear programming would be required, both of which have much higher computational costs than linear programming.

6.4 Growth and Savings

Since the theoretical structure of the models is an extension of existing economic theory rather than an innovation, surprises are not to be expected in the qualitative results. The sectoral and temporal detail generated by the solutions does make those results quantitative and thus more useful in determining strategies for economic growth. The issues of growth policy have many common elements, whether in the context of advanced or less developed, mixed-capitalist or socialist economies. They include relatively abstruse issues, such as the effects on growth of a change in the marginal savings rate and the best relationship between industrialization and agricultural expansion. The implications of the Guidepath Model solutions are by no means final results, but they do approach practical answers to these and other questions. The Guidepath-I Model was solved for six and ten periods covering eighteen and thirty years, respectively. In the Guidepath-I Model the level of savings is not constrained, though minimum levels of consumption are assured by appropriate constraints, as is the capacity of the system to continue to grow at specified rates at the end of the planning period. With such conditions, solutions have been found in which consumption grows smoothly at annual rates which increase steadily from 5 per cent to as much as 12 per cent in 30 years, with postterminal consumption growth at 12.5 per cent assured. These growth rates are achieved in the Model's solutions in part because of the assumptions of foresight and efficiency that are embodied therein. Most important, however, are the high and steadily increasing savings rates realized. The Guidepath-I Model thus demonstrates the potentiality of both higher consumption growth rates *and* high over-all growth rates, if the relatively high savings rates are achieved.

In the Guidepath-II formulation, the savings rate is directly controlled by a constraint. This relates marginal savings and, therefore, consumption to net national product. It combines an effective demand condition with the previous supply conditions. Increases in net national product from any source, e.g., growth in consumption or investment production, lead directly to further increases in consumer demands that must be met. This additional constraint can also be viewed as a behavioral relationship imposing institutional restraints on policy decisions. The consumption growth rates achieved in the Guidepath-II Model solutions are more modest than in the Guidepath-I Model solutions. Even so, with a maximum marginal savings rate of 20 per cent, it is possible to find a Guidepath-II solution in which consumption grows at 5 per cent annually for 18 years with provision for a postterminal yearly growth rate of 6 per cent.

Several different marginal savings rates have been tried in the Guidepath-II solutions, beginning with the average savings rates achieved in the last years of the Third Five Year Plan. The constraints embodying these savings rates are always binding, even up to a marginal net savings rate of 30 per cent. Thus, their imposition has had a significant effect in reducing the over-all growth rates achieved as compared to Guidepath-I solutions, in which the unconstrained marginal net savings rates often exceeded 45 per cent.

The sectoral allocations of the Guidepath-II Model as compared to the Guidepath-I Model reflect the over-all savings constraints. Both the Guidepath-I and Guidepath-II Models generate a long-term program of structural change in the economy leading to an increasing degree of industrialization. In the Guidepath-I versions, however, the change is more drastic and concentrates on the capital goods producing sectors and their major suppliers. With less savings allowed and with consumption related to net national product in the Guidepath-II version, the emphasis in investment and production shifts toward the consumption goods industries. In these cases the industrialization is, to a greater degree, required to support increases in consumption rather than to support increases in the investment goods sectors and, as a result, has a different sectoral content.

The over-all contrasts between the Guidepath-I and Guidepath-II solutions are quite striking and may help explain the different experiences of countries that have, during certain periods, developed quite rapidly under the forced draft of tight controls on domestic consumption, and those countries that have been unable or unwilling to force equally high savings rates. The former have emphasized their capital goods sectors, relatively neglected their consumer goods sectors, and achieved high over-all rates of growth, while improvements in the standard of living took place at a slower pace.

It is assumed that high investment rates corresponding to the high growth rates in the Guidepath-I Model solutions can be attained without drastic reductions in the productivity of capital as the result of technical, manpower, or organizational limitations. Such limitational factors have not been embodied in the models because of the analytical and computational difficulties entailed. Yet they are likely to be of considerable practical importance and must be taken into account in evaluating the Guidepath solutions. It is a characteristic of optimal programs, such as those of the Guidepath Models, that they are a highly interdependent system. If any part cannot function as prescribed, the programs of the other parts must be modified. Thus, it cannot be assumed that the investment allocations called for in a Guidepath solution will be optimal if these allocations, because of declining capital productivity for example, do not produce the originally projected output.

One important lesson of the Guidepath solutions is that there are no simple mottoes or priorities, such as "heavy industry" or "high investment," that necessarily lead to optimal programs. Ambitious plans that cannot be attained may lead to less desirable results than more modest targets set and achieved. As a specific, important example, if high rates of saving and capital accumulation are realized but consumer targets are not met, the welfare objectives of the plan are likely to be seriously impaired. Moreover, there are grave political dangers in setting targets that require high savings rates and in treating consumer goods as residual sectors with only secondary investment and organizational priorities. Yet well-conceived, ambitious plans, purposefully carried out, can assist in achieving growth rates substantially higher than those now being realized in many developing countries.

Index